BLACK, BROWN, YELLOW, AND LEFT

W9-BDJ-899

AMERICAN CROSSROADS

Edited by Earl Lewis, George Lipsitz, Peggy Pascoe, George Sánchez, and Dana Takagi

Black, Brown, Yellow, and Left

RADICAL ACTIVISM IN LOS ANGELES

LAURA PULIDO

UNIVERSITY OF CALIFORNIA PRESS

Berkeley Los Angeles London

University of California Press
Berkeley and Los Angeles, California

University of California Press, Ltd.
London, England

© 2006 by The Regents of the University of California

Library of Congress Cataloging-in-Publication Data

Pulido, Laura.
 Black, brown, yellow, and left : radical activism in Southern California /
Laura Pulido.
     p.   cm. —(American crossroads ; 19)
 Includes bibliographical references and index.
 ISBN 0-520-24519-9 (cloth : alk. paper)—ISBN 0-520-24520-2
(pbk. : alk. paper)
    1. Radicalism—California—Los Angles—History—20th century.
2. Right and left (Political science)   3. African Americans—California—
Los Angeles—Politics and government—20th century.   4. Mexican
Americans —California—Los Angeles—Politics and government—
20th century.   5. Japanese Americans—California—Los Angeles—
Politics and government—20th century.   I. Title.   II. Series.
HN79.C23A-Z.R368   2006
305.8'009794'909047—dc22   2005002624

Manufactured in the United States of America

14   13   12   11   10   09   08   07   06
10   9   8   7   6   5   4   3   2   1

This book is for Mike

The publisher gratefully acknowledges the generous contribution to this book provided by the Lisa See Fund in Southern California History.

Contents

Illustrations

FIGURES

MAPS

Tables

Acknowledgments

I have benefited from the wisdom, experience, and generosity of many people in writing this book. This project required me to go beyond the familiar territory of Chicana/o and Latina/o studies, which was not always easy. This process was greatly facilitated, however, by people like Tony Osumi and Jenni Kuida, who know most politically active Japanese Americans in Los Angeles, as well as by Ruthie and Craig Gilmore, who listened to my ramblings about this project for years, while sharing their extensive library, ideas, and contacts, and who provided a base for fieldwork in Northern California. Special thanks also to Pierrette Hondagneu-Sotelo, Lisa Duran, and Jim Lee, who, besides reading portions of the manuscript, have listened and supported me through the various trials and tribulations it entailed.

Numerous individuals have also contributed their particular expertise or resources to this project. Special thanks to the Yamashita-Oliveras family for providing housing in Northern California; Craig Gilmore and my mom for being wonderful baby-sitters; Clyde Woods for his encouragement and encyclopedic knowledge of the civil rights movement and Black studies in general; Steven Murashige for graphic assistance; Cynthia Cuza, Lian Hurst Mann, Mark and Kathy Masaoka, and Merilynne Quon for sharing documents; Diane Fujino, Dan Hosang, Lon Kurashige and his Asian American History seminar, John Laslett, George Lipsitz, Manuel Pastor, Merilynne Quon, Dana Tagaki, Howard Winant, and two anonymous reviewers for reading and commenting on the manuscript or portions of it; Gloria Gonzalez-Lopez for introducing me to the literature on Chicana sexuality; Shirley Hune for her insights on gender and Asian American women; Jennifer Wolch for endless urban citations; Lisa Lowe, Jorge Mariscal, Betita Martinez, and Melissa Gilbert for their early encouragement of this project; and Miriam Ching Louie for generously allowing me to borrow the title of her paper for this book.

Funding for this project was provided by the Southern California Studies Center at the University of Southern California (USC), for which I thank my colleague Michael Dear. I am extremely grateful for a fellowship from the Institute of American Cultures and the Cesar Chavez Research Center at the University of California, Los Angeles (UCLA), which provided a supportive environment in which I was able to write the first manuscript draft. Many thanks also to USC's Program in American Studies and Ethnicity, which provided me with funding for a research assistant, as well as to the Geography Department, which has been a supportive academic home, and especially to that department's amazing Billie Shotlow. I would also like to acknowledge the significant contributions of the following people who worked as research assistants on this project: Angel Gomez, Donna Houston, Hallie Krinski, Veronica Marin, Nate Sessoms, and Adrianne Stringer. These students tracked down materials, transcribed lengthy interviews, imposed order on an unruly bibliography and endnotes, and offered their insights and ideas.

Research for this project was conducted at various libraries and collections across California. The starting place for my research was the Southern California Library. Many thanks to the terrific people at the library for their assistance with this project. I would also like to acknowledge and thank the librarians of UCLA's Special Collections, the USC, Special Collections of Stanford University, and Special Collections of the Bancroft Library. In addition, the various ethnic studies libraries at UCLA proved invaluable, especially the American Indian Studies Center Library, the Asian American Studies Reading Room, and the Chicano Studies Library. The Los Angeles Public Library was also quite useful, especially the East Los Angeles branch.

I am especially indebted to those people who allowed me to interview them or otherwise shared their knowledge, experiences, and materials of the Third World Left with me: Kumasi Aguilar, Karen Bass, Luisa Crespo, Cynthia Cuza, María Elena Durazo, Roland Freeman, Ronald Freeman, Warren Furutani, Bill Gallegos, Juan Jose Gutierrez, Steve Holguin, Billy X Jennings, Glenn Kitayama, Sid Lamelle, Barry and Paula Litt, Eric Mann, Lian Hurst Mann, Kathy Masaoka, Mark Masaoka, Nobuko Miyamoto, David Monkawa, Carlos Montes, Mohammed MuBarak, Mike Murase, Mo Nishida, Nelson Peery, Merilynne Quon, Margarita Ramirez, Antonio Rodriguez, Talibah Shakir, Victor Shibata, Gerry Silva, Evelyn Soriano, Miguel Tinker-Salas, Amy Uyematsu, Ron Wilkins, Kent Wong, Long John Ali Yahya, Evelyn Yoshimura, Michael Zinzun, and others who requested anonymity. I know that not everyone will agree with my interpretation, but I hope that I have managed to represent their stories and experiences with the care and respect they deserve. Special thanks to those who generously gave permission for use of their materials, including Emory Douglas, Mike Murase, Mary Kao, Antonio Rodriguez, Roy Nakano, James Allen, Eugene Turner, the Russell Sage Foundation, Stanford Special Collections, UCLA Special Collections, the *Los Angeles Times,* and the Southern California Library. Also, my deep appreciation to the several unknown artists whose work I have used. Although I did my best to identify the artists/owners of anonymous works, I did not always succeed and would welcome the opportunity to hear from those individuals whose work appears on these pages.

And finally, *un mil gracias* to Mike Murashige and *mi hijo* Amani. Mike knows what this project has meant to me and has been supportive from the beginning. I would like to unequivocally state that many of the ideas in this book came from him, and, as often happens with couples, it is sometimes hard to tell where one person's ideas end and another's start. Besides benefiting from his remarkable mind, this book has been strengthened by his love, dedication, and commitment. I, of course, remain responsible for all shortcomings. As for Amani, he fortunately was spared most of the grief associated with a book project, but he, more than anyone else, has helped me keep it in perspective.

Introduction

This book compares the historical experiences of African American, Japanese American, and Chicana/o activists who were part of the Third World Left in Los Angeles from 1968 to 1978.[1] The idea for this project grew out of my general curiosity with the sixties, as well as my desire to understand the generation of activists who preceded me. Although I was only a child during the late sixties, I knew that this period was key to understanding contemporary politics, particularly in communities of color. How and why did the seemingly revolutionary politics of the sixties and seventies falter, and what were the consequences for those struggling to challenge capitalism and racism?

Particularly important to my thinking was my involvement with the Labor/Community Strategy Center in Los Angeles, which, in the 1980s, was seeking to create a multiracial left by organizing in low-income communities of color. During my time with the Strategy Center, I learned the importance of organizing beyond the Chicana/o community and the need for an explicit class analysis.[2] I came to appreciate how class consciousness could potentially bring various racial/ethnic groups together and contribute to a larger movement for social and economic justice. Moreover, I realized that although multiracial organizing was new to me, many people had done this sort of work before, and in fact the Strategy's Center project drew upon those experiences. Previous generations of activists had struggled with the tensions inherent in building an antiracist and anticapitalist movement, and I realized that a close examination of these efforts might yield important insights that would cast new light on contemporary efforts—an especially relevant task given the explosion of progressive and social justice activism that characterized turn-of-the-century Los Angeles.[3] As I began exploring this subject, I saw that the left of color had a rich and deep history in Los

Angeles. It included, for example, Japanese American participation in the 1930s Communist Party, the visionary work of Charlotta Bass and the *California Eagle,* and El Congreso de Pueblos de Habla Española, led by Bert Corona and Luisa Moreno.[4] Building upon this base, I sought to learn more about the sixties and seventies, but, despite picking up bits and pieces about organizations like El Centro de Acción Social y Autónomo/the Center for Autonomous Social Action (CASA), East Wind, the August Twenty-ninth Movement, the California Communist League, and I Wor Kuen, with the exception of the Black Panther Party (BPP) I could find little written on the subject.

I struggled to piece together what scattered evidence and historical clues I could gather until I finally had a breakthrough. In 1995 service workers on my campus, the University of Southern California, were at odds with the administration over the university's subcontracting policies, and I became involved with the workers and their unions (Justice for Janitors and the Hotel Employees and Restaurant Employees Local 11). Subsequently, I began researching the political backgrounds of union members and staff— imagining that, perhaps, Central American workers with revolutionary backgrounds were contributing to the rapidly changing labor politics of Los Angeles.[5] Although I did not find much evidence for my "migrating militancy" theory, I did find a group of older organizers who had become politicized through the Third World Left, and thus an entry into this book.

RACE, CLASS, AND THE SIXTIES AND SEVENTIES

Since my initial curiosity, the literature on the radical and revolutionary movements of the sixties and seventies has grown tremendously. One of its most popular genres is the political memoir or biography written by a leading activist.[6] Books in this genre paint an intimate picture of how and why certain individuals became politicized, as well as the structure and culture of various organizations and movements. But, though rich in detail, they are limited by being written from individual perspectives. Another rapidly expanding genre is the sociological or historical study of the activism of a particular ethnic group.[7] Together, these literatures have greatly enhanced our understanding of this era, but they have presented a somewhat skewed picture of radical politics in the sixties and seventies.

One problem is that many chroniclers of the New Left have defined it as a largely white event. The writer Elizabeth Martínez has dubbed this phenomenon "that old white (male) magic."[8] At the same time, though ethnic studies scholars have produced an impressive literature on the antiracist and nationalist struggles that emerged in communities of color, only a hand-ful have seriously studied the left of color. Most have focused on the larger movements centered on questions of identity, community empowerment, antiracism, and culture. This focus is understandable because of the small size of the Third World Left relative to the larger nationalist movements, but I would also argue that it reflects an ambivalence, at best, toward anti-capitalism. The result of these twin practices has been the almost complete erasure of the existence of a Third World Left, or a left of color, in the United States during this period. The primary exception is, of course, the BPP. The BPP is routinely mentioned in almost all accounts of the New Left and fig-ures prominently in the literature on Black Power as well as that of other ethnic struggles. The problem with this emphasis, however, is that the BPP becomes a stand-in for the entire Third World Left and is viewed in isolation from its relationships with other Third World Leftist groups, thus obscuring the larger movement.[9]

The prominence of the BPP indicates another problem: most studies of the Third World Left are rooted in one particular racial/ethnic group, such as African Americans or Asian Americans. This is understandable insofar as many of the scholars studying these movements tend to come from those communities themselves and to be based in specific disciplines, such as American Indian or Chicana/o studies. While there is still much to learn about all ethnic groups in the United States, and reclaiming buried histories is an urgent task, a multiethnic approach enables us to see the interaction among various racial/ethnic groups and their influences on each other.[10] Indeed, the fact that the Third World Left was not just a loose collection of revolutionary nationalists and Marxist-Leninists but a network of organi-zations that drew on each other's ideas led me to pursue a comparative study. I hope that by carefully examining the similarities and differences between these various activists and organizations, as well as the degree of influence and interaction between them, I can offer a new perspective on the movement.

Because this project evolved from a historical study into a comparative analysis, I had to grapple with a challenging set of theoretical issues around race, class, difference, and place. How would I compare the experiences of different racial/ethnic groups? What might the similarities and differences I found actually mean in terms of larger racial and economic processes? Fortunately, I was able to draw on the work of others who have forged a path in comparative and interethnic studies, including Claire Jean Kim, Susan Koshy, Linda Gordon, Neil Foley, Tomás Almaguer, Evelyn Nakano-Glenn, Nicholas De Genova, and Ana Ramos-Zayas. These scholars not only have helped clarify how and why various racial/ethnic groups experience distinct forms of racism but also have shown how racialization is a relational process: that is, how the status and meanings associated with one group are contingent upon those of another.[11] Hence the idea of Asian Americans as "model minorities" exists only in relation to "less than model" Black, Latina/o, and American Indian minorities. The concept of differential racialization, which denotes that various racial/ethnic groups are racialized in unique ways and have distinct experiences of racism, is key to this discussion. Particular racial/ethnic groups are associated with particular sets of meanings and economic opportunities, or lack thereof, and these in turn are influenced by groups' history, culture, and national racial narratives and by the regional economy. I emphasize regions because although all of the United States is informed by a national racial narrative, class structures and racial divisions of labor take shape and racial hierarchies are experienced at the regional and local levels. Because the United States is so large and diverse, it is primarily at the regional level that nuanced and meaningful comparison must take place.

Although discussions of race in the United States are still largely confined to a Black/white framework, the scholarship emerging from American Indian, Asian American, and Chicana/o and Latina/o studies has challenged this notion, with profound implications for how we think about race.[12] A crucial idea to emerge from these debates is the concept of racial hierarchies. Complex racial hierarchies are formed when multiple racially subordinated populations occupy a range of social positions. The precise configuration of any racial hierarchy will depend upon differential racialization, which in turn affects the regional economy, as seen, for example, in the racialized nature of labor markets. Though a growing number of scholars have examined complex racial hierarchies in detail, and though it is well known that resistance varies according to the nature of oppression, few have examined how differential racialization may contribute to distinct forms of revolutionary activism. Accordingly, one of the goals of this book is to examine this relationship in detail. I argue that differential racialization influences a racial/ethnic group's class position and that both of these factors then shape the local racial hierarchy. Thus differential racialization and class positioning have contributed to the distinct radical politics articulated by various leftists of color.

Because of my initial interest in the history of radical activism in Los Angeles, I did not always appreciate that the city also offers an unparalleled opportunity to study complex racial hierarchies. Not only does the Los Angeles metropolitan region defy the Black/white binary, but also the long histories of multiple racial/ethnic groups in the city provide a key to under-standing the evolution of racial hierarchies over time and the relational nature of differential racialization.[13] For instance, how did Asian Americans (primarily Japanese and Chinese) rise from the bottom of the racial hierar-chy in the early twentieth century to a much higher position? And equally important, who took their place? Los Angeles is one of the few metropoli-tan regions that has long been home to a diverse population of Asian Americans, American Indians, Latinas/os, and whites, and it thus offers an ideal setting to study differential racialization, racial hierarchies, and politi-cal activism.

THE THIRD WORLD LEFT IN LOS ANGELES

I define the Third World Left as organizations that explicitly identified as revolutionary nationalist, Marxist, Leninist, or Maoist and had a member-ship of at least half people of color. Having arrived at this definition, I soon confronted a bewildering array of organizations, such as the October League, Workers' Viewpoint Organization, the Socialist Workers Party, and the California Communist League. To make this project manageable, I nar-rowed my study to one organization per racial/ethnic group. Accordingly, this book focuses on the following organizations: for African Americans, the BPP; for Asian Americans, East Wind; and for Chicanas/os, CASA. To be sure, in making these decisions I risked generalizing about an entire racial/ethnic group of activists on the basis of a single organization that, arguably, could have been an anomaly. In addition, some readers might wish that I had chosen other organizations—say, an example of Chicana/o activism less well known or more multinational than CASA. But as any scholar knows, difficult choices have to be made based on the availability of materials, accessibility, comparability, and significance—in this case, a group's significance to the Los Angeles region.

I had originally intended to include American Indians in this study as well. But as I began sifting through the archival material, I learned that while there was indeed a great deal of American Indian activism—not sur-prising, given that Los Angeles has the largest urban Indian population in the United States—there was little evidence of left activity in the area. While this discovery was initially surprising, an explanation began to emerge. Not only did American Indians draw on a somewhat different set of ideologies than other Third World activists, but also the most radical orga-nizing occurred in rural areas. This distinctive geographical pattern was partly a function of American Indians' unique engagement with nationalism. During the sixties and seventies, leftist ideology conceived of racial/ethnic minorities as "oppressed nationalities." Thus, although both Chicanas/os and African Americans were categorized as distinct nations, the nationalist dimension of American Indians' struggles was far more immediate and concrete, as they focused on specific territorial demands and historic land claims.[14] Accordingly, the geographic focus of more radical Indian activism was reservations and rural lands. Reservations became key sites of contestation, and while American Indians' struggles were certainly carried out in the cities, including Denver and San Francisco, they did not loom large in the everyday activities of the Los Angeles left. Instead, Third World activists operating in Los Angeles were more likely to visit and support American Indians in rural areas.[15] For example, at one point East Wind sent a delegation of approximately twenty people to Wounded Knee, and the Black Panthers regularly hosted American Indian Movement activists when they came to town. Because no comparable American Indian group was *based* in Los Angeles, I decided not to include them in this study.

The BPP is the most well known of the groups I investigated. At first, I hesitated to include it because there is already a burgeoning literature on the party. However, the more I delved into its history, the more I realized that I could not ignore it. Whether organizations patterned themselves after the BPP or not, the party created the political space and inspiration for other activists of color to pursue more militant and radical forms of political action. The BPP was a revolutionary nationalist organization created in Oakland, California, in 1966. The Southern California chapter was established in 1968 by Alprentice "Bunchy" Carter. Like the larger history of the sixties, representations of the BPP are often polarized: mainstream society has typically depicted the Panthers as gun-toting thugs, whereas lefties and liberals have often romanticized them as revolutionaries. The reality is inevitably more messy, and there is, thankfully, a growing body of literature that portrays this complexity.[16] The BPP was significant in that it was the most prominent organization of the era to embrace self-defense, but it also developed a remarkable set of "serve the people" or "survival" programs. I argue that these two concerns, self-defense and community service, emanated from the distinct racialization of African Americans and their particular class and racial position in U.S. cities during the 1960s and 1970s. Not only were urban Blacks an impoverished population in need of basic resources, but also, as "the Other" upon which whiteness was based, they were at the bottom of Los Angeles's racial hierarchy and represented an ever-present threat to a system of white privilege, requiring constant containment by the police.

The Chicana/o group I examined, CASA, was a Marxist-Leninist organization formed in 1972 that focused on immigrant workers. Its political ideology can best be summarized by its slogan *Sin fronteras* (without borders), which signifies its understanding of the Chicana/o and Mexicana/o working class as one. CASA was a vanguard group that sought to unite the workers of the world, or at least workers of Mexican origin. It was active in challenging the *Bakke* decision[17] and, most important, attempted to effect policy changes toward immigrant workers. When CASA was formed, many Chicana/o organizations, including the United Farm Workers, viewed immigrant laborers as a problem rather than as workers to be organized. CASA contributed a great deal toward changing that position. I argue that Chicana/o leftists' preoccupation with questions of labor organizing and immigration reflected Chicanas/os' intermediate racial position as a "problem minority." Their racial status and particular historical experiences cemented their position as low-wage workers in the region and all that such a position entails.[18] Thus their ambivalent racial identity facilitated their incorporation into the formal economy, but only in a subordinated status.

Inevitably, when I tell people about this project, I am asked, "Are you studying the Brown Berets?" The Brown Berets, basically fashioning itself after the BPP, was active at roughly the same time and looms large in the Chicana/o imagination. I did not include it because, while it was radical, it was not left. In fact, the leader of the Berets, David Sánchez, was a strident anticommunist and espoused a much more nationalist politics. The Berets had members who openly embraced leftist ideologies, but the organization as a whole did not.[19] The distinction between nationalists and revolutionary nationalists is an important one that will be discussed at length in chapter 5.

The final group that I consider is East Wind, a Japanese American collective that began in Los Angeles in 1972. Initially composed of revolutionary nationalists, it later became Marxist-Leninist-Maoist. Activists focused on politicizing the larger Japanese American population by doing community work and organizing. Although its roots were in study groups, community service, and numerous collectives, East Wind was significantly influenced by the BPP. East Wind became a highly disciplined organization that strongly emphasized serving the people by engaging in local struggles around drug abuse, worker issues, community mental health, and the redevelopment of Little Tokyo, to name but a few. Although relatively few, East Wind and other Japanese American leftists made significant contributions, as seen in their early organizing around the movement for redress and reparations. East Wind activists, like activists in the larger Asian American movement, concentrated on issues of identity, community service, and solidarity work, concerns that I believe reflect their mixed economic position and their status as a "middle minority."

I focused on Japanese Americans, since they were the largest Asian American population in Los Angeles County in the late sixties and early seventies.[20] To be sure, we already know far more about Japanese Americans than about other groups, such as Filipinas/os or Vietnamese Americans, in the diverse Asian/Pacific Islander population because many Japanese Americans have become successful writers and academicians and because they have simply been around longer to tell their stories. Moreover, in light of post-1965 immigration, Japanese Americans are rapidly becoming numerically insignificant in Southern California. These points underscore the need for more research on other Asian/Pacific Islander groups. For my study, however, I felt it was crucial to include Japanese Americans because not to do so would preclude a thorough interrogation of the racial dynamics of the time: the Nikkei[21] were a central part of the Los Angeles racial hierarchy in the 1960s and 1970s, owing to both their size and their tenure in the region.

A ROAD MAP

Part 1 of this book provides a theoretical and historical context for understanding the Third World Left. Chapter 1 is primarily theoretical and discusses differential racialization, racial hierarchies, and political activism. In it I develop a framework for analyzing the racial dynamics of the Third World Left. While this chapter is important conceptually, it can be skipped by those more interested in the Third World Left itself. The second chapter describes Southern California during the 1960s and 1970s to establish the setting for the larger story. In particular, I consider the racial and economic positions of Japanese Americans, Mexican Americans, and Blacks in terms of the racial hierarchy. I take up political consciousness in chapter 3: How and why did leftists of color became politicized? I highlight major political events that not only contributed to the prevailing political culture but also led to the rise of the Third World Left.

The second part of the book centers on the Third World Left itself. Chapter 4 introduces the key organizations—the BPP, CASA, and East Wind—and provides a brief overview of the history, structure, and demise of each. The fifth chapter compares the political ideologies and cultures of the various organizations, particularly on how the relationship between race, nation, and class was conceptualized. To portray a greater range of political ideologies, I compare each organization to a competing group within each respective racial/ethnic community. While revolutionary nationalism was certainly a dominant theme, it was by no means the only one at work. As Daryl Maeda has argued in the case of the BPP, these groups were simultaneously about the business of revolutionary nationalism, cultural nationalism, socialism, armed struggle, and worker and community organizing.[22] Interethnic relations is the subject of the sixth chapter. Here I explore the politics of solidarity: To what extent did each organization work with other racial/ethnic groups? What do such practices reveal about each group's political ideologies and contradictions and about the larger racial hierarchy? In the seventh chapter I explore gender relations. While all the organizations can be called patriarchal, there were important differences stemming from each group's unique history and experience of racialization, as well as the politics they embraced. For instance, some political ideologies encouraged more egalitarian gender relations than others. Finally, in chapter 8 I consider where the activists and organizations are today, the legacy of the Third World Left, and some of the lessons to be learned.

METHODOLOGY AND CAVEATS

A word on methodology: I am not a historian. While this book is very much about the past and I have borrowed heavily from the works and tools of historians, I am a social scientist—one deeply concerned with how race and class play out in the field of political activism. Accordingly, I do not offer a definitive history of each organization; I leave that task to the professionals. I seek to understand *why* activists developed the politics they did and how their actions might (or might not) make sense in light of larger racial and economic structures. My secondary goal is to analyze the breadth and diversity of racism. Over the years I have been frustrated by the assumptions that a person or action either is or is not racist and that there is only one kind of racism.[23] I hope to show that the forms and expressions of racism can vary greatly and need to be examined from multiple viewpoints.

As I completed this manuscript, it occurred to me that this study should have included a predominantly white organization. As explained earlier, I did not include one precisely because of the paucity of material on the left of color. However, as the analysis progressed, I realized that inclusion of a predominantly white organization would have provided a useful contrast to the Third World groups. I trust that other scholars will pursue this line of inquiry.

A final caution: the case studies that make up this work are not contemporaneous. The BPP began in 1968 in Southern California, was in decline by

1970, and managed to hang on for a few more years. In contrast, both East Wind and CASA did not begin until 1972, and both dissolved around 1978. Although only a few years apart, the BPP is closely associated with revolutionary nationalism and Black Power politics, whereas East Wind and CASA are more aligned with the sectarian politics of the New Communist movement. Despite the differences between the left politics of the late sixties and the seventies, they are fundamentally linked and represent a historical trajectory. While this disjuncture precludes easy comparisons, I try to consistently take this into account.

Data for this study came from three sources: secondary accounts, archival materials, and personal interviews. With the exception of the BPP, the secondary literature on leftists of color is sparse, but a sizable body of work on the larger movements and politics of the time provided both valuable context and clues. Libraries and archives across the state contained newspapers, special collections, and ephemera related to the relevant organizations. In addition, I interviewed numerous individuals, venturing beyond members of the BPP, CASA, and East Wind. I found it enormously useful to interview activists of color in related or competing organizations as well as white activists. This gave me access to more viewpoints and deepened my appreciation of the political landscape by providing outsiders' views on specific organizations. Needless to say, my most valuable resources were the individuals who consented to be interviewed. I am extremely grateful to all those persons who gave of their time, memories, and experiences in helping me reconstruct this period. And while I know that not everyone will agree with what I have written, I hope this book will be seen as a serious effort to better understand the Third World Left.

Direct quotations from activists are not attributed to particular individuals in this book because of the numerous interviewees who desired anonymity. Early drafts included both pseudonyms and actual names, but this system grew unwieldy, so I dropped all references to individuals' names and just included brief descriptions of the sources. Only in a few cases where individuals have already made public their political past and there is some insight to be gained from revealing their identities have I disclosed names.

Writing about a movement that I was not part of posed special challenges. Some people did not wish to talk with me because I was an outsider—and, worse, an academic. Tensions still existed regarding this recent history, I quickly learned, and as an outsider I did not always detect the political minefields I was walking into. On the other hand, I did not have the prejudices of an insider. Although I still might seem overly sympathetic to some readers, I have tried to be critical, while honoring my responsibility to represent accurately what informants told me, by contextualizing their comments and pointing out contradictions. One reason for the seemingly positive slant is that the most critical individuals declined to be interviewed, not wishing to revisit their experiences or share them with me. Thus, despite my best efforts, my interviewees were somewhat self-selected. In addition, given the current political climate, many emphasized the positive aspects of their activist experiences, knowing what was at stake and the negative nature of previous portrayals of the Third World Left. No doubt an insider would provide a different perspective, and I encouraged numerous interviewees to consider writing their memoirs.

Authors choose to spend a part of their lives on projects that mean a great deal to them. I am no exception. This book addresses issues that I have thought about for decades: How do we mobilize to create a more socially just world? How do we overcome racial tensions to build a stronger movement? How can we mobilize around a specific class politics? Despite my initial fascination with the mystique of the Third World Left (partly because of its inaccessibility), any romantic notions I might have had were dispelled by my research. Though I have tried to be candid about the many problems and shortcomings of the Third World Left, my research also gave me a deep respect for the individuals who made up these organizations. In most cases they cared passionately about their communities and social justice. Besides daring to dream of a new world, they were often willing to give of their lives. While I did not always agree with their actions, I admit to admiring their conviction, and I believe that if we wish to create a different world— one free of racism, poverty, human rights abuses, and environmental degradation—we can learn a great deal from the passion and commitment of the Third World Left, albeit tempered with more wisdom, honesty, kindness, and flexibility.

PART I

Race, Class, and Activism

ONE **Race and Political Activism**

The experience of growing up in Los Angeles partly explains my interest in the issues of race, class, and political activism that this book addresses. Born in East Los Angeles, I lived for a number of years in San Pedro and subsequently moved to Westminster in Orange County. Throughout these various moves, one constant was riding in our station wagon with my brothers and sister while driving to visit relatives throughout the area. Throughout the 1960s and 1970s I regularly traveled the Harbor Freeway to visit Grandpa and Tía Lola in East L.A.; the Pomona Freeway to see my aunt in Pico Rivera as well as my *ninos* (godparents) in Monterey Park; and the San Diego Freeway to visit my cousins in Canoga Park (see map 1). Little did I know that the history and geography of my extended family was in many ways typical of working-class Mexican Americans: with a decrease in residential segregation, as well as a strong Fordist economy, many of my relatives began leaving the greater East L.A. barrio around 1970.[1] Nevertheless, the maintenance of family ties was highly valued, and we managed to see some set of relatives at least once a week, usually on Sundays. The Southern California freeway system was key to maintaining this connection.

Aside from the usual childhood complaints stemming from seemingly interminable car rides, including such things as being touched and looked at by one's siblings, what I remember most was the landscape and geography of the region: eerie industrial buildings, dramatic mountains and palm trees, the downtown skyline, endless housing tracts, and of course, the racial patterns associated with them. Who lived in those vast expanses of South L.A. or the Westside, in which we knew no one? And why did our family seem to be strung out along the Pomona Freeway?

It was clear to me that East L.A. was the heart of the Mexican American community, and I suspected that Watts served a similar function for Blacks,

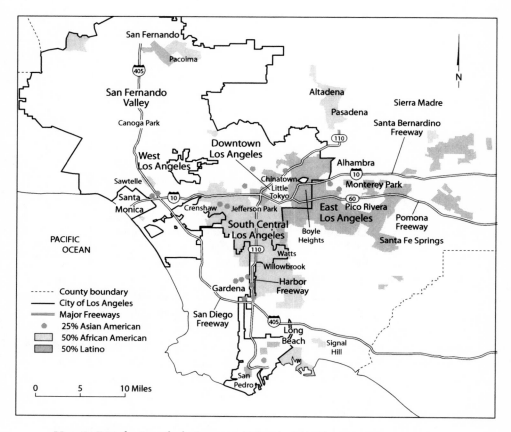

Map 1. Distribution of ethnic groups in Los Angeles County, 1970.

but I could not identify a comparable place for Asian Americans. In my mind, Chinatown and Little Tokyo were tourist spots with only a limited connection to contemporary Asian Americans. Such partial knowledge stemmed from intense residential segregation and a resulting lack of familiarity with either Black or Japanese people. My world was largely brown and white.

As a youngster, I struggled with being brown. Living in San Pedro, I learned early that being Mexican was far from desirable. At various times I detested my brown skin, was embarrassed by the Spanish spoken in our household, and was envious of light-skinned Mexicans, wondering why I couldn't be a *güera*.[2] My painfully limited consciousness concerning my Mexican identity was complicated by my awareness of other peoples of color. Although I did not really know any African Americans, I knew that Blacks were a devalued racial/ethnic group, and I sensed that my racial position was somehow tied to theirs—how that worked out exactly I wasn't sure, but I understood that what it meant to be brown in Los Angeles was somehow linked to what it meant to be Black. I vaguely recall one incident in which I came home from school crying one day. My mom, seeing my anxiety, inquired, "*M'ija*, what happened?" Apparently, a girl at school, who was white, had asked if I was Black, and this had caused me great anguish. What indeed if I *was* Black? It was a frightening thought to a little Mexican American girl who knew she was racially problematic but sensed that things could be worse. My mom assured me that no, I wasn't Black, but she also stressed, in her very Catholic way, that even if I were, what would be wrong with that?

In contrast, I actually did know some Japanese Americans, a family down the street in San Pedro. While they were nice enough, I considered them to be "foreign." Several things stood out about them: their yard was landscaped in a distinctly Japanese style, they did not wear shoes in the house, and they enjoyed a cuisine that was totally unfamiliar to me. But what was significant was how I perceived them relative to me: *they* were foreign. And while I was uncomfortable with my Mexican background, which I equated with being both inferior and different, I had somehow absorbed the dominant reading of Asian Americans as the ultimate foreigners. Moreover, I sensed that my Japanese American neighbors occupied a distinct social position. I did not feel that they were as despised as Blacks and Mexicans, but they clearly were not on the same level as whites either. They were somewhere in between.

I share this bit of autobiography to introduce a basic premise of this book: what we know as racial/ethnic groups (I use the term *racial/ethnic* to emphasize that racial groups may also function as ethnic groups) can be grasped only in relation to *other* racial/ethnic groups. In other words, racial/ethnic groups, the meanings attached to them, the economic positions they occupy, and the status conferred upon them can be understood only in the context of the larger racial landscape. Further, the dynamics that produce racial/ethnic groups are so profound that a grade school child living through them can discern them. Unfortunately, what most kids know social scientists, myself included, are only beginning to pay close attention to.

My first political awakening centered on issues of racial oppression, particularly the plight of African Americans. I certainly did not learn these things in school, but as an avid reader I became aware of the civil rights movement and slavery (Harriet Tubman was my hero—I was deeply inspired by her courage). In addition to reading, popular culture contributed to my nascent consciousness. In particular, I recall the deep impact that Stevie Wonder's song "Living for the City" had on me. I experienced deep moral outrage upon learning how Blacks had been treated, and, having no idea what other groups had undergone, I came to believe that African Americans were the only oppressed racial/ethnic group in the United States. I knew that I was not Black, so it was impossible for me to think of myself as affected by racism. But I also knew that I was not white, and I struggled with being rendered invisible by the Black/white binary—despite living in a city with deep Mexican roots.

In addition to racial oppression, however, I was concerned with the plight of workers and the poor of all colors. Coming from a union family, I was all too familiar with the power that the "contract," which was negotiated every three years, had over our lives. In addition, I became acquainted with strikes, the rhythms of the hiring hall, and the idiocy of waterfront bosses that we heard about every night from my dad. These events provided a framework in my mind of what it meant to be a worker. Thus it was hardly surprising that when I learned about the United Farm Workers (UFW) and its struggle, it resonated deeply within me. Here at last was a group of Mexicanas/os giving voice to the inchoate feelings and consciousness that were stirring in so many of us. Not only did the UFW announce our presence to the world, but it mobilized around a series of issues that most poor and working-class people could readily identity with. When I was young, I had a very romantic vision of the UFW. I was appalled at the conditions that Mexicana/o field workers labored and lived under, but I was proud of this seemingly organic and charismatic form of Mexican American resistance. Although I sensed that Mexicans had long been subordinated in California, before I learned of the UFW I knew of no instance of collective resistance and/or struggle. Accordingly, my impression was not only that we were invisible but that we lacked the ability to mobilize and fight for our rights. Maybe we really were the "dumb Mexicans" that everyone said. Not surprisingly, I took the UFW struggle, as perhaps one of the most profound instances of Chicana/o resistance, to heart, and explored it more closely in my dissertation.[3] One of the things I learned from that project, which compared how two Chicana/o communities mobilized around environmental issues, was how deeply anti-communist the UFW was. Yet I also knew that many people considered the

UFW to be "radical." This led me to question the term. What is radical? Who is a radical? If nothing else, I have learned that *radical* is a relative term. While the Chicana/o movement was indeed radical, there was tremendous diversity within it, with some groups assuming far more conservative positions than others. Further, it struck me that much of the scholarship and teaching of *el movimiento* centered on a few themes and groups, such as the UFW, the Brown Berets, La Raza Unida Party, New Mexican land-grant struggles, and the Crusade for Justice.[4] Though this work was of tremendous importance and had a great impact, I knew that it was not complete, as my own experience at the Strategy Center suggested otherwise.

I wished to study the Chicana/o left for this project because I was intrigued by this missing piece of history and was keen to learn how such organizations handled race and class. As I began the research for this book, however, I quickly became immersed in a larger set of racial/ethnic relationships. I realized that I could not grasp the Chicana/o left without addressing the Black Panther Party. The Black Panther Party loomed large in the national, including Chicana/o, consciousness, and it seemed to me that in addition to inspiring other peoples of color it had created the necessary political space for the development of a Third World Left. This could not be ignored. Thus I found myself having come full circle and needing to explore the very issues I had first become aware of as a child regarding the interconnectedness of racial meanings and structures. Accordingly, I decided that the project needed to be comparative so that I could examine the racial dynamics associated with these radical groups, as well as the relationships between them.

Several questions are at the heart of this book. They come from my personal experiences, the empirical research I conducted for this project, and larger debates within the literature. My primary concern was to examine the extent to which differential racialization leads to distinct forms of radical politics. Scholars have long noted that wherever domination exists, resistance will follow. Often resistance is invisible to all but the participants themselves, but at other times it evolves into a broad-based opposition. This book examines one moment when "revolution was in the air," engendering extremely public and overt forms of resistance, and thus offers an exceptional opportunity to explore the extent to which resistance is shaped by domination.[5] To adequately explore this question, however, I needed to analyze how and why various populations of color are racialized in distinct kinds of ways. What are the processes of differential racialization, and what do they look like on the ground? To what extent are these processes shaped by racial dynamics and class relations, and how are these two factors linked?

Finally, assuming that different peoples of color are racialized in different ways, what does this mean for the larger racial landscape? In particular, how do these processes translate into racial positions and hierarchies, and how do they change over time?

COMPARATIVE RESEARCH: TALKING TO EACH OTHER

Although comparative research within ethnic studies is hardly new, scholars have only recently begun seriously theorizing differences and relationships between various racial/ethnic groups. When ethnic studies first became a formal discipline in the early 1970s, each racial/ethnic group, including African Americans, American Indians, Asian Americans, and Chicanas/os and Latinas/os, operated from a largely bipolar racial approach centered on whites. In other words, the experience of, say, Asian Americans, was studied relative to the dominant white population. This meant both exploring how white society contributed to the subordination of Asian Americans and documenting various outcomes and indicators—educational, social, health related, and political—relative to whites.[6] From a historical perspective, this approach is understandable given that whites were considered the norm.

Thirty years later the struggle for ethnic studies continues at the institutional level, but the intellectual content and focus of the discipline have changed considerably.[7] While the initial focus of ethnic studies was corrective, challenging previous racist assumptions and scholarship,[8] ethnic studies scholars have begun engaging each other in new ways. Researchers have come to appreciate that power relations, particularly racial and class dynamics, cannot be understood in a bipolar framework. Accordingly, there has been a growing effort to develop alternative approaches that capture the complexity of how race and class work in the United States.

One catalyst in the development of new strategies to the study of race and ethnicity came from the humanities. Heavily influenced by theoretical developments in literature, social scientists, including historians, began in the 1980s to conceptualize race and racial/ethnic groups not as given and natural but as socially constructed. To say that race is a social construction simply means that the idea of race has no real biological significance and is largely the product of human social systems. This does not imply that race is not "real" or a powerful force shaping our lives. But by recognizing it as the product of human activities and imagination, we can shift the focus of our inquiry to questions of process: *How* are racial/ethnic groups constructed? What are the boundaries for inclusion and exclusion, and how do they shift over time? How do groups and individuals challenge and (re)produce processes of racialization? By asking such questions scholars began to realize that individual groups could not be understood in isolation. Whereas before the emphasis had been on whites, researchers began looking increasingly to other groups of color in order to sort out the complex processes and meanings that produce racial dynamics and patterns.[9]

The work of historians has been especially helpful to me in developing a comparative approach. In *Racial Fault Lines,* Tomás Almaguer showed not only how white supremacy worked to dominate all people of color historically in California but also how each group fared differently. He illuminated the particular meanings associated with various racial/ethnic groups, as well as the economic resources and/or opportunities they presented to white aspirations. This text was critical in forcing a reconsideration of the history of particular places and in insisting that racial positions are shaped by both discursive meanings and economic structures. Building on this work was Neil Foley's *The White Scourge,* which focuses on the central Texas cotton belt and analyzes how the racial meanings and attitudes associated with poor whites, Mexicans, and Blacks translated into particular economic outcomes, as well as how they played off each other. Thus the meanings attached to poor whites could not be understood outside the meanings and economic purpose embodied by Mexican workers.

The political scientist Claire Kim has sought to clarify this growing body of literature by developing a model to explain complex racial hierarchies. She argues that the racial position of "intermediary" or ambiguous minorities, such as Asian Americans, can be ascertained only through a process of triangulation. That is, it can be understood only relative to whites, as the universal dominant, and Blacks, as the universal subordinate. She conceptualizes the racial landscape as a field in which various groups have fluid but distinct positions.[10]

This work has been invaluable in my efforts to build a comparative framework to explain the distinct forms of activism that developed among the Third World Left. But before launching into that discussion, I would like to take a step back and say a few words about race itself.

RACE AND RACIAL IDEOLOGY

Having established that race is a social construct, we can define it more specifically as an ideology that functions to separate the human population into various groups based on supposedly significant biological features, including skin color, hair texture, and eye structure. Although many of us were taught about race in school (I recall learning about Caucasians, Mongoloids, and Negroids and wondering where I fit in), racial groups and ideology are fairly recent developments. Humans have always found ways to distinguish ourselves, but only within the last five hundred years or so have we created the notion of inherent biological difference. The problem with the idea of race is that the closer one looks, the less viable the concept is. Numerous writers have demonstrated that there is more biological diversity within any given racial group than between racial groups. And when one examines how societies interpret these biological "facts," especially with regard to categorizing people, the contradictions mount. Our historical practice, for example, of categorizing as Black any person with as little as one drop of "Black" blood suggests that more is at work than rational scientific practice. Moreover, the fact that some people who are categorized as "non-white" but *appear* to be white can at times "pass" in order to access greater opportunities suggests the complex ways racial ideology is constructed and employed toward particular ends.[11]

Because of such manipulations race is best understood as a relationship of power. The idea of racial groups and race itself is rooted in attempts to assert control over particular populations in order to enhance the position and well-being of others. The idea of race essentially developed as an ideology in conjunction with imperialism and colonization. A justification was needed to help rationalize taking over other countries and peoples, whether by usurping their resources, appropriating them as colonies, or enslaving them. The notion of biological difference and, more specifically, the corollaries of biological inferiority and superiority gave conquering forces ideological tools to dehumanize their victims and legitimize their actions.[12] That racial ideologies are still with us, despite a radically different global political economy, not only indicates the longevity and deeply entrenched nature of such ideologies but also suggests that they are still useful in shaping contemporary power relations.

As we go about creating our world as humans, we cannot help drawing upon prevailing ideologies in the production of everyday life. This occurs both consciously and unconsciously. Hegemonic ideologies, or what Gramsci calls "common sense," are ideologies that become so widespread and accepted that they not only become naturalized but determine the boundaries of acceptable thought.[13] Appreciating hegemonic ideologies is necessary for understanding how race works in the contemporary United States, as they help explain why racial inequality persists in a society that advocates equality and has made some forms of discrimination illegal. This is not to deny that, as George Lipsitz has pointed out, discriminatory policies and practices that accrue to the benefit of whites exist and play a role in perpetuating inequality. But it is meant to stress that unless individuals develop an explicitly antiracist consciousness, they will inevitably reflect and act upon hegemonic racial ideologies, which, in turn, reproduce structures of inequality.[14]

Although I have defined race as an ideology, it is important to appreciate its material dimensions as well. Race is composed of both ideological and material components that are manifest in the creation of structures, institutions, and practices. One example of how racialized discourses and structures work together to produce racial inequality is that of urban housing markets, particularly housing segregation and property values. Urban housing markets, which are considered to be free markets, produce highly skewed and racialized outcomes that can be seen in the urban landscape. It is well known that U.S. cities are highly segregated, particularly in terms of Blacks and whites. Many whites do not wish to live in Black communities, and while many will accept Black neighbors, Black *neighborhoods* are a different story.[15] The widespread nature of this pattern reflects pervasive and deeply held prejudices that translate into real material structures: segregated cities. Segregation, in turn, translates into real material disparities that perpetuate inequalities between Blacks and whites and further reinforce racist ideologies. For instance, Black property is less desirable and therefore is worth less than white property. This fact has enormous implications for the distribution of wealth and resources. Because real estate is the basis of most individual wealth in the United States (including intergenerational transfers of wealth), white property owners benefit from the devalued nature of Black property in the form of higher property values and greater wealth.[16] But the white community benefits as well in the form of enhanced resources, such as better schools. Urban segregation and inequality are predicated on racial ideologies, or "common sense," that is enacted by millions of people every day, resulting in the sedimentation of racial inequality in the physical environment. Yet although Blacks are clearly disadvantaged, the majority of whites rarely consider their greater wealth to result from any sort of privilege; instead, they assert that it is entirely due to their own industriousness.

Differential Racialization and Racial Hierarchies

Differential Racialization   As a geographer I am keenly interested in how racism plays out across various landscapes. In different places and times and at various scales, particular groups may be subordinate, dominant, or in some intermediate position. Two ideas in particular can help us understand how race varies over time and space: differential racialization and racial hierarchies. Differential racialization refers to the fact that different groups are racialized in distinct kind of ways. What this means is that a particular set of racial meanings are attached to different racial/ethnic groups that not only affect their class position and racial standing but also are a function of it. Thus there is a dialectic between the discursive and the material.

Today, the word *racism* is used so frequently, particularly among progressives and the left, that I sometimes feel there is a loss of nuance. While *racism* is a powerful word, and many people correctly understand it to mean the production of inequality between various racial/ethnic groups, I am frustrated that there is insufficient attention directed to *how* different communities of color may experience racism. People of color are not homogenous and do not experience the same types of racialization. The concept of differential racialization can help us understand these subtle and not-so-subtle differences.

The process by which a people becomes racialized is highly specific. The particulars of history, geography, the needs of capital, and the attributes of various populations all contribute to it. In analyzing contemporary forms of differential racialization, one must always consider a group's history of incorporation and economic integration. Under what conditions and circumstances did they become part of this country—undergoing what Espiritu calls "differential inclusion"?[17] Were they already here and conquered by Anglo Americans, as in the case of indigenous people or Mexicans in the Southwest? Were they brought here in chains as forced labor? Or did they come as immigrants in search of better opportunities? In each case, we need to determine the political economic forces that led to the initial contact. Was a particular fraction of capital in need of workers? If so, what was the structure and culture of the existing working class? Or was capital in need of new workers because the existing ones were organizing or dying due to inhumane conditions? Alternatively, it could be that the state and capital wished to expand and acquire the land and resources of another people. Each scenario can engender a distinct racialization process, depending upon the political economic specifics and available racial ideologies.

Another factor in differential racialization is the "cultural distance" between the groups in question. Almaguer's study of California found that in the nineteenth century whites were far more amenable to accepting Mexicans than to accepting Indians and the Chinese: both of the latter were considered to be heathen savages, whereas Mexicans, though problematic, could be included on the margins of society due to their Christian background, Spanish tongue (a European language), and racial diversity and whites' general familiarity with Mexican and Spanish culture, given its long presence in the region.[18] Such readings have enormous implications for a group's relationship to the nation. If, drawing on Benedict Anderson, we define a nation as an "imagined political community," it becomes clear that the United States as a nation has historically been defined in explicitly racial terms.[19] In particular, citizenship has been reserved for those categorized as white. Not only did such practices supposedly protect the racial purity of the nation but, perhaps more importantly, as Anthony Marx has argued, the subordination of nonwhites has allowed the state to appease and consolidate potentially marginalized and fragmented whites. The somewhat arbitrary nature of acceptance into the nation in turn profoundly affects the racialization process. If the dominant group is willing to accept the minority group as part of the nation, this bodes well for a relatively smooth incorporation process and works against the most dehumanizing forms of racialization. If, on the other hand, the dominant population sees the minority group as objectionable or a threat to the nation—despite the needs of capital—then the group in question is likely to be highly marginalized and to experience a brutal form of racialization. In short, differential racialization affects how each group is treated legally, socially, and economically and can even determine life and death.

Racial Hierarchies   A racial hierarchy is a specific configuration of power relations in a given place and time based on racial ideology. Racial hierarchies are the mapping of power relations: Who is on top? Who is on the bottom? Who is in between? And how are racial groups related? By connecting the lines between various locations and nodes we can ascertain the status of various racial/ethnic groups and their positioning relative to each other. Racial hierarchies are composed of several elements, including local demographics, history, and economic structures, as well as national racial narratives. They can be relatively simple, such as the hierarchy of whites over Blacks in the South during slavery, which featured clear dominant and subordinate groups whose inequality became increasingly codified over time.[20] More complex racial hierarchies existed in many eastern industrial cities during the late 1800s, when, in addition to Blacks and whites, there were a number of "not quite white" groups, including Jews, the Irish, and Italians.[21] The same was also true for California starting at the time of Spanish conquest, when a racially mixed group of conquerors and settlers—who brought with them their own complex racial order—confronted the indigenous population. The resulting hierarchy was further complicated by the arrival of various Asian peoples and later African Americans. Because California has historically been so racially diverse, with populations that could not readily pass into whiteness, it remains an exceptional place to study complex racial hierarchies.

Racial hierarchies are not static: they respond to both geographic and historical processes. One example of the transformative capacity of racial hierarchies is the case of Chinese and Japanese Americans in California. In the late 1800s and early 1900s, Asian Americans were arguably the most despised racial/ethnic group in the state. They were regularly lynched, occasionally massacred, excluded from large sectors of the economy, prohibited from living among and marrying whites, denied citizenship, and eventually banned from immigrating. Although California was home to a large and varied population of color, Asians received the brunt of racial animosity. This is in dramatic contrast to today, when Chinese and Japanese Americans are no longer the most detested racial/ethnic group. They have experienced not only economic mobility but improvement in their racial position. In some circles, Asian Americans are almost considered "honorary whites."[22] A century ago it was inconceivable that the hostility directed toward Asian Americans could ever change—but it did. Thus, whenever we speak of racial hierarchies, we must be sensitive to issues of temporality.

Regional Racial Hierarchies. The case of Chinese and Japanese Americans also illustrates the importance of spatiality to racial hierarchies. Racial hierarchies exist at multiple geographic scales.[23] We can discern the general contours of a global racial hierarchy in the admittedly crude division between the "First" and "Third" Worlds, which correspond roughly to patterns of colonization. But racial hierarchies also exist at smaller scales. For example, while Asian Americans were under attack in California, the national racial hierarchy was structured along largely Black/white lines. The influence of the national racial narratives could be seen in the fact that many of the discriminatory tools and techniques directed against Asian Americans had been originally deployed against Blacks. On the other hand, regional racial hierarchies can also affect the national one, as when problematic "regional minorities" become national threats.

While we must always be cognizant of national racial narratives, studying racial hierarchies solely at the national level poses several problems. In particular, it precludes a fine-grained analysis of the relationship between economic structures and racial ideologies because economic processes get worked out and shape individual lives primarily at the regional and local levels. Although national economic patterns and policies certainly matter, the importance of regional variation should not be underestimated. One need only reflect on the historical importance of slavery to the South, industrialization to the Northeast, and mining to the West to appreciate the significance of regional economies.[24] Hence it is primarily at the regional or local scale that more nuanced discussions of the relationship between race and class emerge. Such scaled analyses allow us to see the intersection of labor markets, class relations, and racial ideologies—all of which contribute to racial hierarchies. These hierarchies, in turn, can have profound implications for the nature of regions themselves.

Class and Racial Hierarchies. Let us look more closely at how local labor markets are racialized, as this is key to the creation of racial hierarchies. Labor markets are significant not only because are they fundamental to the process of class formation but because they are primarily regional and local phenomena. Most people commute to home and work on a daily basis, so this activity sets the potential geographic parameters of labor markets and divisions of labor. The exact nature of local labor markets is determined by the needs of capital, the nature of the commodity or service, state policies, the available labor pool, and racial and gender ideologies. These last two factors are instrumental in suggesting which groups will occupy what positions.[25] It is at the intersection of economic processes and racial discourses that racialized class structures and divisions of labor are created.

The intersection of labor markets and racial ideologies can have profound consequences reaching far beyond the local labor market. Consider, for example, the intimate relationship between Mexicans and farm work, which has been central to the racialization of many Latinas/os in the western United States. Over time California farmers decided that Mexicans were an ideal workforce and generated a whole set of stereotypes and ideologies to justify their intensive exploitation. For example, it was believed that Mexicans, in addition to tolerating stoop labor better than whites (because they were relatively short and thus would not have to bend down as far as a white person would), would work long hours for cheap wages without complaining, would have no ambitions (or capabilities) beyond farm work, and would "disappear" when the harvest was over. They were thought to be content with illiteracy and dirty living conditions. These attributes, it was felt, rendered them an efficient and pliable workforce ideally suited to the shifting conditions of California agriculture.[26] Such ideas, regardless of their accuracy, developed into a racial ideology that justified the treatment of farmworkers and was extrapolated to many Mexicans and Mexican Americans throughout the Southwest, regardless of their actual class positions. Thus we can see the dialectic nature of racial ideologies and processes of class formation.

Today, Mexican labor has expanded far beyond California's fields. There is even a growing professional class, yet these stereotypes and images linger. We can see their staying power in the fact that the vast majority of Mexicanas/os are located in the working class, receive inferior educational opportunities, are poor, and continue to face discrimination in many arenas. In effect, these ideologies, combined with immigration flows and a postindustrial economy, produce highly racialized outcomes. Care must be taken not to suggest that such is the plight of all Latinas/os. I myself, for example, am a professor at a research university. Yet despite a radically different class position I am affected by prevailing racial ideologies, as some students resist seeing me as a legitimate professor. Not infrequently I am asked, "Are you a *real* professor?" For some, it is difficult to believe that a Mexican American woman can have a position of authority. Certainly, the racial hierarchy has not dictated my economic position, but it does inform my daily experience.[27]

I have suggested that racial hierarchies change over time. I now wish to consider *how* that happens and the role of crisis in change. Crises, which are endemic to capitalism, can be defined as moments when the prevailing formation can no longer reproduce itself. At such times racism may be used to help "work out" the crisis, with profound implications for the racial hierarchy.[28] In such instances racial hierarchies not only become more vivid but also can be transformed. Typically, during a crisis, as large numbers of people are being dislocated and are feeling pain and uncertainty, so-called leaders may channel the resulting anxiety into hostility toward those at the bottom of the racial hierarchy. Scapegoating is nothing new and can fall on any marginalized group depending upon how the lines of difference are drawn. In California, both today and in the past, they are primarily drawn racially. As Omi and Winant have pointed out, race remains a central organizing principle in U.S. society.[29] Scapegoating a racial/ethnic group serves to subordinate that group, but it also contains the possibility of movement for others. Groups that are not held responsible for the current crisis may attain an improved status and position within the racial hierarchy.

One recent example of a change in the racial hierarchy is California's Proposition 187. In the late 1980s California entered a deep and painful recession, leading then-Governor Pete Wilson to make immigrants, particularly undocumented immigrants, the centerpiece of his 1994 re-election campaign. He argued that California could not afford the cost of undocumented immigrants and that they were responsible for the recession. This resulted in tremendous public hostility toward immigrants, particularly Latina/o immigrants and by extension those who looked Latina/o. According to the immigrant-rights activist Susan Alva, "The immigration issue, particularly in California, has very much turned into a Latino issue." This sentiment eventually culminated in Proposition 187, which sought to ban undocumented persons from a whole range of social, educational, and health services.[30]

What was significant about this episode was not that it demonized Latinas/os but that it provided a fleeting opportunity for both Blacks and Asian Americans to improve their racial position. Conservative pundits catered to the African American vote, emphasizing that Blacks were negatively affected by immigration and that they were citizens and thus included in the body politic. In short, part of the politics of Proposition 187 was about giving Black people a chance to be "Americans," something they have systematically been denied because of the extent to which the nation has been defined as white.[31]

For Asian Americans the situation was somewhat different. Proposition 187 ostensibly targeted all undocumented persons and thus would have certainly affected the Asian/Pacific Islander population. Various progressive Asian groups knew this and saw the occasion as a valuable opportunity to ally with Latinas/os. In the public's mind, however, Proposition 187 was not about Asian/Pacific Islanders. It was a referendum on the Latinization of California. In fact, both Asian Americans and Blacks voted for the initiative in fairly highly numbers: 57 percent and 56 percent, respectively (compared to 31 percent of Latino voters). In short, Proposition 187 reworked the racial hierarchy insofar as it exerted downward pressure on Latinas/os' position while offering a temporary reprieve to Blacks, who were suddenly part of the nation, and to Asian/Pacific Islanders, who were rendered a much less problematic immigrant population.[32]

To summarize, the racial hierarchy is an ever-changing landscape composed of distinct racial positions. Racial hierarchies are shaped by local demographics, regional economies, local history, and national racial narratives. Differential racialization is key to the production of racial hierarchies, as it produces a variety of racial meanings, all of which are in continuous engagement with each other. Finally, although the racial hierarchy is in a continual state of flux, moments of crisis are pivotal to its transformation. However, racial hierarchies may also be transformed from the bottom up by activism.

RACE AND POLITICAL ACTIVISM

To Act or Not to Act

Because racial hierarchies are predicated on inequality and domination, they are also sites of resistance and contestation. People struggle not only to change their own positions but in some cases to dismantle the structures of inequality that oppress others as well as themselves. Within ethnic studies, much energy has been directed at unearthing the rich but often obscured histories of racial resistance. Such instances of political awareness and mobilization beckon researchers, not only because we wish to uncover submerged histories but because such accounts provide historical linkages with more contemporary forms of activism.[33]

While this work has been invaluable, we must not give the impression that all people of color are poised for revolution.[34] Only a small number of people take the step from private individual to public actor and become activists. For various reasons, most persons choose not to act publicly, regardless of how exploited or oppressed they may be. This does not mean they are content with the injustice; it means only that they are not willing or able to openly challenge it. Fear is one of the most powerful forces that prevents people from acting. Depending upon how repressive the situation is, people may fear, with good cause, retribution in the form of unemployment, the denial of basic services and needs, the destruction of their property, and, in some instances, violence and death.[35] Another factor is the pervasive nature of hegemonic discourses and the internalization of self-hate. It never fails to amaze me how many people, in the face of grave injustice and inequality, will justify their marginalized positions by drawing upon "common sense." They, in effect, buy into dominant discourses that have been deployed by more powerful actors to justify what may be an immoral set of arrangements, often by naturalizing the conditions of the most subordinated.[36] Finally, many people choose not to act because of apathy and a limited faith in their ability to effect change. Disillusion and cynicism are widespread throughout U.S. society, and people of color are no exception. It takes an enormous amount of time, energy, hope, and creativity to initiate change from below.[37]

Consequently, some writers, such as Gregory Rodriguez, have questioned the significance of social movements and political activism, pointing out that the vast majority never participate in them: "The Mexican American experience has largely been interpreted through the actions of advocacy groups. No matter that surveys find that Mexican Americans are much less likely to join civic groups than are, say, Anglos, most writers still adhere to the rule that the collective, organized minority activity is the only minority behavior that's worth writing about. . . . With few exceptions, the history of an organized few has obscured the more revealing story of the lives and daily struggles of the unorganized mass of people."[38] Rodriguez's point, though true enough, reflects a limited understanding of *how* social change occurs. Among dominated communities, fundamental change does not occur through the ballot box, or even through mass uprisings, although both can play important roles. Rather, it centers on producing a shift in consciousness— an alternative vision of what the world might look like, an expanded sense of personal efficacy (often called empowerment), and a clear set of demands—and on systematically mobilizing. Such changes constitute the beginnings of a movement. Creating these changes, or at least the conditions for them, is the job of the political activist and organizer.

Changing Racial Hierarchies through Racial Projects

Over the course of history, millions have initiated countless attempts to create a more socially just society. Some have done so out of anger and a refusal to be dehumanized, others have responded to the suffering of fellow human beings, and still others have been motivated by an awareness that not to act is to support a particular social formation. Just as motivation may vary, so do the content and form of resistance itself. Some individuals have acted alone, some have banded together in acts of rebellion, and some have built elaborate organizations and movements to help them achieve freedom, liberation, and equality.[39]

The Third World Left, which existed at the intersection of the New Left and the more nationalist movements embedded within communities of color, constituted a social movement. The sociologist James Jasper defines a social movement as "conscious, concerted, and relatively sustained efforts by organized groups of ordinary people (as opposed to, say, political parties, the military, or industrial trade groups) to change some aspect of their society by using extrainstitutional means."[40] The Third World Left sought to dismantle the racial hierarchy and alter the class structure of U.S. society, particularly as it related to people of color. It engaged in what Howard Winant calls a racial project: that is, an "interpretation, representation or explanation of racial dynamics and an effort to organize and distribute resources along particular racial lines."[41] In the case of the Third World Left, this project sought to end numerous discriminatory practices that were part of the racial hierarchy and class structure. Activists targeted such issues as police abuse, unfair treatment of immigrants, exclusion from social services, the exploitation of workers of color, U.S. domination of Third World countries, and the general marginalization of communities of color. They did this by challenging policies, withholding cooperation, mobilizing large demonstrations, educating and politicizing others to take up the struggle, and, in some cases, arming themselves. Ultimately, their hope was to create a radically different society, which would feature a redistribution of economic and political opportunities along both class and racial lines in the United States.

The extent to which activists or organizations are successful is decided not only by their skills and abilities but also by the forces arrayed against them. While there will always be resistance to oppressive conditions, the precise nature and content of that resistance are often determined by history. The alternatives people envision, the methods they employ, and the way they mobilize all occur within a particular historical and cultural milieu. Thus, during the Cold War, antiracist activists were able to mount only relatively small challenges to the racial formation, given the pressure to conform and be patriotic.[42] The 1960s and 1970s presented a very different set of possibilities. George Katsiaficas has described this era as a "world historical moment" when seemingly the entire world was rising up and challenging imperialism, economic and racial inequality, and societal norms and conventions.[43] Hence the boundaries of what seemed possible were greatly expanded, and people engaged in behavior and practices that may sometimes be difficult to understand today. But, for many, revolution *was* in the air, and within this context the Third World Left was born. The following quote from a New Left activist describes how many perceived the world at the moment.

> Every left idea is winning right now. That's very important for people to understand about not rewriting history. . . . King is moving on the war [and] towards the Black working class and trying to build a multiracial movement of the poor. The Vietnamese are winning in Vietnam. The Panthers are saying armed struggle. SDS chapters that used to have a hundred people now have five hundred people in them. There was the Harvard strike—1967–68—everyone thought that a world revolution was happening and there was no limit to what was possible at that point. All of Latin America, all of Asia, all of Africa was going communist, the protests in France, the French workers' strike. So we were part of this world historical moment.[44]

Given that so much was going on, the task of analyzing the political activism and social movements of the 1960s and 1970s presents a challenge. Not only is it difficult to distinguish between various political tendencies, but establishing causality or priority in terms of race and class is no easy task. Was the Third World Left equally committed to struggles against racism and class exploitation, or did it tend to privilege one over the other? How do we untangle and make sense of these multiple forces? Is it accurate to depict activists as engaged in a racial project? Or should such activism be more appropriately categorized as anticapitalist? Although I argue that the

Third World Left was simultaneously about race and class, I locate this activism in racial terms, a decision some may disagree with. Stuart Hall's work, in particular, has furthered my conceptualization of such activism by pointing out the extent to which class may be lived through race (and I would add, gender): "Race performs a double function. It is . . . the principal modality in which the black members of that class 'live,' experience, make sense of and thus *come to a consciousness* of their structured subordination. It is through the modality of race that blacks comprehend, handle, and then begin to resist the exploitation which is an objective feature of the class situation."[45] Hall indicates that, especially for the working class in a highly racialized society, one's class position is largely *experienced* through race. This is meant, not to reduce class to race, but to show the extent to which they intersect in shaping the everyday life of the poor and colored and to suggest the important work that race does in creating a particular social formation.

I find this analysis compelling insofar as activists in the Third World Left did in fact organize along racial lines. Although there were many multiracial (or multinational, as they were called) groups, all the organizations I studied were composed overwhelmingly of a single racial/ethnic group and focused their efforts on that community, in particular the poor, marginalized, and lower-class members of that community. Thus, although activists developed elaborate class ideologies and were anticapitalist, their frame of reference was always their racial/ethnic position. It was through race that they came "to a consciousness of their structured subordination." Indeed, the emphasis on race was what distinguished the Third World Left from the larger New Left. Numerous individuals departed from the New Left precisely because of their discomfort with its approach to race. The Third World Left gave expression to activists' longing and need to articulate a politics centered on their understanding of the racialized nature of capitalism.

Clarifying the nature of this relationship is crucial because I argue in this book that the distinctive nature of each organization's politics is linked to the larger process of racialization and the racial position of each racial/ethnic group. Without being too reductionist, I hope to show throughout the remainder of the book the extent to which the unique concerns, ideology, and cultures of the various organizations were produced by a particular racial and economic experience, as well as by a selective borrowing from other movements and places, ranging from Cuba and Vietnam on the international scene to the ghettos, barrios, and Nikkei clusters of Los Angeles at the local level.

TWO

**Differential Racialization
in Southern California**

Historical accounts of contemporary Southern California often emphasize
World War II because during this time the region reinvented itself and its
contemporary foundations were established, including a major restructuring of the regional racial hierarchy.[1] Accordingly, it was the racial and class
structure of the post–World War II era that Third World Left activists grew
up in. This same formation led to the differential racialization of African,
Mexican, and Japanese Americans that activists ultimately rebelled against.
My goal in this chapter is to consider how the demographic, political, economic, and social changes initiated by World War II affected communities of
color and thus provided the backdrop to activists' lives.

WORLD WAR II IN SOUTHERN CALIFORNIA

Five key shifts associated with World War II were critical to refashioning
Southern California's racial hierarchy and its concomitant distribution of
economic and political opportunities. First, the war triggered a tremendous
population explosion, which in turn altered the racial/ethnic composition of
the region. Second, population growth was coupled with massive economic
development, particularly in the military and aerospace industries, which
provided unprecedented employment opportunities for communities of
color. Third, population and industrial expansion together produced a new
spatial structure—urban sprawl—with important implications for interethnic relations. Fourth, in one of the greatest mass violations of civil rights,
Japanese Americans were placed in concentration camps and returned to
Los Angeles not only impoverished but with traumatic memories that
would play themselves out in subsequent generations. Finally, African and
Mexican American veterans returned from the war with an enhanced sense
of empowerment and a commitment to fight against racial inequality.

Table 1   *Population increase in Los Angeles*
            County, 1920–1970

Year	Population Total	% Increase
1920	936,455	—
1930	2,208,492	235
1940	2,785,643	126
1950	4,151,687	149
1960	6,038,771	154
1970	7,041,980	165

SOURCE: B. Marchand, *The Emergence of Los Angeles: Population and Housing in the City of Dreams, 1940–70* (London:
Routledge and Kegan Paul, 1986), 70.

Demographic, Economic, and Spatial Changes

Although Southern California's prosperity has always been based on population growth and land speculation, World War II brought a period of unparalleled expansion.[2] Los Angeles County's population quadrupled from less
than one million in 1920 to over four million by 1950. Table 1 charts the
county's growth before and after the war. Although all decades were characterized by phenomenal growth, the greatest increase occurred in the two
decades after the war, as literally millions of people came to the region seeking jobs and the California lifestyle.

While the majority of World War II immigrants were white, there was also
a large influx of African Americans, thus bolstering the small but long-standing Black community. In 1920 there were 15,579 Blacks in Los Angeles,
whereas by 1950 there were 170,880.[3] Although this influx was relatively
small given the overall population, it not only resulted in a sizable Black community but marked a transition in Los Angeles's racial hierarchy. Before then,
Black Angelenos had often been considered better off than other urban
African Americans, primarily because there were other, larger, nonwhite
groups targeted by white racism. So, for instance, in Southern California,
American Indians were lynched and sold into slavery, Chinese American communities were destroyed by race riots, Japanese Americans were terrorized by
white vigilantes, and Mexican Americans were subject to intense police
harassment.[4] This is not to deny the discrimination that Black Angelenos
faced but rather to suggest the distinctive nature of Los Angeles's racial hierarchy. In Los Angeles, not only were there other more reviled populations of

color, but there were arguably too few African Americans to pose a threat, economic or otherwise, to white Angelenos. Consequently, the 1920s are often referred to as the "Golden Age" of Black Los Angeles. Unfortunately, this was not to last. The increase in African Americans, as well as the decline of American Indians, transformed the racial hierarchy, and over time Black Angelenos found themselves sharing the plight of other urban Blacks.

Regardless of whether they were "Okies," southern Blacks, or urban whites, Southern California transplants came for similar reasons: jobs, the climate, and hopes for a better life. The demand for workers during World War II was such that not only were white arrivals absorbed into the workforce, but, with the notable exception of Japanese Americans (who were evacuated), people of color encountered unprecedented opportunities—although federal intervention was required to end exclusions against Black workers. Between 1940 and 1943, employment in Los Angeles County grew from approximately 900,000 to 1,450,000, a 60 percent increase.[5] While most of this growth was in defense, defense was not the only industry that propelled the region into becoming a manufacturing powerhouse. Before the war, city boosters attracted industry via the "branch plant" strategy, which encouraged major industries to establish a West Coast operation. As a result of these efforts, auto and ancillary industries, such as rubber and glass, invested heavily in the Los Angeles region in the thirties.[6] Together, this array of Fordist industry, including auto, shipping, aircraft, and later aerospace, created singular prosperity, especially for whites.

Concomitant with such dramatic changes in population and industry was the transformation of the region's geography. While suburbs have a long history in the United States, Southern California recast suburbanization as the new urban model. From early on, elite whites created suburbs and residential enclaves to insulate themselves from immigrants, the working class, and people of color. But beginning in the 1920s the region distinguished itself by building suburban housing for the working class. Becky Nicolaides has pointed out that there was actually a diversity of working-class suburbs, including many "homemade" units for poorer residents.[7] Nonetheless, they were still relatively segregated by race and class, so that by the 1950s early Mexican suburbs had become *barrios* that endure to this day. Given such a history of segregation, it was not surprising that as whites arrived in the 1940s they too sought to distance themselves from nonwhites: People of color were simply not part of the Southern California dream that millions of whites wished to buy into. Although such patterns reflected individual preferences, the state also played a crucial role in promoting racially exclusive communities. Because Los Angeles was a center of wartime activity, the state needed to ensure sufficient shelter, as a housing shortage could poten-

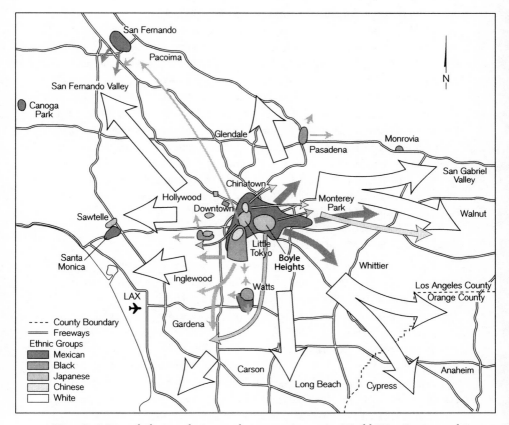

Map 2. Major shifts in ethnic populations, 1940–1960. World War II triggered a massive outmigration of all groups, especially whites, from the urban core. SOURCE: Based on James Allen and Eugene Turner, *The Ethnic Quilt: Population Diversity in Southern California* (Northridge: Center for Geographical Studies, California State University, Northridge, 1997), 51; courtesy of Allen and Turner.

tially jeopardize production. In addition to wartime policies, new housing initiatives promoted segregated suburban housing, including the adoption of the Home Owners Loan Corporation and the Federal Housing Act, both of which, among other discriminatory practices, institutionalized redlining.[8]

The result of these various measures was an outmigration of whites from central Los Angeles. Whites took advantage of new, high-quality, inexpensive, subsidized housing in the suburbs, while people of color remained largely concentrated in the core of Los Angeles. Such spatial shifts had a profound effect on subsequent social relations. Map 2 shows the outmigration of various racial/ethnic groups during this period.

While it is apparent from map 2 that all groups participated in outmigration to some degree, the white exodus was most dramatic. The consequences and boundaries of segregation were further intensified by incorporation, which gave municipalities more autonomy. Between 1940 and 1960 almost sixty cities incorporated in the metropolitan area.[9] Such a move not only had profound implications for the city of Los Angeles in terms of its tax base and community well-being but also established a geographic basis for unequal opportunity, as incorporated cities were able to exert far more control over who lived, entered, and shopped in their communities. This spatial relationship was also racial, as shown in the geographic distribution of whites and nonwhites: the reproduction of white privilege was predicated on distancing oneself from the poor and people of color.[10]

Racial Politics during and after the War

Changes in the racial hierarchy accompanied the economic and population shifts of World War II. Accordingly, this era should be understood as a transition period. While the war provided great opportunities, this was also a time of virulent racism as wartime anxieties were projected onto various communities of color. The "old" racial order could be seen in the zoot-suit riots, the Japanese American internment, and the refusal to accept Black workers. After the war, however, the "new" racial hierarchy was evident in the unprecedented possibilities for advancement that Mexican Americans, Asian Americans, and middle-class Blacks enjoyed. Yet despite growing racial tolerance in the postwar years, the Japanese American internment, a trauma that affected all racial/ethnic groups, would continue to play itself out over subsequent generations.

The Japanese American Internment Racism against Asian Americans has been long-standing and intense in California, and appreciating its breadth and depth is necessary for understanding why, on February 19, 1942, President Roosevelt signed Executive Order #9066, establishing the basis for placing Japanese Americans in concentration camps. Because Los Angeles had the largest Japanese American population in the United States, this was a critical event for the entire region.[11] By 1940 there were almost thirty-seven thousand Japanese persons living in Los Angeles County.[12] Because of historical animosity toward Japanese Americans, support for internment was strong in Southern California, with one in three people supporting it (versus one in seven along the remainder of the Pacific Coast).[13] Mass evacuations began in the spring of 1942, and within a matter of weeks the entire Japanese American population of Los Angeles had been forced into temporary facilities. From there, 120,000 Nikkei were sent to ten "relocation centers," primarily in the West.

In January 1945, Japanese Americans were released from the camps. Although relieved to be free, they faced new hardships upon their return to Los Angeles. Because of the haste under which they were forced to depart, many businesses and homes had been sold for a pittance. Other possessions had been stolen or misappropriated during their absence. As a result, Japanese Americans returned destitute to a city already suffering a severe housing shortage. Many sought to return to their old communities, including Boyle Heights, Crenshaw, Sawtelle, and San Pedro; others were forced to live in trailers on the rural edges of the city. In some cases, previously Japanese spaces had been taken over by others: for example, Bronzeville, near downtown, was now full of African Americans. Through heavy reliance on entrepreneurship and the ethnic economy, many Japanese Americans were eventually able to rebuild at least the material foundations of their lives.[14] The pain of racism and the violation of their civil and human rights, however, took a much longer time to heal. One activist, interned as a child, recalled the devastating impact of internment on his family:

When the war broke out we were shipped to Santa Anita [racetrack]. My sister was born in 1941, so she is just an infant . . . and gets the chicken pox or something. There were rumors circulating in the camp that they were killing the children in the hospital. So my mother is going nuts and then the riot [happens]. Me and my mom are sitting there watching the soldiers come in, these big trucks with 50-caliber machine guns pointed directly at us. I remember this one truck stopping right in front of us, and we were looking at this white, blond, young man who was probably more scared than we were, with this goddamn machine gun aimed at us. Anyway, my mother is freaking out, she couldn't protect nothing, she couldn't protect her baby daughter, she couldn't protect me from those sons of bitches. The next day my mother has a nervous breakdown. I recall my dad explaining to me that my mother was sick and that she wasn't going to be with us for a little while. I really didn't understand that. . . . My mother never fully came back. But we were never allowed to talk about it while she was still alive. The idea of being crazy was taboo in the community. When she passed away, I was able to talk a little bit about it with my dad.

The difficulty of reconstructing one's life after internment was further exacerbated by a climate of conformity and the celebration of white America. Japanese Americans responded by trying to blend in, becoming model citizens, and suppressing any criticism, in the hope that they would never again be targets of such discrimination. The Nikkei's behavior eventually drew the begrudging respect of the white majority but further marginalized Mexican Americans, Puerto Ricans, American Indians, and Blacks and, of course, created problems for Japanese Americans themselves.

Racial and Class Politics   Mexican and African Americans had wartime experiences radically different from those of Japanese Americans. Black and brown soldiers returned home with a new sense of possibility and a determination to resist domestic inequality. Soldiers of color were keenly aware of the contradictions: they were fighting for "freedom" abroad, yet they were second-class citizens at home.[15] Their renewed commitment to democracy and equality resulted in increased political activity in all communities of color. Activists joined civil rights organizations like the GI Forum, the League of United Latin American Citizens, the National Association for the Advancement of Colored People (NAACP), the Congress of Racial Equality (CORE), and the Japanese American Citizens League.

Although assimilationist politics dominated this era, real progress was made in the fight against racism. Mary Dudziak has argued that African Americans' ability to portray domestic racism as contradictory to U.S. claims of democracy in the international arena eventually bore fruit in the 1960s.[16] Despite such strides, however, the racial and class politics of the Cold War were radically different from those of the 1930s, or even the war years. During the 1930s, for example, Los Angeles was home to a vibrant left that was second in size only to New York's. During the Great Depression millions of people moved to the left, and the war produced new opportunities for political work in the defense industry.[17] Despite the absence of a strong tradition of organized labor, a traditional source of left membership, Los Angeles's left was bolstered by Hollywood, the International Longshoremen's and Warehousemen's Union, politically conscious Blacks, and Mexican and Japanese workers. Like other leftist formations, the Communist Party actively opposed racism and had some success in recruiting Japanese immigrants, many of whom had first been exposed to socialism in Japan, but was less effective among Mexicans, despite a tradition of Mexican radicalism. Showing its uneven commitment to antiracist politics, the Communist Party did not protest the internment of Japanese Americans, even though some of its members, including Karl Yoneda, were interned.[18]

Despite various shortcomings, the left took the lead in challenging racism and developing, however tentatively, an antiracist class-based politics. While the left never became mainstream, its demise in the 1950s, triggered by both McCarthyism and Khrushchev's revelation of Stalin's atrocities, bolstered conservatism and paved the way for more nationalist and conformist politics among people of color. Because there was no longer a regular flow of radical ideas, the political space of Los Angeles, indeed, the entire nation, contracted dramatically. Gerald Horne has argued that the demise of the left was partly responsible for the Watts riots of 1965, as there was no longer an ideological alternative to explain the oppression of communities of color, which might have been able to effectively challenge Black nationalism.[19]

In short, the war opened many doors and led to concrete material, political, and social advancements. But the postwar era was also an extremely difficult time. While elements of discrimination's legal apparatus were being dismantled, the culture of the 1950s placed a premium on white conformity, and the Red Scare threatened those who dared challenge it. The silence and conformity of the fifties nurtured deep frustrations on the part of youth of color that would erupt in the sixties.

SOUTHERN CALIFORNIA IN THE LATE SIXTIES AND EARLY SEVENTIES

By 1970 the Los Angeles region was the second largest metropolitan area in the United States. During this time the region's population was still largely white, with Latinas/os constituting the largest minority group and African Americans the second largest (see table 2). Among Latinas/os, 80 percent were of Mexican origin, of which the majority were native born. Japanese Americans constituted almost 50 percent of the Asian population. Both the Latina/o and the Asian American populations were far more homogenous than they are in Los Angeles today.[20]

Shifts in the Racial Hierarchy

By the late sixties Los Angeles's racial hierarchy looked increasingly similar to that of other large cities in one important regard: the position of African Americans. As previously mentioned, before and during the war, the lives of all people of color were narrowly circumscribed by discrimination and institutionalized racism, but by the late sixties most people of color, including many middle-class Blacks, enjoyed a less hostile environment and a greater range of housing, employment, and educational options. Such was not the case for low-income Blacks, however, who had come to occupy the

Table 2 *Los Angeles County population by race/ethnicity, 1970*

Racial/Ethnic Group	Population	% of Total Population
White	7,083,500	73.7
Hispanic	1,399,600	14.6
African American	781,000	8.1
Asian American	256,200	2.6
Middle Eastern	52,400	0.5
American Indian	20,500	0.2
Other	15,800	0.2
Total	9,609,000	99.9

SOURCE: Adapted from Georges Sabagh and Mehdi Bozorgmehr, "Population Change: Immigration and Ethnic Transformation," in *Ethnic Los Angeles*, ed. Roger Waldinger and Mehdi Bozorgmehr (New York: Russell Sage Foundation, 1996), table 3.2, "Population of Specific Ethnic Groups by Nativity, Los Angeles Region, 1970–1990," pp. 95–96. ©1996 Russell Sage Foundation.

lowest rung in the racial hierarchy. This was clearly a shift from earlier days when Asian and Mexican Americans were the targets of racist hysteria, as seen in the zoot-suit riots, the Sleepy Lagoon murder case, Mexican repatriation, countless Asian exclusions, and, of course, the internment.[21] Blacks' earlier relatively privileged position was due not only to their relatively small numbers but more importantly to their distinct experiences in the region. Although the first Spanish expedition to arrive in Los Angeles included Blacks, any distinctive history and culture were soon dwarfed by the overwhelming Spanish, Mexican, indigenous, and Anglo presence. For example, Mexican Blacks were subsumed under Hispanic culture. That culture, while certainly racist, did not rest on a Black/white racial binary, like Anglo-American culture, but instead featured a racial ideology predicated on a range of racial categories, color gradations, and class. As a result, for much of Los Angeles's early history, Blacks were located in a Hispanic racial order, in which they were one of many subjugated groups.

In addition, because of their relatively small numbers and marginalization, African Americans did not pose a significant political-economic threat. Almaguer has shown how in nineteenth-century California whites struggled with Indians over land, with Asians over labor, and with Mexicans over both land and labor—but not with Blacks. Even in the late 1930s, evidence from a Home Owners Loan Corporation survey suggests that as long as Blacks "kept their place" and were relatively few they were not considered to be a problem.

Negroes do not constitute a racial problem . . . for although they too
have been increasing rapidly in number, their ratio to the total county
population has remained constant since 1890. The Negro race is fairly
well confined to a few sections within the county. They occupy one
larger area southwest of the business district. . . . Although Beverly
Hills shows a larger than average number of Negroes, these are made
up entirely of servants and they do not own property in the community. . . . The major racial problem existing in Los Angeles, and one
which is not revealed by the census data, is that created by the large
numbers of Mexicans, who are classed as Whites by the Census
Bureau. . . . While many of the Mexican race are of high caliber and
descended from the Spanish grandees who formerly owned all the territory in southern California, the large majority of Mexican people are a
definite problem locally and their importation in the years gone by to
work the agricultural crops has now been recognized as a mistake.[22]

Clearly, as long as Blacks remained spatially and socially subordinated, they
were not considered a threat, as their numbers and actions did not intrude
on the acquisition of white property, wealth, and status.

This all changed with World War II, however, as Southern California's
racial hierarchy came to more closely reflect the national one. The redefinition of race along Black and white lines required a change in status for
Mexican and Asian Americans. This was partly achieved by simply ignoring
both groups and allowing them to become less prominent in the racial hierarchy, but also by granting them some movement toward whiteness. This
shift is attributable to several events. First, as previously mentioned, there
was a significant increase in the Black population, and some described the
newer immigrants as poor, rural southerners who did not readily embrace
an urban, middle-class lifestyle and ideals. Accordingly, many whites and
Blacks maintained that this population diminished the status of all Blacks.

In addition, the war drew many southern whites to the region in what
Leonard calls "the southernizing" of Los Angeles. White southerners
brought with them the foundations of a southern racial order. Asians and
Mexicans did not readily fit in that order, so southern whites were more
willing to tolerate them and instead directed their racial animosity to the
"other" they were most familiar with, Blacks.[23] Consequently, there was
both a rise in Ku Klux Klan activity and a hardening of Black segregation
that did not diminish until 1970. In 1963, for instance, when CORE waged
a sustained campaign to integrate Torrance, an industrial suburb, they faced
fierce white opposition from both Nazis and the Klan.[24]

The development of the "model minority" myth also affected the racial
hierarchy by enhancing the position of Asian Americans to the detriment of

Blacks and Mexican Americans. Upon their return from internment, Japanese Americans, while still facing hostility, began to occupy a racial position somewhat similar to that of Jews in earlier times. Because of the enhanced postwar status of Japan, as well as the particular way Japanese Americans responded to internment—not making waves, striving to "out-white the whites," and focusing on becoming professionals—by 1966 their "success" drew the attention of journalists, scholars, and policy makers.[25] Don Nakanishi has pointed out how, in a perverse way, the internment and Japanese Americans' response to it paved the way for greater acceptance by whites.

> Two frequently used themes—that no acts of sabotage were committed by Japanese Americans during the war, as well as the stories of Japanese American soldiers who provided "proof in blood" of their loyalty to America—served to buttress the view that the Internment was wrong, and yet, it provided Japanese Americans with unexpected opportunities to demonstrate their worth as American citizens.
>
> The Internment came to symbolize a test of character for Japanese Americans, particularly the Nisei. Although the test may have been unnecessary and unconstitutional, the Nisei passed with flying colors. They deserved recognition as full-fledged and equal American citizens, much as did World War II veterans of other racial and ethnic minorities at the time.[26]

If Japanese Americans could prosper without being "disorderly," why couldn't Mexican and African Americans? Such comparisons were especially acute in places like Los Angeles, where Japanese Americans often attended the same schools as Blacks and Mexican Americans. Not only was the development of the "model minority" myth problematic—although that was bad enough—but its embrace by some Nisei, and their belief that they *were* superior, served to make other people of color appear deficient. It is important to understand how the myth itself is a function of racism. Besides underscoring the relational nature of race, the myth serves to maintain white privilege and status. It does so by denying the diversity and humanity of Asian Americans and by further marginalizing other minorities.

Another shift in the racial hierarchy was the erosion of housing and employment barriers. Many Mexican and Asian Americans were able to avail themselves to new opportunities, but not all. Light-skinned Mexican Americans, for example, as well as those with solid middle-class credentials, were more likely to "pass" or to be accepted by whites, though to varying degrees.[27] Such was not the case for more dark-skinned or working-class Mexican Americans. The Black experience was also highly uneven. Although Blacks as a whole still faced discrimination, class distinctions became more pronounced by the late sixties, as the middle class began leaving South L.A. to distance themselves from the poor. Despite their upward (and westward) mobility, however, they were still largely confined to Black spaces.[28]

Finally, the growing visibility of Blacks on the national scene had important local consequences. Black unrest, in the form of the civil rights movement as well as the riots that marked the sixties, including the Watts riot of 1965, served to draw significant attention to African Americans. Not only was the entire population more aware of Blacks, but many whites (and others) grew resentful and afraid of them.[29] This, in turn, intensified white animosity toward Blacks while reducing it toward other people of color. This tension was particularly pronounced between the Los Angeles Police Department (LAPD) and the African American community.

In short, as prospects increased for Mexican and Japanese Americans, opportunity was distributed more unevenly for Blacks. The Watts riot of 1965 served to solidify the new racial hierarchy. Blacks, who were most closely associated with the events of August 1965, were seen as the most problematic of all communities of color. Mexican American East L.A., although it would have its share of unrest, did not erupt at that time. Such differing responses to domination contributed to whites' viewing Mexican Americans as less hostile, "better behaved," and more socially similar to themselves. Of course, such attitudes did not necessarily translate into better conditions or opportunities. One could even argue that the Watts riots signaled that African Americans and their concerns would have to be dealt with. And in fact, the attention and resources directed toward African Americans *did* affect their economic status, but it was nowhere enough to prevent the hardships that would befall the Black working class in the coming years.

Communities of Color in the Los Angeles Economy

Changes in the racial hierarchy were also accompanied by economic shifts. Although the Southern California economy was unable to sustain full employment after the war, the region continued to enjoy general prosperity. While many people of color advanced economically during this time, whites still garnered the lion's share of the region's wealth and opportunities. By examining more carefully the economic position of each racial/ethnic group, we can see the relationship between the racial hierarchy and class position.

Although by 1970 other regions were already undergoing the pains of deindustrialization, manufacturing remained an important part of Los Angeles's economy. Besides providing significant employment, manufac-

Table 3 *Manufacturing employment by racial/ethnic group,*
Los Angeles, 1970

	No. in Manufacturing Employment	% of Total Manufacturing Employment
White	717,300	70.9
Hispanic	209,800	20.8
African American	60,600	6.1
Asian American	20,500	2.0
Other	3,800	0.3

SOURCE: Adapted from Allen Scott, "The Manufacturing Economy: Ethnic and Gender Divisions of Labor," in *Ethnic Los Angeles*, ed. Roger Waldinger and Mehdi Bozorgmehr (New York: Russell Sage Foundation, 1996), table 8.6, "Employment in Manufacturing by Ethnic Group, Los Angeles, 1970," p. 222. ©1996 Russell Sage Foundation.

turing has traditionally served as an economic ladder for immigrants and the poor. In 1970 manufacturing accounted for 26.2 percent of all jobs in Los Angeles.[30] Table 3 depicts manufacturing employment by racial/ethnic group and shows that while whites still composed the bulk of manufacturing workers, Latinas/os were making serious inroads.

Mexican Americans   The role of Mexican Americans in the manufacturing sector is central to explaining both their position in the racial hierarchy and the importance of working-class politics to Chicana/o leftists. Although Mexicans have been a crucial part of the Los Angeles economy since the early twentieth century, their situation changed dramatically with World War II, as they were no longer confined to the secondary labor market and agriculture and became more fully integrated into the industrial working class. By 1970 Latinas/os constituted almost 21 percent of manufacturing workers, though they were only 14.6 percent of the total population. This attachment to manufacturing was both deep and broad. Latinas/os were represented in both durable and nondurable manufacturing.[31] A 1965 study that focused on East Los Angeles found that 37 percent of men were employed as operatives and kindred workers, while 40 percent of women were (table 4). Despite their participation in the manufacturing economy, many residents of East Los Angeles still suffered from unemployment and poverty. In 1965 the average unemployment rate for both men and women in East Los Angeles was 7.25 percent, while almost one-fourth of all households in the community were below the poverty line.[32] Such widespread

Table 4 *Occupations of residents of East Los Angeles, 1965*

Occupation	% of Men	% of Women
Operatives and kindred	37	40
Craftsmen and foremen	16	—
Laborers	11	—
Professional/technical	5	—
Clerical	—	24
Service	—	7

SOURCE: California Department of Industrial Relations, Fair Employment Practices Commission, "Negroes and Mexican Americans in South and East Los Angeles: Changes between 1960 and 1965," 1965, p. 28, box 69, Los Angeles Area Chamber of Commerce Collection, Department of Special Collections, University of Southern California Library, Los Angeles.

poverty, which was relatively consistent throughout East Los Angeles, was due less to joblessness than to Latinas/os' overrepresentation in low-wage employment. Only 5 percent of East Los Angeles men were employed as professional or technical workers, whereas 15 percent of all men in the Los Angeles–Long Beach Metropolitan area were. Given the experiences of Mexican Americans, including their low-wage work, it seems inevitable that radical activists would focus on issues of labor, immigration, and workers' rights.

African Americans   African Americans' situation was somewhat different. Black Angelenos, while also largely working class, were less attached to the manufacturing sector and indeed to the formal economy as a whole. Structural unemployment has been a persistent problem for Blacks throughout the twentieth century and into the twenty-first. Often considered the least desirable workers, they have typically been the last hired and the first fired or laid off. During the war, African Americans were eventually absorbed into the workforce, but many faced unemployment as soldiers returned home and the country shifted out of wartime production. Ironically, Blacks' proximity to the vast concentration of Fordist industry along the Alameda Corridor did not translate into widespread employment, due to both employer and labor union discrimination. Black Angelenos faced two painful periods of industrial job loss. First, beginning in the 1950s and 1960s, many industries began leaving the urban core for the suburbs, but few Blacks could follow them because of persistent residential discrim-

Table 5 *Occupations of residents of South Los Angeles, 1965*

Occupation	% of Men	% of Women
Operatives and kindred	30	26
Craftsmen	17	—
Service	14	19
Laborers	12	—
Clerical	—	17
Private household	—	17
Professional/technical	4	—

SOURCE: California Department of Industrial Relations, Fair Employment Practices Commission, "Negroes and Mexican Americans in South and East Los Angeles: Changes between 1960 and 1965," 1965, p. 19, box 69, Los Angeles Area Chamber of Commerce Collection, Department of Special Collections, University of Southern California Library, Los Angeles.

ination in outlying areas. Second, in the 1970s the Southern California region began undergoing a larger deindustrialization that was part of the national shift from a Fordist to a Postfordist economy. Thus no sooner did Blacks get a toehold in the auto industry, for example, than such industries began closing down. Table 5 shows employment by sectors for residents of South Los Angeles in 1965.

There are several important distinctions between the economic conditions of South and East Los Angeles. For one, residents of South Los Angeles suffered from 11 percent unemployment, significantly higher than the 7.25 percent Eastside unemployment rate and twice the regional average. In addition, while Blacks were approximately 8 percent of the county population, they constituted only 6 percent of the manufacturing workforce.[33] While men in East Los Angeles were more likely to be employed in manufacturing than men in South Los Angeles, this difference was even more pronounced for women. Twenty-six percent of women in South Los Angeles were employed as operatives, but 40 percent of East Los Angeles women were. Women in South Los Angeles were far more likely to work as domestics (17 percent), a category that did not even register for East Los Angeles women.[34]

Although the overall poverty rates between South and East Los Angeles were relatively comparable, 26.8 percent and 23.6 percent respectively, these figures obscure important spatial differences. As table 6 indicates, there was a tremendous range of poverty rates throughout South Los Angeles. For

Table 6 *Percent of families below poverty line for selected South Los Angeles communities, 1965*

Community	% below the Poverty Line
Watts	41.5
Central	32.2
Avalon	31.5
Florence	25.8
Exposition	23.0
Willowbrook	18.7

SOURCE: California Department of Industrial Relations, Fair Employment Practices Commission, "Negroes and Mexican Americans in South and East Los Angeles: Changes between 1960 and 1965," 1965, p. 21, box 69, Los Angeles Area Chamber of Commerce Collection, Department of Special Collections, University of Southern California Library, Los Angeles.

instance, the poverty rate was over 40 percent in Watts but less than 20 percent in Willowbrook.

These economic differences have important implications for political activism. The fact that Mexican Americans were more firmly embedded in the formal economy suggests a different relationship to work, which translates into specific political concerns. It is possible, for example, that greater employment militated against Mexican American participation in the 1965 Watts riots. One African American interviewee, who had been a young man at the time of the uprising, explained that he had just been waiting for East Los Angeles to erupt, and that if it had, the political trajectory of the city might have been altogether different. That East L.A. did not explode is significant. Possibly Mexican Americans were more invested in the prevailing social formation, as they were not locked out of jobs to the extent that Blacks were. As a result, they were less likely to participate in a mass insurrection.

One way that structural unemployment played itself out was in community-police relations. The high rates of unemployment among Black Angelenos coupled with the racism of the LAPD resulted in a severe and continuous disciplining of the African American population, which was felt to threaten the social order. Mexican American communities were also subject to police harassment, but it appears to have been less intense. One former Panther reflecting on the role of the LAPD explained, "Their job wasn't to protect us, their job was to protect the white community from us, protect the white community's properties from us, and to keep us in our place so we wouldn't get out of line." Not surprisingly, joblessness and, by extension, police relations would become focal points for radical Blacks.

Another consequence of differential employment patterns is exposure to labor activism. Working in a factory, one is far more likely to be exposed to, if not to actually participate in, unions and other forms of collective action. In contrast, such opportunities do not readily exist among, for example, domestics—an occupation that, as Pierrette Hondagneu-Sotelo has argued, is notorious for its ability to erase the "work" of caregiving by obscuring its status as wage labor.[35] As a result, not only were many Chicana/o activists already familiar with industrial work, but they had often accompanied parents to union meetings, and they saw unions as a part of everyday life and a useful tool for addressing economic inequalities. Among the African American activists I interviewed, not one mentioned a parent working in a factory or belonging to a union, whereas the vast majority of Chicana/o activists had at least one parent employed in manufacturing. Most Blacks described households where parents, often the mother, worked at a variety of different jobs to support the family. As a result of these conditions, which were similar to those of other urban Blacks, we can see why the Black Panther Party focused on both self-defense programs (against police abuse) and "survival" programs that sought to meet people's basic needs.

Japanese Americans   Japanese Americans represent still another economic picture. Not only was there greater economic diversity within this population, but the Nikkei had much higher rates of self-employment and participation in the professions than either African or Mexican Americans. By 1970 Japanese Americans had one of the highest rates of self-employment in Los Angeles County (18.6 percent), second only to Chinese Americans (20.5 percent). In contrast, Mexican and Black self-employment averaged 4.75 percent and 6.3 percent respectively.[36] Table 7 shows the employment patterns of Japanese Americans in 1960.

Several distinct features characterize Japanese American employment. To understand these patterns, however, we must place them within the larger context of the Japanese American experience. Because of discrimination before the war, Japanese Americans found entire occupations and industries closed off to them and were thus restricted to a limited set of industries, particularly agriculturally related ones.[37] Eventually, through entrepreneurship and self-employment, they gained entrance into the pro-

Table 7 *Japanese American employment by industry, Los Angeles, 1960*

Occupation	% of Men Employed	% of Women Employed
Professional/technical	16.9	10.8
Farmers/farm managers	19.8	1.8
Craftsmen	12.3	1.0
Clerical	7.5	34.9
Operatives and kindred	10.6	22.2
Private household	0.6	7.1
Services	3.1	5.8

SOURCE: California Department of Industrial Relations, Fair Employment Practices Commission, "Californians of Japanese, Chinese, and Filipino Ancestry," 1965, p. 36, box 69, Los Angeles Area Chamber of Commerce Collection, Department of Special Collections, University of Southern California Library, Los Angeles.

duce market, nurseries, and gardening, as well as serving the larger ethnic economy. According to table 7, a sizable percentage of Japanese American men were still involved in agriculture (20 percent) in 1960. After internment, however, Japanese Americans, including a significant number of women, sought to become professionals as a means of gaining acceptance and respectability. As one activist described Japanese Americans, "Their thing after the camps was to out-white the whites and don't rock the boat. So many of my generation, my classmates, were doctors, lawyers, pharmacists, and optometrists."[38]

Japanese Americans' ties to manufacturing were tenuous at best not only because they were excluded from that sector during the war but because even before their incarceration many had been barred from federal, state, and defense employment.[39] As a result, Japanese Americans were underrepresented in manufacturing and as wage workers in general. *All* Asian Americans were underrepresented in these sectors and occupations, but especially the Nikkei. In 1970 Asian Americans constituted 2.6 percent of the county's population but only 2 percent of manufacturing workers. Moreover, almost half of the Asians in manufacturing were foreign born. Because there was little Japanese immigration at this time, we must conclude that most of these workers belonged to other nationalities, including Chinese, Korean, Filipina/o, and Vietnamese.[40]

Japanese American women were about twice as likely as men to be employed in manufacturing (see table 7). Given the high rates of family formation among Japanese Americans, it is reasonable to assume that their higher household income was partly due to female employment in this industry. Because of patriarchy, however, a family's class position and identity were largely defined by the male earner. Men's limited involvement in manufacturing, plus the fact that the Nikkei were in a transitional period of racial and economic advancement, contributed to Japanese Americans' ambiguous class identification, even though over 50 percent of women worked in clerical or manufacturing occupations.

It is important not to equate Japanese Americans' enhanced economic mobility with the end of racism. Far too often we reduce racism to poverty, and while it is true that the U.S. economy is racialized and that poor people of color may experience class through race, racism exists in multiple arenas, as the experiences of both middle-class Blacks and Asian Americans have attested.[41] In this case, the diminishment of certain types of anti-Japanese racism allowed for mobility, but many other types persisted.

In short, Nikkei economic activity in Los Angeles was clustered along several occupations and activities, including self-employment/entrepreneurship, the professions, and working-class jobs. Given such a fragmented economic background, we can see why Japanese American activists did not develop a politics grounded in either workers' or class struggle. Instead, their politics focused on the racism that the Asian American community as a whole faced, with particular emphasis on the disempowered and economically marginalized sectors of that population.

Residential and Spatial Changes

Changes in the racial hierarchy and regional economy were also reflected in Los Angeles's spatial structure. The region continued its outward expansion, but, despite incremental steps toward integration, it remained characterized by what Philip Ethington calls "segregated diversity."[42] One of the key factors responsible for these patterns was the outmigration of industry. As previously mentioned, beginning in the 1950s, expanding firms encountered an expensive land market, and large lots were increasingly difficult to find—a requirement for industries such as aerospace. Accordingly, Northrop, Hughes, and Lockheed began an exodus, creating industrial agglomerations along the way and taking high-paying jobs with them.[43] This intensified white outmigration as firms took their employees with them and/or became the economic centers for new white enclaves. Although there was still a significant white presence in central Los Angeles, whites moved outward in large numbers, particularly toward the coastal zones and into Orange

County. Between 1960 and 1965 Orange County's population had grown by 137.5 percent, almost all of which was white.[44] By the late sixties residential discrimination was illegal, but it persisted, particularly in the planned communities of Orange County, epitomized by Irvine. One housing developer, explaining why his corporation chose not to reach out to low-income and nonwhite persons, noted that a multiracial advertisement "would scare off every white person I had even the slightest hopes of getting."[45]

Despite such attitudes, barriers *were* breaking down, especially in older, more mature suburbs. One Chicana activist described how her family was a "blockbuster" in the city of Lakewood.

> In the early sixties there were several white neighborhoods that had laws that prohibited realtors from selling to African Americans and Latinos. The way we were able to get the house was my mom found someone who was selling without a realtor, because a realtor would not sell it. They would sell to my mother, because she looks fairly European, but once they saw my dad, who looks like a Toltec, it was like, "No, I'm sorry, this is off." So that's how we got in. Once we got in, there was a lot of reaction. For about two years we were constantly having different political groups like the Democratic Party and the FBI involved because there were a lot of physical threats.

The residential clustering and segregation patterns that characterized the region in the late sixties testify to the deep racial and class anxieties that accompanied the pursuit of the American Dream.

Residential shifts were also propelled by population growth. Housing pressure on the Eastside, for example, both overcrowding and substandard housing, pushed Mexican Americans beyond the East Los Angeles barrio.[46] Consequently, historic Mexicana/o communities in Pacoima, San Fernando, San Pedro, Watts, and Santa Ana were complemented by new concentrations in Pico Rivera, Monterey Park, and Alhambra. By 1965 just under one-third of Mexican Angelenos resided in East Los Angeles.[47]

Japanese Americans encountered a similar situation. Though discrimination persisted, Asian Americans had a greater choice of neighborhoods by 1970. One activist recounted how, despite a struggle, her family moved to Sierra Madre, an overwhelmingly white community. Her family had a nursery and wanted to build a house on the property but encountered resistance. "It was property my grandfather owned from before the war. The neighbors circulated a petition trying to get us not to build a house there . . . we'd be their neighbor, right? This would be in the early sixties. It's kind of shocking if you think about it. It never got any place, and Dad built the house and we lived right there." As can be seen in map 1 (p. 16), Japanese Americans were

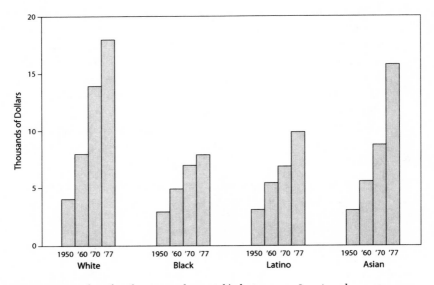

Figure 1. Median family income by racial/ethnic group, Los Angeles, 1950–1977. Median income reflects the larger racial formation in Los Angeles. Source: "New Middle Class Emerging in City—Persevering Asian," *Los Angeles Times*, April 13, 1980. Graph by Patrick Lynch. Copyright 1980, *Los Angeles Times*. Reprinted with permission.

clustered in several districts, most of which had been Nikkei neighborhoods before the war, as they sought to rebuild old communities. Because of the relatively small size of the Japanese American population, however, they never dominated an area the way Mexican Americans or Blacks did. Instead, they were located in the interstices of nonwhite spaces. Crenshaw, for example, was a predominantly Black neighborhood, while Boyle Heights was part of the greater Mexicana/o Eastside. This geography would have important implications for subsequent political activism and consciousness, as Japanese Americans became comfortable and familiar with other minority cultures. As one Japanese American described these sociospatial relations, "If you lived in Boyle-Heights, you hung out with Chicanos and acted Chicano. If you grew up in South Central, you hung out with Blacks and acted Black."

While African Americans were also beginning to enjoy more residential options, their experience was distinct from that of both Mexican and Japanese Americans. More than any other population, African Americans remained concentrated in central Los Angeles, regardless of the westward movement of

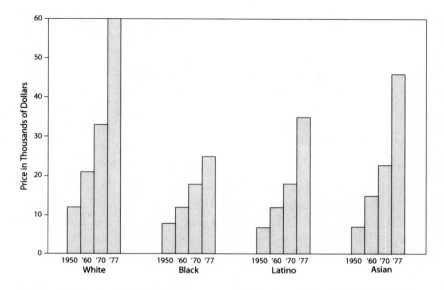

Figure 2. Median housing price by racial/ethnic group, Los Angeles, 1950–1977. Housing values skyrocketed in the 1970s, particularly among whites and Asian Americans and to a lesser extent among Latinas/os. Source: "New Middle Class Emerging in City—Persevering Asian," *Los Angeles Times,* April 13, 1980. Graph by Patrick Lynch. Copyright 1980, *Los Angeles Times.* Reprinted with permission.

the Black middle class (see maps 1 and 2, pp. 16, 37). Indeed, a full 40 percent of Los Angeles's Black population lived in South Los Angeles in 1965.[48] Below, a Black activist describes four different moves, all in South Los Angeles: "I was born near Avalon and Florence. From there we moved to 29th and Central. And in 1959 we moved to Figueroa Street, off of Vernon Avenue, and all the neighbors came out to tell us goodbye. In those days moving to Figueroa was like moving to Beverly Hills. We were the big shots in the neighborhood. We stayed at 46th and Figueroa from 1959 to 1965, and then we moved to 88th Place, and our greeting there turned out to be the Watts riots." Such limited movement contrasts with that of Mexican and Asian Americans, who were venturing miles away into suburbia.[49]

The end product of these racial, economic, and spatial shifts was a distinct set of social outcomes for whites, Latinas/os, Blacks, and Asian Americans. Figures 1 and 2 depict the evolution of median family income and housing values for these groups from 1950 to 1977.

One cannot help noting the overall superior economic position of whites.

Observe also that Asian Americans' housing values and incomes were similar to those of Latinas/os and Blacks until 1970 but increased significantly afterwards, suggesting greater economic and residential integration with whites. Finally, although Blacks and Latinas/os had similar incomes, after 1970 housing values for Latinas/os increased far more than they did for Blacks. This reflects both reduced discrimination and increased suburbanization among Latinas/os, as well as the extent to which Black land was/is devalued in comparison to the land of other groups.

Discrimination and Political Consciousness

When I began conducting interviews, I assumed I would hear how personal experiences of discrimination contributed to activists' political consciousness, but I did not anticipate how deeply residential patterns would figure in these accounts. Activists' political development was affected not only by residential discrimination but also by *whom* one lived near. Most activists, particularly Japanese and African Americans, shared stinging memories of racism that required them to analyze their place within the larger society at a tender age. Despite the decline in institutional racism against Japanese Americans, they still encountered prejudice, especially in neighborhoods in transition, where they were likely to find themselves.

> After camp my family settled in what is now the Crenshaw area. At that time, they wouldn't rent even to Asians. We had an apartment, and then my parents saved up to buy a house, and I remember them being told that they didn't want Japs in the area. They had one of those covenants. But during that time the Fair Housing Act passed, so we moved, as did a lot of other Japanese Americans and other people of color. So the area changed very quickly. This is the fifties and the sixties. By the time I was in high school, Dorsey was about one-third Black, one-third white, one-third Asian, there were a few Latinos, but not too many. A lot of the whites were Jewish. Later, I realized that they were red-diaper babies. That's why they didn't move, because they didn't have a problem with being in a multicultural area, and the people who did left. I think growing up at this time of great change had a lot to do with my politicization.

These geographic and economic complexities had an impact on activists. Living near other people of color facilitated their ability to make connections and to identify with other oppressed groups. But Third World activists quickly learned that they were not typical and often had to fight prejudice within their own families and communities. For example, Japanese American activists, despite living in mixed neighborhoods, often reported that their parents felt superior to other racially subordinated populations.

"My dad's family used to own nurseries, and his employees were Mexican. At an early age I remember being conscious of little offhand racial comments. I saw their particular way of viewing Mexicans or Blacks." As will be seen, Japanese American activists were much more aware of and concerned with their relationship to other people of color than were African Americans and Chicanas/os.

Those Chicanas/os that grew up near Blacks, though relatively few, had a particularly strong connection that informed their political consciousness. Carlos Montes, for instance, lived for a period in Florence (a.k.a. Florencia) in South L.A. "They [Blacks] were from the South, and we were from Mexico, so [we shared] a rural background. I saw that later on. I went to school with Blacks, so I started identifying when I heard about the Black liberation movement and the rhetoric of militant Blacks. For me, it was a natural link."[50] Still, Mexican American prejudice toward African Americans was not unknown. Indeed, numerous writers have pointed out that Mexican Americans have occasionally sought to distinguish themselves from Blacks and to claim whiteness. Ambrecht and Pachon found that between 1965 and 1972 the percentage of Mexicans who favored coalition building with Blacks jumped from 16 to 32 percent, illustrating the wariness with which many Mexicanas/os had traditionally viewed Blacks.[51] Indeed, fighting against the prejudice and narrow nationalism of their own community has been a constant struggle for some Chicana/o leftists.

Similarly, Black Angelenos did not automatically gravitate toward other people of color. This was perhaps most evident in the uneven relations between Japanese and African Americans, who often lived in close proximity. Though Nikkei youth seemed to have absorbed a good deal of Black culture, it was not always a two-way street. This pattern was at least partly due to the fact that Japanese Americans were a minority in predominantly Black spaces, but social distance also appeared to increase with age, so that interaction diminished between older African and Japanese Americans. Such patterns derived both from potentially antagonistic class positions, since some Nikkei functioned as "ethnic middlemen" in the ghetto economy, and from racial hierarchies. Some Blacks resented Japanese Americans, seeing them as "foreigners" or as having few problems. The tendency of some African Americans to disregard the plight of other minorities is an ongoing problem that militates against multiethnic cooperation. At the same time, some Nikkei sought to distance themselves from Blacks. One activist explained her mother's admonishment "Don't play with the *Kurocha*" (a pejorative for Black children) as due to a dislike of Blacks she had learned from the larger society, as well as fear that her Asian daughter would incur even more racism and discrimination if she associated with Blacks. Such attitudes speak volumes about the racial hierarchy.

Despite the possibility of close relations, those connections had to be carefully articulated and cultivated by political activists and leaders—by no means were they inevitable. One former Panther explained that although the structural conditions for coalition building were in place by 1970, it was not readily apparent if and how Third World unity could be forged. "Before I became conscious, I saw that it wasn't white folks getting knocked on the head. It became very obvious that it was basically people of color. I didn't call them people of color, I called them Mexicans, Indians, and whoever else. I began to see that, and because I didn't understand it, it stayed in there [my head]. But it was only through formal study that I began to put these various pieces together." The next chapter explores precisely how these pieces began falling into place in Los Angeles in the late 1960s.

THREE

**The Politicization
of the Third World Left**

Although popular images of the sixties and seventies often portray a period
of widespread political activism, only a minority, albeit a significant one,
became politically active, and even fewer became leftists. Instead, the vast
majority of activists from communities of color, particularly Chicanas/os and
Blacks, supported either a nationalist or a civil rights political ideology, thus
requiring us to ask what set the members of the Third World Left apart.
What led them to this path, and how did that process differ from those who
adopted more conventional movement politics? What was the draw of an
anticapitalist critique, and how did it relate to activists' experiences?

In this chapter I explore the process of individual politicization and how it
was linked to larger events of the day. Drawing on Doug McAdam, I argue
that the politicization of the Third World Left was a two-step process.[1] First,
almost all individuals either were confronted early on with racial or class
inequalities leaving a lasting impression on them or were initially politicized
by a family member. While such experiences served to encourage individuals to question the "system" and perhaps led them to embrace more radical
analyses, they were not in themselves sufficient to produce activism. The second requirement was the presence of an opportunity, or an opening, that pro-
voked individuals into action, thus allowing them to act upon their beliefs.
Because the historical moment offered an abundance of such opportunities
complemented by a storehouse of discriminatory and racist memories, a significant number of young people were drawn to the Third World Left.

The political spaces and opportunities associated with the late sixties
must be placed in a larger historical context. In particular, the Third World
Left should be seen as part of an unfolding political trajectory that dates
from at least World War II and goes something like this: the civil rights
movement blossomed in the 1950s and early 1960s. It was superseded by

the various racial/ethnic power movements of the late 1960s, which was then followed by the development of the New Communist movement. This latter formation reached its culmination in highly sectarian political parties that eventually collapsed because of their own internal contradictions and growing conservatism. The year 1980 often serves as the final marker of this period of social unrest, as it denotes Ronald Reagan's presidency. Although U.S. revolutionaries still exist, the structural conditions necessary to support such movements are not fully present today. In short, a particular set of historical circumstances led many to see the Third World Left as a potential vehicle to create a more socially just world.

A secondary aim of this chapter is to address a somewhat politically thorny issue: the centrality of Black political mobilization. Within Chicana/o, Asian American, Puerto Rican, and, perhaps to a lesser extent, American Indian studies, a subtle and carefully worded debate questions the degree to which these movements were inspired by African American protest. To varying degrees, non-Black scholars of color have sought to emphasize the organic and singular nature of their respective struggles. This is understandable when we consider the number of writers who have reduced the indigenous, Chicana/o, Puerto Rican, and Asian American movements to mere copycat status or, more typically, simply ignored them. But although it is important to stress the individuality of each movement, I believe there is no denying that non-Black people of color were greatly inspired by, and in some cases emulated, Black Power.[2] As people of color we must come to terms with the role that African Americans played in the development of a Third World consciousness. As longtime activist Anne Braden has pointed out, "The '60s were so important because the country had to confront the . . . racism which it was built on. When African Americans began to organize, they were the foundation, [and when they] moved, the whole building shook. That is why people were able to organize against the War. That's why women were able to organize."[3] And I would add, other people of color. Acknowledging this role should not be seen as disempowering or as in any way devaluing ethnic-specific struggles. Instead, such recognition can contribute to greater solidarity, as it underscores the centrality of racial oppression and the power of broad-based collective action.

THE PROCESS OF POLITICIZATION

It would seem that politicization, or how one becomes politically conscious, should occupy a privileged position within the social movement literature. After all, people cannot fully participate in social movements without undergoing a process of political awakening. Yet with a few prominent exceptions the question of politicization has received surprisingly scant attention in the literature on social movements, despite spanning many disciplines.[4] Early studies of political socialization, as it was called in the 1950s, were often quantitative and sought to understand the bases of political attitudes and awareness, as well as how various demographic, political, and personal factors influenced political participation, particularly around electoral politics. Rarely did this literature address radical or left activism, as such forms of political expression were considered "deviant." But over time, as protest became recognized as a necessary part of democratic politics, researchers began studying politicization. During the 1970s and 1980s, when Marxism was still influential in the social sciences, many scholars took a somewhat formulaic approach to political consciousness and activism, assuming that these would flow automatically from structural conditions of domination and exploitation. The rise of identity politics, feminism, and postmodernism, however, has posed a direct challenge to such approaches and has demonstrated the need for greater sensitivity and nuance if we truly wish to understand politicization.[5] Currently, some of the most dynamic work in the field consists of ethnographic studies as well as autobiographies and *testimonios*. While limited in their ability to generalize, they provide detailed, textured analyses of how the politicization process works and its implications. This is especially significant because women of color have been an important force in this genre. Given that most research addresses people of color only occasionally, and women of color even less frequently, this is one of the few ways we can learn about the politicization of an important part of the Third World Left.[6]

Politicization can be defined as the process of becoming politically aware. While there are almost always certain moments that stand out in a person's political development, politicization should be viewed as an ongoing process, as new understandings are always available in response to political shifts and individual change. If politicization is the process of political awakening, *political consciousness* refers to the quality of one's awareness. Paulo Friere has observed that full political consciousness requires two levels of awareness. First, one must understand the structural conditions that shape one's existence (including one's relationship to the oppressor), and second, one must understand that these relations can be transformed and the individual's role in doing so. The classic example that Friere uses to illustrate political consciousness is the tenant who despises his or her condition.[7] Several responses are possible. The tenant might decide to become a landlord and thus end his or her misery as a tenant. An alternative, however, would be to analyze the relationship between the tenant and the landlord, identify the sources of domination and exploitation, and articulate a new set of social arrangements. For Friere, the second response is an example of political consciousness: understanding the problem beyond individual remedies. There are always strong ideological forces at work to ensure that the oppressed seek to emulate the landlord rather than to challenge the larger social formation itself. But if politically conscious individuals choose to challenge the existing social structure, they can also consciously direct their lives toward personal and social transformation, as seen in such activists as Malcolm X, Amiri Baraka, Yuri Kochiyama, Cesar Chávez, and Rigoberta Menchu.[8]

POLITICIZATION IN THE THIRD WORLD AND WHITE LEFT

In contrast to the Third World Left, significantly more is known about the politicization of the white New Left, particularly student activists.[9] When I compared the existing literature with my interviews, it became evident that although there were some commonalities, there were also important distinctions. The most striking similarity, which is hardly surprising, was the extent to which all activists were deeply affected by the same events, namely the civil rights movement and opposition to the Vietnam War. Yet there were important distinctions in how individuals encountered these events, which were in turn based on activists' racial and class positions.[10] For example, while virtually all activists were outraged by the conditions of southern Blacks and felt compelled to act, this awakening led both urban Blacks and other people of color to view their own communities anew, as they saw parallels between the South and their own conditions. For whites, in contrast, their involvement was about helping others and fighting larger injustices, but not necessarily within their own communities. A similar set of dynamics can be seen with regard to the Vietnam War. While the white New Left (and millions of others) opposed the war for numerous political and moral reasons, the Third World Left shared those concerns but in addition mobilized against what they saw as the genocide of their people(s). Because the white New Left was composed overwhelmingly of students and the middle class, they were not dying in the same numbers as those from the working class and communities of color.

In discussing the motivations for activism among the New Left, David Horowitz has suggested that "radicalism was a displacement of personal grievance."[11] On the basis of my interviews I disagree with this conclusion. While radical activism may provide a vehicle to either work out or hide from one's demons, such an attitude belittles the very real structural forces limiting people's lives. One Japanese American woman shared how when she was thirteen her teacher told her, "If you want to be a dancer, you have to be twice as good as everyone else." Later, when auditioning, she was regularly told, "You're a very good dancer, but we can't use you because you will stick out." I would argue that this woman's decision to become an activist was not a case of "displaced personal grievance" but a logical response to her experience of racism.

Nevertheless, the dynamic between the self and the external world is complex.[12] For this reason we cannot automatically assume that because someone is poor, or belongs to a subordinated group, that person will become political, or, if he or she does, the content of his or her politics. Witness, for example, the proliferation of nonwhite conservatives.[13] The fact that many respond to them with confusion and anger is indicative of the assumptions we make. Clearly, care must be taken in ascribing causality, and we must strive to balance an individual's story with larger historical events.

Another important distinction between white activists and the Third World Left was the role of the Old Left. Todd Gitlin and others have observed that many in the New Left were influenced by the legacy of the Old Left. "The majority of the original New Leftists were not the children of Communist or socialist parents, but sometime in adolescence were touched, influenced, fascinated, by children who were. From them the rest of us absorbed, by osmosis, the idea and precedent and romance of a Left."[14] Such was not the case for leftists of color. None of the activists I interviewed came from leftist households or even mentioned someone from the Old Left. To the contrary, a tremendous void was created by McCarthyism, especially among Asian and Mexican American radicals. Because of their immigrant backgrounds and "unassimilable" nature, nonwhite leftists were more vulnerable during the Red Scare. Already suspected of being un-American, they would be flirting with disaster by affiliating with communism.[15] Contributing to the scarcity of older radicals of color was the exodus of many African Americans and Puerto Ricans from the Communist Party (CPUSA) in the 1950s. Under Harry Haywood's leadership, many departed in response to the party's position on the "national question" and its policies toward racial minorities.[16] The fact that activists of color left the CPUSA en masse, as well as the party's subsequent reluctance to actively support Third World and antiracist struggles, is pivotal to understanding the development of the New Communist movement and particularly the Third World Left: The CPUSA was simply not seen as a viable or welcoming political home.[17] Accordingly, while white activists struggled to negotiate their relationship to the Old Left, Third World Leftists rarely did. On the other hand, members of the Third World Left had relatively few leftist traditions and resources to draw upon. In Southern California only a handful of non-white members of the Old Left worked with youth of color, including Nelson Peery and Bert Corona.[18] Thus, for the most part, activists of color created leftist organizations outside the shadow of the Old Left.

A final issue is the relationship between leftist traditions and particular ethnic groups. No group illustrates this more strikingly than Jewish Americans. Not only did Jews loom large in all the activism of the sixties and seventies, but their experience illuminates the nature of leftist traditions. Because of anti-Semitism, European Jews were disproportionately urbanized and entered the working class in large numbers, where they were exposed to socialist, communist, and anarchist thought. As Jews immigrated to the United States, they brought such traditions with them. Thus not only did Jews form a vital part of the Old Left, but a generally progressive character can be ascribed to the population as a whole in the sixties. Indeed, until fairly recently, some suggested that a commitment to social justice was part of what it meant to be an American Jew in the post-Holocaust era. Although there are no reliable figures, Jews composed a disproportionate number of civil rights, New Left, and New Communist movement activists. Jews got involved for numerous reasons, including responding to their own discrimination, feeling empathy with racially oppressed groups, and having grown up in politicized households where capitalism, socialism, and racism were routinely discussed. In other words, a progressive Jewish tradition served to politicize many members of the white left, and while there are deep histories of resistance and activism among communities of color, none of these traditions matched that of Jewish Americans.[19] Instead, most members of the Third World Left came from relatively apolitical households.

EARLY POLITICIZATION: FAMILY BACKGROUND
AND OVERT RACISM

Although few activists of color came from explicitly political households, a number of interviewees traced the beginnings of their political consciousness to their parents. Exceptions to the pattern of apolitical families included several Chicana/o families with strong union ties, a Chicana/o family involved in Democratic politics, a Black Garveyite household, and a Japanese American activist-oriented mother. Regardless of this limited political involvement, however, many parents transmitted critical values to their children through their behavior, by lectures, and by interpreting events and history in a politically progressive way. Following are two examples of parental influence:

My mother was very concerned about neighborhood issues, but not an activist. I think all of my sisters and I are strong women. . . . We're very vocal, very strong, very opinionated, and very open, and I think we attribute that to Mom. She was self-employed, she did taxes and immigration papers, primarily for the neighborhood. People who were low-income, *imigrantes, Mexicanos.* She was against discrimination of all kinds. She had an openness to the plight of African Americans, immigrants, poor people, and gays and lesbians. She felt really bad for people who had to fight for what they were. She just had a passion and a rage for a lot of things.

My family was not political and was terrified . . . [when] I became politically involved, even though it was really my father who introduced me to politics. We used to watch the news together when I was a child, [but] he did not realize that he was providing the seeds for my political education. He was from the South, and being a kid from California watching the news, and seeing these people sitting on lunch counters and other people dumping food over their heads, it was very hard to understand. It was very hard to understand segregation. Even though stuff was segregated here, it was not apartheid law, so my father interpreted that news for me. And in interpreting it, he politicized me.

In both cases we can see how parents subtly politicized their children. Indeed, most parents sought to instill antiracist and social justice values, but not all. A few Japanese Americans whom I interviewed identified an attitude of racial superiority on the part of their parents and grandparents toward Mexicans and Blacks. These activists not only saw their elders' attitudes as problematic but consciously strove to develop a different set of beliefs.

Some parents ensured that their children had an alternative framework to evaluate the world from the one provided by the dominant society. One woman recalled her mother subscribing to *Ebony* to guarantee that she and her siblings understood Black history and the power relations associated with racial differences. In another case, two former Panthers (twin brothers) came from a Garveyite household in Detroit. They were raised as Black nationalists and were keenly aware of how history was taught from a white supremacist perspective.

Only one interviewee came from an explicitly political family: a mother involved in mainstream politics, particularly at the interface of the Democratic Party and the nascent Chicana/o movement.

You didn't really have a choice over whether you could be political or not, it was a matter of survival. My mother was part of John Kennedy's presidential campaign. She was basically [into] mainstream Democratic politics, and we moved through that with her. In 1965 she started working with the UFW [United Farm Workers] because part of her work with the Democratic Party was to raise funds and get the Latino vote. She worked with labor unions, the UAW [United Auto Workers], the URW [United Rubber Workers], and the UFW. So we learned a lot about political organization, political campaigning, union organizing, grassroots organizing, that was sort of our supplemental education, doesn't everybody do this? I felt we couldn't make a political issue out of everything, but my family's view was, "Yes, you can!"

A second important source of politicization was the urban geography of activists' early lives. As previously mentioned, the 1950s and 1960s were a time of demographic and spatial transitions. Mia Tuan has shown how such geographies can help make young people conscious and aware of their racial and class identity at an early age.[20] One woman, who grew up in the rapidly changing Crenshaw district, recalled how the juxtaposition of Blacks and Japanese Americans influenced how she saw herself.

I remember the first time anybody called me an "Asian sister," as opposed to a "Japanese girl," or an "Oriental girl." It was this guy who was selling the Black Muslim paper at the Boy's Market. I'll never forget it, because I thought, "Hey, I like the way that sounds." I can even picture him still with his bow tie and everything. . . . The Black Muslims were one of the active groups then. I remember people in high school talking about Malcolm X and stuff, and I didn't have any direct experience with it, but because of where I was and the ethnic makeup and the historical period, they impacted me and made me very curious.

In another instance, an African American man described himself and his cousin as "amateur anthropologists." As boys they would ride their bikes through Los Angeles and study the different neighborhoods, trying to figure out how and why they varied. This process helped him understand the structural factors oppressing Blacks but also enabled him to articulate connections with Mexicans—a political commitment he still carries.

Place was also important in terms of the opportunities it offered. The harsh reality of the ghetto and barrio helped to make activism an attractive option. One Chicano from City Terrace explained that activism was an alternative to joining a gang.

What else do you have? For somebody on the Westside [there was] football, or tennis, or anything else recreational. For people who grew up in my community, [activism] was our way out. If you don't have a job, you don't have a recreational release, then what do you have? The street. And if the street offers you only violence and drugs, then that is what you do. But if the street offers you a chance to be a fighter, not a gang, but a street fighter for the community, boy, what an option that was. For a lot of people who really didn't want to be in gangs, who had smarts, who wanted to do something good, it was terrific. It was like our own gang, but we were doing good work, accomplishing good things, and felt good about ourselves.

While all of these formative experiences, whether living in a barrio or growing up in a Garveyite household, resulted from racialized social relations, overt discrimination also played a role in politicizing activists. At such moments young people grasped the nature of structural inequalities and realized that they had a responsibility to address them, in what McAdam calls "cognitive liberation."[21] One woman, for example, who grew up doing farm work, was forever marked by the death of her younger brother. He had become sick and could have easily been saved if he had had access to health care.[22] Once active in the Chicana/o movement, she yearned for an explicit class politics that would enable her to improve the rights and well-being of workers and their families. Another Chicana was acutely aware of how racism negatively affected her social life: "If a boy came up to me and wanted to talk to me and his parents saw this, he could get beaten. The racism was that intense." A Black man who had faced innumerable hardships recalled the moment when he understood how Blacks were denied class mobility. He noted that his school, which was predominantly Black, taught primarily the trades, and when he voiced an interest in engineering he was told that "wasn't for him." He subsequently drifted into a gang.

I have tried to briefly present a range of discriminatory experiences that activists incurred. As can be seen, they range from life-and-death matters to less serious, albeit painful events. What is important, however, is that they taught young people that society was organized along racial and class lines and that they and their people were clearly disadvantaged.

POLITICAL OPPORTUNITIES: MOVEMENTS AND EVENTS

While family background and overt discrimination may have predisposed young people to see the world in a particular way, they needed an opportunity to become politically active. Given the highly politicized nature of the era, young people not only were aware of injustices but encountered ample opportunities to get involved.

The Civil Rights Movement

The first event that served to politicize activists was the civil rights movement. The movement affected activists in two ways. First, all minority activists in Los Angeles saw the civil rights drama on television and felt a strong sense of moral outrage that caused them to rethink hegemonic narratives of democracy and freedom. Televised images of nonviolent protestors being brutalized generated support for the movement and served to politicize viewers. Second, the civil rights movement contributed to young activists' political consciousness through direct experience. Several soon-to-be activists participated in nonviolent protests and were subject to police abuse. One former Panther went downtown to take a postal service test and found himself suddenly involved in a civil rights protest.

> The day I was supposed to take the test was the same day as a demonstration about Selma, Alabama. I went where the people were blocking the driveway, hundreds of nonviolent protestors. The police, the news media, everybody was there. The deputies, or the U.S. marshals, or whatever they were, came out of the building, about fifty of them. They waded into the crowd and started beating and arresting [people]. I'm standing on the side just watching this, and the next thing I know a guy runs over and grabs me. Then four guys are beating me up. They arrested me as part of the demonstration. I went to jail and I got bailed out by the civil rights people.

Upon his release from jail, the budding activist felt somewhat obligated to the movement and began exploring various civil rights organizations, but he was dissatisfied with their nonviolent philosophy, especially in light of his experience. He eventually helped establish the Southern California chapter of the Black Panther Party (BPP) because he felt strongly about community defense against the police.

Another Black activist, while attending California State University, Los Angeles, participated in demonstrations organized by the Congress of Racial Equality (CORE).

> We went and demonstrated at the Board of Education. One of the things I remember most was sitting in the hallway while board members came in. We had gone through self-defense training, passive resistance, and had been told that if somebody starts beating on us we should ball up, that sort of thing. So a group of us were sitting in the hallway and a few of the board members came in and somebody said something. This woman became upset and kicked this guy in the face. Growing up in South Central L.A., I had seen violence before, but this was so unexpected: we were well dressed and at a peaceful demonstration. I think something clicked at that point, like, "I don't know if I want to do this again, because I want to be able to defend myself."

The significance of being beaten while engaging in nonviolent protest cannot be overstated. Besides provoking moral outrage, it made activists seriously rethink nonviolence as a strategy.[23] Edward Escobar, in his study of police relations among Mexican Americans found that law enforcement experiences perceived as unfair not only angered people but also contributed to further politicization.[24] This process was clearly evident in the civil rights movement and both contributed to and intensified the Watts riot and Chicano Moratorium, with important implications for the Third World Left.

The civil rights movement also politicized non-Black people of color, including this former East Wind member, as it forced Chicanas/os and Asian Americans to rethink their racial position and identities.

> When I was at Cal State Los Angeles the civil rights movement was in full swing in the South, and Asians were getting a lot of flak from Blacks. Those of us who had Black friends, most of us did at the time because we lived in the ghetto and barrio, we were being asked, "So, what side are you on?" There were demonstrations at the Federal Building, and just watching it on television freaked me out. And then my friend in chemistry disappeared for a while. When I saw him again he said he had been in jail. He explained that during the demonstration "a couple of police deputized all these rednecks, beat up the kids, and put them in jail." I said, "Wow, fuck this shit. Let's go out there and demonstrate." When I went down there I saw a couple of Buddhahead [Japanese American] guys. I was self-conscious and feeling kind of weird, but I was watching these older guys and they were really angry.

This recollection is interesting for several reasons. First, we see how the political struggles of one racial group had a definite impact on others. Being neither Black nor white, Japanese Americans found themselves in the position of having to assert some racial/ethnic identity in response to this bipolar racial conflict. Would they identify as white or as nonwhite? In addition, when the activist did join the protest he encountered older Nikkei. This not only indicates Japanese Americans' historic position as a racially subordinated population but also hints at the remnants of a Japanese American left.[25] Their presence, while somewhat comforting, was perhaps more important insofar as it urged the activist to reconsider what it meant to be Japanese American.

While major events, including the Watts riot and the Vietnam War, served to politicize individuals, they also forged connections between various groups and refashioned the political culture of the region. Watts was one such event that forever changed the nature of Black politics, the meaning of Blackness in Southern California, and, ultimately, what it meant to be Mexican, Asian, or white.

Watts 1965

August 11, 1965, is an important date not only in Los Angeles's history but also in the nation's. Considered one of the most significant urban rebellions of the late sixties, Watts was the most costly and deadly to date. In the end, thirty-four people were dead, almost four thousand were arrested, and property damage was estimated at $40 million.[26] Watts also marked a turning point in Black/white relations: Blacks were tired of waiting for white justice, and young people, in particular, were ready to take matters into their own hands.

Watts, similar to other civil unrest episodes, began in response to a routine traffic stop. A white policeman pulled over a Black motorist suspected of drunk driving. A crowd gathered, the driver's mother exchanged words with the police, and the conflict began. The insurrection had a distinct flow to it—people clashed with the police at night, went to bed, and got up and did it again the following evening—a pattern that lasted for six days and that the police had not previously witnessed. Gerald Horne describes Watts as initially "a black 'riot' aimed principally at the police [but one that] became quickly a police riot aimed principally at blacks."[27]

Though many dismissed Watts as simple lawlessness, such a view overlooks the multilayered meanings and motives that constituted the event. Watts, like other instances of civil unrest, included both random acts of cruelty and violence and targeted acts of resistance and rebellion. For instance, though there was a great deal of looting and vandalism, much of it was geared toward merchants perceived as unfair. Likewise, it is difficult to interpret Black attacks against the police as random.[28] Former Panthers who participated in Watts were clear on their motives and saw it as an insurrection, as well as retaliation against the police. One former member of the Slauson gang who was instrumental in leading the rebellion on the second night described the police as an "occupying force." In his view, the police were just another gang, one that upheld the interests of the merchant class. Another activist, who subsequently joined the Student Non-violent Coordinating Committee (SNCC), vividly recalled standing at the corner of Avalon and Imperial and telling the police that they would not win this site. The contrast between the politics, style, and method of the civil rights movement and urban rebellions could not have been more distinct, yet the two were clearly related. The following quote not only conveys the attitude and thinking of some Black youth at the time but also suggests *why* Watts happened and how it helped set the stage for the BPP.

> Things like Emmett Till and the civil rights struggle in the South came
> to our attention, even though here on the West Coast we didn't agree
> with the civil rights tactics. We saw people being lynched. Every time
> they took to the streets we saw them being washed down with firehoses,
> dogs being sicced on them, having rocks thrown at them, spit upon, and

physically attacked. Out here we were not willing to allow anyone to carry out those types of abuses against us and get away with it. You got to remember that we came up in gang culture, so we were already with a combative spirit. We were already organized to fight anything and anybody that didn't agree with us. [That] set the stage for the fight we had in 1965 with the police. When they asked us what this was all about on the second night of the so-called riot, what we refer to as the rebellion, we explained it to their faces: "We don't see you as the police. You are an occupying force. You don't protect us and serve our interest. You only serve the interest of the merchant class that doesn't even live among us."

Time and again Black male activists emphasized that Watts clarified the role of the Los Angeles Police Department (LAPD): it was a white gang. This attitude towards the police is significant for several reasons. First, it hints at the tense relations between Black Angelenos and the police. This was a widespread problem, but especially so in Los Angeles, where the LAPD, under the direction of Chief Parker, was notoriously antagonistic toward the Black community, as well as activists in general.[29] Police abuse was perceived as a major problem by African Americans, and challenging it became a cornerstone of the BPP. The third part of the police/community equation, however, was gangs. The presence of a gang structure was not insignificant in South Los Angeles (indeed, across the city) during the 1950s and 1960s.[30] Prominent gangs, or clubs, as they were called, included the Bartenders, the Businessmen, the Executives, and the Slausons. The Slausons, easily the largest, eventually controlled all of South Los Angeles. Under the leadership of Bunchy Carter, a former Slauson, the existing gang structure became the basis for the Southern California chapter of the BPP.

While Watts was significant on numerous levels, perhaps its greatest impact was that it presented an alternative. With the exception of one Black activist imprisoned at the time, virtually everyone recalled August 1965 vividly as a turning point: Blacks were no longer going to accept police brutality and white injustice. The days of the cautious and patient Black activist were over.

It [Watts] had a tremendous impact on me. . . . I guess it had quite an impact on most young Black men. [It] was like when a slave realizes that there is such a thing as freedom. I had moved out here in 1961, and the LAPD dogged young Blacks, just treated them any kind of way. And in 1965, during the riot, you see the police getting run out of town. They were just as vulnerable and human as anybody else. People saw that as powerful as the government projects itself to be, it's still just a paper tiger. Any time masses of people rise up, the government has a serious problem. And you just can't riot every day, so what do you do? It took Bunchy Carter to start the Black Panther Party for a lot of people to find a vehicle they could use.

Although there was a distinctly gendered character to the Watts uprising, a significant minority of Blacks residing in the curfew zone supported it.[31] Others, while perhaps not condoning the tactics used, readily understood the need to challenge law enforcement and to voice pent-up resentment. One former Panther who was then a young girl recalled: "I was fourteen when Watts happened, and I thought it was as exciting as hell. I was glad to see Black people standing up, doing something. And I kept thinking to myself, 'This must be like the slave revolts that grandma told me about.' Every time the National Guard would pass I would stick my tongue out and give them the finger. My mother would get upset and tell us to get in the house. We thought it was the beginning of the revolution. We watched it on TV, the whole city going up in flames."

While the previous two quotes reflect an obvious hostility towards law enforcement, Watts also served to politicize those whose ideas were less fully developed. For some, the extraordinary nature of the event forced them to begin asking hard questions: "What [Watts] did was push me to try to find answers to questions. I saw [the] National Guard and the LAPD driving down my street. I can't tell you the shock, the utter amazement that here I am standing on the corner of Florence and Figueroa, several blocks from my house, and watching a state of war in my neighborhood. I remember watching this caravan of tanks and just being paralyzed. It was the shock of living in an area that was literally being militarily occupied. It had a deep, deep impact on me."

Watts had the greatest effect on Black activists, but it was also significant for Japanese Americans and Chicanas/os. Both Asian Americans and Chicanas/os who lived in the curfew zone reported being so shocked by the police presence that they became further politicized. But the biggest impact was in terms of the racial hierarchy. Like the Japanese American internment, Black participation in Watts was instrumental in shifting the racial hierarchy and contributing to Japanese and Mexican Americans being seen as more "deserving" minorities. Subsequent investigations emphasized that many of the conditions facing African Americans were also present among Mexican Americans—yet *they* did not engage in an outbreak of lawlessness. The McCone Commission, the state-sponsored report on the Watts uprising, comments: "In this report, our major conclusions and recommendations regarding the Negro problem in Los Angeles apply with equal force to the Mexican Americans, a community which is almost equal in size to the

Negro community and whose circumstances are similarly disadvantageous and demand equally urgent treatment. That the Mexican American community did not riot is to its credit; it should not be to its disadvantage."[32] Mexican American leaders and academics also sought to distinguish Chicana/o activists from Black lawbreakers.[33] The end result of these various moves was the continued demonization of the African American population. Ironically, while many whites, particularly working-class Angelenos, grew more hostile toward Blacks, the African American community gained political power. This was seen in an expansion of resources, increased social and economic opportunities, and a growing number of Black elected officials. Such shifts also signaled the simplification of Los Angeles's complex racial hierarchy toward a bipolar Black and white one, with Asian Americans, American Indians, and Mexicans occupying an increasingly irrelevant place.[34]

The Antiwar Movement

Another major force in politicizing the Third World Left was opposition to the Vietnam War. People of color not only actively opposed the war but, in places like Southern California, assumed a leadership role, as seen, for example, in the Chicano Moratorium. Unlike the Watts riots, which chiefly affected African Americans, the antiwar movement involved all people of color, as the war was fought primarily by the working class. Interestingly, although many African Americans actively opposed the war—at one point Huey Newton offered the services of the BPP to the North Vietnamese— the antiwar movement was not a major factor in the *politicization* of young Black radicals in Southern California. Rather, their opposition to the war reflected an already existing political consciousness. In contrast, many Chicana/o and Asian American leftists were *transformed* by the war itself. Opposition to the war became a catalyst for a larger political awakening.

Chicanas/os   Chicana/o opposition to the Vietnam War is a complicated phenomenon that must be appreciated in its historical context. Although the military did not count Hispanic soldiers, there are indications that Latinos, particularly Mexican Americans and Puerto Ricans, served, and died, in disproportionately large numbers. This was partly because, for most of the war, students were exempt from the draft, and because most Latinos, on account of their relatively limited participation in higher education, could not claim student status. In addition, recruitment programs like Project 100,000 ensured that low-income minorities were disproportionately channeled into combat troops.[35] Finally, and perhaps most significantly, military service has always represented a vehicle of upward mobility for the poor and working class. This socioeconomic ladder, however, has extra significance for immigrants and nonwhites. Military service offers a way to prove one's Americanness, what Jorge Mariscal calls "warrior patriotism."[36] While many Mexican American soldiers felt it was their duty to serve, others realized that they had few options: to resist would humiliate one's family and one's community. Warrior patriotism explains the special meaning that military service has had to Asian Americans, Latinas/os, and Blacks, as well as any others who have been deemed "not quite American."[37] As a result, Mexican Americans have been deeply connected, both ideologically and bodily, to the military. This attachment is such that Lorena Oropeza has argued that Mexican Americans have essentially relied on their exemplary military service record to emphasize that they deserved equal treatment. How military service, civil rights, and support for the Vietnam War came together can be seen in the GI Forum, a fairly conservative Mexican American political organization: "Faithful to the Mexican American political tradition that sought civil rights on the basis of military service performed, Forumeers proudly had made note of Mexican American loyalty and service to the United States during the Second World War, in Korea, and now, in Vietnam. Strongly opposed to communism as well, members were thus doubly disinclined to question their president's policy in Southeast Asia. To the contrary, with another war looming, Forum leaders again saw an opportunity to emphasize patriotism—and by implication, the well-deserving nature—of their ethnic group."[38] Given this history, it took a powerful combination of events to propel Mexican Americans to oppose the war, but once they did, the size of the population and the strength of its opposition had a major impact, not only on the antiwar movement, but on the politicization of many Chicanas/os.[39] The large number of Mexican Americans that served, particularly in combat troops, created a death toll that the people back home found increasingly hard to justify.

In her study of Chicana/o opposition to the war, Oropeza found that the Chicana/o antiwar movement was distinct in several ways from the white struggle. For one thing, activists were less antagonistic toward Mexican American soldiers, for these were their brothers, sons, homeboys, and boyfriends. Simply put, the class distinctions that characterized the white movement did not exist for Chicanas/os. A second difference was the Chicana/o emphasis on the struggle for equality at home. "*La batalla está aquí*" (the battle is here) stressed the need for Mexican Americans to put their energy into changing conditions in the United States, not waging war against peasants in a far-off country.[40] Third, the fact that the majority of the Vietnamese were rural peasants enabled many Mexican Americans to identify with them. Although by 1970 the vast majority of Mexican Americans were urban, rural imagery was still powerful, as many were only a generation or two removed from the soil. In addition, the rural loomed large in the Chicana/o movement itself, as seen in the land grant struggles of New Mexico and the UFW in California. Oropeza argues that while Chicana/o antiwar activists' primary concern was never the Vietnamese people, the war did serve to introduce many to internationalism. Not surprisingly, this dimension of the war resonated with would-be leftists. In addition to the belief that this was a "white man's" war, the United States' escalating involvement in Southeast Asia made it increasingly difficult to sustain the War on Poverty. While these programs were of paramount importance to all poor communities and people of color, the results were especially disappointing for Mexican Americans, as these programs were partly seen as their reward for not having resorted to rioting, as African Americans had done.[41] Below, one former member of El Centro de Acción Social y Autónomo/ the Center for Autonomous Social Action (CASA) explained the connection between the antiwar and Chicana/o movements.

> I finally settled down with a combination of the anti–Vietnam War movement and the Chicano movement, which was then forming around 1969. It seemed to make sense, "We're against the war and we're also pushing for our community." Before it was just survival and we had no idea there was an outside world. And then guys came back from the military and said, "Hey, something else is going on besides just here." People were dying, we were fighting communism, all these things were being thrown around while everyone was getting high. I mean, you are chewing on a rag with glue and people are talking about the war in Southeast Asia, and then African Americans had a struggle, and people were saying, "Well, what about our struggle?" So, finally, when the two came together . . . it made sense to a lot of people. There was something worthwhile we could do. It was not only for us, it was for our community. When you can identify with something that is definitely wrong, it is easier. In the abstract, you can say, "We're oppressed," but when people are coming home in boxes, you have something to really look at.

On August 29, 1970, Chicana/o activists organized the largest antiwar demonstration ever by a community of color, the Chicano Moratorium. What started as a peaceful protest of twenty to thirty thousand demonstrators turned into a major police confrontation that left three dead, including the journalist Rubén Salazar, and hundreds wounded. Strong evidence exists that local law enforcement, working in conjunction with the FBI, were intent on curbing the demonstration.[42] While they did succeed in brutally ending it, their actions also served to politicize a large number of Mexican Americans who were either political neophytes or simply in the wrong place at the wrong time. That the police responded violently to what many considered a peaceful event had an enormous effect on young people who were not necessarily opposed to authority or even politically conscious.

> I graduated in 1970, and that summer my friend had become somewhat involved in the Chicano movement and told me, "Let's go to this parade in East L.A. Let's go check it out." So I said, "Ok, that sounds good." I invited my little sister. Well, little did I know that we were in the middle of this huge demonstration and march. There were a lot of speakers, Dolores Huerta, and then all of a sudden, we see people screaming. It looked like a school of fish when the tear gas hit, because people were running one way, and then they went another. . . . Pretty soon we found ourselves screaming and running and trying to get out of there. That was my first sort of "hit" to any social movement or political activism.

The parallels between Blacks who participated in nonviolent civil rights demonstrations and Chicanos/as in the Moratorium should be apparent. "I guess August 29th was a turning point for me. I attended it with a group of priests to oppose the war in Vietnam and then witnessed ourselves being chased by the police, tear-gassed, and being harassed and pushed around. In many ways reflecting upon my own political history, I would say that's an important turning point, not only for myself, but I think for a generation that was becoming involved in politics."

While police abuse is an everyday occurrence in communities of color, these mass events were significant for several reasons. For one, it wasn't individuals that were being attacked, but thousands of people. In addition, although people from across the Southwest came to participate in the Moratorium, it was composed largely of locals, for whom it became a political touchstone. Finally, a political infrastructure existed that enabled young people to channel their anger and confusion.

> The Chicano Moratorium was my defining moment in terms of thinking that we could actually change something and make a difference. When I was fifteen, I marched, I got tear-gassed. I recognized that it was a life-and-death situation in order to achieve certain goals. There was a requirement that you be committed to certain ideals, and it meant sacrificing some of your youthful pursuits. The greater cause was going to be the priority. I think the thing that the Chicano Moratorium showed me was that we had tremendous power that day and it frightened the pow-

ers that be so much, that they crushed it. [They] just overwhelmingly came down on us in a way that was very brutal, and it was clear to me that it was going to be an "us against them" proposition. Although I knew that Cesar's [Chavez] movement and his commitment to nonviolence was extremely important, I knew at that point that the establishment was not going to allow this to happen. There had been so many assassinations, it was very clear that there was enormous power to stop these movements. So I became very radicalized by it.

Japanese Americans   The Vietnam War also served to politicize a large number of Japanese Americans.[43] Because their economic and racial position was distinct from Chicanas/os', their politicization process was also somewhat different. Japanese Americans served in the war, but their firmer footing in the middle class and higher education shielded them from disproportionate representation in combat.[44] Yet as Asian Americans they were forced to confront the racism of the war itself, the racist nature of the antiwar movement, and questions regarding their identity. Because the war was against an Asian people, there was a generalized racism against all Asians in the United States that had to be confronted—what William Wei refers to as "gookism."[45] In addition, because the Vietnam War was considered by many to be an act of imperialism, it served to dramatize the struggle of Third World countries at precisely the same moment that U.S. racial minorities were beginning to identify as Third World people and thus became a crucible for the politicization of many Asian American activists.

Most Japanese American activists interviewed were somehow involved in the antiwar movement. This is not surprising, since many Japanese Americans attended universities, which became leading sites of antiwar activity. Several activists joined campus groups opposed to the war but eventually left because of political differences, particularly around race: "I was interested in some of the antiwar stuff. I checked out a few meetings, but I definitely felt like I didn't belong there. I remember one guy in a small grouping saying stuff like, 'You know, those Blacks, they just don't listen to us, and they just don't feel like they have anything to learn.' And I looked at him and I thought, 'He's saying this in front of me. I'm invisible. I'm Asian and he doesn't see me as having any connection to that.' That really made me feel like I didn't belong there." This activist's alienation and discomfort among white antiwar activists were echoed by most people of color who ventured into the movement.[46] Such frustration led to the creation of ethnic-specific antiwar organizations, such as Asian Americans for Peace, based in Little Tokyo. The quote is also significant, however, in the extent to which the activist identifies with African Americans yet is treated as an "honorary white." This is a persistent and crucial theme that surfaces repeatedly throughout the era: What is the racial position of Asian Americans? Politically, what does it *mean* to be Asian American?

In addition to the racism of the peace movement, many Japanese Americans were critical of its larger political analysis, which was felt to center on U.S. troops.

> A lot of us felt that the white anti-war movement had these slogans like "Bring the boys back home," as if what was wrong with the war was that American boys were dying—not that the U.S. was an invasive force in an Asian country and that there were Asians dying too. A lot more Asian people that looked like me. There was a gradual politicization of the whole movement around the role of U.S. imperialism, the role of capital. The war was fought under the guise of stopping communism, but Ho Chi Min was Vietnamese, he was coming from an invaded country. Then you start looking at it in terms of your own identity. Who do you identify with? Do you identify with the Vietnamese, or do you identify with oppressed people in this country? Or do you identify with the U.S.?

While this activist identifies the multiplicity of themes that Japanese Americans activists had to contend with,[47] the following quote from a different Nikkei activist frames the relationship between Asians and U.S. militarism in starker terms. "First there was the H-bomb, then the Korean War, then the Vietnam War. For all these decades I've been watching them kill Asians. I considered them my cousins." Figure 3 illustrates how Japanese Americans emphasized the experience of the Vietnamese in their approach to the war. At this particular teach-in organized by Japanese Americans, the primary focus is the Vietnamese people and their struggle. In her study of the Asian American left, Miriam Ching Louie has argued that the movement's greater embrace of Marxism-Leninism, relative to the Chicana/o or Black movements, is at least partially explained by the existence of revolutionary activity in Asia itself. This is a crucial point: Chicana/o and Black leftists developed partly in *response* to both civil rights and more nationalist movements in the United States, whereas the Japanese American left developed as part of the larger Asian American movement, which was generally more left-leaning. Encouraging this leftward tilt was the fact that many Asian Americans were inspired by and took their cues from Asian struggles and revolutionaries, including the Vietnamese peasantry, Ho Chi Min, and Chairman Mao.

> The Asian national liberation movements were highly ideologized. This has nothing to do with anything we did, but was a formative influence on us. Compared to liberation movements in Africa and Latin America at

Figure 3. Anti–Vietnam War flier. Japanese American antiwar activists emphasized the experience of the Vietnamese. Source: Vietnam War Subject File. Courtesy
of Southern California Library for Social Studies and Research.

> the time, Asian movements were led by Marxist forces who were part
> of the international communist movement. There was the Chinese Com-
> munist Party, the Vietnam Workers Party, the Korean Workers Party. A
> new communist party was soon formed in the Philippines, and a militant
> left student movement existed in Japan. Here we were just figuring out
> what it meant to be Asian. . . . [B]eing Asian in our minds came to be
> synonymous with being progressive, and being Marxist.[48]

Thus opposition to the Vietnam War provided a concrete opportunity not
only to establish one's identity but to develop it along leftist lines. Of course,
most Japanese Americans were never part of either the Asian American movement or the left, but many *were* affected by the generalized racism of the
period. This was true both for Asian American troops stationed in Vietnam,
who looked similar to the "enemy," and for Asian Americans on the home
front. The experience of wartime racism served to heighten the contradictions
and to further radicalize them, as it did for this one East Wind member.

> I had this really horrible experience once. I had taken the midnight flier
> and I was walking down the corridor at L.A.X. and there were these two

guys walking near me. They were white guys with buzz cuts and they were obviously in the military. They were saying things like, "I wonder if she has a slanted cunt?" I thought, "oh shit,'" and then my reaction was, "Wait a minute, there is no one else around here." I was trying not to panic, but one of them was drunk, and I was getting scared because they were saying really awful things. It was making me mad, but I didn't think I could do anything about it. But then this guy came along on a cart. He was an older, African American guy and stopped and said, "Excuse me, miss, do you need a ride?" I think he caught the vibe. I'm such a chicken, when I was on the cart I [told them], "Fuck you!" I don't know what I would have done without him.[49]

This incident demonstrates not only how racist attitudes toward the "enemy" can be extrapolated onto a domestic group but also the gendered nature of racism. While racism is always gendered, we can see how the soldiers' images of Asian American women were deeply sexualized. This is a long-standing construct that Asian American women must contend with and has been fueled by U.S. military excursions into Asia. The Vietnam War was the latest instance of reproducing racist/sexist imagery. Overall the war added a powerful new dimension to the racism that Asian Americans experienced, which in turn, encouraged the development of a political framework that underscored the connections between imperialism, racism, and sexism.

The Struggle for Ethnic Studies

The final political struggle that helped to politicize Third World Leftists was the creation of ethnic studies programs. Student activism was central to all the movements of the sixties and seventies, and, as Carlos Muñoz has pointed out, this activism cannot be divorced from the demographic and generational shifts of the baby boom. This trend was especially pronounced for students of color, many of whom were first-generation college students, and contributed to universities becoming sites of political fermentation. The struggle for ethnic studies, as well as more general efforts to support students of color, was something all racial/ethnic groups participated in.[50]

However, as a politicizing force among Los Angeles activists, these issues were especially relevant for Chicanas/os and Asian Americans. It wasn't that Blacks weren't actively involved in student organizing.[51] Huey Newton was a student at Merritt College when he and Bobby Seale founded the BPP, and several Panthers (along with other people of color) participated in the High Potential Program at the University of California, Los Angeles (UCLA). However, the BPP was more rooted in the community than either CASA or East Wind. In addition, few of the Panthers I encountered were actually enrolled in school at the time. Most did not attend college as young people, and those that did typically enrolled for only a semester or two. Moreover, such individuals tended to be already politicized through either the civil rights movement or the Watts uprising. For instance, one former Panther attended Los Angeles City College for a few semesters but subsequently quit in order to join the party full time. While the BPP was more community based, both CASA and East Wind were characterized by greater student representation.

Campus-based activism produced a slightly different political trajectory than community-based work, as students were often initially politicized through nationalist frameworks and only later sought a more materialist approach. In comparison, Panthers, regardless of educational attainment, were more apt to eschew cultural nationalism from the beginning and adopt a more internationalist and/or revolutionary nationalist perspective. Because these individuals were typically politicized through the civil rights movement or the Watts uprising, they felt that a more radical politics was necessary. For instance, when asked about cultural nationalism, one former Panther replied, "No, I guess at that time I had enough sense to know that what they were talking about wasn't realistic. They didn't offer any solution to the problem. [If] the police are just harassing you and putting their foot up your ass all day, a bone in your nose isn't going to change anything, wearing a dashiki isn't going to change anything. The only thing that is going to change it is having enough courage to challenge it. The only way you are going to challenge them is with the same force that they use to oppress you with." In contrast, the vast majority of activists who spent any significant time in college had to grapple with cultural nationalism to some degree. Cultural nationalism was most intense for Chicana/o students because the Chicana/o movement, a significant element of which was campus based, was far more nationalistic than the Asian American movement. As discussed in chapter 5, the sheer diversity of Asian Americans precluded the development of a simple nationalism. While Chicana/o students adopted an increasingly narrow vision of what constituted "Chicana/o," Asian Americans were beginning the process of developing a panethnic identity.[52]

The story of ethnic studies in California begins at California State University, San Francisco in 1968. After two years of wrangling with the administration over minority recruitment and control of the Black Studies Department, Black, Latina/o, American Indian, and Asian American students formed the Third World Liberation Front (TWLF). Although composed of students, the TWLF was deeply rooted in the community and articulated a vision of ethnic studies linking the university and community. The

TWLF, with the support of progressive white students, including Students for a Democratic Society, called for a strike beginning November 6. Strike demands included the creation of a School of Ethnic Studies, faculty positions, student control, minority admissions, and the reinstatement of George Murray, a terminated Black instructor.[53] The strike lasted five months and ultimately succeeded in establishing ethnic studies on campus. Similar protests spread quickly to other campuses, including UC Berkeley,[54] while administrators at other schools, such as UCLA, sought to head them off. "The San Francisco State strike involved not only the students from that campus, but it also mobilized thousands of other students, people from Third World communities all over the state, rank-and-file members of unions, an overwhelming majority of the faculty, and ultimately, the whole political apparatus of California."[55]

In Southern California, California State University, Long Beach and UCLA were two of the leading campuses fighting for ethnic studies.[56] Ethnic studies affected students in two ways: first, it offered classes on their history and culture from a new perspective that radicalized them, and second, many students became familiar with coalition building, and, on the basis of that experience, gravitated toward an internationalist politics. Recall that before the widespread adoption of ethnic studies, almost the entire curriculum was grounded in a white perspective. The experiences of students of color were routinely ignored and sometimes denigrated. Not only was the San Francisco strike an inspiration, but the TWLF encouraged others to organize similar campaigns. According to one East Wind member, "We started hearing about the Third World Liberation Strike up north. And then in 1968 we started having Asian American meetings, and people from San Francisco actually came down to speak at different campuses, including ours [Cal State Long Beach]. That had a huge impact on everybody. Because they were actually running a strike where they had an instructor, community, and labor support, it was amazing. Very inspirational. They helped people clarify their political demands. It wasn't just these classes to learn about cultural stuff, it was classes to develop political leaders to help solve problems in the community." The process of demanding ethnic studies was itself transformative and enabled students to experience political efficacy while learning basic organizing skills. This training would serve them well as they later sought to develop off-campus organizations. In one case, there was a direct link between the struggle for Chicano studies at St. Mary's, the Northern California chapter of CASA, and eventually the Southern California office.[57]

> When I went to St. Mary's the fight for Chicano studies was really strong, and because it was an all-white school, it was unheard of. We

demanded Chicano studies, and when they didn't deliver it, we basically took over the chapel for a week. We had a fast and a sit-in at the church. We just took our sleeping bags and took over. We were very much supported by the priests, so it was good. We got our demands met, started a Chicano studies program, and hired our own teacher, Carlos Vásquez, a historian teaching at Berkeley. We hired him and a number of other teachers and got involved in that way in Chicano studies and Chicano rights.

Eventually, Carlos Vásquez became involved in CASA and introduced his students to the organization, with some later working in the Los Angeles offices.

Both the ethnic studies course content and the experience of being with other co-ethnics in a classroom had a profound impact. Ethnic studies offered a safe space for students of color that was empowering. As one Japanese American activist put it,

> Student energy started to snowball around Asian American stuff. It was the same group of people that ended up in the first Asian American studies class that Yuji Ichioka taught. That was like a lightning rod for me. It was wonderful, saved my life. It was actually the first class at UCLA that I felt I was getting something that was important to me. It was called "Orientals in America," that was before *Asian American* became a term. It was kind of an early energy when the movement is young and the people are just so high on everything they hear.

The mobilization for ethnic studies created numerous student organizations. Typically, students of color formed both ethnic-specific and panracial organizations. For instance, at UCLA, Asian American students formed Orientals Concerned; at the University of California, San Diego, the Third World College was born; and at California State University, Long Beach, Chicana/o students formed United Mexican American Students, which was also part of a larger Third World Coalition. Once again, the struggle of African Americans loomed large in the formation of Chicana/o and Asian American organizations, as one East Wind member recalled:

> That first year I was there the Black students started to organize. My friend and I actually went to a few meetings. It really made a lot of sense because it was so alienating for students of color. We used to get together and listen to music and practice dance steps and discuss stuff. So when the group started to meet, they invited us. A lot of it really resonated—I could just substitute the word *Asian* for *Black* and it was still true. Like we weren't learning our own history, you never see yourself on TV, all these different things applied. But obviously I realized that I didn't belong there.

As ethnic-specific organizations proliferated, they sometimes engendered competition and friction. One former member of CASA who was also a member of MEChA (El Movimiento Estudiantil Chicano de Aztlán/Chicano Student Movement of Aztlán) explained, "I was really disillusioned with a lot of the politics. It became very nationalistic and idealistic and turned me off. Everything was 'us against them.' Everybody was trying to get grants. We were fighting over grant money that was going to go to the African Americans in North Long Beach. They were fighting against us because the money was going to us in East Long Beach." Such disillusionment not only led some activists to develop multinational organizations but paved the way for their subsequent embrace of Marxism-Leninism, as it offered a more internationalist perspective.

In addition to being highly nationalistic, many of these organizations were quite sexist. Although there are many types of nationalisms, most are inherently gendered, and the Black and Chicana/o movements were no exception. Both movements cultivated and affirmed an identity that was explicitly male centered, as one Chicana interviewee described:

> In the early Chicano movement, everybody had to be a "vato loco" or have this gangster affiliation. But the majority of us were middle class or from the working class. I was always tired of the Chicano nationalist perspective because it was extremely narrow. Not all Chicanos lived in East L.A. Not all Chicanos were men. The Chicano issues that were being addressed pretty much discounted women, single-parent moms, [and women's concerns with] adequate child care, health issues, violence against women. Those were completely outside of this political platform. I went to Cal State Long Beach and became involved in MEChA. Anna Nieto Gomez was there at the time, so we were very much part of the development of a Chicana feminist movement, including Hijas de Cuahtemoc. [The founders] were purged from MEChA, hung in effigy. MEChA was very upset with us. The MEChA women were not allowed to speak to us because we were the lesbian feminists. Eventually, we were able to integrate the feminist perspective into the movement.

Precisely these types of frustrations, centered on cultural nationalism, sexism, and a desire for a more materialist and internationalist politics, led to the formation of a Third World Left.

As can be seen, the politicization of activists of color was due both to personal experiences that predisposed them to challenging the social order and to the larger historical moment and the opportunities it presented. Virtually all activists were affected by the same events, but there was significant variation in how groups were affected and why, differences that could be traced to their class position and location within the racial hierarchy. In any event, many were inspired to fight against the conditions of their own oppression and embraced an anticapitalist perspective. Regardless of their goal, however, they required a political organization to carry out their work.

PART II

The Third World Left

FOUR

**Serving the People
and Vanguard Politics**

The Formation of the Third World
Left in Los Angeles

The previous chapter demonstrated how both the historical moment and the larger political culture contributed to the development of individual political consciousness. While politically conscious individuals are essential to social movements and political struggle, they are not enough. Without the presence of political organizations, counterhegemonic activity would be limited to rebellion and random acts of protest. Organizations and groups are the essential building blocks of movements, as they provide the space where like-minded individuals coalesce and can accomplish a great deal more collectively than alone.

This chapter examines the creation of the Third World Left in Los Angeles, particularly the Southern California chapters of the Black Panther Party (BPP), CASA, and East Wind. I first discuss Black Power, which is key to understanding the development of the New Left, nationalist struggles, and the Third World Left. Then I present overviews of the BPP, East Wind, and CASA, as well as the nationalist movements that gave rise to them.

THE CIVIL RIGHTS MOVEMENT AND BLACK POWER

The Black civil rights movement is central to the development of the Third World Left, as it destabilized the social formation, enabling activists to envision a new reality. Although the civil rights struggles of both Mexican and Japanese Americans were significant in their own right, they were largely eclipsed by the Black/white conflict that engulfed the nation in the early 1960s.[1] As a result of its greater visibility, the Black civil rights movement had a profound impact on society and became a source of inspiration to other people of color. As William Wei has noted, "Not until the civil rights movement of the 1960s exposed the pervasive problem of racism in US society and raised questions about exactly how democratic the nation's political system in fact was did members of the various Asian ethnic groups begin to think of themselves, and to act politically together, as Asian Americans. Thus was the Asian American movement born."[2]

The nonviolent civil rights movement lasted from approximately 1955 to 1966, but the energy it unleashed fueled a host of oppositional movements that were not extinguished until the late 1970s. Why the civil rights movement transitioned into more radical politics has been analyzed by many scholars, but one key was the state's hesitancy to respond to activists' concerns. In many cases, activists were only asking that federal laws be enforced, given that the police, courts, and vigilantes worked in concert to punish and exile "outside agitators" and "upstart Negroes" alike. Despite repeated pleas for protection, the federal government, particularly the Kennedy administration, turned a deaf ear toward activists, preferring instead to protect the interests of Dixiecrats.[3] As the death toll mounted, a growing number of activists became disillusioned with nonviolence as a strategy and ideology. Why subject oneself to repeated beatings when little was changing?

As in all political struggles, there were conflicting ideologies within the civil rights movement itself. On the one hand, there was a fairly radical tradition, as manifested in the Mississippi Freedom Democratic Party, that was rooted in extensive community networks and a long history of resistance.[4] Upon its defeat by the Mississippi Democratic Party in 1964, however, many began questioning the efficacy of the civil rights strategy, and the process of radicalization accelerated. Blacks not only voiced more militant demands but became critical of Black subjectivity implicit in civil rights ideology. Black leaders, inspired by revolutionary movements in the Third World, grew cognizant of how they had been colonized in the United States and the need to develop an independent and liberated Black consciousness. This new reality could be attained only if Blacks assumed leadership in their struggle and redefined the terms of the debate. This new ideology was powerfully expressed by Stokely Carmichael and Charles Hamilton in their book *Black Power*.[5]

Black Power was fundamentally different from but related to the civil rights movement. It was a direct extension of a politics that Black militants saw as inadequate and thus refashioned into a more far-reaching critique. The political transition from civil rights to Black Power was accompanied by a shift in the center of action from the rural South to urban centers. Elaine Brown described the moment in 1968 when she realized that the Black Power movement had replaced the civil rights paradigm in Los Angeles.

> Seated in a row on the huge stage . . . was the entire leadership of the
> new black militant movement, a national movement neither supported
> by, endorsed by, nor involving white people. They were a new genera-
> tion of black men, divorced completely now from the . . . civil-rights
> movement of the NAACP and the Urban League and . . . Southern
> Christian Leadership Conference. They were young black men no
> longer concerned with the business of segregation and integration.
> They were young black men who were calling for an end, not only
> to discrimination[,] . . . to the denial of civil rights, but to all forms
> of oppression of blacks—social, political *and* economic—on all fronts.
> This new leadership was not begging the question but making a de-
> mand, a demand it declared it was backing up with armed force, as
> symbolized in the hero of that new movement: Huey P. Newton.[6]

Black Power itself was not a single ideology or political strategy; rather, the
term included an array of ideologies, organizations, and personalities.
Inspired by Malcolm X, Black Power symbolized a deep radicalization of
African Americans' (and others') struggle for equality with a focus on self-
determination and self-defense. Black Power included cultural nationalist
organizations, such as US; more territorially oriented groups, such as the
Republic of New Africa; Marxist organizations, such as the League of
Revolutionary Black Workers; and the revolutionary nationalist BPP.[7]

The implications of Black Power were significant for all those involved in
social protest. One of the more dramatic consequences was that whites could
no longer assume leadership roles in the struggle for racial equality. As Tom
Hayden described the situation, "Whites . . . suddenly lost their legitimacy
and their roots in SNCC [the Student Non-violent Coordinating Com-
mittee]. Ideologically, they could not disagree with the demand for black
control, but the personal consequences were shattering. . . . In time, [whites]
began to see new identities for themselves, in the fledgling consciousness of
women's rights or the antiwar movement, where new barricades of oppression needed breaking."[8] Of course, whites did not stop working with Blacks,
but the rules of the game had been fundamentally altered.

A second consequence of Black Power was the extent to which it inspired
other people of color to mobilize. In Los Angeles this included, in addition
to Chicanas/os and Japanese Americans, smaller groups like Arab Americans, Vietnamese, and Filipinas/os.[9] While the civil rights movement raised
the consciousness of potential activists, Black Power pushed them into
action, eventually resulting in the Red, Yellow, and Brown Power movements. These movements, which I collectively refer to as the "Power movements," ultimately gave rise to the Third World Left. In some cases, Black

Power directly inspired activism, as in the Yellow Power movement, whereas in others it contributed to a deeper radicalization, as was the case with Brown Power. From the Power movements came such organizations as the BPP, the Young Lords, the American Indian Movement, the Brown Berets, and the Red Guard. A Chicano activist describes below his political trajectory from engaging in fairly conventional student politics to becoming the Brown Berets' Minister of Defense.

> I was at ELAC [East Los Angeles College] and ran for student government. At that time ELAC was mostly white, maybe one-third Chicano. The older GIs started a group called MASA [Mexican American Student Association]. I went to a meeting to find out what it was all about— they were into tutoring, scholarships, mentoring. Up until this time I had bought into the American way of life, the Bill of Rights, and all this bullshit.
>
> But at the same time as MASA was going on there was also the Teen Post in Lincoln Heights, the newspaper, La Piranya Coffeehouse, and UMAS [United Mexican American Students]. I started going to UMAS meetings and identifying with the Black student movement, what was happening in the South, SNCC, the Black Panther Party, Stokely Carmichael, H. Rap Brown. So I started talking to these older Chicano guys [in MASA] about Stokely and H. Rap Brown, but they weren't into it. I saw the difference between them and the Young Citizens for Chicano Action [the predecessor of the Brown Berets], and I started hanging out with them. That's when I split from more traditional student politics and into more community activism.[10]

This comment illustrates several themes. For one, it suggests the breadth and diversity of activism. Young people mobilized around numerous issues and developed a range of ideologies. In addition, it hints at the rapidity with which things happened. In a fairly short time, this activist went from being a stalwart citizen to becoming a leader in one of the most militant Chicana/o groups in the country. Finally, he openly acknowledges the influence of the Black Power movement, as in his references to Carmichael and Brown.

One of the things that made Black Power so compelling to other people of color was its multidimensionality. Unlike the civil rights movement, which focused on gaining access to the white world, Black Power addressed the multiple sources of domination that affected oppressed and colonized people. Black Power was simultaneously about racial pride, self-respect, self-determination, and, in some cases, self-defense and economic well-being. It was through the Power movements that most of the membership of the Third World Left initially became politically active within their respective communities.

A final outcome of Black Power was that it set the stage for the development of a Third World and international consciousness among U.S. activists. As Blacks and others began grasping the nature of imperialism, people of color in the United States began identifying with and acting in solidarity with Third World people across the globe. It took Black Power to make this connection because it emphasized the pervasiveness and power of white supremacy. The movement was no longer just southern Blacks struggling against a racist order; it was the dispossessed of the world rising up against their oppressors. This shift in consciousness was evident when James Forman declared 1967 as "the year of internationalization" and when SNCC began identifying as a human rights organization rather than a civil rights group.[11] In addition, the development of an international consciousness paved the way for a greater exposure to various forms of Marxism, as they were the basis for many Third World revolutions.

WHITE RADICALS AND RACIAL POLITICS

Black Power had a deep effect on the white New Left. Because it arose in the context of the civil rights movement, race, and more specifically a commitment to antiracist politics, had been a defining element of the New Left. In fact, this commitment was one of the things that set the New Left apart from the Old Left and forced the Communist Party USA (CPUSA) to struggle for relevance. But just because Black Power forced many white activists to find new organizational homes did not mean that they abandoned their antiracist politics. Rather, it led to a new configuration of movement politics. As one member of the New Left explained, "It's not like we didn't talk to each other. We were closer than in a coalition with the Panthers, but not in the same organization."[12]

Students for a Democratic Society (SDS) was one of the most influential New Left organizations. As the civil rights movement was eclipsed by Black Power, SDS became increasingly radicalized, until, for a variety of reasons, it splintered into a number of groups. This evolution, however, was anything but straightforward and was due in no small measure to the differing racial politics of SDS and the Progressive Labor Party (PL). PL was a Maoist organization that infiltrated SDS in the hopes of further politicizing its membership along its ideological lines. Originally, PL was characterized by strong antiracist politics, but this changed as the organization became increasingly impatient with Black nationalism, arguing that it did little to help the working class. Eventually, PL opposed Black studies, affirmative action, and other aspects of Black liberation—goals that SDS held dear.

Nonetheless, a significant element of the SDS membership was attracted to the PL because of its emphasis on the working class and its discipline, which contrasted with SDS's more informal culture.[13] The PL eventually took over SDS, and those who didn't support it created other organizations, including the Revolutionary Youth Movement and Weatherman. In contrast to the PL, Weatherman maintained race at the center of its analysis, as it believed that the struggles against imperialism and racism were the pillars of the revolution. In recognition of their white privilege, the Weatherman Underground sought to open up a second front in the struggle against white supremacy and imperialism. Acknowledging the threat that the police posed to the continuation of the Black struggle, white (and a few Asian) youth sought to divert some of the mounting pressure on Black revolutionaries by engaging in highly disruptive, sometimes violent actions.[14]

Questions of race, and more specifically how much emphasis to give it and how best to change a racist society, were addressed in very different ways among the white left. While some organizations, such as PL, came to repudiate most nationalist and antiracist struggles, others, such as the Revolutionary Union and the Peace and Freedom Party, saw their primary mission as promoting an antiracist politics among whites. Because of the separatist impulses embedded within Black Power, as well as the challenges associated with building multiracial organizations, people of color, in addition to forming their own groups, sought to create their own spaces within larger political formations. For example, at the founding convention of the Peace and Freedom Party a Black and Chicano Caucus "voted to establish itself as a permanent ongoing body." Eventually the party ratified the California Coalition Treaty, which emphasized the right to self-determination.[15] Although such negotiations were highly contested, the fact that they occurred suggests how seriously the New Left, or at least parts of it, took the question of racial inequality.

Other segments of the left, including the CPUSA and the Socialist Workers Party, presented a somewhat different picture. Like other organizations, they underwent dramatic growth and change during this period as they sought to emphasize race more. As a result, most left organizations at least produced a document stating their position on the struggle for racial equality.[16] Nonetheless, some, including the CPUSA, were hesitant to embrace Black Power and more generally the antiracist struggle because they saw them as potentially divisive. According to the CPUSA leader Dorothy Ray Healey, "The Party's hostile attitude toward the New Left was probably the greatest political liability we had to contend with in the 1960s."[17] Needless to say, such a position did not help in the recruitment of people of color. One way the CPUSA tried to compensate was by organizing Che-Lumumba clubs in Southern California. The cell, or club, was the basic organizational unit of the party and was typically organized along either neighborhood or work lines. The Che-Lumumba clubs, named after Che Guevara and Patrice Lumumba, were basically clubs for African Americans. While they were technically counter to official CPUSA policy, Healey noted that if not for the clubs there would have been few Blacks in the party.[18]

Because of the left's uneven track record on racial politics, activists of color who desired a more materialist politics than that offered by the nationalist movements created a "thirdspace"[19] where they could pursue their political commitments unencumbered by white leftists. This was the space of the Third World Left. Ideologically, the variant of Marxist theory most compelling to leftists of color was Maoism. Maoism, discussed in chapter 5, was a relatively recent offshoot of communist theory developed by Mao Tse-tung in the 1950s. What resonated with activists was Mao's concept of the "Three Worlds." Building on Lenin's insights concerning uneven development, Mao conceptualized inequality in terms of the nation (rather than race), emphasizing both the role of U.S. imperialism and the centrality of national liberation—a view that many groups understood as applicable to their struggle. This position allowed revolutionary nationalism to be seen as a legitimate struggle, rather than as secondary to class. Maoism was also important insofar as it facilitated an international consciousness among U.S. activists, thereby promoting solidarity with Third World peoples. Some Maoist organizations were the Black Workers Congress, the Communist League, the Congress of Afrikan People, the Revolutionary Communist Party, the Communist Party (Marxist-Leninist),[20] the October League, the Revolutionary Workers League, the Puerto Rican Revolutionary Workers' Organization, the August Twenty-ninth Movement, Wei Min She, Workers' Viewpoint Organization, and I Wor Kuen.[21] Many of these organizations were composed of a single nationality, but some, including the August Twenty-ninth Movement, the October League, and the Communist League, were multinational. The splintering along national lines was a stumbling block for the CPUSA and like-minded organizations, which believed fervently in integration and saw nation-specific organizations as divisive. The popularity of these organizations, however, suggests that people of color had a genuine need to create their own spaces outside the purview of whites. Such organizations, nonetheless, continued to engage with multinational and noncommunist groups associated with the various Power movements. Together, nation-specific and multinational organizations should be seen as the two threads that made up the richly textured fabric of the Third World Left.

THE THIRD WORLD LEFT IN SOUTHERN CALIFORNIA

The Black Panther Party

The BPP was a leading organization in the Black Power movement. Its slogan "All Power to the People!" and the imagery of Blacks carrying guns were symbolic of a new political moment. Although the BPP began in Oakland, California, in 1966 under the leadership of Bobby Seale and Huey Newton, its roots can be traced to various traditions of Black self-defense, including the Defenders, the Deacons, and the Black Panthers of Lowndes County, Alabama.[22] Even in Los Angeles self-defense cadres had begun patrolling the community before the establishment of the BPP, suggesting the centrality of these issues to African Americans. What made the BPP different, however, was that in addition to self-defense it developed an impressive social and political program to both serve and politicize urban Blacks.

After the Watts uprising, Newton and Seale saw the need for an alternative political formation. In particular, the two were deeply concerned with police abuse, poverty, and the need for self-determination. Thus it was no coincidence that one of their first public acts was to stand about armed (as was then legal in California) and defiantly observe police conducting an arrest. The momentous nature of this event cannot be overestimated. It galvanized thousands as it directly challenged state power. According to one interviewee, "When Newton stood up and made the police back down, it just caught on like wildfire." Soon afterwards, Huey and his comrades instated themselves as officers and developed a Ten-Point Platform listing their demands. Although the platform evolved over time, the initial document suggests what the early BPP was about (see table 8).

Several themes emerge from a careful reading of the platform. First, there is a clear emphasis on *social reproduction* issues: that is, what people need to reproduce themselves, including housing, food, education, and employment. Such concerns would ultimately be expressed through an array of survival programs. Survival programs, including the widely publicized Free Breakfast Program, sought not only to meet people's basic needs but also to politicize them. Services varied by location, so that, for instance, the Los Angeles BPP provided transportation to take people to visit their incarcerated friends and family, whereas other cities offered medical and dry-cleaning services. Figure 4 shows an advertisement for some of Los Angeles's survival programs.[23]

The second major theme of the platform is the issue of state control and terror. Urban Blacks were heavily controlled by the state, as seen in their

Table 8 *Black Panther platform and program, October 1966*

1. We want freedom. We want power to determine the destiny of our Black community.
2. We want full employment for our people.
3. We want an end to the robbery by the CAPITALIST man of our Black community.
4. We want decent housing, fit for the shelter of human beings.
5. We want education for our people that exposes the true nature of this decadent American society. We want education that teaches us our true history and our role in the present-day society.
6. We want all black men to be exempt from military service.
7. We want an immediate end to POLICE BRUTALITY and MURDER of black people.
8. We want freedom for all black men held in federal, state, county and city prisons and jails.
9. We want all black people when brought to trial to be tried in court by a jury of their peer group or people from their black communities, as defined by the Constitution of the United States.
10. We want land, bread, housing, education, clothing, justice and peace. And as our major political objective, a United Nations-supervised plebiscite to be held throughout the black colony in which only black colonial subjects will be allowed to participate, for the purpose of determining the will of black people as to their national destiny.

SOURCE: *Black Panther*, August 9, 1969, 26.

relationship to the police, courts, and systems of incarceration. One former Panther explained the deeply historical roots of police repression.

> The only ones who really get to kick you in the ass are those who are under the color of authority. The courts, the judges, and the police are able to do it and get away with it. The police have a system behind them that was very similar to how the settlers would call on the army to attack the Native Americans. Because they had the military behind them, they were able to successfully wipe out whole areas of Native Americans, who were simply saying, "This is our land, and we have a right to defend ourselves." The Black Panther Party is simply an extension of that kind of conflict in a racist society.

As a result of this structural oppression, the Panthers demanded such things as the release from prison of all Blacks, an end to police violence, and a call

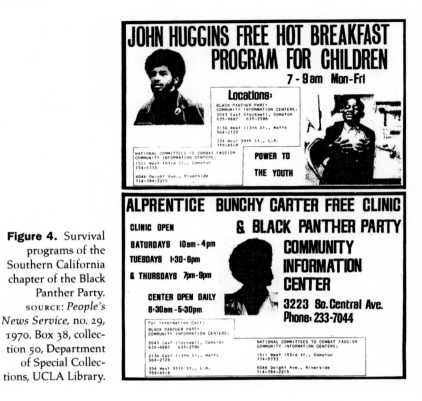

Figure 4. Survival
programs of the
Southern California
chapter of the Black
Panther Party.
SOURCE: *People's
News Service*, no. 29,
1970. Box 38, collec-
tion 50, Department
of Special Collec-
tions, UCLA Library.

for fair trials. The drawing shown in figure 5 illustrates the degree to which
the BPP believed that all Blacks, including men, women, and children,
needed to defend themselves against the police. Because of its rhetoric and
graphics, the visibility of guns, and the reality of police raids and shoot-outs,
this element of the BPP is perhaps most widely recognized, although it is
only one of several themes.

A third political focus is the call for self-determination, evident in the
demand for freedom and, specifically, a plebiscite. Although never achieved,
this loomed as one of the larger and more abstract goals guiding the BPP. The
fourth and final theme of the party centers on economic justice. Besides
demanding that the material needs of African Americans be met, the Platform
recognized capitalism as an economic system detrimental to the Black community. While this may seem vague, it is critical because recognizing the
power of capitalism enabled the BPP, unlike other Black Power groups, to
work with non-Blacks. In addition to working with whites, the BPP engaged

Figure 5. The importance of self-defense to the Black Panther Party. SOURCE: Drawing by Emory Douglas. *Black Panther Party Community News Service,* no. 29, 1970, p. 6. Box 38, collection 50, Department of Special Collections, UCLA Library. Courtesy of Emory Douglas.

in coalition and solidarity work with other oppressed people across the United States and around the world, including Palestinians, the Vietnamese, Puerto Ricans, Africans, and people from Northern Ireland. Indeed, the BPP was treated as a foreign dignitary in some Third World countries.[24]

The rhetoric, goals, practices, and style of the BPP spread rapidly, and chapters were established in major cities, including New York, Philadelphia, Baltimore, Newark, Chicago, New Haven, Houston, Dallas, and Los Angeles, and some minor ones as well. Although the BPP lasted well into the seventies, its apogee was relatively brief. Shortly after Newton and Seale established the party, Newton was charged and imprisoned for shooting a police officer. While he was in prison, the BPP underwent phenomenal growth, part of which was due to the "Free Huey" campaign. Upon Newton's release and return to leadership, however, the party shifted, placing greater emphasis on political work than on self-defense and, as one interviewee explained, causing a major rift.

> Actually, when Huey got out of jail, I believe that was in '70 or '71, a lot of changes started happening like putting down the gun, like no longer defending yourself. When he went to [jail] it was a few hundred people,

when he got out there were thousands. There were chapters nationwide, we even had a couple of international chapters. I don't know if it over-whelmed Huey or what, but there were a lot of differences. He was in the penthouse, with tailor-made suits, Jane Fonda was there, and most of us were kicked out of our homes, living fifteen to a house, sleeping in parks, sleeping in our cars.

As the quote implies, the BPP was seriously hampered by internal factors, particularly tensions stemming from trying to balance self-defense and political organizing. At one point, for example, Elaine Brown ran for city office in Oakland, while in other cities the focus was still on self-defense. Such schizophrenic behavior reflected not only a political divide but also larger class tensions. Nonetheless, the central question was how much to emphasize politics (electoral politics, survival programs, coalition building, etc.) versus self-defense. Eldridge Cleaver thought Newton was going soft, while Newton, concerned about the violence and bloodshed, wanted to lead the party in another direction. Eventually, these differing philosophies led to a party split.[25] Complicating the situation was Newton's extravagant spend-ing on personal luxuries, which contradicted his expressed ideals. Some felt that he had sold out, while others attributed the change in his leadership style to his abuse of drugs. In any event, problematic leadership, coupled with a whole series of internal contradictions, including sexism, violence, substance abuse, the murder and incarceration of large numbers of its mem-bership, and a lack of political agreement, all contributed to the party's end.

It would be wrong, however, to assume that the BPP's demise was due solely to its own internal dissonance, as it was continually beset by state repression. The FBI, under J. Edgar Hoover, declared the BPP to be the great-est threat to the internal security of the United States. Accordingly, the FBI, working in conjunction with local law enforcement, sought to destroy the party. They did so by sowing discontent, planting outright lies, deploying informants and provocateurs, and assassinating Panther leaders, such as Fred Hampton of Chicago. As the BPP came increasingly under attack, and some chapters, including Southern California's, were literally destroyed by police attacks, the leadership decided to regroup in Oakland, where, although they focused more on political organizing, the problems continued.[26]

The Southern California Chapter   The Southern California chapter of the BPP was established in 1968 by Alprentice "Bunchy" Carter. Carter, a leader of the Slauson gang, met Eldridge Cleaver while in Soledad prison, and Cleaver then introduced him to the BPP. Upon his release, Carter returned to Los Angeles and established a chapter. By the time he was assassinated in 1969, he had managed to create one of the largest and most distinctive chapters in the party. The Southern California chapter was notable for its size, commitment to self-defense, intense police repression, and leadership.

In *A Taste of Power,* Elaine Brown recounts how Carter introduced the BPP to the Los Angeles Black community. At a poetry event organized in 1967 by the Black Congress, an umbrella organization for local African American groups, Carter proclaimed,

> I came here to make an announcement: We have just officially formed the Southern California chapter of the Black Panther Party for Self-Defense. . . . I also came here to let you know that it is the position of the Black Panther Party for Self-Defense that we are the vanguard of revolution in the United States. . . . And the vanguard party is declaring all-out-war on the pig. We are declaring war, and we are declaring that from this point forward, nobody will speak about Black Power or revolution unless he's willing to follow the example of the vanguard, willing to pick up the gun, ready to die for the people.[27]

Founding members of the Southern California chapter recall the beginning as somewhat less dramatic but as demanding the same level of commitment. A small group was invited to a meeting, and from that a dedicated nucleus emerged. Initially, the chapter emulated the Mau Mau, a group of Kenyans who resisted colonial power, but it was difficult to maintain such a commitment among the growing membership, as one founding member described: "The Mau Mau took an oath that they wouldn't give in, nor give up. So when the party started we took a [similar] oath . . . . Then, as it expanded and more people got involved, we had to back away from that because a lot of people joined that weren't that serious. But when it started, that was the commitment. They understood what we were fighting against. We didn't have any illusions as far as victory, but we also knew that unless we stood up and made a stand, the repression would just continue."

The Southern California chapter stretched from San Diego to Bakersfield. Most states had one chapter, but because of California's size there was a northern and a southern one. The Los Angeles office was considered a regional one, signaling its somewhat higher status. Aside from being second in size only to the Northern California chapter headquartered in Oakland, the Southern California chapter played a leading role in establishing other chapters, such as Houston and Dallas. All chapters were under the Central Committee in Oakland, and within each chapter was a hierarchy that included field marshals, section leaders, subsection leaders, members, community supporters, and the underground. The party divided the city into sections, and each section had a leader who was basically responsible for everything that went on in his or her territory, including selling the newspaper, political education classes, defense, security, and the general well-being of the membership. Each section, in turn, was then divided into subsections. Each subsection was composed of small squads of two or three people who reported directly to the subsection leader, who in turn reported to the section leader. There were approximately ten BPP offices in the Los Angeles area, including ones in Pasadena, in Venice, and throughout South Los Angeles. The following quote from a former Panther outlines how a member could move through various positions.

> I started as a community supporter for about a week; then I decided I wanted to be a Panther. I was ready to die for the people. It began with a probation that was several weeks in length. I was given an orientation to the party, I had to memorize the Ten-Point Program, conduct myself as a Panther at all times, I had to understand and relate to the chain of command and the discipline process. I underwent survival training, the use, safety, and care of weapons, law, and emergency medical treatment.
>
> Upon completion of my probation, I put in a lot of work at the 84th and Broadway office. I participated in various missions and soon became a section leader. As a section leader, not only was it my duty to be abreast of things, I had to resolve conflicts, explain politics affecting my area, make sure provisions were made for the needy, provide protection and awareness for community residents. It was also my responsibility to investigate shootings, murders, and the incarceration of community residents by the local police.

The chapter was noted for its emphasis on self-defense. One reason for this was that nascent self-defense efforts existed before the introduction of the BPP, as seen in the Community Alert Patrol, whose purpose was to observe and monitor the police. In fact, one former patrol member said that Newton and Seale saw the organization on a visit to Los Angeles and were so impressed that they decided simply to modify the tactic by adding guns.[28] In addition to such organized activity, armed individuals patrolled together informally, as one founding member recounted:

> Our history has been one of slavery, segregation, lynching, and burning, and every generation has found some kind of reason to excuse it and say, "Well, it'll get better." We just decided that that wasn't the position we were going to take. We took the position that we would go tit-for-tat, bullet for bullet, whatever it took. And basically that's what the Black Panther Party represented. When [Newton] came down here, there was a bunch of people ready for it. It wasn't like I had to change my opinion or philosophy or anything because it was already my opinion and

philosophy. So we got involved right at the beginning, ten, fifteen, twenty people, and it grew.

A second factor contributing to the chapter's focus on self-defense was significant gang membership and the leadership of Geronimo Pratt. Pratt, who had served in Vietnam and was a member of the chapter, played a pivotal role in training the BPP in self-defense. This, coupled with Los Angeles's widespread gang structure and the extraordinarily repressive nature of the Los Angeles Police Department, resulted in a chapter with a large underground and a self-defense orientation. As one interviewee recounted, "What happened in Los Angeles was a unique experience. Bunchy Carter was the leader of the Slauson gang. What he did was [make] his gang the only gang."

The overall size of the Southern California chapter is unclear. No interviewee was sure, and estimates ranged from five hundred to several thousand. One reason for such ambiguity was the underground, which was structured so that no one knew it in its entirety. That way, if someone was forced to talk, he or she could reveal only limited information. The underground was composed of small cells that carried out missions together and individually. Some of the units had names, such as the Wolverines. Also complicating the situation is uncertainty over what constituted membership. As one former Panther pointed out, do you count those that are willing to house and harbor Panthers at great personal risk or only those engaged as public activists?

That African Americans in Los Angeles (and other cities) gravitated so quickly to the BPP suggests that they were on the same page politically *before* the party developed and were facing similar conditions. It also suggests the extent to which the ideology of the civil rights movement had collapsed in urban ghettos. Thousands joined the BPP partly because it was a genuine expression of the experiences of a generation of urban Blacks. All that was needed was a charismatic leader to make it happen. At the national level, that person was Huey Newton. In Southern California, it was Alprentice "Bunchy" Carter. According to one former Panther,

> Bunchy was a natural leader, he had been the leader of the renegade Slausons, he had been to prison, he was well educated, he was a poet. You name it, he could do it. And he knew history. He knew Black history, he knew world history, he was almost a scholar of history. He could fight. He didn't have any fear. He could dance, he could drink, and he could lead. The Los Angeles chapter was really built around his personality, and it started expanding and getting bigger, and going in different directions. Until his assassination, he was the leader. There was no question, there was no doubt. And he ran it the way it should have been run.

Although Carter was a legendary leader, he was not alone in building the chapter. Pratt contributed to the party as a whole, and so did Masai Hewitt. Hewitt (deceased) was well regarded by all interviewees and eventually became the party's minister of education. In addition, there was significant female leadership, as seen in such women as Gwen Goodlowe and Elaine Brown. Despite this wealth of leadership, however, the chapter faltered after Carter's assassination.

Carter and John Huggins were shot to death in a conflict with US, a rival organization, in January 1969. As cultural nationalists, US eschewed working with whites (and other people of color) and developed a highly patriarchal, Afrocentric philosophy. This was at odds with the BPP's politics and stated desire to fight on behalf of *all* oppressed people. Not surprisingly, the conflict was exacerbated by the local police. The BPP believed that US was working with the L.A. Police Department, and it did in fact receive some local monies. The BPP felt that these funds were part of a larger effort to weaken the more radical organizations and support the less overtly political ones, such as US. It is also known that the FBI was aware of this conflict and sought to use it to its advantage. Realizing the potential damage that such a conflict could engender, the BPP decided that all tensions with Black organizations were to be settled nonantagonistically. Unfortunately, this executive order was not adhered to and there were violent episodes between the BPP and US, culminating in the assassinations of Carter and Huggins at UCLA.[29] These deaths were tragic in their own right but also contributed greatly to the demise of the chapter. Indeed, several interviewees said that the chapter died with the murders—they just hadn't known it at the time.

In addition to interorganizational conflicts, the chapter was beset with other problems. As previously mentioned, Newton becoming increasingly out of touch, and his right-hand man, David Hilliard, alienated some of the membership with his harsh treatment. But the greatest problem, by far, was the split between Newton and Cleaver on self-defense. Many chapter members were deeply attached to the principle of self-defense, so the dispute had devastating consequences for the chapter. For instance, Pratt was being considered for the Central Committee but was replaced for several reasons, including his commitment to self-defense. Subsequent efforts by the party leadership to eliminate Pratt led to expulsions, betrayals, and the abandonment of other party members. Such chaos and callous treatment were devastating to chapter members and led some deeply committed individuals to leave the organization.

The conflict was also an expression of the organization's class tensions. The lives of the rank-and-file members were far different from those of the

BPP leadership. Life was a constant struggle for many members, as they were essentially in a state of war. For such individuals, many of whom had never gone to college and had limited hopes of upward mobility, it was unthinkable that the party could shift its focus to politics. In contrast, Panthers who were students, or came from the middle class, were apt to embrace a more political strategy. Such individuals were often assigned to teach political education classes, published the newspaper, and assumed leadership roles within the organization. In turn, many of the rank and file held such individuals responsible for pushing Newton toward a political path.

As can be seen, there were many substantive political disagreements within the BPP, but as a nondemocratic organization it was ill equipped to resolve them productively. Instead, the organization's hierarchical decision-making apparatus, reliance on force, and paranoid tendencies led many individuals to leave the party, despite their continuing commitment to the Black community, social justice, and self-defense. In December 1969 the Los Angeles Police Department initiated a devastating attack on the chapter's headquarters at Central and 41st that essentially destroyed the chapter.[30] This, coupled with the party's retrenchment in Oakland, led to the temporary suspension of the Southern California chapter. While some party members went to Oakland, some followed the Cleaver faction, and others tried to maintain the spirit of the party through other initiatives, such as the Coalition Against Police Abuse (CAPA). In the late 1970s, under the leadership of Kwaku Duren, a new organization was established that called itself the New Panther Vanguard Movement, although its ties to the original BPP are disputed. The Southern California chapter of the BPP lasted only briefly and preceded both East Wind and CASA, but it had an enormous effect on the radical politics of both Chicanas/os and Japanese Americans.

Yellow Power

> Unlike the Panthers, we weren't heroes.
> —Art Ishi, quoted in Martin Wong,
>   "Art Ishi and Guy Kurose"

Although I have emphasized the importance of Black Power to the Third World Left, the rise of an Asian American left must be appreciated on its own terms. Indeed, the Asian American movement was distinct in many ways from both the Black and Chicana/o movements. Though inspired by Black Power, it arose in response to the concrete problems facing Asian Americans.[31]

The development of an Asian American movement posed special challenges. For one, most Asian Americans did not yet identify as a group; rather, they identified along national lines.[32] In addition, many, including the majority of Japanese Americans, were not altogether comfortable with political agitation. Exacerbating the situation was the fact that the pre–World War II radical tradition among Japanese Americans had all but vanished. Finally, more than a few Japanese Americans had bought into the model minority myth and did not see themselves, or wish to see themselves, in the same light as their Black and Latina/o neighbors.[33] In recounting early organizing efforts in New York, Wei has described the painstaking way early activists had to reach out to each Asian American they encountered at antiwar demonstrations.[34] Such was not the case in Southern California, where many young Asian Americans were poised for action based on their growing political consciousness.

Asian American radicalism differed from Black and Chicana/o activism in several respects. One key difference was that activists, including those predating Yellow Power, were more likely to support and join organizations associated with *other* racial/ethnic groups, especially African Americans. For example, Yuri Kochiyama was active in the Congress of Racial Equality and African American Unity, Richard Aoki was a field marshal in the Oakland BPP, Grace Lee Boggs devoted her life to the Black struggle, Shinya Ono joined Weatherman, and Wendy Yoshimura was associated with the Symbionese Liberation Front.[35] Asian Americans joined such organizations out of solidarity, an awakening identity as people of color, but also because nothing comparable existed in their community early on. Such interethnic participation accounts for some of the ideological and political overlap between the Black and Yellow Power movements, but certainly not all. In contrast, Chicanas/os and African Americans were much more likely to focus on their own communities.

A unique feature of the Asian American movement was its historical trajectory. Because there was no Asian American civil rights movement comparable to those of African and Mexican Americans in the 1950s and 1960s, the Yellow Power movement did not evolve from an earlier political ideology. Of course, the Japanese American Citizens League existed, but even in more conservative eras its overly cautious politics were contested by many Japanese Americans.[36] Because Yellow Power was not hindered by the same historical baggage and conflict as the Black and Chicana/o movements, it developed more independently and moved quickly to the left.[37] On the other hand, Asian Americans were basically starting from scratch without an array of organizational institutions to draw upon.

In Los Angeles both universities and the community were sites of movement activism.[38] College campuses were crucial to the development of Asian American activism, as young people were grappling collectively with questions of politics, identity, and strategy. A first step for many was articulating an alternative consciousness and identity. This was actually a three-part process. First, activists rejected the label *Oriental*, because of its colonial connotations, in favor of *Asian American*, which was more accurate geographically and emphasized a shared U.S. experience.[39] Second, individuals began to add a pan-Asian dimension to their already existing national identities. Finally, radical activists changed the meaning of *Asian American* to an identity rooted in Third World ideology. Amy Uyematsu's article "The Emergence of Yellow Power" helped facilitate this process:

> Asian Americans can no longer afford to watch the black-and-white struggle from the sidelines. They have their own cause to fight, since they are also victims—with less visible scars—of white institutionalized racism. A yellow movement has been set into motion by the black power movement. Addressing itself to the unique problems of Asian Americans, this "yellow power" movement is relevant to the black power movement in that both are part of the Third World struggle to liberate all colored people.
>
> . . . Frightened "yellows" allow the white public to use the "silent oriental" stereotype against the black protest. The presence of twenty million blacks in America poses an actual physical threat to the white system. Fearful whites tell militant blacks that the acceptable criterion for behavior is exemplified in the quiet, passive Asian American.
>
> . . . The yellow power movement envisages a new role for Asian Americans: It is a rejection of the passive Oriental stereotype and symbolizes the birth of a new Asian—one who will recognize and deal with injustices. The shout of Yellow Power, symbolic of our new direction, is reverberating in the quiet corridors of the Asian American community.[40]

Uyematsu identifies several of the impulses that were shaping the nascent Asian American movement. For instance, she underscores the extent to which Asian Americans were conscious of their ambiguous role in a bipolar racial structure and the way that supposedly positive stereotypes were used to further oppress African Americans. Nonetheless, Uyematsu is not suggesting that Asian American activism is merely a response to Black-white political tensions. Rather, there is a call to form a movement that addresses Asian Americans' own experiences of discrimination and oppression. "The Emergence of Yellow Power," originally published in *Gidra*, was rapidly disseminated and had a powerful effect on many young activists. Its publication was soon followed by such conferences as "Are You Yellow?" and the

"Asian American Experience in America—Yellow Identity," both of which provided forums to discuss issues and inspired young people to organize.[41]

Asian American organizations developed on several campuses in Southern California. While some of these groups focused on providing support and cultural activities, many others, such as the Asian American Political Alliance and Orientals Concerned on the UCLA campus, were more explicitly political. Ethnic studies, as mentioned in chapter 3, also played a pivotal role in the development of the movement, as it contributed to students' political consciousness and encouraged community ties. Community involvement, in fact, was a cornerstone of early ethnic studies programs.

Mo Nishida has argued that by 1969 two key themes could be identified within the movement: Identity and Serve the People. As he has described the dominant thinking, "We are people with no identity except the white man's and the only place and ways you could find your identity was to serve the people in our respective communities."[42] The burgeoning Asian American movement did in fact embody these themes. There was a burst of activism, and new organizations proliferated across the country, especially in New York, the San Francisco Bay Area, and Southern California. In Los Angeles a range of groups and programs covered numerous topics and interests, including community and social services, the arts, media, labor, education, women's issues, and politics.

Key among movement institutions was the newspaper *Gidra*, begun by UCLA students who later went off campus.[43] Working solely as volunteers, the *Gidra* collective managed to produce a monthly publication for five years with a national readership. *Gidra* was extremely important because it provided a regular forum for the exchange of ideas and documented and analyzed the movement in fairly self-conscious ways. Besides highlighting the activities and histories of movement organizations, *Gidra* provided news coverage and analysis. Moreover, because it was not the organ of a single group, it illustrated the breadth of the movement. According to one founding member, "Because the newspaper was mobile and in ink, it had a real permanence to it. We found out similar things were going on with Asians in New York, in the Midwest, [and] in Canada. . . . So there were all these connections that were made nationally."

Community was the second anchor of the movement. During the late sixties, both drug abuse and gang participation reached crisis proportions among Japanese American youth, prompting widespread activism. The reasons for these problems were complex.[44] First, Sansei were largely the children of camp internees, and many grew up in homes affected by the pain and confusion of unexpressed and unresolved trauma. Simply put, the internment created a crisis in Nikkei families. One Japanese American activist cogently summarized its influence: "It was not until I was in college that I learned about the camp experience. Prior to this time I was told that Manzanar was a small town in California where Japanese people lived. When I learned more about the camps, many aspects of my life and identity as a Nikkei person began to fit into place—the family pressure to 'blend' into the society and not rock the boat; the pressure to act the right way and the stress upon education as a means to overcome racial hostility."[45] Or, as another activist put it, "It was like there was an elephant in the room and nobody would talk about it." Certainly not all Nikkei families responded this way, but the approach was quite widespread. Second, and relatedly, because many Nisei parents felt that the best way to ensure the acceptance and well-being of their children was for them to become professionals, Sansei were under intense pressure to succeed, and many found themselves unwilling and/or unable to meet such expectations. Some youth internalized the racist ideologies of the larger society and sought professional and social success to prove their "Americanness." But many found themselves struggling against discriminatory barriers. Unlike other groups, Japanese Americans were expected to be quiet and behave and thus did not have sanctioned outlets to express the anger and indignation that accompanied their racially subordinated status. A clear set of expectations was imposed on Japanese American youth by the society, community, and family. Consequently, many young people turned to drugs in an effort to cope.[46]

Janice Tanaka, in her film *When You're Smiling,* reports that in 1971 thirty-one young Sansei in the Los Angeles area died. Despite the efforts of the *Rafu Shimpo,* the Japanese American daily, to obscure the causes of death by, for example, attributing deaths to heart attacks, she and many others believe they were drug related.[47] Activists realized that the larger Japanese American community was ignoring the problem and that mainstream service organizations were ill prepared to serve them. Besides the general reluctance of social service agencies to address the needs of particular ethnic groups, there was an assumption that Japanese Americans took care of their own and did not need assistance, although this was simply untrue. Thus young people in Los Angeles took it upon themselves to address this problem and formed organizations such as the Yellow Brotherhood, Asian American Hardcore, and Japanese American Community Services—Asian Involvement (JACS-AI). Activists aimed not only to rebuild their community but also to do political intervention. The Yellow Brotherhood was composed primarily of streetwise Nikkei, including former prisoners and/or drug users. Not everyone was comfortable with the Yellow Brotherhood's occasional use of force, however, which prompted Asian American Hardcore to develop an alternative approach. Eventually, Hardcore aligned itself with the BPP and began working with JACS-AI.[48]

While many organizations were male centered, women did participate, and there was a vibrant Asian American women's movement, which included such organizations as Asian Sisters.[49] Though many groups served a particular constituency, several drew the "lumpen" elements of the Japanese American community, including former gang members and ex-convicts (many of whom were older), into political organizations. Due to the social and spatial fragmentation that the Nikkei were undergoing, many young people did not realize the diversity of their community. As one former East Wind member suggested,

> For a lot of Asian students, it was a new experience connecting with the poor of the community, the ex-gang members, and people who had been to prison. It's probably true in every community, but especially in the Japanese American community there was this sense of shame, the sense of being the model minority and being good students and high achievers and all. In that kind of culture you have a separation with people who were "bad guys" and that was engrained in kids, "You don't mess with people who are from the streets." That was broken down in the sixties. The movement was created by a combination of students, graduate students, and also people whose experiences were mostly on the street, the working class.

The Yellow Brotherhood and Asian American Hardcore helped drug users become sober and rebuild their lives. Besides addressing drug abuse, they became sites of political discussion and one of the launching pads for the community-based left. While some of these individuals later established social service organizations geared toward Asian Americans,[50] others pursued community-based arts, while still others followed an explicitly political path, joining the New Communist movement in the 1970s.

As both students and community residents became more politically aware, study groups proliferated. Study groups were extremely popular and could be found in the women's, antiwar, and antiracist movements. Within the left, study groups have a long tradition, as study has always been part of Marxism-Leninism. Besides introducing people to theory, study clarifies larger social and economic processes, promotes political development, and fosters discipline. Numerous activists, including Japanese Americans, were drawn to study groups in order to better understand the world and how to transform it. According to one interviewee, "As people learned more history, about the world and society in terms of economics and politics, there was a corresponding thirst for more understanding of what makes things the way they are and how you change. [Unlike today], people were looking for a coherent ideology that explains social processes and history. So naturally we looked to those forces that were fighting what we considered to be the common enemy, U.S. imperialism. There were a lot of people who started study groups. That was one step beyond teach-ins, people reading the same books together and discussing them." According to Roy Nakano, Garbagemen, named after a New York garbage collectors' strike, was the first Marxist-Leninist Asian American study group to emerge in Los Angeles, and although it lasted only one and half years, it was instrumental in laying the groundwork for future left organizations.[51] Among Los Angeles–area Asian American study groups, two tendencies emerged: multinationalism and nationalism, a parallel seen among other leftists of color. Multinationalism emphasizes working with other nationalities, whereas nationalism privileges working with co-ethnics. Although chapter 5 discusses these issues in detail, clarifying the distinctions now is important for understanding the development of East Wind. According to one interviewee, "There were a large number of political collectives that were forming within the Asian American community. There was one in Chinatown, there was KDP [Katipunan ng Demokratikong Pilipino] in the Filipino community. A couple of them were substantially Japanese American but had other Asian Americans in it [them] as well, [such as] Storefront, on the Westside." While several organizations worked closely with other oppressed nationalities, others focused on Asian Americans or nation-specific groups. East Wind was representative of this latter tendency.

East Wind East Wind was created in 1972 in response to the desire of some activists for a "political cadre organization in the community to give analysis and overall direction and to be involved in the party-building process."[52] Initial membership drew from study groups, the Community/Workers Collective, the Westside Collective, Asian American Hardcore, JACS-AI, the *Gidra* collective, and assorted individuals. One interviewee described the membership as consisting primarily of the main leaders of local mass organizations within the Los Angeles Asian American movement. Essentially, two streams of activism, campus and community, merged in the Community/Workers Collective, a predecessor of East Wind. The collective was formed when some members of Asian American Hardcore sought to develop a politics that went beyond drug issues.[53] One interviewee who had been a member of both groups recalled,

The group [Hardcore] evolved to the point where they decided they needed a political living collective. Some people decided to go with it and others decided to leave. It was a real commitment. They also invited some women to live in this collective. . . . I don't remember what the criteria [were], but there was a big discussion and you were [voted on] by the whole group. It wasn't like you joined because you were related to somebody, but you [had to be] on your own, involved, and committed to some sort of principles. You had to be willing to really, totally, collectivize your life, everything you owned.

There were thirteen of us at the beginning in this collective in East L.A. We lived in this two-story house, that interestingly enough, a group of people in the community collected money to pay our rent. John Saito spearheaded it. So there was a lot of support. . . . There was people's work going on out of the JAC's office and people thought that it was a good thing. Not everybody, but this segment of progressive Nisei supported it. I look back on it and I don't think we appreciated it as much as we should have.

As a Marxist-Leninist organization, East Wind was highly disciplined, and members' lives were filled with meetings, study, and community work. The collective consisted of twenty-five to thirty members, but with a core of fifteen. East Wind had two key organizational structures: the Central Committee and work units. The Central Committee, which was elected annually, was the primary decision-making body, while the work units were composed of those engaged in mass work around labor, community, youth, and so forth.

East Wind was different from the BPP in that its community work was not limited to its own programs. Although East Wind took the lead in some projects, including the takeover of the Resthaven mental health facility in Chinatown, activists were dispersed throughout the community, working in labor, the redevelopment of Little Tokyo, *Gidra*, and the Pioneer Senior Center, to name just a few projects. Besides providing necessary services and creating social change, East Wind supported other minority groups and sought to raise the political consciousness of all Japanese Americans.

The living collective was another distinct feature of Japanese American activism. Although both Chicana/o activists and the Panthers had versions of collective living, the practice was most developed among Japanese Americans. In fact, Japanese American living collectives existed before East Wind, whereas Panthers, for example, began living together only after joining the party. Besides providing inexpensive housing, living collectives offered the opportunity to forge alternative lifestyles as part of a larger revolutionary practice.

When East Wind initially formed it was composed primarily of Japanese American activists with similar political tendencies. Early on, revolutionary nationalism was the dominant ideology, but in conjunction with larger political shifts it became more Marxist-Leninist and Maoist in the mid-seventies. While most members' time was spent literally serving the people, some members argued that the cadre required more time for study, theory, and political development. The group agreed to try this approach, but some members were frustrated with this shift in emphasis, even leaving because of it. Eventually, it was decided to reduce the commitment to study and prioritize community work once again.

As the seventies progressed, the New Communist movement shifted toward party building and consolidation. East Wind spent considerable time exploring commonalities with other groups before joining the League of Revolutionary Struggle, a multinational organization that had already incorporated I Wor Kuen and the August Twenty-ninth Movement. Not all made the move, as some objected to the shift, but the majority made the transition.[54] The League of Revolutionary Struggle formally dissolved in 1990, at which time the remnants of East Wind also died, although individuals from both East Wind and the League of Revolutionary Struggle are still active in the community today.

The Chicana/o Movement

The Chicana/o movement can be described as a series of community and campus-based struggles across the southwestern United States "agitating for social and political change and promoting a militant version of self-help and racial solidarity."[55] Community activists mobilized around long-standing grievances and concerns, including poverty, political disenfranchisement, land rights, and working conditions. Student activists served the community and were deeply engaged in questions of Chicana/o identity and politics.

The political landscape of Chicana/o activism shifted in the mid-sixties in response to the Vietnam War, growing ethnic consciousness, the influence of Black Power, and frustration with Mexican Americans' social and economic marginalization. These forces resulted in an expansion of struggles, organizations, and activists and a growing militancy. As among African Americans, the younger generation became disillusioned with the strategies and tactics of their parents and were no longer willing to accept and tolerate what previous generations had endured.

One arena that dramatically illustrated this shift was identity. The previous generation encouraged the assimilation of Mexican Americans and even argued for their designation as white. Organizations such as the League of United Latin American Citizens and the GI Forum hoped to "Americanize" their constituents by emphasizing hard work, education, English, and patriotism.[56] Such politics reflected the civil rights and integrationist strategies of the Cold War era. In contrast, the Chicana/o movement of the sixties and seventies sought to validate *mestizaje*[57] and affirm Chicanas/os' indigenous roots.

In addition to racial pride, the movement tapped into long-standing frustrations and unleashed a torrent of activism. The early movement was diverse not only in terms of the issues addressed but also in terms of its range of ideologies. It included such struggles as La Alianza Federal de Pueblas Libres, a northern New Mexico group fighting for the return of communal grant lands; a series of walkouts in East L.A. high schools; and, of course, the United Farm Workers. Born in California's Central Valley, United Farm Workers attained international prominence as it urged consumers to boycott grapes, with its leader, Cesar Chávez, becoming an icon of *el movimiento*. Other pivotal organizations included the Crusade for Justice in Denver, focused on youth organizing and led by Corky Gonzales, and La Raza Unida Party, an alternative third party begun in Texas that eventually spread throughout the Southwest. Many Chicanas/os felt strongly that a third party was necessary to achieve political power since neither the Democrat or Republican parties were willing to attend to their concerns.[58] La Raza Unida was so promising initially that more than a few Black leaders studied it as a possible model.

One of the legacies of *el movimiento* was the creation of a consolidated regional identity among Chicanas/os. Given the geographic concentration of Mexican Americans in the Southwest at the time, it was inevitable that political activity would be spatially concentrated. This led Chicana/o activists across the region to begin seeing themselves as one people with a common heritage. Like Japanese Americans, Chicanas/os had to figure out who they were and how they fit into a bipolar racial structure. Mexican Americans were neither white nor Black, and although nominally more accepted by whites, they had a low socioeconomic position and were even more politically marginalized than Blacks.

In March 1969 activists gathered in Denver for the National Chicano Liberation Conference, where they adopted "El Plan Espiritual de Aztlán." The poet Alurista argued that Aztlán, the mythical homeland of the Aztecs, was located in the contemporary southwestern United States, which Chicana/o activists sought to reclaim. "El Plan" established nationalism as the ideology of the Chicana/o movement:

With our hearts in our hands and our hands in the soil, we declare the independence of our mestizo nation. We are a bronze people with a bronze culture. Before the world, before all of North America, before all our brothers in the bronze continent, we are a nation, we are a nation of pueblos, we are *Aztlán*.

Nationalism is the key to organization that transcends all religious, political, class and economic actions or boundaries. Nationalism is the common denominator that all members of La Raza can agree upon.[59]

This emphasis on nationalism was crucial to the subsequent development of the Chicana/o movement and contributed to activists' identifying themselves as a colonized people, one whose land had been stolen by Anglo America. Nationalism provided a powerful framework to help Chicana/o activists understand their experience.

I got involved in the movement in 1969 through the first Chicano studies class the University of Colorado offered. We had a guest lecturer, Corky Gonzalez, who was the director of the Crusade for Justice. He just had a tremendous impact on my political consciousness. As he began to describe Chicano history and discussed Chicanos' contributions to the Southwest and their oppression, I realized that that was my own family's history. [It was] the stories I had been hearing from grandparents and my aunts and uncles and parents over the years. Our family were coal miners and railroad workers, and owned land and lost land. I realized how much of that was a part of the history of an oppressed people. That really motivated me to get involved.[60]

In this quote we see the loss of land, and of the Southwest in particular, as crucial elements in the formation of a dispossessed people.[61] The activist later joined the Brown Berets, La Raza Unida, the August Twenty-ninth Movement, and finally the League of Revolutionary Struggle.

One movement organization that merits special attention is the Brown Berets. While many campus-based organizations existed, including MEChA (El Movimiento Estudiantil Chicano de Aztlán/the Chicano Student Movement of Aztlán), United Mexican American Students, and the Mexican American Youth Organization, the Brown Berets offered a political vehicle to the many Chicana/o youths who did not attend college. Because the Berets were a militant, Los Angeles–based organization, many have considered them to be the Chicano version of the BPP. But though the Berets were certainly inspired by the BPP, they were more nationalist than revolutionary nationalist. In fact, understanding the politics of the Berets is necessary for understanding CASA.

The Brown Berets evolved from a mainstream organization called Young

Citizens for Community Action (YCCA). YCCA was a city-sponsored initiative spearheaded by David Sánchez. In 1967 YCCA opened a coffeehouse, La Piranya, which became a meeting ground for Chicana/o activists. Young people held meetings, participated in history and cultural classes, and organized around various issues, particularly educational concerns and police abuse. On November 24, 1967, police responded to a family disturbance on the Eastside and beat the residents. YCCA protested the beating, and soon after, the Brown Berets were born. The Brown Berets considered themselves to be the shock troops of the movement. Like the Panthers, they wore a semiuniform, stressed self-defense, developed a platform, and adopted a military culture. The Berets published a newspaper, *La Causa,* and engaged in service projects, including a volunteer health clinic, but were best known for protecting the community. One former member described their role: "During the high school 'blowouts' [walkouts], the Brown Berets acted to protect, support, and advise the striking students. The Brown Berets placed themselves between the police and the students, taking the brunt of the beatings." By 1969 there were ninety Beret chapters stretching from Los Angeles to Chicago to San Antonio.[62]

The Berets embraced a Third World ideology. They saw the Chicana/o struggle as rooted in this paradigm and believed the loss of the Southwest was central to their oppression. Yet despite this seemingly radical position the Brown Berets were in some ways quite conservative. Besides hesitating to join coalitions and responding tepidly to internationalism, Sánchez often opposed such efforts, arguing instead that the Berets should concentrate on their own community. Most important, however, Sánchez held deep antipathies toward communism. He eschewed Marxism and Leninism as irrelevant European theories that did not speak to the struggle of Chicanas/os.[63] Although there were a number of leftist Berets, they represented individual tendencies, not the official position of the organization. Carlos Montes, who served as minister of information, described the political tensions within the organization:

> Vietnam made a big political impact on me and the Berets. Even though we weren't Marxist-Leninist, we supported the Vietnamese because they wanted their own country. We went from civil rights to more revolutionary politics. We started talking about Che Guevara, the Cuban revolution. We started forming a Third World ideology, we started reading Mao, Fanon, etc, but we didn't go beyond that really.
>
> David Sánchez, the prime minister, he didn't make that political change, however. He stayed in a cultural nationalist stage, and we became more revolutionary nationalists and internationalists. He became anti-red. There was a struggle within the Brown Berets for more revolutionary positions within the newspaper and in what we

talked about and did. He would always say, "We got to think about our own backyard." That was his way of saying, "Don't talk about this other shit." He would rationalize, "We got to think about the issues here, the police abuse, the housing . . . ," which all sounded real good, but I knew what he meant. He didn't want to talk about international issues.

The above distinguishes between cultural and revolutionary nationalism. Nationalism is advocating for the social or political interests of a nation. Cultural nationalism suggests a greater emphasis on one's own nation and heritage, whereas revolutionary nationalism implies a concern with other subordinated groups as well and often anticapitalism. As can be seen, there were tensions within the Berets between cultural and revolutionary nationalists. To his credit, Sánchez allowed such political diversity. For instance, the newspaper would have a different political line depending who was putting it out. Likewise, when members were invited to speak at events, they were not required to adhere to a uniform position. Nevertheless, tensions mounted until eventually a group of more leftist Berets broke off to form La Junta.[64] As the Chicana/o movement continued to evolve, a growing number of activists were confronting the limits of cultural nationalism and felt the need to adopt a more materialist and internationalist politics, thus giving rise to groups like CASA.

CASA   CASA was founded in Los Angeles in 1968 by Bert Corona, Chole Alatorre, and the Mexican American Political Association. Initially, it was a chapter of La Hermandad Mexicana Nacional (the National Mexican Brotherhood), a San Diego group established in the 1950s to defend the rights of immigrants. Corona admired its work and decided to pursue similar activities in Los Angeles, where he developed a multifaceted organization—part *mutualista*,[65] part social service organization, and part legal defense center—geared to Mexican immigrants. In addition to protecting immigrants' rights, La Hermandad organized immigrant workers.[66] Before then most unions eschewed immigrants, assuming that they were "unorganizable," but La Hermandad helped to change this.

> [T]he unions in the building trades and the metal trades, as well as the big service unions, would have nothing to do with the undocumented. Their organizers told me that they weren't interested in organizing plants with mostly undocumented workers; they believed that these workers were not organizable, because the INS [Immigration and Naturalization Service] could come in and threaten them with deportation, and the people would run like quail.
> This attitude didn't begin to change until we proved during the 1970s

that immigrant workers could organize and win contracts. . . . Some of the unions didn't have enough Spanish-speaking organizers, they couldn't communicate with the workers . . . but many of our people could. So we talked to the workers outside the plants in the mornings and in the afternoons. We also had *Hermandad* members who worked inside some of these plants, and they organized internally. The fact was that most of the workers trusted us rather than the regular union organizers.[67]

Because of La Hermandad's successes and popularity it grew rapidly. Eventually, the leadership decided to create a series of separate centers that would focus on meeting the daily needs of immigrants, while La Hermandad would function as more of an umbrella organization. These individual centers were called CASAs (Centros de Acción Social Autónomo/ Centers for Autonomous Social Action). As the name implies, the individual centers were fairly autonomous, but they were united under the larger Hermandad. Many volunteers, often Chicana/o professionals, staffed the CASAs and carried out much of the work. Through their efforts, CASAs spread throughout Los Angeles and as far away as Chicago.

At the same time that CASAs were developing, an organization called Casa Carnalismo (Brotherhood House) formed in East Los Angeles. Casa Carnalismo, which provided legal services and information, was led by several young Chicanos, including Antonio Rodriguez. In 1973 activists associated with Casa Carnalismo became involved in a police abuse case when three Chicanos trying to uncover police corruption in the barrio were falsely accused of shooting an officer. The national Committee to Free Los Tres (CFLT) was formed to support the accused, with strong participation from Casa Carnalismo. Their participation in the case led some members of the CFLT to become increasingly politicized so that they "began serious study into the drug question, and through their study of marxism, ultimately analyzed it as a tool of the capitalist system against working people."[68] As the campaign began to wind down, these individuals began to see CASA as a potential vehicle to carry out their political work and hopefully build a mass movement. Consequently, a large number of students and young Chicanas/os (versus immigrants) became active in CASA, beginning with the Los Angeles CASA on Pico Boulevard. According to Bert Corona, the young people sought to take over some of the CASAs in order to use them as building blocks in the creation of a revolutionary movement. Though Corona and Alatorre thought the young people were somewhat misguided, they agreed to it, with the stipulation that the immigrant services be maintained. The young activists were ready to assume the role of the vanguard, but it was uncertain whether CASA's membership would serve as the requisite masses.[69]

Under the new leadership, CASA changed radically. First and foremost there was a profound ideological and political shift as the new leaders embraced Marxism-Leninism.

> We are not negative towards the Chicano movement. Most of us in
> C.A.S.A. are a product of the movement and were formed politically
> in that movement. But we must recognize that in the world there is
> consistent change and that one must move in tune with the laws of
> social development and especially in revolutionary times one must be
> careful to learn the lessons of practice and to advance our theoretical and
> political actions according to that. Once we apply a scientific outlook to
> our history and to our struggle, the possibilities of our liberation are
> that much greater and our clarity and confidence in our identity and
> our destiny will truly be in our hands.[70]

This quote emphasizes CASA's roots within the larger Chicana/o movement but also illustrates the extent to which it moved beyond it, embracing a scientific Marxism-Leninism.

Given activists' desire to build a vanguard movement, it should hardly be surprising that the immigrant services suffered. Dues-paying membership dropped from an estimated high of two thousand in 1972 to less than one thousand in 1977.[71] Nonetheless, CASA continued to do important work in terms of immigrant organizing and defense and was pivotal in providing the leadership necessary to push the larger Chicana/o movement to adopt a more progressive position on immigrant workers. It did so by organizing around immigration legislation, co-founding a conference that led to the establishment of the National Coalition for Fair Immigration Laws and Practices, calling for worker amnesty and an end to deportations, and shifting the discourse within the Chicana/o movement itself.[72]

As a Marxist-Leninist organization, CASA was highly disciplined and offered differing levels of membership, ranging from *militante* to *aspirante*. Being a *militante*, the highest level, required one to attend study groups and meetings, sell the newspaper, and take on a major piece of work, whether it was helping to publish the newspaper or organizing workers. An *afiliado* had somewhat fewer responsibilities and rights, an *aspirante* hoped to become a *militante*, and a member was simply someone who needed CASA's services and was not necessarily interested in building a revolutionary movement. Such individuals were simply required to pay their dues and abide by the slogan "An injury to one is an injury to all." As in other organizations, membership requirements varied over time, but they always included a high level of commitment and political agreement.[73] One member recounted how he joined the organization: "I went and asked them,

'How do you join CASA?' because nobody would recruit me. They said, 'Oh, we're going to have to give you a test.' So I had to go and read up on everything. I remember going into this building on Pico and spending about six hours just writing. It was really intense. It was like, 'Write until you finish answering your questions.' Then I got a call saying, 'Yes, we are going to accept you.'"

CASA also had a fairly elaborate organizational structure. At the highest level, key decisions were made by the Political Commission. Each individual CASA had a Local Committee, which oversaw the work and activities of various secretaries, including Labor Affairs, Finance, Information and Propaganda, as well as the *nucleo*. The *nucleo* or cell, was the smallest unit of CASA, and its leader reported directly to the Local Committee. CASA also created a Centro Legal, which was akin to a legal collective. The Centro focused on immigration, as well as family and work-related matters. Besides providing much needed services to the community, the Centro Legal generated revenue for CASA.[74]

Arguably, CASA's greatest work was in changing attitudes toward immigrant workers in the political arena. Figure 6 presents a list of CASA's demands, which convey a great deal about the organization itself. In addition to immigration, CASA was actively involved in mobilizing against the *Bakke* decision, which challenged affirmative action in California. Given its politics, CASA developed close ties to some Third World countries and movements, including Cuba and the Puerto Rican Socialist Party. In this way, CASA enlarged the terrain of Chicana/o politics by making important connections with other Latinas/os.

CASA was far less successful, however, at building a social movement, let alone a revolution. Its primary problem was its inability to translate the dues-paying immigrant membership into a viable base that the cadre could lead. In addition, CASA, like many other organizations of its time, suffered from severe internal problems, including undemocratic practices, a patriarchal culture, and sectarianism, and, of course, police surveillance.[75] In the late seventies there were severe tensions over the political direction of CASA, and the contradictions between the organization's political rhetoric and its actual practices mounted. The Political Commission decided to adopt an increasingly leftist line, and as a result several chapters pulled out. This began a long downward spiral, culminating in the resignation of Carlos Vásquez, a key leader, in December 1977. Soon after, the entire Political Commission resigned en masse and the organization folded in 1978.[76]

As can be seen in these brief sketches, the BPP, East Wind, and CASA had a great deal in common but were also quite distinct. One of the most impor-

Unconditional Amnesty!

Resistencia y Unidad - Nuestro Pueblo Vencerá!

WE DEMAND

UNCONDITIONAL AMNESTY - The total recognition of democratic rights undocumented people; an end to the constant persecution of our people; full access to s services, bilingual and bicultural education; the right to be with our families; the rig due process.

STOP DEPORTATIONS - An end to the deportation raids that create panic in communities and work places, divide our families, break organizing campaigns, and f people to sidestep badly needed social services. An end to the conspiracy between bo and La Migra in planning factory raids.

JOBS FOR ALL - RIGHT TO ORGANIZE - Employment is a basic right and government must assure socially useful jobs for all workers, without separating a sect/ the working class for persecution nor deny them the right to organize.

END THE BRACERO PROGRAM - We must demand an end to bracero-type progr. modern day slave labor systems. It denies workers the right to organize, to decent w and working conditions. It is used to break organizing campaigns. It does not benefit worker - the only profiteers are the bosses.

MIGRA - OUT OF THE FACTORIES - The collaboration between La Migra and the bc permits the super-exploitation of Mexican labor. This must stop and full protection mu: given workers who are deported under existing labor laws and collective bargai agreements.

OVERTURN THE BAKKE DECISION - The Bakke Decision denies Mexican and c Third World students our rights to higher education by threatening special admission affirmative action programs. Now, gains won through struggles in the 60's face elimina under the smokescreen that they are forms of 'reverse racism'.

RESPECT THE RIGHTS OF UNDOCUMENTED PEOPLE - We must protect our hu rights and fight to defeat sterilization practices, police brutality and mass deportations are workers, we have rights, we create the wealth!

CASA - HGT

California   Illinois   Texas   Washi

Figure 6. List of CASA's demands. CASA's demands and accompanying graphic reflect both its commitment to worker rights and its tendency toward Mexican nationalism. Source: Box 31, folder 12, CASA Collection. Courtesy of Antonio Rodriguez and Department of Special Collections, Stanford University Libraries.

tant distinctions was the different foci of each organization. The BPP was focused on self-defense and survival programs; East Wind concentrated on community service, leadership, and identity issues; and CASA devoted itself largely to immigrant rights and labor organizing. In addition, we can see how the organizations developed along different historical trajectories. The BPP was established first as the fullest expression of Black Power. Both East Wind and CASA were born in 1972, but whereas East Wind was created almost from scratch, CASA represented a new stage in Chicana/o politics, one that can be traced to the Old Left, as seen in the activism of Corona. While these are significant differences, the commonalities, such as undemocratic practices and the emphasis on serving the community, underscore the extent to which all groups were influenced by the larger political culture of the time. The next chapter explores the political ideology of each organization, specifically, how each one conceptualized race, class, and nationalism—the theoretical pillars of the Third World Left.

FIVE

Ideologies of Nation, Class, and Race in the Third World Left

Popular depictions of sixties radicalism, as seen in movies like *The Big Chill* and *Forrest Gump*,[1] tend to reduce political activism to rallies, marches, and speeches, thereby glossing over the vibrant theoretical debates that characterized the movement. Though most of the Third World Left identified as revolutionary nationalist, Marxist-Leninist, or some combination, there was profound ideological diversity within the movement, as most organizations developed highly nuanced political positions informed by the history and experiences of the organization's membership. Such ideologies offer valuable insights into how different racial/ethnic groups understood societal problems, their proposed solutions, the distinctive nature of each organization, and the larger political culture of the time. I am especially interested in how activists articulated the relationship(s) between nation, race, and class, the fundamental inequalities identified by the Third World Left. Building a political ideology required deciding how much weight each relation should be given, developing positions, and crafting strategies to create the desired change.

Concepts of nation, class, and race, along with gender, are still some of the most vexing for social justice activists today, as they remain key axes of difference and inequality. They raise basic questions that all those engaged in oppositional struggle must contend with: What is the source(s) of oppression? How do multiple forms of inequality, such as racism and class domination, affect subordinated groups? And what is the best path for mobilization and coalition, given the political landscape?

These are big questions to which there are no easy answers. To varying degrees, CASA, East Wind, and the Black Panther Party (BPP) all turned to Marxism for guidance. They did so, as previously mentioned, because of the limits of reformist politics and the influence of international revolutions, many of which were Marxist in orientation. The relationship between U.S. revolutionaries and anticolonial struggles was not inconsequential. Indeed, Fanon Che Wilkins has argued that Black Power was internationalist from the beginning, thus paving the way for a connection between internationalism and the U.S. Third World Left. Activists also turned to Marxism because issues of domination, oppression, resistance, and revolution have been the most fully developed within this tradition.[2] Thus it was hardly surprising that Third World Leftists, feeling that the white left had not adequately addressed issues of race, would turn to Marxism, as well as their own history and experience, to develop their own analyses.

Further, many activists of color carved a separate space for themselves because of concerns with how the left treated its nonwhite members, despite its commitment to antiracism. "The left was not very creative in their application of Marxism or the national question. I think there was a lot at stake—particularly among the white left—they didn't like the idea that this country might somehow not look like it does . . . that there might actually be a very different political-geographic shape to the United States if there was significant revolutionary change, [such as the Chicano nation]. I think a lot of folks were just not ready to accept that."[3] Such attitudes contributed to activists' wanting to shape their own positions removed from the chauvinism and paternalism that sometimes characterized the white left.

CASA, East Wind, and the BPP all identified as revolutionary nationalists to varying degrees. They conceptualized themselves as oppressed nationalities and, in addition to fighting for their liberation and that of other oppressed groups, had some vague notion of a goal of socialism, which they associated with equality and a more humane society. The distinctive ways in which revolutionary nationalism and other radical politics were articulated can be traced to the unique racialization and attendant racial and class position of each group. Though considerable ideological overlap existed among the organizations, I emphasize their differences to highlight their distinctiveness and to illuminate key themes in Marxist-Leninist and Maoist thought as articulated by Third World Leftists. To better convey the ideological breadth of the movement, I also discuss the ideology of competing organizations: CASA in relation to the August Twenty-ninth Movement (ATM), East Wind in relation to Storefront, and finally, the BPP in relation to US.

CASA

CASA's political ideology centered on the class position and national status of ethnic Mexicans, particularly immigrants and workers. Although CASA was arguably the leading Chicana/o revolutionary organization in Los Angeles during the 1970s, it was not the only one. In fact, many Chicanas/os participated in interethnic organizations, including the Communist Labor Party, the October League, the ATM, the Socialist Workers Party, and the Communist Party (CPUSA).[4] Except for the CPUSA, all these organizations were composed primarily of people of color and were Marxist-Leninist. Chicanas/os who joined such organizations often felt that the most effective path to social change was working with other peoples.[5]

In contrast, CASA was largely by and for ethnic Mexicans, despite a few white members. Careful to distance themselves from cultural nationalists, CASA sought to reconnect Mexican Americans with Mexico, regardless of how many generations removed, by stressing political economic ties. Thus, despite its socialist leanings, it was quite nationalistic, a pattern common to the Third World Left. Its nationalist leanings were most vividly expressed in a debate over whether Mexican Americans were Mexicans or Chicanas/os.

The National Question: Chicanas/os in Aztlán versus Mexicans *sin Fronteras*

The most distinctive and controversial feature of CASA's ideology was its denial of a Chicana/o identity. Instead, CASA saw all ethnic Mexicans as part of the Mexican nation and the same international working class.

> The position of CASA-HGT [Hermandad General de Trabajadores (General Brotherhood of Workers)] is that Mexicans in the U.S., whether born north or south of the imperialist border[,] are part of the same nationality, the Mexican nationality. It is our duty to take our position amongst the masses of our people and to debate it against the position that the Mexicans born here in the U.S. form part of another nationality, the Chicano nationality.
>
> Our organization considers that the central political task of all the progressive Mexican forces is . . . resistance against repatriation and repressive immigration laws. The attacks of the armed forces of immigration directed at expelling millions of Mexicans from our historic lands and of denying us our right to work and survive, constitute the most racist political attacks of imperialism against the Mexican people as a whole, as a nationality and as part of a class.[6]

The twin concepts of nationality and national oppression, which today we would simply call racism, were dominant issues in the sixties and seventies. Because Marxism had a more sophisticated understanding of the national question than of racism, minority activists drew upon this work and began exploring their experience in light of nationalism, leading CASA to conclude that Mexicans and Mexican Americans were one nation. The radical nature of this position cannot be overstated, as the *movimiento*, for the most part, was predicated on the assertion that Chicanas/os were distinct from Mexicans. Not only did many activists identify with the Chicana/o nation, but they claimed the Southwest, or Aztlán, as their homeland.[7]

In contrast, CASA insisted that Chicanas/os and Mexicans were the mirror image of each other (see figure 7). CASA argued that the perceived differences between the two populations were due to the international border, itself the result of U.S. imperialism. This politically imposed boundary, which tore asunder the Mexican nation, coupled with the belief that all Mexicanas/os were part of the same working class, enabled CASA to deny any distinction between the two. CASA conceptualized Mexicanas/os as an oppressed nation by Stalin's definition: specifically, "a historically constituted, stable community of people, formed on the basis of a common language, territory, economic life, and psychological make-up manifested in a common culture."[8]

This was a highly innovative move insofar as it nullified the very real differences that characterized Mexican Americans, Mexican immigrants, and Mexicans. David Gutiérrez's work has shown that Mexican Americans' and Mexicans' attitudes toward each other have historically been ambivalent. Mexicans often dismiss Mexican Americans as *pochos* (assimilated Mexicans), while Mexican Americans have used their U.S. citizenship to exclude or marginalize Mexicans.[9] Though these two groups are certainly connected and imperialism has contributed to their separate but linked evolution, the notion of a single Mexican nation was not well received by most Chicana/o activists. Indeed, even some of CASA's membership resisted it. For instance, CASA promoted the Spanish language to reinforce Mexican culture. This meant always providing translation and requiring those not fluent in Spanish (who were more than a few) to engage in extra study, which was not always appreciated. In another example, CASA supported the Mexican student movement, and when activists were forced to flee in response to intense government repression, CASA became even more involved.[10] Not only did some members believe that too much energy was focused on Mexico, but some felt that Mexican members occupied a privileged position within CASA because of their authenticity. According to one activist, "There was an enormous emphasis on Mexico . . . which was fine. I didn't object to that. But it took precedence over the analysis that we should have had here."

National oppression requires an oppressor, and CASA, like many others, targeted U.S. imperialism. CASA agreed with the larger Chicana/o move-

Figure 7. Mexicans and Chicanos are one people. The mirror image illustrates CASA's belief that Chicanas/os do not exist separately from Mexicans. Source: Drawing by John Alvarez. "National Chicano Forum," *Sin Fronteras*, June 1976, p. 6. Courtesy of Antonio Rodriguez and Department of Special Collections, Stanford University Libraries.

ment that racism and colonialism contributed to the impoverishment and marginalization of Mexican Americans, but they went further. First, CASA insisted that racism itself did not explain the subordination of Mexicans. Rather imperialism was the culprit and racism its tool. Second, CASA insisted that both Mexico and Mexican Americans were part of the Third World.

Despite the primacy of nationalism, racism was considered essential to the functioning of imperialism. Racism was the ideology that justified discriminatory treatment and, more importantly, led to Mexicanas/os being raced as "nonwhite" and therefore considered inferior. CASA was especially conscious of institutional racism, as seen in widespread police abuse, Immigration and Naturalization Service (INS) policy,[11] and challenges to affirmative action. The discrimination that ethnic Mexicans experienced, whether in the case of a union not providing translation or the INS targeting brown-skinned people, simultaneously illustrated national oppression and racism. For CASA the two were linked:

> We are constantly forced to prove to the state of the imperialists that we have a legal right to be in our historical lands. On the basis of our language, on the color of our skin we are singled out for harassment.
>
> We call for the united resistance of the Mexican people. We must refuse to produce any documents in response to the racist demands of the immigration agents. This is not only an act of solidarity to undocumented workers. It is an act of resistance to racism and brutality toward all Mexican people in the U.S.[12]

Given CASA's emphasis on imperialism, it was hardly surprising that activists identified as part of the Third World. They did so by juxtaposing the oppression of Mexican Americans in the United States with that of Mexico in the global arena. Imperialism provided the conceptual basis to connect the relationship between the United States and Mexico, immigration, and the continued subordination of ethnic Mexicans in the United States.

> Imperialism is the main enemy of the Mexican people today. It is by the very dynamics of imperialism . . . that millions of Mexicans have been dispersed from their national territory and are forced . . . to migrate to the U.S. The forces which impel these migrations as well as the forces which receive and exploit their labor are those mechanisms of Imperialism. In its incipient stages of development monopoly capitalism impelled the annexation of half the national territory of Mexico in an expansionist war. It annexed the lands of the Southwest in a war of aggression and imprisoned within its boundaries members of an already formed nationality—the Mexican nationality.[13]

Imperialism was recognized as a global system and members of CASA felt that it was incumbent upon them as revolutionaries to prepare the Mexican people to challenge it. "It should be clear that while the center of the storm of revolution against Imperialism is presently in Africa, it is only a matter of time until defeat for Imperialism will center that storm in Latin America. When this occurs, it will have been our responsibility to prepare our people in this country and in Mexico for the correct posture vis-à-vis Imperialism. We must develop among our people a deep commitment to the Latin American revolution."[14] Though CASA was in many ways internationalist, it was clearly more committed to events in Latin America than other parts of the world. Hence close ties were cultivated with Puerto Ricans, Cubans, and of course, Mexicans.

A Working Class *sin Fronteras*

Related to CASA's belief in a single Mexican nation was its assertion that Mexicans constituted a single working class. While CASA fought on behalf of all ethnic Mexicans, it paid particular attention to the working class, viewing immigrants as the embodiment of both class exploitation and national oppression. However, to link class and national oppression, CASA had to conceive of all ethnic Mexicans as part of the working class, which, as Ernesto Chávez has pointed out, ignored significant class distinctions.[15] Of course, Mexican Americans *were* predominantly working class, but not entirely. Ironically, CASA's privileging of workers tacitly acknowledged the existence of other class positions. "Our organization has set itself the task of going among the Mexican people in this country and organizing our people for class struggle. In doing so we recognize that it is the Mexican worker who will be the central force in our struggle but that we have also the duty to organize and bring class and national consciousness to the *rest of our people*."[16]

Undocumented workers were the main focus of CASA's work: not only were they Mexican, but they were, by definition, workers. Thus *los indocumentados* provided a vehicle for class solidarity among all Mexican Americans.

> Although since 1968 over three million undocumented workers have been forced out of the country by deportation or political and economic pressure, there has been a growing resistance among Mexicans to the threat of deportations, which is another form of class and national oppression. We as a national organization are a part of that resistance and call for all sectors of the Mexican people and progressive sectors of the overall society to participate in this resistance. Since we recognize that the most important base of the Mexican population is its workers, we especially make a call to workers to defend their class and national brothers and sisters.[17]

The importance of undocumented workers cannot be overestimated. As immigrants, *los indocumentados* belonged to two countries, and their very action of unauthorized migration defied the international boundary. In short, they were the incarnation of *sin fronteras*. The phrase *sin fronteras* (without borders) refers to a working class that is not constrained by political boundaries but is international, as seen in CASA's logo, which shows a connected North and South America without boundaries (figure 8). As

Figure 8. CASA's logo. Note how the logo does not include any national boundaries. Source: "CASA General Brotherhood of Workers Salutes National Chicano Forum," box 2, folder 11, CASA Collection. Courtesy of Antonio Rodriguez and Department of Special Collections, Stanford University Libraries.

noted earlier, CASA dismissed the U.S./Mexican boundary as an imperialist move. Thus *sin fronteras* was a spatial expression of Mexican subjectivity and class politics, one distinct from Aztlán, which placed Chicanas/os firmly *within* the United States and did not dispute the U.S./Mexican boundary.

The absence of a national boundary also served to reinforce a shared class position. Only by uniting would ethnic Mexicans be able to resist the INS, corrupt Mexican unions, exclusion from U.S. unions, and U.S. imperialism. Although limited to Mexicanas/os, this was a very progressive stance, as many U.S. unions eschewed immigrant workers and Mexican unions themselves were rejected as statist unions (which they were). Not until the 1990s, when the North American Free Trade Agreement (NAFTA) and globalization were underway, did unions on both sides of the border begin to see each other in more productive ways.

CASA and the ATM

Many Chicana/o leftists disagreed, sometimes vehemently, with CASA. Not only did they believe that CASA's position was wrong, but they felt it was dangerous to deny the existence of the Chicana/o nation. After all, what was the Chicana/o movement if there were no Chicanas/os? CASA was in greatest ideological conflict with the ATM,[18] another Los Angeles-based left organization that spent considerable time and energy theorizing the Chicana/o struggle and reached a conclusion different from CASA.

The ATM evolved from several collectives and the Labor Committees of La Raza Unida Party (LRUP). Initially, leftists within LRUP sought to develop a cadre organization, but they eventually realized their mistake— LRUP was a *mass* organization, not one centered on highly disciplined revolutionaries. Still desiring this type of political space, however, activists created the ATM in 1974. The ATM was composed of dedicated revolutionary nationalists and focused heavily on workplace organizing. Its goal was to democratize unions and support worker organizing efforts, especially among Chicanas/os. Because they operated at workplaces, however, the ATM inevitably absorbed a diversity of peoples, thus becoming multinational. Whites, Asian Americans, and African Americans joined the ATM, but it always remained a predominantly Chicana/o organization.[19]

While CASA argued that Mexican Americans and Mexicans were one, the ATM insisted on the existence of the Chicana/o nation. Its position was laid out in *Fan the Flames: A Revolutionary Position on the Chicano National Question*, the publication of which was a major event. As one member recalled, "When we developed our position on the Chicano Nation, we had a national campaign. We went all over. We set up forums and we had workshops and we had discussion with people. We put up posters and all of that. So we had a national campaign to really spark a lot of discussion around the character of the Chicano liberation struggle and its relationship to the larger working class's struggle for socialism." The ATM's analysis of the Chicana/o struggle was an advance over previous formulations. Before then, most leftists had simply applied Lenin's and Stalin's ideas of the nation to the Chicana/o experience, with unsatisfactory results. As early as the 1930s, the CPUSA had argued that Chicanas/os were *not* an oppressed nation and therefore did not have the right to secession or self-determination.[20] In contrast, the ATM insisted that Chicanas/os were a distinct nation and had the right to self-determination. Self-determination did not necessarily imply secession; rather, it referred to a people's right to decide their future. As a consequence of this position, the ATM also recognized Aztlán. It described its goals as

> fighting and liberating the homeland of the Chicano people in the Southwest which was annexed by the U.S. capitalists in 1848, from Mexico. By this act we will be contributing in defeating U.S. imperialism which controls economically and politically the Mexican and the Chicano nation.
>
> The Chicano people in the Southwest represent a nation oppressed by U.S. imperialism. Like the Afro-American nation in the South, the Chicano nation lacks self-rule, all important political decisions which affect it are made by the Imperialists and not by the Chicano people.[21]

Like CASA, the ATM made imperialism part of its ideology, but it paid less attention to the international working class, stressing instead the subordination of the Chicana/o nation by the United States. Moreover, the ATM privileged the working class by devoting considerable resources to organizing workers. Despite these similarities, however, there was a schism between the two regarding Chicanas/os and Mexicans.

> The Mexican nation is the result of three revolutions. The war of Independence (1811–1821), the liberal-bourgeois revolution *de la Reforma,* and the Mexican Revolution of 1910–1920. Chicanos in the Southwest were not part of these revolutions and only a handful minimally participated in the 1910 revolution. Chicanos as a people developed under different historical circumstances, those of colonization and national oppression within the borders of the U.S. The Mexican masses, for example, do not suffer from racial or national discrimination, the Spanish language is not suppressed in Mexico but is the "official" language, the Mexican culture is not systematically attacked by the state. These particular conditions of oppression have given rise to a distinct psychological make-up (although there are some similarities to Mexican culture), reflected culturally in their language, their art, their music, etc. of the Chicano people.[22]

Such radically different interpretations of the Mexican American experience led to conflict between the organizations. CASA described the ATM as a "dangerous and destructive" force, and the ATM responded accordingly.[23] Unfortunately, such conflict undermined individual efforts as well as the larger movement. Such destructive sectarianism, however, in which a handful of people fight over what appear to be relatively minor distinctions, was commonplace in the New Communist movement, as Max Elbaum has shown.[24]

To focus solely on the conflict, however, overlooks the significant ideological overlap between the two groups, which can help us understand the concerns of Chicana/o activists as a whole. For instance, both organizations focused on workers and were deeply committed to a class-based analysis. In addition, both felt a genuine concern for the oppression that ethnic Mexicans faced in the United States. Likewise, they opposed the racist actions of the state, as seen in the *Bakke* decision and the persecution of undocumented workers.

Thirty years later, it is easy to critique both CASA and the ATM. The ATM clearly overstates the distinction between Mexicans and Mexican Americans, and CASA's insistence that there were no differences is contrary to both popular sentiment and research findings. Moreover, both positions have become increasingly tenuous in light of the immigration waves of the 1980s and 1990s, which fundamentally altered the ethnic Mexican population.

While many of the activists interviewed had forgotten the details of the conflict, the antagonism left lasting scars. In retrospect, some conceded that there was no reason why the ATM and CASA could not, at the very least, have been civil to each other, as there was violence on more than one occasion. Moreover, it was clear that what people recalled and cherished most was their commitment to immigrants and the working class. It was the actual community work that people, especially women, were drawn to, and that had a transformative capacity—not the ideological debates. The organizations were vehicles that provided individuals with the opportunity to organize, educate, and otherwise serve the community, but their work was often overshadowed and diminished by ideology.

EAST WIND

East Wind focused ideologically on the development of a Third World identity, the national question, and serving the people. Unlike CASA or the BPP, East Wind was not created by like-minded individuals; rather, it was a collection of activists with similar tendencies who sought to deepen their understanding of the Japanese American experience and become more politically developed. For this reason, along with a conscious effort to avoid sectarianism, East Wind was the least ideologically rigid of the three organizations. Although members devoted considerable energy to studying Marxism-Leninism and adopted specific positions, East Wind did not require the same level of political agreement, as, for example, CASA. As a result, some members of the collective were revolutionary nationalists, some Marxist-Leninists, and some Maoists.[25]

East Wind struggled to strike a balance between study and action. In terms of revolution, one interviewee theorized, there are basically two options: study and action. "There are those people who want to intellectualize the revolution. Then there are those who want to go out and work. The medium is for the study to help solve problems in your mass work. There was the tendency to get away from that and just do book study." While East Wind never abandoned one for the other, the collective did shift its emphasis over time. Dedication to study was not unique to East Wind but was characteristic of the New Communist movement.[26] This partly explains East Wind's greater attention to study, at least in comparison to the BPP, which, it must be recalled, preceded the New Communist movement. Other explanations for East Wind's relatively greater focus on study are that it was not caught in the same life-and-death struggle as, for example, the BPP, which was engaged in almost daily police conflicts and devoted the fewest resources to ideological development. Indeed, several interviewees noted that even though the BPP sold Mao's *Little Red Book*, it was Asian Americans that actually studied it.[27] In addition, Asian Americans arguably faced a greater theoretical challenge than Blacks and Chicanas/os, as they were more diverse both economically and in terms of nationality, thus requiring greater analysis. Finally, the fact that Asian American activists were grappling with questions of identity and were inspired by Asian revolutions might have given additional meaning and significance to key Asian texts. Not only were they reading authoritative political documents, but studying revolutionary Asian works became an act of performing one's Asian American identity.[28]

This observation has generated some intense reactions, particularly among young Asian Americans. Some take exception, feeling that it reinscribes Asian Americans as "model minorities," while others feel that study is less revolutionary than other activities. While I can appreciate such concerns, especially given Asian Americans' invisibility in most accounts of the era, the fact remains that differences did exist. To deny them would overlook important patterns. Perhaps more significant are the anxieties they suggest. In this case, there is an assumption that guns, for example, are more revolutionary than study or community work. This is simply untrue. While the use of guns is certainly more dramatic, it does not necessarily translate into greater social change—which was the desired goal.

Maoism: The Third World and the National Question

Within mainstream Marxist thought, Mao was a secondary figure, perhaps best known for his work on peasants and revolution.[29] Among the Third World Left, however, he was a leading theoretician. While many Asian

Americans were inspired by Mao's commitment to the peasantry, as well as his contributions as a nonwhite philosopher, it was his theoretical work on the national struggle and the Third World that was critical to U.S. activists. Inspired by him, a growing number of Blacks and other people of color began conceptualizing themselves as nations. Indeed, in his comparative study of the United States and France, Fields found that Maoism was far more popular and complex in the United States precisely because of the greater racial/ethnic diversity there. More than any other philosophy, Maoism, or some version of it, enabled nonwhites to engage Marxism in a meaningful way, as it allowed them to merge their commitments to class and racial politics under the rubric of the nation.

The relationship between socialism, Marxism, and nationalism is complicated and at times contradictory. Marx was generally dismissive toward nationalism, viewing it as an obstacle to class consciousness that would soon become obsolete. Of course, nationalism persisted and spread throughout the early twentieth century, and Stalin, Lenin, and Mao all theorized it. While Lenin concluded that *all* nations have the right to self-determination, Mao placed the national struggle on an equal footing with class struggle. Because of China's colonial experience, the question of national liberation was crucial to Mao. Besides arguing that the national and class struggles were comparable, he maintained that it was necessary for the proletariat to make alliances with the bourgeoisie during revolution—something most Marxists disagreed with. Nonetheless, the centrality of the national struggle resonated with U.S. minority activists. Aside from describing the nature of national oppression, Mao also made clear the source, imperialism.[30]

The second conceptual contribution of Mao's was the "three worlds." Mao theorized that "[t]he world was divided into three areas: the first world was composed of the two superpowers, the second world was an 'intermediate zone' (the middle class) composed of the other advanced industrialized countries, and the third world was composed of the underdeveloped or 'proletarian' nations."[31] This analysis clarified the nature of national struggle and grounded it in a set of material relations similar to class. Though many critiqued this as more rhetorical than real, there was no denying that the colonized world *was* the leading site of revolutionary activity during the 1960s, and such struggles, along with figures such as Che Guevara, were enormously compelling to U.S. Third World activists.

Ideologically, East Wind and the larger Asian American movement were preoccupied with the development of an oppositional identity. Asian American leftists affirmed their identity as members of the Third World, but this was not always easy, given their diversity and fragmentation.

> The concept of "Asian American" is diverse, with opposition and contra-
> diction a part of its character. We are Chinese, Japanese, Korean, Filipino,
> Indian; we speak Cantonese, Japanese, Toysan, English, Okinawan, Man-
> darin, Pidgin English. We are women, we are men. We range from fifth-
> generation descendants of the earliest immigrants to Hawaii, to recent
> arrivals from Hong Kong; we are old, middle-aged, young; rich, middle
> class, solid working class, poor; college kids, freaks and street people
> inside of prison; we can count among ourselves super-macho Sansei
> Samurai, and sisters struggling against male chauvinism; the most tight-
> assed scholastic who spends 80 percent of his waking hours reading Mao,
> to totally spaced-out freaks; loyal Amerikans and revolutionaries.[32]

Contending with such diversity also entailed challenging Asian Americans'
ambiguous racial position. While there was no doubt that Asian Americans
were affected by white racism and imperialism, their partial acceptance by
whites, which enabled both upward and spatial mobility, necessitated that
activists clarify their position within the racial hierarchy. As a revolutionary
organization, East Wind was not interested in developing an antiracist politics predicated on integration. Such a strategy would not only exclude
many Asians but reproduce white hegemony, which was recognized as key
to racial inequality. Thus a truly radical antiracist identity and politics was
needed, and Mao's concept of the "Third World" provided one answer. "My
political consciousness as a Japanese American and member of the Third
World progressed step by step from initial support for the Civil Rights
Movement (brotherhood of all people) to 'revolutionary nationalism' (yellow power in unity with other Third World people and progressive whites)
to self-determination of Third World people within the context of a socialist society."[33]

A Third World identity offered several advantages to Japanese American
leftists. Since people of color throughout the United States were beginning
to identify as part of the Third World, its adoption reinforced their status as
nonwhites. While many Japanese Americans were acutely aware of their
nonwhite status due to daily discrimination, they nonetheless received the
societal message that they were distinct from other communities of color,
and indeed Chicanas/os and Blacks did not always recognize them as
minorities. Thus a Third World identity solidified their minority position
and offered a more politicized and oppositional reading of their status.

Another benefit to a Third World identity was its connection to the colonized world. By emphasizing global inequality and Mao's three worlds,
Japanese Americans aligned themselves with oppressed people globally. For
example, aside from opposing the Vietnam War, East Wind supported self-
determination for Okinawa, the reunification of Korea, and the ousting of

Marcos from the Philippines. Such acts of solidarity drew parallels between the subordination of U.S. minorities and Third World countries.

East Wind also drew on Maoism to help clarify other issues, including nationalism. Articulating a national identity was challenging because Asian Americans did not readily fit the description of a nation, at least as outlined by Stalin. Asian Americans did not share a language, territory, history, and so forth. East Wind, as a relatively homogenous Japanese American collective, wished to remain open to other Asian Americans and saw itself as part of the larger Asian American movement. Accordingly, East Wind explored the concept of an Asian nation. Several members wrote an essay in *Gidra* exploring the concept of the nation-community.

> The concept of building an Asian nation here in North Amerika is an attempt at finding unity. There are two main premises that we can think about: first, Asians of all kinds, regardless of where their heads are at must be reached out to, and touched. . . . Second, every form of activity, service, organizing, struggle and digging each other that makes us more aware of our oppression and also makes us feel more powerful and human is valid and legitimate as part of the movement. Beyond these two premises, the idea is a simple one: to build a power base as Asians—culturally, geo-politically, economically, and as it becomes necessary, militarily. The base we build must be broad in scope, touching all levels of our social existence, so that we can grow, together, towards forging our own nation right here in Amerika. . . . What we must begin to build is our own culture— one that relates to our experiences of struggling to survive mentally and physically in this crumbling thing called Amerika. . . . As we begin to build our culture, we will feel the necessity more and more to start building our own parallel institutions within and for our communities, manned and serviced by us. For instance: legal, medical and social services, day-care centers, liberation schools, food co-ops, garages, dress and garment shops, churches, Pioneer centers [for seniors], and our own media. The only thing new about them is that they will be a part of one, unified theme: our own nation-community.[34]

One former member of East Wind explained that, borrowing from Chinese ideology, the group was conceptualizing Asian Americans as an oppressed nationality with the right to develop as a people, rather than as a nation by the more conventional definition. Essentially, East Wind argued that liberation could not be equated with voting or the absence of discrimination; rather, it referred to minorities, regardless of their size and geography, "ha[ving] the right to develop themselves as a people, with all the necessary institutions and cultural development."[35] This was an innovative move insofar as activists departed from a close reading of Stalin and theorized from their own experience.

Despite significant theoretical debate, however, the idea of an Asian American nation did not catch on. A former member recalled, "I think it seemed just fairly impractical and difficult. Like where? Where would this be? I think only a couple of people really thought it was real. It was the concept that the Asian nation gave you a land base. It was inspiring, but it wasn't something that I think people could really grasp."[36] As further evidence of the lack of fit, other Asian American groups called East Wind narrow nationalists, soundly rejecting the proposal. One activist described the processes as follows:

> At that time one of the people, he was from New York . . . wrote this long essay called "The Asian Nation." The essence of it was that the movement was creating a nation, a people who felt some kind of identity with each other. And I think he used the term *nation* very loosely, it was symbolic. You know how people say "Asian America." Nobody is saying that there is a separate territory or anything. It's just sort of a concept. It [the article] was in *Gidra,* and it was very long and substantive, and it talked about revolutionary nationalism. So what happened is that some group in New York read this and wrote this whole polemic against East Wind for their narrow nationalism and promoting the nation. They went into this whole thing about a nation defined by Stalin has to be "this and that. ". . . There were differences in the group as to how we responded. Some people said, "Fuck them, who cares, we don't even know who they are." But [some of the members] actually knew some of the people because [they were] from New York. . . . I don't know, maybe it was a guy thing, but they felt like they had to respond. We, as a group, never responded.

The whole incident, especially confusion over the nation, contributed to East Wind devoting more resources to studying. Though it drifted from the concept of an Asian American nation, East Wind remained committed to working within the Nikkei community, resisting national oppression, and identifying as part of the Third World. Though some members worked with other nationalities, especially those in the labor movement, and the collective regularly supported other people of color, most worked with Asian Americans. "At no time were we 'narrow nationalists'—seeing white people as the enemy. We always understood the enemy [to be] the economic political *system* that survived and thrived on racism, sexism, and war."[37] To this day, many former members of East Wind continue to be active primarily, though not exclusively, in the Japanese American community.

Serving the People

East Wind's final ideological concern was serving the people, as community work was both an activity and a theoretical subject. As previously suggested, the organization's emphasis on community work arose from the organic needs of Japanese Americans but was also inspired by the BPP. Members took pains to differentiate themselves from service organizations, emphasizing how community work politicized both the doer and the receiver. As one former member recalled, "We were not a social service group, we were revolutionaries, we tried to organize our people to help themselves. Like the mental health stuff, we took over the institution of Rest Haven . . . but the mental health stuff was to bring the Panther model of redemption out into the movement and openly propagate that. . . . Helping others, that's the best thing for your own ego and finding out who you are."

East Wind's appreciation of community work as potentially transformative is significant. Though the BPP and CASA may have also grasped it, there is little evidence that they made this an explicit part of their ideology. One East Wind member explained, "We should build caucuses, collectives, parallel and alternative institutions in [the] social service[s], professions, mass media and culture. These will serve as our 'base areas' for accumulating our strength and for self-change and growth."[38] Recognition that community work is a dialectic and can change individuals and cultures helped East Wind maintain a flexible attitude and a self-conscious organizational culture.

Much of East Wind's community work was directed toward the Nikkei community, especially the elderly, youth, and the working class, but not all. Because Japanese Americans were a relatively small population, many of their initiatives, including Rest Haven and labor organizing projects, required them to work with other racial/ethnic groups. This was especially true for those involved in labor issues, who inevitably encountered Mexican Americans. Such associations were typically valued as opportunities to build ties with other oppressed nationalities. However, choosing which groups to work with is not the same as working cooperatively with others in a campaign. Hence East Wind prioritized the Nikkei population, as one member described: "My job as a Japanese American was to work in the Japanese American community, to raise consciousness, get us organized, and fight this colonization that was going on. And to bring a significant contingent of our people to the front lines of the struggle. . . . We never took a hard line, but those of us who identified with our people saw that as our primary responsibility."

One campaign that gave East Wind ample opportunity to serve the Japanese American community was the redevelopment of Little Tokyo. Little Tokyo, or J-Town, was a historic district that housed older and low-income Japanese Americans and that began to be threatened by Japanese capital in the 1970s. Although few activists lived in J-Town, it served as the heart of the community. In addition to ethnic restaurants, temples, and funeral homes, J-Town was the site of numerous community services and institutions. East Wind, along with other activists, fought to maintain the community nature of Little Tokyo. Jim Lee has suggested the centrality of redevelopment battles to Asian American activism during the seventies.[39] Considering that this was a period of intense spatial and social fragmentation for Japanese Americans, we can understand the significance that Little Tokyo held for East Wind. J-Town was something that held the community together and rendered it identifiable on a map. Its disappearance would not only entail the loss of a historically Japanese American space but symbolize the demographic demise of the Nikkei.

East Wind and the Storefront

The Storefront represented a different approach to Japanese American revolutionary politics. The organization was created when a group of activists saw a vacant storefront and envisioned it as an ideal place for community activities.[40] Based in the Westside, Storefront sought to promote Third World unity, primarily between African and Asian American people, through a series of "serve the people" programs. Activists provided day care, a food co-op, youth programs, movie nights, and a newspaper, *Come Unity*. Defining itself as multinational, Storefront was basically a group of Japanese Americans serving both the African American and Nikkei communities, as few Blacks actually joined.

Storefront described itself as "a political organization that believes in the liberation of all people oppressed by imperialism, racism, and sexism." Central to its ideology and strategy was geography and urban space. Storefront took a highly geographic approach to organizing by working with all oppressed nationalities in a particular area.

> The Storefront is dealing with community organizing on the grass roots level. We are relating to a geographical community and believe that this is a concrete basis upon which to develop the principle of self-determination. The community is composed of blacks and Asians with a few whites, Chicanos, and Latinos. The question of nationalism is relevant and has provided a serious topic of struggle. The outcome has been that revolutionary nationalism would be used to enhance our community organizing which is based on Third World Unity. . . . [T]he Storefront plans to use and share with each other these points of revolutionary nationalism, but just as importantly the common bond [of] geography provides a basis for unity. The people live next door to each other, go to the same schools, buy from the same stores, are affected by the same drug peddlers and police. Therefore, they share the same oppression.[41]

Though not oblivious to the differences between Asian and African Americans, Storefront stressed their similarities. Unfortunately, it was never particularly successful at creating a multinational organization. As one former member explained, "Although in principle it was trying to be a multinational organization, the Storefront in practice became more or less Asians attempting to serve a black community."[42] Although African Americans did not join Storefront in large numbers, many participated in its programs and services, including its child care and film series. One reason for the limited Black membership was that at this time of intense nationalism, few Black activists were interested in joining a predominantly Asian American group. Storefront also faced another problem that was common among other groups: young radicals trying to connect with and serve a more mainstream and demographically mixed population. The following interview from *Come Unity* features a conversation with a local Black resident and suggests some of the difficulties Storefront (and similar groups) encountered:

MS. HENDERSON: They're not interested. Because they are old and everybody here is young. And these people are more mature people—and they're kind of set in their ways. I was kind of scared when I came over here.

INTERVIEWER: What do you think of Third World Unity?

MS. HENDERSON: I think you should explain it more to the parents and the children because I don't think even half of them know what it means. It's just a word to them. They think of the war—but it doesn't even mean that. Tell it to them until they understand.[43]

Ms. Henderson's comments suggest the generation gap and how extraordinary much of the Third World Left was relative to the populations it served. Not only did Storefront hope to serve *other* people of color, but much of its work was done at the grassroots level, which was characterized by widely varying degrees of political consciousness. In contrast, the organization was quite successful in working with politicized individuals. For instance, members of the Old Left and Panthers worked closely with Storefront's food co-op, which lasted long after the organization's demise.

Storefront clearly represents a distinct ideology from East Wind. Activists firmly believed in Third World unity but also realized that while both Blacks and Japanese Americans occupied the same space they also occupied different locations in the racial hierarchy. Thus Storefront sought to ally itself with the more subordinated group as an act of solidarity and support, an act that also solidified its status as a Third World organization. Although numerous other multinational organizations existed, Storefront was unique in its racial politics. For instance, although the ATM was predominantly Chicana/o, it attracted others by working in the labor movement. However, Chicanas/os in the ATM considered *themselves* to be the oppressed nationality, whereas the Storefront served Blacks and Nikkei, rather than focusing on Japanese American oppression per se. Such differences underscore the logic informing each project. Storefront attracted considerable attention because it was one of the few organizations to really attempt Third World unity. "We consciously organized the Third World. It took us out of the realm of just the Asian movement, the broader left looked at us as just a small component. But when we tried to organize [the] Third World, everybody started coming around. Dorothy Healey from the Communist Party–USA . . . Irwin Sillwood from the *Guardian* at the time; Bobby Avakian from the Revolutionary Union—all these people were coming in."[44] Despite their political differences, East Wind and the Storefront were not antagonistic. Indeed, one interviewee described them as simply having different emphases. That, plus the fact that both organizations had leaders who understood that there was room for differing ideologies, contributed to a very different scenario from that between CASA and ATM.

THE BLACK PANTHER PARTY

The Black Panther Party and the Lumpen Proletariat

The BPP was part of a long line of Black nationalists.[45] It was unlike other groups in that "the Negro question," including Blacks' role in revolutionary struggle, had been well theorized. As early as the Sixth World Congress of the Communist International, southern Blacks were declared a subject nation, meaning that they were "capable of engendering a national revolutionary movement."[46] The BPP drew on this tradition as well as more contemporary work by Malcolm X and Mao Tse-tung in formulating its political ideology. The hallmark of the BPP's politics was its emphasis on the lumpen proletariat, or what today might be called the "underclass."[47] Traditionally, Marxism had placed the greatest agency in the working class, while the lumpen proletariat had been dismissed as unorganizable, lacking class consciousness, and basically out for themselves. The BPP reversed this long-standing tradition by naming the lumpen proletariat as the revolutionary vanguard.

Marx theorized that the central contradiction in capitalist societies was between capital and labor. The extraction of surplus value from workers was deemed a sufficiently powerful contradiction to drive a revolution. Further, it was assumed that workers would identify as a class. This, coupled with their discipline, led them to be designated as the leading revolutionary forces. Unlike other groups, workers are disciplined by daily routines and having one's activities monitored by a boss or machine. Such discipline is considered essential for building political parties, creating worker leadership, and waging sustained struggle.

Within capitalist societies, however, there is a need for unemployed persons, also known as "surplus labor," or structural unemployment. Surplus labor serves several functions. First, it can be used when labor supplies tighten and then released when demand eases. Second, it serves to dampen pressure on wages and working conditions. Should too many workers demand higher wages or resist speed-ups, the threat of replacement by surplus labor always exists. Because of their weak attachment to the formal economy, surplus workers are often involved in the informal economy, participating in such activities as crime, drugs, and the sex trade. Moreover, they are unlikely to be a disciplined force, as their lives are not circumscribed by a time clock. Nor do they typically identify as a class—indeed, many reject the lumpen proletariat as part of the working class. Marx warned that because they had no class consciousness, the "lumpen" would sell their services to the highest bidder, potentially betraying the working class.[48] As a result, the lumpen proletariat (along with peasants) have generally been discredited as a revolutionary force. While I understand structural unemployment to be a feature of the working class, there is no denying the diversity of this population, especially in terms of consciousness.[49]

Because the United States has historically been racially constituted, the lumpen proletariat have largely been nonwhite, specifically African American.[50] As previously discussed, throughout much of the twentieth century Black labor has been considered somewhat expendable. And while it would be a gross error to ignore the centrality of labor to the Black experience, we must also recognize the significance of the lumpen proletariat to the Black community. Geography is important for understanding the differing roles of Black workers and the lumpen in revolutionary activity. In old industrial cities, Black labor has historically been a powerful force, as seen, for example, in the American Negro Labor Congress. Building on this tradition, Black workers in the 1960s and 1970s developed radical organizations such as the Dodge Revolutionary Union Movement, based in the Detroit auto industry.[51] But in places like Los Angeles, Black labor declined significantly after World War II, becoming increasingly concentrated in the public sector. Historically, other groups, namely Mexicans, have performed the most undesirable work in a highly racialized division of labor. As a result, African Americans have been disproportionately represented in the ranks of the lumpen proletariat, and it was this class that the BPP mobilized.

While at Merritt College, Newton and Seale were members of Soul Students Advisory Council, which promoted Black studies and student empowerment. From the beginning, however, they were more interested in the "brothers off the block."[52] This desire emanated from their own experience, recognition of the tremendous energy generated by mass Black uprisings, and their belief that campus struggles were ultimately rooted in the community.[53] Eventually, Newton and Seale created their own organization—one that placed the "brothers off the block" at the center. Over time they organized the men, women, and children who belonged to the lumpen proletariat and other segments of the working class, and they rationalized their actions by making the lumpen proletariat central to their ideology.

Political analysts and scholars have debated the merits of such a strategy. Chris Booker and Errol Henderson, for example, have noted the problems associated with building an organization composed disproportionately of the lumpen proletariat, including a lack of discipline, a tendency toward violence, the importation of street culture, including crime, and the use of weapons.[54] Others have been harsher in their assessment. Hugh Pearson, for instance, dismisses the very notion of organizing the lumpen proletariat, criticizing both SNCC and the BPP for putting all poor Blacks in the same category. "The blurring of the line between blacks at the bottom who had a street mentality and those sincerely interested in improving their lives began to set the stage for Newton's BPP to gain legitimacy."[55] Pearson is correct that the BPP did, in fact, try to consolidate poor, urban Blacks, who were indeed a diverse population. But his condemnation overlooks two things. First, this is the way *most* political movements operate. Connections between various groups are not inevitable or automatic but must be articulated. Recall CASA's efforts to define ethnic Mexicans as workers, thereby overlooking real class and legal distinctions, as well as East Wind's attempts to forge a pan–Asian American identity. Second, despite the Black working class's diversity, members did have a great deal in common and shared at least some material and political interests, although significant differences existed in terms of consciousness, risk taking, and preferred tactics. It was the BPP's willingness to overlook such distinctions that made it so revolutionary: few were willing to work with the lumpen and forge connections with other working-class Blacks. Was the BPP ultimately successful? No. Was it a flawed strategy? Yes. But it was an attempt to deal with a serious problem. There was a large group of poor urban Blacks that the civil rights movement and integration strategies had done little to assist.

By functioning as an open organization the BPP was accessible to all segments of the working class. This accessibility contributed to its overall popularity but, as Booker has pointed out, also created problems. For instance, such an open policy facilitated infiltration. At one point, some Panthers stopped wearing their trademark berets because they felt it enabled anyone to pose as a member. Another problem was gender relations and sexism. Because people with limited political consciousness joined the organization, they inevitably brought sexist attitudes with them. As one member explained, "We had a lot of people that that [male chauvinism] was the only thing they knew. They had to be retrained in the party. A lot of the men thought women were sex objects. A lot of men thought women were supposed to bring food to them. The party embraced everybody, so a lot of people brought those attitudes. We had to retrain them." While the participation of such persons was not without risks, the real question is, Where else might the "brothers off the block" have become politicized and learned to work with women as their equals? Aside from the Nation of Islam, few political groups have been willing to engage this population.

The BPP's focus on self-defense was connected to its relationship to the lumpen proletariat. Though all Blacks might be disproportionately affected by police harassment and abuse, not all African Americans were willing to pick up a gun or make resisting the police a political priority. The lumpen and other segments of the working class who were most familiar with crime and violence as well as police repression were the ones who supported such a stance. Of course, not everyone agreed with the BPP's position, and many on the left criticized it.[56] They insisted that it was folly to trust the lumpen, given its lack of discipline and political consciousness, and that the Panthers' use of guns was simply adventuristic and dangerous; true revolution first occurred in people's minds, through a shift in consciousness, not through weapons.

Regardless of these debates, we must appreciate *why* guns and self-defense loomed so large for the BPP, particularly in comparison to Chicana/o and Asian American groups. One obvious factor was that neither CASA or East Wind was so deeply rooted in the lumpen proletariat. Consequently, they faced less police abuse and harassment and were more vested in the existing social formation. For instance, CASA sought to change laws, policies, and institutional practices, particularly those of labor unions and the INS, to make them more supportive of immigrants. Hence it was invested at least to some extent in the prevailing employment structure. The BPP was not vested in workplaces or any comparable set of institutions and thus took quite a different approach. Its goal was to politicize Blacks so that they would eventually be able to mobilize on their own behalf and meet their own needs.

The BPP and US

The emphasis on the lumpen was only half of the BPP's overall philosophy; the other half was revolutionary nationalism. Although some, including cultural nationalists, have questioned the BPP's nationalist credentials, given its engagement with whites, it was deeply rooted in Black unity and autonomy. As David Hilliard succinctly described the BPP's ideology, "The ideology of the Black Panther Party is the historical experiences of black people in America translated through Marxism-Leninism."[57] The BPP's commitment to Black nationalism can be seen in the Ten-Point Program, which calls for the self-determination of the Black nation through an African American plebiscite. The party saw African Americans as a Black nation, albeit one with pronounced class divisions. No attempt was made to gloss over such divisions; instead, it was argued that the lumpen, as the most marginalized, should lead the revolution. "The Black Panther Party was forced to draw a line of demarcation. We are for all of those who are for the promotion of the interests of the black have-nots, which represent about 98% of blacks here in America. We're not controlled by the white mother country radicals nor are we controlled by the black bourgeoisie."[58]

In contrast to the Panther's revolutionary nationalism stood cultural nationalism. Alphonso Pinkney describes Black cultural nationalism in the following way: "Cultural nationalism assumes that peoples of African descent share a way of life, or culture, which is fundamentally different from that of Europeans and other non-Africans. This way of life, it is assumed, is permitted greater freedom of expression on the continent of Africa than in the Western Hemisphere, but it is shared by Afro-Americans as well. Generations of American social scientists have rejected this notion, preferring instead the positions that Afro-American culture did not exist, [and] that it represented a 'pathological' version of the larger American culture."[59] The general disparagement of African American culture and life is crucial to understanding the potentially oppositional nature of cultural nationalism and its importance to all oppressed racial/ethnic groups. Its relevance was evident in CASA's efforts to promote the Spanish language, as well as the desire of Asian American radicals to connect with Asian revolutionaries and their pleasure in beginning to identify as Asian Americans. As oppressed people, activists went through a period of reclaiming themselves, their bodies, culture, and history.

White leftists have historically rejected cultural nationalism as misguided or a case of false consciousness. Leftists of color have been somewhat more tolerant, but they often conceive of it as a first step and are critical of those who remain wedded to it. According to Linda Harrison, "Cultural nationalism is recognized by many who think in a revolutionary manner as a distinct and natural stage through which one proceeds in order to become a revolutionary. Such is not always the case, and many people remain at the level of a cultural nationalist all of their lives."[60]

There were many cultural nationalist formations in the sixties and seventies, but one of the more Afrocentric ones, US, was located in Los Angeles and served as an ideological opposite to the BPP. Given their differing political ideologies, conflict between the BPP and US was perhaps inevitable, but ideological rigidity, the widespread use of guns, and intense police interference exacerbated the tensions between the two organizations, culminating in the deaths of John Huggins and Bunchy Carter.

US, like Sons of Watts and Slant, was established in the aftermath of the Watts riot. It and related organizations saw themselves as providing a positive alternative, but the Panthers considered them to be "containment organizations"—that is, groups intent on preventing future violence and uprisings. Cultural nationalists hoped that if they offered African Americans an alternative cultural framework and identity, their anger and frustration could be more positively channeled. Maulana Karenga (a.k.a. Ron Karenga and Ron Everitt), the acknowledged leader of US, attracted a large following, particularly among Black men. "Karenga viewed cultural revolution as an indispensable and primary aspect of the black liberation struggle. US was designed to be a vanguard formation that would ignite the black cultural revolution by introducing an alternative value system, rituals, and aesthetic expressions to the broader African American community."[61] US offered lessons in Swahili, promoting it as a potential lingua franca for African Americans, led study groups centered on Karenga's writings, and pioneered the development of Kwanzaa, an alternative Christmas celebration that has now become mainstream. Even the attire and appearance of members of the two organizations underscored their political differences. Men in US were known for their shaven heads and African-style clothing, while men in the BPP favored leather jackets and naturals.

US and the BPP differed in their gender relations, political strategies, relationships with whites, and perhaps most importantly, views on the significance of class. US saw race as the primary determinant shaping Blacks' lives, whereas the BPP also weighed one's class position. Although hardly shy when it came to challenging white racism, the BPP did not immediately categorize all whites as the enemy. Rather, one's class and politics were also considered. The key question was, Which side are you on? Are you willing to align yourself with the interests of the dispossessed? The BPP's attitude was highly unusual because this was a time when Black nationalists treated all nonblacks warily. Thus the BPP rejected cultural nationalism.

> Cultural nationalism, or pork chop nationalism, as I sometimes call it, is basically a problem of having the wrong political perspective. It seems to be a reaction instead of responding to political oppression. The cultural nationalists are concerned with returning to the old African culture and thereby regaining their identity and freedom. In other words, they feel that the African culture will automatically bring political freedom. Many times cultural nationalists fall into line as reactionary nationalists.
>
> Papa Doc in Haiti is an excellent example of reactionary nationalism. He oppresses the people but he does promote the African culture. He's against anything other than black, which on the surface seems very good, but for him it is only to mislead the people. He merely kicked out the racists and replaced them with himself as the oppressor. Many of the nationalists in this country seem to desire the same ends.
>
> The Black Panther Party, which is a revolutionary group of black people, realizes that we have to have an identity. We have to realize our black heritage in order to give us strength to move on and progress. But as far as returning to the old African culture, it's unnecessary and it's not advantageous in many respects. We believe that culture itself will not liberate us. We're going to need some stronger stuff.[62]

Newton's belief that cultural nationalism was wrong, coupled with the larger tensions between US and the BPP, led the Panthers, as Errol Henderson has noted, to caricature cultural nationalism. One need only consider the more nuanced forms of cultural nationalism, as seen in the work of Amiri Baraka, to understand its potential value. Moreover, such a caricature has enabled observers to overlook the BPP's own cultural nationalism, as seen in its art, its poetry, its references to "Black is beautiful," and the widespread image of Newton sitting majestically in his rattan chair, which, as Daryl Maeda has pointed out, is strongly reminiscent of Africa.[63] The BPP's chief criticism of cultural nationalism, however, was the degree to which it was divorced from political economy. By abstracting cultural practices from material relations, it reproduced the status quo.

> Cultural nationalism manifests itself in many ways but all of these manifestations are essentially grounded in one fact: a universal denial and ignoring of the present political, social, and economic realities and the concentration on the past as a frame of reference. . . . Those who believe in the "I'm Black and Proud" theory—believe that there is dignity inherent in wearing naturals; that a buba makes a slave a man; and

that a common language, Swahili, makes all of us brothers. These people usually want a culture rooted in African culture; a culture which ignores the colonization and brutalization that were part and parcel, for example, of the formation and emergence of the Swahili language. In other words cultural nationalism ignores the political and concrete, and concentrates on a myth and fantasy.[64]

The BPP conceptualized the cultural and economic as two distinct realms. Although few scholars hold this position today, such thinking was common at the time and was strategically used to highlight differences. Contemporary scholarship seeks to understand the economic as cultural, while simultaneously appreciating the economic dimensions of cultural activity. While this constitutes a major improvement, discussion of the cultural has tended to emphasize fashion, art, music, and poetry to the exclusion of consciousness and everyday forms of living. This is particularly salient to the Panthers, who, as Henderson writes, developed a potentially revolutionary culture insofar as it was predicated on self-transformation. Converting a street hoodlum into a politically aware individual who was willing to serve the people and make the sacrifices that many committed Panthers did was a revolutionary act. It was also very much a cultural process. Thus, although the Panthers were deeply engaged in a cultural project, it was not acknowledged as such, partly because of the problematic conceptions of culture and political economy that existed at the time.[65]

Instead, the BPP stressed the material bases of oppression and poverty. Black poverty was believed to stem from capitalism, which in turn was linked to white racism. The term *pig* was reserved for the agents of such oppression, including the police, capitalists, and imperialists.[66] Though most of the "pigs" depicted by the Panthers were white, such hostility was not directed against white people per se; rather, it reflected whites' disproportionate power. In figure 9, for example, *pigs* refers to the police. The problem, according to the BPP, was a racialized economic system, the state's role in upholding white privilege, and whites' desire to maintain their position. Another arena where the class politics of US and the BPP clashed was Black capitalism. The BPP initially condemned Black capitalism (see point 3 of the platform) and although that position changed over time, such a line differed markedly from that of US.[67]

The final ideological difference between US and the BPP concerned gender relations. Although both organizations were patriarchal, the BPP struggled with questions of sexism and gender relations, while US openly advocated different roles for women and men, as well as polygamy. Angela Davis reported that at one point Karenga criticized her for doing a "man's job."[68]

A PIG IS A PIG IS A PIG
And the people see it

IN LOS ANGELES...

On Saturday afternoon, June 17th, 1970 the people witnessed another fascist attack by the hired guns of this foul power structure. Three servants of the people, Gail Williams, Gilbert Parker and Simba were out among the people spreading the truth in the form of distributing the Black Panther Party Community News Service on the corner of Sixth Street and Broadway in Los Angeles (Dodge City).

Gail was taken to Sybil Brand Women's Institute, where the money which was donated for the Free Breakfast Program that the Black Panther Party has implemented throughout the black colony, was stolen by the pigs and she was charged with 'begging'

By the end of the day, the fascist funnies of LAPD found an excuse to kidnap two more servants off the streets. Simba and Gill were arrested for 'disturbing the peace' and 'beg-

Four pig cars loaded with pigs came to a halt alongside of the curb followed by a pig wagon. Then the H.P.I.C. (Head Pig In Charge) walked over to Gail, the seventeen year old sister and without a word grabbed her by the arms and pushed her forward. The masses of people in that area had stopped and were looking on. But the pigs kept on oinking to show they didn't even respect the masses of people that gathered.

ging while they stood waiting for the bus.

If begging is getting funds to feed hungry children in Babylon, that the U.S. government neglects, and if it disturbs the pig's peace for the people to receive the Black Panther Party Community News Service then Right On!

con't on page 13

Figure 9. The Panthers and the "pigs." Article depicting officers of the Los Angeles Police Department as "pigs." Source: *People's News Service*, no. 29, 1970, p. 11. Box 38, collection 50, Department of Special Collections, University of California, Los Angeles.

Likewise, Elaine Brown noted that at an US meeting in San Diego, it was made clear that the men were to eat first, even though everyone had contributed toward buying the food. Unfortunately, there was no food left when it was time for the women to eat.[69] In contrast, the BPP, while still characterized by intense sexism, espoused the rhetoric of gender equality, and women were allowed to become organizational leaders. Sexism has traditionally been one of the Achilles' heels of nationalist movements, which are often predicated on reclaiming the masculinity of colonized and subordinated men. Nonetheless, revolutionary nationalism can carry the seeds of gender equality, and, if nothing else, its rhetoric may encourage recognition of multiple forms of domination, which some may ultimately act upon. Cultural nationalism as practiced by US precluded such a possibility.

Intercommunalism

The political ideology of the BPP evolved over time. This was apparent in changes in the Ten-Point Platform as well as in the party's political rhetoric.[70] Intercommunalism was a later theoretical innovation of Newton's that not all Panthers understood or agreed with. Essentially, Newton's study of political economy led him to believe that nations no longer existed because they were ultimately controlled by empires. Instead, communities were identified as the most relevant political unit, as it was at the local level that people lived their lives. Newton called for a radical form of community solidarity, one intent on retrieving power from the imperialists.

> In 1966 we called our Party a Black Nationalist Party (BNP). We called ourselves Black nationalists because we thought that nationhood was the answer. Shortly after that we decided that what was really needed was revolutionary nationalism. That is, nationalism plus socialism. After analyzing conditions a little more, we found that it was impractical and even contradictory. Therefore we went to a higher level of consciousness. We saw that in order to be free we had to crush the ruling circle and therefore we had to unite with the peoples of the world. So we called ourselves Internationalists. . . . We sought solidarity with what we thought were the nations of the world.
> But then what happened? We found that because everything is in a constant state of transformation, because of the development of technology, because of the development of the mass media . . . and because of the fact that the United States is no longer a nation but an empire, nations could not exist, for they did not have the criteria for nationhood. Their self-determination, economic determination, and cultural determination has been transformed by the imperialists and the ruling circle. They were no longer nations. We found that in order to be Internationalists we had to be also Nationalists, or at least acknowledge

> nationhood. Inter-nationalism . . . means the interrelationship among
> a group of nations. But since no nation exists, and since the United
> States is in fact an empire, it is impossible for us to be Internationalists.
> These transformations and phenomena require us to call ourselves
> "intercommunalists" *because nations have been transformed into
> communities of the world.* The Black Panther Party now disclaims
> internationalism and supports intercommunalism.[71]

Although Newton spoke eloquently on his position and openly advocated it at the Revolutionary People's Constitutional Convention, many were unable to either understand or support intercommunalism, particularly its denial of the Black nation.[72] A former Panther described how individuals responded to this idea: "Actually, when Huey got out of jail . . . a lot of changes started happening like putting down the gun, like no longer defending yourself. And he had this thing of intercommunalism. Huey was real deep. He was a brilliant man, but a lot of people didn't understand intercommunalism, and I think that is what helped split the party, because they didn't understand where Huey was going." Whether intercommunalism actually contributed to the demise of the BPP is beyond the scope of this project, but clearly the ideology was not embraced by the larger rank and file.

Although both the BPP and US were Black nationalist organizations, they differed markedly. Yet, despite their differences, two similarities stand out. First, both organizations were essentially competing for the same audience: young, urban Blacks (especially males); second, both were rooted in the community, as opposed to schools, the workplace, or other institutions. In effect, both organizations offered a political path to the young Black working class and lumpen proletariat, who were seeking answers and alternatives to the reality of the ghetto.

This chapter has tried to illuminate the ideological concerns of each organization. While each group differed in its political focus and ideological interpretations, there is a commonality that helps us understand the Third World Left in its entirety. To a certain degree, each group adopted some form of revolutionary nationalism and struggled to define their people and cause as a nation. In addition, each sought to develop an economic analysis. Although they assigned different significance to the working class, the lumpen proletariat, the community, and the Third World, they essentially drew from a shared set of concepts and ideological tools. The exact configuration of those ideas reflected both the economic and racial positions of the larger racial/ethnic group to which members belonged, the constituencies they served, their particular interpretation of Marxism-Leninism, and larger political events.

SIX

The Politics of Solidarity

Interethnic Relations in the Third World Left

Movements are more than the sum of their parts. Their character, size, and shape are also determined by their interactions with other organizations and individuals. I am particularly interested in the interethnic politics of the Third World Left, given the movement's emphasis on internationalism and revolutionary nationalism (versus cultural nationalism). What were the attitudes of East Wind, the Black Panther Party (BPP), and CASA toward whites and toward other people of color? To what extent did they actually engage in coalition building or interethnic activism, and how does the reality correspond to the rhetoric?

I make two main arguments in this chapter. First, the racial politics of Southern California's Third World Left can best be understood as a tension between nationalism and internationalism. All three organizations identified as internationalists and as such were committed to supporting the struggles of other colonized and oppressed peoples. This political commitment, for example, led Huey Newton to offer the services of the BPP to the South Vietnamese.[1] On the other hand, these organizations were also quite nationalistic at heart. Besides focusing on their respective racial/ethnic groups, they were uncertain to what extent they should work with other communities.

Second, the larger racial hierarchy, and specifically each group's position within it, influenced how the group negotiated these dynamics. Those at the bottom of the racial hierarchy, in this case African Americans, enjoyed an elevated status within movement circles. African Americans, particularly the BPP, were considered authentic revolutionaries, so whites, Asian Americans, and Latinas/os sought to align themselves, to varying degrees, with the Black struggle. The converse is also true: Asian Americans, who occupied a relatively more privileged place within the racial hierarchy, were the least sought after in terms of coalitions and partnerships. In fact, Asian

Americans were largely absent from many of the historical documents reviewed, as well as from interviews with Black and Chicana/o activists. This pattern sheds light on the local racial hierarchy and its politics but also raises difficult questions. For example, what does the term *people of color* actually mean when some nonwhites are only marginally included? What is the real criterion for membership?

Hopefully, a close reading of interethnic dynamics will provide valuable insights into each organization and the movement and facilitate a larger discussion on contemporary racial politics. While most social justice activists recognize the importance of multiracial movements and coalitions, building them is another matter and raises challenging issues regarding leadership, differences, and acknowledging other's histories. Yet if we are to build a broad-based movement for social change these concerns must be addressed.

EAST WIND

Of all the organizations, East Wind was arguably the most self-conscious in its efforts to work with other people of color. Although the organization was centered in the Japanese American community, it connected with other Asian Americans, as well as with Blacks, American Indians, and Chicanas/os. The importance of cultivating relationships with other Asian American groups should not be underestimated. In many cases, there had been only minimal contact between these diverse populations—as recently as World War II Chinese Americans had worn buttons distinguishing themselves from Japanese Americans.[2] Given such a history, Third World activists were truly forging a new path. As one member of East Wind explained, "We had to consciously link up our own communities. It wasn't like it was all of us Asians together. We knew that we were a small community. . . . We just didn't register in the same sense that we do today." East Wind frequently worked with activists from Chinatown and established close relationships with other Asian and multinational groups, including the mostly Chinese I Wor Kuen, the Filipina/o Katipunan ng Demokratikong Pilipino (KDP), the August Twenty-ninth Movement, and Seize the Times. In addition, many of the initiatives that East Wind participated in, including *Gidra* and the Amerasia Bookstore, were essentially pan-Asian undertakings.[3]

Other People of Color

Besides working with other Asian American groups, East Wind did extensive support work with Blacks, Latinas/os, and American Indians. Such acts

Figure 10. Asian American contingent at a march against deportations, East Los Angeles, summer 1976. Example of Asian American solidarity with Chicanas/os. © 2004 Mary Kao.

of solidarity included participating in proimmigrant events (see figure 10), sending a delegation to Wounded Knee, assisting in a soup kitchen in Chinatown, and supporting the United Farm Workers (UFW) and the BPP. In addition, they joined various coalitions and ad hoc committees, such as International Women's Day, which became an annual event. Participation in such activities was not random or accidental but reflected Japanese Americans' position within the racial hierarchy and a clear set of political commitments on the part of East Wind.

Several factors help explain the prominence of interethnic work in East Wind and the larger Asian American movement. One reason the movement took solidarity so seriously was Japanese Americans' position as supposed "model minorities" and their relatively more privileged economic and social status. Because they did not share the same levels of poverty, unemployment, or incarceration as Blacks and Mexicans—the "typical" evidence of racism—Japanese Americans had to reiterate their status as Third World people to the larger world, despite feeling grounded in such an identity themselves. One way to do this was to work with other people of color. This was evident in groups like the Storefront but also in more nationalist projects like East Wind. A former member of East Wind described some of the challenges they encountered in working with other groups:

> We were in Boyle Heights and our work [was] in Little Tokyo. A lot of us were living there and looking for ways to link. We clearly identified with other people of color, and we felt that we had to link up to build our struggles together, but other people didn't seem to see it as much. I mean, we were reaching out to the Raza Unida Party, etc. I remember it always seemed like we were trying to make a connection, but we weren't really being seen . . . . [T]hey didn't understand our struggle and what our community was about. Everything was very narrow for them then.

East Wind took racial solidarity very seriously, but, as evidenced below, this was rarely reciprocated by Blacks and Chicanas/os. Nonetheless, this outward orientation was evident in the language, rhetoric, and actions of East Wind. Indeed, whenever East Wind discussed the oppression of U.S. Third World peoples, they almost never mentioned Japanese Americans exclusively but rather included other racially subordinated populations, especially Blacks. The drawing in figure 11 illustrates this multiethnic thinking.[4]

Additional factors contributing to a strong interethnic practice were demographics and geography. Relatively speaking, the Asian American population was much smaller than the Mexican and African American communities at the time. Hence activists realized that given their group's size they had to forge coalitions with others to achieve anything. This was hardly the concern of either Chicanas/os or Blacks, who, given their larger numbers, felt more empowered to act alone. This discrepancy was not lost on East Wind, as one interviewee attested: "The reality [is] that we are such a small minority in America that there's no way in hell that we could do it ourselves. There's an illusion amongst Blacks and browns that they think they can do it by themselves. And that's sad. We can't have that illusion, reality just kind of kicks our ass every time we turn around. And being this middle-man minority also makes it really important to do that outreach if you don't want to get isolated."

Closely related to demographics was *where* Nikkei activists grew up. As previously mentioned (see map 1), Japanese Americans lived in predominantly Black and Latina/o spaces and thus were familiar with multiracial environments. One activist described how the Crenshaw district, where he was raised, was mixed, as were his schools and even the gangs he joined (the Little Gents and the Ministers, respectively). Accordingly, he felt it was only natural to carry a multiethnic sensibility into his political work.

The tendency of Chicana/o and Black activists to overlook Japanese

Figure 11. People power. Popular image from *Gidra* that expresses solidarity with the struggles of other minority groups. Source: Artist unknown. *Gidra*, January 1970, p. 14.

Americans that was evident in the actions of CASA and the BPP seemed to characterize the larger movement as well. Even in Northern California, where Asian Americans had a greater presence and there was significantly more interaction, they were written out of history to a remarkable extent. Consider the Third World Strike at San Francisco State University, for example. The strike, which began in November 1968, is considered a watershed in the history of the Third World Left and particularly the Asian American movement. Yet, as Karen Umemoto has pointed out, the role of

Asian American students is largely glossed over. She notes that although many articles and books have been written on the subject, and although three of the six groups who made up the Third World Liberation Front were Asian American, they are scarcely mentioned.[5] Indeed, *On Strike, Shut It Down*, published by the San Francisco State Strike Committee, makes almost no mention of Asian Americans and devotes only one paragraph to conditions in San Francisco's Chinatown. Instead, the publication presents the strike largely as a Latina/o and Black event. "The administration needs to suppress the developing student movement. It needs to divert our potentially revolutionary direction, particularly our growing ties to Chicano and black working people in the brown and black communities. The power structure fears a united front of Third World students and militant off-campus groups in the brown and black communities. The power structures fear that we will wage an uncompromising struggle for Third World liberation. We urge Third World students to join the liberation struggle and carry out a protracted battle until all the Third World demands are met."[6]

There is some evidence of a more reciprocal set of relationships in the Bay Area, such as David Hilliard speaking at a Red Guard rally, Richard Aoki's position within the BPP, and the presence of Filipino members in some Brown Beret chapters, but the evidence is hardly overwhelming.[7] Further, much of the activity centers on *individuals* rather than organizations. Assata Shakur, a New York Panther, described how other Panthers could not understand why she wanted to meet with members of the Red Guard while in San Francisco:

> Finding the Red Guard was not at all easy. Half the people I ran into had never heard of them, and the other half only had a minimal knowledge of who they were and what they were all about. . . . I got a brother to drive me over to Chinatown to look for their headquarters. . . . He couldn't understand why a black woman wanted to hook up with Chinese revolutionaries in the first place: "ain't nobody gonna free black folks but black folks"; "those Chinese don't give a damn about you and me. All they care about is their own people and what's going on in China."[8]

Despite such stereotypes and prejudices on the part of African Americans, the irony was that the Red Guard was greatly inspired by and patterned itself after the Panthers.[9]

Although coalition work was another site for multiracial activity, even this was not always easy. Speaking of her experiences as a student at California State University, Long Beach, one member of East Wind recalled the struggles that Ana Nieto Gomez, a pivotal force for Third World unity, faced: "She really tried to keep the coalition going. And it was hard. There

Figure 12. Third World revolutionaries. In this BPP depiction of international revolutionaries, note that three are Asian, one is Black, and one is Latino. Source: Artist unknown. *Black Panther,* February 6, 1971, p. 12.

were people who were saying, 'Why should we do this? Why are we with these Orientals? They don't have any problems, they're all rich.' "[10]

Because of such attitudes the *Black Panther* rarely mentioned Asian Americans. They seemingly did not exist as a group for the BPP. There were, of course, numerous references to Asian people, and in particular to the struggles being waged in Vietnam and China. Figure 12, taken from the *Black Panther,* depicts a host of revolutionary leaders, over half of whom are Asian. The Chinese people were recognized for their struggle and the contributions of Mao, while the Vietnamese were respected for their willingness to fight the U.S. military. Yet few Chicana/o or Black interviewees mentioned Asian Americans at all, despite being asked pointedly about interracial politics. Activists were more likely to discuss Asian visitors than Asian Americans themselves. One former Panther volunteered that his chapter had a relationship with a Japanese group active in nuclear issues. But obviously, Asians and Asian Americans are two distinct populations.

> The Japanese dealt with a lot of nuclear things that we participated in. Every year they would come and we would have annual sessions to educate people around nuclear issues. The Japanese would have connections with other Asians here and Japanese [Americans]. But I think the biggest force was probably the Chinese, because of the influence that Mao had. . . . A lot of their activities came right out of Chinatown. In fact, until a few years ago, you could easily go up to Chinatown and buy a *Red Book,* which is where we bought a lot our *Red Books* from.

Only one interviewee mentioned a concrete instance of working with an Asian American organization. In this case, a Panther recalled the Storefront and the food co-op it had established and the exemplary work of Nobuko Miyamoto.[11]

During my interviews it became apparent that some recalled and interpreted the past through the lens of the present. Although this is always true to some extent, I sensed that it was more pronounced in discussions of Asian Americans. I attribute this to the tremendous expansion of the Asian American population and heightened Black/Asian tensions in contemporary Los Angeles. Over the last two decades the Asian/Pacific Islander (A/PI) and Latina/o populations have exploded while African American numbers have stagnated. Exacerbating such numerical shifts are class and racial tensions between various population segments, most notably Korean immigrant merchants and inner-city Black residents. Thus, if anything, Black and A/PI relations have become more complicated and potentially strained over time, and these developments may have eclipsed more positive memories and readings.[12]

Despite the seriousness with which East Wind pursued interracial work, it still had revolutionary nationalist tendencies. Its primary focus was the Nikkei community, and there was a question of just *how much* East Wind should work with other racial/ethnic groups. For instance, during the struggle at Rest Haven, the mental health facility in Chinatown, two Chicana/o employees began working closely with East Wind. Both were members of the working class and committed to Third World liberation, and at least one member encouraged their membership in East Wind.

> There were two Chicanos, a real good sister and brother. Some of us really wanted them to join East Wind, we're talking about multinationalism, let's practice it. But [another member] came up with all this bullshit about how culturally they would have a problem. There was no reason in the world to deny them, at least the chance, to come and meet us. But they [the membership] went for it. . . . Then, the very next draft . . . brought in this Chinese lady, a lawyer, another petty bourgeois. I guess she was a professor at a university . . . and here we had two working-class candidates, and we're supposed to be a Marxist-Leninist organization?[13]

Although it is uncertain why the Chicanas/os did not join the organization, some have suggested that there was a concern over how they would feel in a predominantly Asian American organization, whereas others intimated a more nationalist dynamic, and still others insisted that the issue was never presented to the group. In any event, the incident hints at the larger class and racial tensions underlying organizational membership: At what point does an organization's class commitment conflict with its nationalist tendencies? When does interracial and multinational work begin to threaten one's national focus? Perhaps for different reasons, both East Wind and, as we shall see, the BPP, drew the line at membership.

Whites

One group that East Wind worked little with was whites, and few whites attempted to work with the organization. If anything, because of their proximity to whiteness, Japanese Americans sought to distance themselves from the dominant racial/ethnic group. They did so partly because much of the Asian American movement, including East Wind, was focused on identity issues and developing a pan-ethnic identity—a process that was in opposition to whiteness. Moreover, there were genuine differences in whites' and Asian Americans' concerns, as seen, for example, in their opposition to the war. Finally, there was white racism. Japanese Americans, like all people of color, desired a space free from the daily prejudice, discrimination, and expectations that they encountered with whites.

Although East Wind worked with whites in the context of a united front, there were not close organizational relationships. In fact, it was common for Asian Americans to disaggregate themselves from white initiatives, as seen in the women's movement. Most of the Japanese American women interviewed had some exposure to white feminism, having attended colleges where feminism was flourishing. Women's studies was emerging at this time, and feminist study groups and women's group were proliferating. Asian American women were drawn to such activities, but many, especially those in the Third World Left, eventually broke with white feminist organizations, as they did not adequately address issues of race and class.[14]

Likewise, there is sparse evidence of whites seeking to work with Asian American leftists. Whites were far more likely to support the Black struggle and, to a lesser extent, the Chicana/o movement. Because Asian Americans were not readily seen as an oppressed group, given the model minority myth and Blacks' position within the national racial hierarchy, white activists were not drawn to their cause in large numbers. Indeed, one alternative newspaper, the *Los Angeles News Advocate,* ran a story entitled "Asian Community Beset with Woes." Apparently the "discovery" of problems among Asian Americans was considered newsworthy.[15]

One interesting exception to the pattern of limited interaction was Asian American participation in white-dominated radical groups. Just as individual Asian Americans were more apt to join Black and Chicana/o organizations, they were also more likely to join white ones. Consider, for instance, Wendy Yoshimura's participation in the controversial Symbionese Liberation Army (SLA) or Shinya Ono's membership in Weatherman.[16] Such participation reflected the nascent state of the Asian American movement and the fact that some Asian Americans were able to move easily within the white world, with all of its political implications.

THE BLACK PANTHER PARTY

The BPP, like East Wind, participated in an array of interethnic collaborations and multiracial coalitions. The nature of the relationships was different, however, insofar as many non-Blacks sought out the Panthers. The BPP occupied a privileged place within the larger revolutionary movement, and, with perhaps the notable exception of the Communist Party USA, working with the Panthers conferred political legitimacy and a touch of "revolutionary authenticity" upon non-Black leftists.[17] The BPP was the acknowledged leader of the revolutionary nationalist movement because of the positions it took, the claims it made, its style and rhetoric, and its ability to inspire, and because it was Black. As one former member put it,

> We became a threat because thousands and thousands of people began joining. Latinos, began forming the Brown Berets and other activities. We began linking with other organizations, like AIM [the American Indian Movement]. We began linking with the Weather Underground, or SDS [Students for a Democratic Society], at that time. And so it was not just the Black Panther Party. . . . While we were singled out because of the initiative we took and the call for our right to self-defense, we found that in linking with others [we] created the kind of threat against the capitalist, who maintained the kind of control over our community that brought them the profit and us the misery.

The interethnic politics of the BPP can be divided into two categories: its work among whites and among other people of color. Such a distinction arises from the different positions that whites and people of color occupied in the racial hierarchy as well as the nature of the relationships. The relationships between the BPP and whites varied and were often unequal. In all cases, whites provided resources, and, while often their political motivations were genuine, sometimes the desired payback was the "revolutionary chic" the party offered. In contrast, its ties to other people of color were more reciprocal and predicated on an exchange of solidarity (although not entirely devoid of such desires). Both types of relationships were necessary for building a broad-based movement. Bobby Seale summarized these differing dynamics. "Alliances with groups like Los Siete have worked out a lot better than coalitions with white liberals because the brown American people are suffering from the same things black Americans are. The Young Lords, a Puerto Rican gang that turned political, works in alliance with the Black Panther Party in Chicago and New York. They're suffering the same oppressive conditions that black people are subject to. There's also the Young Patriots who are a vanguard in the poor white communities, we can relate well with them because they are in opposition to the power structure's oppression."[18] As suggested, what distinguishes these relationships is not race per se but the group's position vis-à-vis larger power relations.

Whites

Among the general public the perception existed that the BPP was antiwhite and an exclusively Black political project. This belief was fostered by the FBI and local police in an effort to discredit the BPP but was also attributable to the Panthers' scathing critiques of mainstream society and their inflammatory rhetoric, in which they railed against whites and "pigs." Nonetheless, such a position is simplistic and ignores significant evidence to the contrary. Despite such apparent hostility, the BPP worked closely with many whites in numerous capacities. Instances of collaboration include the BPP's close ties to the Peace and Freedom Party (PFP), its relationship to SDS, and its practice of turning to wealthy whites, particularly the Hollywood crowd, for financial and legal support. Moreover, many white lawyers, particularly Jewish ones, figured prominently in the pantheon of behind-the-scenes supporters.

While no one has researched systematically the relationship between whites and the BPP, several autobiographies and personal memoirs suggest that the BPP was more closely involved with whites than with other peoples of color, despite its rhetoric of Third World solidarity. Although such a conclusion comes from a largely biased data set—whites writing about their own political experiences—such a finding is not inconceivable. Undergirding such patterns, of course, was the power of the Black-white racial binary. In a society that saw itself largely in Black and white terms, it was inevitable that the Panthers would direct their political analyses and ire toward whites and white privilege and that they would target white support. Though some whites were certainly driven by guilt, many recognized the racist nature of U.S. society and were committed to changing it, including challenging racism within white communities.

The simple fact that Blacks were considered to be *the* most oppressed and visible group in the United States meant that sympathetic whites were apt to be drawn to their struggle. In addition to their subordinated status, however, the Panthers articulated what appeared to be the most revolutionary politics around, which inevitably caught the attention of white radicals. According to Todd Gitlin, "The Panthers were streetwise, disciplined, fearless, Marxist-Leninist, revolutionary, and most miraculously of all, at a time when most other black militants donned dashikis and glowered at whites, they welcomed white allies. . . . In that supercharged atmosphere, there was a law of the transferability of revolutionary credentials. Late New Left factions played the Panther card to certify themselves as righteous revolutionaries."[19] In addition to self-promotion, however, whites had resources, skills, and connections that the Panthers desperately needed. This was especially true in the legal arena. Besides breaking the law and engaging in armed conflict with police, the BPP was constantly harassed by local law enforcement, thus necessitating a small army of lawyers. One Panther interviewed, for example, recounted how he was stopped by the Los Angeles Police Department (LAPD) and how the officer measured the distance from the ground to the fender of his car. After the officer concluded that the vehicle was too low, he arrested the Panther. Such harassment required a constant stream of legal representation that was not readily available within the BPP itself. While many individuals volunteered their services, in Los Angeles a legal collective called Bar Sinister was formed to provide legal support to the BPP and other radicals.[20]

Gitlin's point regarding the BPP's willingness to work with whites is significant. Though whites had a range of responses to their displacement from the movement by Black Power, many still carried a deep commitment to Black liberation, and the BPP was one of the few organizations to engage them. Even though the BPP never allowed whites to actually join the party, it accepted white support and encouraged whites to organize within their own communities.

One example of such an approach was the BPP's relationship with the PFP. The PFP was a mass-based electoral movement created in California to promote a viable third party. Although there is a long history of Blacks and whites working together, this relationship was unique because, "for the first time in the history of this country, a black organization, the Black Panther Party, was in a position to initiate a principled relationship between blacks and whites."[21] This relationship began in 1968 with the campaign to free Huey Newton. Subsequently, numerous Panthers ran on the Peace and Freedom ticket, with Eldridge Cleaver eventually running for president. Although the PFP and the BPP worked in coalition, it was uncertain how people of color should be incorporated into the PFP. Despite the potentially reciprocal nature of the partnership, the coalition eventually floundered over such stumbling blocks as policing. Not all PFP members were comfortable with the BPP's line on community policing—a disagreement that points to the different racial and class positions of each organization's membership.[22]

The BPP had a more complex relationship with SDS. Many members of SDS highly esteemed the Panthers and recognized them as the leaders of the U.S. revolutionary movement. By 1969 SDS had offered its full support to the BPP: "When the leading black revolutionary group is continually harassed, its leaders jailed, hounded out of the country and brutally assassinated, when Panther members daily face the provocations of the ruling class and its racist pigs, when their blood has been spilled and their list of revolutionary martyrs—Huey, Eldridge, Bobby Hutton, Bunchy Carter, John Huggins—increases daily, then the time has come for SDS to give total and complete support to their defense efforts. To do less would be a mockery of the word, 'revolutionary.' "[23]

SDS assisted the Panthers in various ways. Aside from according the organization the respect due the vanguard, SDS formed Newton-Cleaver Defense Committees, produced and disseminated information on the Black struggle, and cultivated relationships with local chapters and the national leadership. Things grew complicated, however, as SDS became increasingly Marxist-Leninist and dominated by the Progressive Labor Party (PL), which was hostile to nationalist struggles. Tensions between the PL and SDS, as well as assorted factions, came to a head at the 1969 SDS convention. Representatives of revolutionary nationalist organizations, namely the BPP, the Brown Berets, and the Young Lords, issued a statement condemning the PL for not supporting oppressed nationalities and warned that SDS would be judged by the company it kept. While this produced ample tension in its own right, the individual Panthers who spoke at the conference were misogynist, which, in addition to the larger PL/SDS conflict, threw the entire convention into disarray.[24]

This event, while small in and of itself, sheds light on the Panthers' contradictory behavior and attitudes toward whites. While the BPP worked closely with whites and the party condemned white racism and privilege rather than white people per se, not all individual Panthers shared these positions. For example, some Los Angeles Panthers' only exposure to whites was the police, so it was difficult for them to overcome distrust and hostility toward whites. Complicating such prejudice was the Panther practice of "liberating" money and other necessary resources from Blacks, whites, and others. Moreover, several whites were victims of violence and murders linked to the Panthers, and while such attacks have appropriately been condemned, the reality was that Blacks were far more likely to be victimized by

Panther violence. In yet another instance, Eldridge Cleaver, in *Soul on Ice*, discussed raping white women as a means of avenging whites. In short, an antiwhite undercurrent permeated elements of the BPP membership.

The PFP, SDS, and Weatherman all represent primarily national-level relationships, but the PFP also had a significant presence in Southern California. In both the Bay Area and Los Angeles, the PFP attracted a wide following and enabled whites to support the BPP without actually working in the organization itself.

Aside from such formalized activities, there was a larger circle of white support. Although white support for the BPP existed across the United States, Southern California was unique because of Hollywood. The entertainment industry was flush with cash, and Hollywood had long supported left-wing causes. Elaine Brown has documented the numerous ways in which relationships were cultivated with wealthy whites in the entertainment industry, including Don and Shirley Sutherland, Don Freed, Jon Voigt, Susan St. James, Jane Fonda, Bert Schneider, and Jean Seberg. Their support took a variety of forms, including hosting fund-raisers, paying the party's bills, and contributing to the breakfast program.[25]

Not all white supporters were wealthy or famous, however. Shirl Buss, then a white UCLA undergraduate, invited Elaine Brown and Joe Brown (no relation) to her sorority, Kappa Alpha Theta. The Panthers educated the sorority sisters about their struggle and raised money. Buss recalled that the pair brought a LAPD bullet to demonstrate what they were up against. Needless to say, bullets were not part of the daily lives of most sorority women, and they were duly impressed.[26] I tell this anecdote to illustrate the degree to which the Panthers were willing to engage a variety of populations, even the most unlikely candidates.

During my research, I asked interviewees about the nature of the Panthers' relationships with other organizations. Each person assured me that the party had excellent relations with all revolutionary groups, with the notable exception of US. However, as I probed further, I realized that few actually had personal contacts with either whites or other people of color, suggesting that perhaps such relationships were managed at a higher level and did not involve the daily participation of rank-and-file members.[27] This finding would apply even more so to the underground, which, by definition, kept its Panther identity secret. Such patterns provide important clues as to how the Panthers managed their relationships with whites: whites could donate funds, provide legal services, raise bail money, build ancillary movements, and furnish contacts and advice, but they could not join the organization itself.

Other People of Color

Any consideration of the relationship between the Panthers and other people of color must acknowledge the degree to which other organizations were influenced by and emulated the BPP. Such groups include the AIM, the Young Lords, the Brown Berets, the Red Guard, and the Black Berets. Many organizations developed programs similar to the BPP's platform. Groups studied the Panthers' program and crafted points particular to their needs and concerns. Moreover, numerous leaders, such as Leonard Peltier of AIM, have explicitly acknowledged the role of the BPP in the formation of their organizations. "They're [the BPP] the ones who came out and showed us how to organize successfully."[28] Individuals from various communities of color frequently sought out the Panthers to learn about them and to find out how they could build similar organizations. Such initiatives led to an assortment of relationships, ranging from the very close, such as that between the Young Lords and the BPP in New York, to the more distant, such as that between the Panthers and the Red Guard. In Southern California, the Brown Berets were somewhat close to the BPP. As one former Beret described the relationship between the groups, "We had good working relations [with them]. Whenever a Panther got killed, we would go to their funerals, we would march with them. I remember one time we were in the parking lot of the funeral parlor and the Panthers and the Berets were lined up and Bobby Seale came by to greet everyone and review us."[29]

One reason for the BPP's wide appeal was its internationalist framework. Despite its base in the Black community, a close examination of BPP texts reveals that the party called for the freedom and liberation of *all* poor and oppressed people, not just African Americans. A brief comparison of the 1966 and 1972 Ten-Point Programs suggests how the BPP broadened its horizons over time (table 9). As can be seen, the community of concern, while still centered on Blacks, had expanded by 1972 to include both "other people of color" and "oppressed communities." Oppressed communities was a useful catch-all category insofar as it could, theoretically, include whites without explicitly naming them.[30]

I found that virtually all Panthers interviewed were aware of the Brown Berets and saw them as a parallel organization in the Chicana/o community. There were, however, varying levels of familiarity and involvement with Chicana/o activists and organizations, even though the *Black Panther* often reported on Mexican American issues. Carlos Montes recalled that at one of the Berets' first actions many Panthers came and joined in a vigil, a gesture that meant a great deal to the fledgling organization. Likewise, the BPP (and

Table 9 *Comparison of selected elements of the 1966 and 1972 ten-point programs*

1966 Ten-Point Program	1972 Ten-Point Program
1. We want freedom. We want power to determine the destiny of our black community.	1. We want freedom. We want power to determine the destiny of our black and oppressed communities.
3. We want an end to the robbery by the capitalists of our black community.	3. We want an end to the robbery by the capitalists of our black and oppressed communities.
7. We want an immediate end to police brutality and murder of black people.	7. We want an immediate end to police brutality and murder of black people, other people of color, all oppressed people inside the United States.
8. We want freedom for all black men held in federal, state, county, and city prisons and jails.	9. We want freedom for all black and oppressed people now held in U.S. federal, state, county, city and military prisons and jails. We want trials by a jury of peers for all persons charged with so-called crimes under the laws of this country.

SOURCES: *Black Panther,* August 9, 1969, 26; Huey Newton, *War against the Panthers: A Study of Repression in America* (New York: Harlem River Press, 1996), 123–26.

its offspring, the Coalition Against Police Abuse) worked with CASA on police abuse and surveillance issues. Nonetheless, most Panthers' knowledge of Mexican Americans did not extend significantly beyond name recognition and recalling a few joint events—although some went to great lengths to emphasize the parallels between the two communities.[31]

While the Panthers and Berets were often seen as parallel organizations, the BPP also cultivated relationships with those who did not share its revolutionary ideology, including the UFW. The Panthers viewed the UFW as the leading organization of the Chicana/o movement and sought to stand in solidarity with it. Besides reporting regularly on the UFW in the *Black Panther,* the Panthers orchestrated a meeting between Cesar Chávez and Bobby Seale at which Chávez pledged to send UFW members to work on Seale's mayoral campaign in Oakland. In turn, the BPP sent the following message to "Brother Chávez": "[W]e wish to express to you, Cesar Chávez, to the entire membership of the United Farmworkers Organizing Committee, and to the countless Mexican-American and other minority men, women, and children whose lives are currently and callously being parleyed for profits by deceitful growers and opposition unions, our complete and open solidarity and support with your efforts to secure the basic human rights for the farmworkers of this country."[32]

Though Los Angeles was not a key site of American Indian revolutionary activity, the Panthers were aware of and supportive of the larger Native struggle, particularly AIM. Once again, the *Black Panther* reported regularly on American Indian issues, and AIM and the BPP made overtures to support each other. For instance, the BPP attended various AIM events, and members of AIM, when in Los Angeles, would visit the Panthers.[33] The revolutionary status of American Indians was somewhat analogous to that of the Panthers in that they were considered to have suffered grievously at the hands of whites, the United States, and capitalism, so that, regardless of their population's size, they were seen as bona fide revolutionaries and their struggles were taken seriously.

> There were several groups that we linked with. . . . [O]ne was AIM and the demands that they were putting forth for sovereignty; their right to determine their own destiny . . . was right up our alley. We always said that everybody already knows how the Native Americans were wiped out, and those who were left were talking mucho shit. We could relate to that, and the whole Alcatraz situation, and the various walks that took place. They [were] willing to come to where we were at, to rallies, and to participate. While it may have been too late to really change history, as the people should have, we all embraced the Native American struggle. Almost every movement I knew of embraced it. But again, it may have been too little to roll back the kinds of abuses and attacks that Native American people suffered. That doesn't mean it can't be changed now, but we're talking about change for a handful of people. The rest of them were denied it, genocide. So to that extent, it was too late. They did a walk every year and stopped by here [Los Angeles], and did a powwow. Different people come and we have food for them. We have Native Americans come down here from Lone Pine, they stay right here in our office.[34]

In contrast to the BPP's relationship to American Indians was their relationship to Asian Americans. Asian Americans, as previously mentioned, though actively supporting the BPP in a variety of capacities in both Northern and Southern California, rarely registered on the BPP's political radar. This relative invisibility is a good example of how hegemonic ideology operates: while only a handful of Blacks and Latinas/os recognized Asian Americans as an oppressed group, even fewer voiced an awareness of what the racial role assigned to Asian Americans meant for them. Instead, most just dismissed Asian Americans as a nonoppressed group without considering how the "model minority" image was oppressive to all people of color, as seen in its ability to erase noneconomic forms of racism and the humanity of Asian Americans. Because they were not characterized by the widespread poverty and misery of Mexican Americans, Puerto Ricans, and American Indians, and because they lacked the numbers, wealth, resources, and power of whites, Asian Americans were rendered invisible.

In summary, the BPP, while very much a Black Power organization, consciously forged links with whites, international revolutionaries, and other people of color in the United States. These relationships were highly uneven and reflected to a degree each group's racial and class position and what they could contribute to an alliance, including resources, connections, solidarity, and revolutionary credentials. While such relationships were highly strategic, they also embodied a real desire to create a new political culture and broad-based movement predicated on Third World unity.

CASA

CASA represents a third approach to interethnic politics, sharing elements of both East Wind and the BPP. While CASA was perhaps the least concerned with developing relationships with other racial/ethnic groups, it was the only organization to admit whites, and it did extensive solidarity work with other Latinas/os. Though CASA joined numerous coalitions and participated in united front work, it was less inclined to emphasize multiracial activism for its own sake, focusing instead on its target population, Mexicanas/os—hardly surprising given CASA's nationalist roots. Although CASA distanced itself from the narrow and cultural nationalist tendencies that characterized *el movimiento,* it was still very much a product of that historical moment.

CASA's relatively less aggressive outreach to other people of color was due partly to Mexican Americans' racial position. CASA was based in a fairly sizable population that was clearly recognized as a "minority" and that offered a large working class from which to potentially build a mass movement. Consequently, CASA was not overly preoccupied with its identity as an oppressed people, and, as alluded to earlier, because of its size, it often felt that it could "go it alone." Yet unlike the BPP, which, as the acknowledged leader of the Third World Left, understood its responsibility to promote solidarity, CASA occupied a more intermediate location. In short, CASA did not feel overly responsible for fostering such ties, and while white radicals were not clamoring to join CASA, numerous whites, Latinas/os, and some African

Americans *did* want to work with the organization. These patterns reflect Mexican Americans' place within the racial hierarchy: they were clearly recognized as an oppressed group, but not to the same degree as Blacks.

Whites

CASA was the only organization among those studied that allowed whites to become members. The whites who joined tended to be deeply interested in questions of immigration and the unjust treatment of undocumented workers. Such individuals were frequently lawyers or otherwise involved in immigrant and workers' rights rather than active supporters of the Chicana/o movement itself (although some overlap existed). Hence whites often focused more on immigration and work issues than on questions of political ideology. In addition to addressing a compelling set of issues, CASA enjoyed dynamic leadership, including the Rodriguez brothers, who were known for their powerful oratorical style and political analysis. One former CASA member noted, "There were some pretty charismatic people running CASA at the time, real community leaders. And the opportunity to learn from these individuals was important. That was my goal, I'm sure it was the same for everybody else." Such leadership served to attract the support and membership of Latinas/os, whites, and others.

Underscoring its ties to the immigration community and its relationship with whites was CASA's location. At one point the Los Angeles chapter was located in a building on Pico Boulevard, the first floor of which was devoted largely to immigration services, thus encouraging an exchange between CASA and immigration advocates of all colors.

Although whites were allowed to join CASA, they were not actively recruited. In contrast, some African Americans were. For instance, a Black activist with the Venceremos Brigade who worked closely with a wide spectrum of the left was invited to join the organization but preferred to maintain her focus on Cuba. Initially, because of CASA's structure as a series of autonomous centers, the question of white membership was decided locally by each chapter. As the organization developed, however, pressure mounted to systematically address the issue. CASA's eventual decision to allow white membership was unprecedented within the larger Chicana/o movement. Marisela Rodríguez Chávez has argued that the organization's class and internationalist framework contributed to this decision.

> While CASA saw itself as the vanguard for Mexicanos/Chicanos in the U.S. and Mexico, their class vision allowed them to form ties and allegiances with other people of color. It even allowed them to form allegiances with Euro-Americans committed to social change.

The incorporation of Euro-American women did not come without challenges. Jana Adkins became a member of CASA in Seattle through her work in the Chicano/Mexicano community there. After moving to Los Angeles in 1976 to work on *Sin Fronteras,* some CASA members questioned her nomination to the Interim Political Commission because she was Euro-American. Others[,] . . . however, supported her nomination. . . . "As progressive activists of all colors and nationalities, we try to understand that the nationalism of an oppressed nationality has a progressive character when it is directed against the source of national oppression. However, it loses that character when it becomes narrow, especially within an organization fighting racism and national oppression." Adkins [did] not recall any negative feedback due to her race, but [did] recall consciously not seeking leadership and power because she did not feel it her place to do so.[35]

In addition to its political ideology, CASA may have been open to whites because few members felt threatened by them, either personally or politically. As one member explained, "There were definitely [those] who felt that there was a need to focus on people who were sensitive to Latino issues, sensitive to the plight of immigrants. . . . I just remember there being that openness, and I think it partly was because we already had people that filled those roles." This is an important point that distinguishes CASA from earlier Chicana/o political activism and reflects the empowerment that had occurred because of the movement.

Another exceptional characteristic of CASA was that it was the least likely of the groups to engage in antiwhite rhetoric. Such language was part and parcel of the BPP's style, and it was not unheard of for East Wind and certainly more nationalist Chicana/o organizations, such as the Brown Berets, MEChA (El Movimiento Estudiantil Chicano de Aztlán/the Chicano Student Movement of Aztlán), and La Raza Unida Party, to demonize whites. In contrast, adhering to a Marxist-Leninist analysis, CASA interpreted white racism as a function of capitalism and imperialism and not of white people per se. This approach, while principled, may have affected who was drawn to CASA. The absence of such strident rhetoric may have made the organization seemingly "safe" for whites, but by the same token, nationalist and antiracist activists may have been less attracted to it.

In addition to organizational membership, CASA interacted with whites in various fronts and coalitions. CASA regularly participated in coalitions covering an array of issues and events, including the Bicentennial, the *Bakke* decision, police harassment, International Women's Day, and the National Coalition for Fair Immigration Laws and Practices.

Other People of Color

CASA also had a range of relationships with other people of color. Most notably, it cultivated intense alliances with Puerto Ricans and Mexicans, while enjoying more formal coalitional relationships with Blacks. As in the BPP, there was limited acknowledgment or recognition of Asian Americans within CASA, despite the potential link of immigration. This contradiction was not entirely unnoticed by CASA members. As one interviewee observed, "We were organizing around immigrant workers, but [only] Latinos. But yet, we were in an immigrant community of Asians of many different cultures." Part of this is attributable to CASA's view of Asians as not quite Third World people, but, equally important, few Asian American radicals were concentrating on Asian immigration at that time. Indeed, when Asian American activists reported working with CASA and participating in pro-immigrant events, the goal seemed to be more solidarity with Chicanas/os than immigration per se. Of course, all of this would change shortly—by the 1980s immigration would become an issue of paramount importance for Asian American activists as well.

CASA invested far more resources in building coalitions with African Americans. Although CASA and the BPP appear to have had different areas of concern, there was one important area of overlap—police abuse. One of the community initiatives that preceded the formation of CASA was the Committee to Free Los Tres (CFLT) (see chapter 4). Given this history, plus the surveillance and harassment that CASA was subjected to, the organization was vigilant against police abuse, a perspective shared by the BPP. For instance, at a rally supporting the Reverend Ben Chavis and the Wilmington 10, speakers included both African Americans and members of CASA,[36] in what the latter considered to be an important moment of Black-Latina/o solidarity.

Of particular concern to both organizations were political prisoners. The BPP counted numerous political prisoners among its ranks, and, though to a far lesser extent, so did CASA. "Neutralizing" revolutionaries was one of the goals of the FBI's Counter Intelligence Program (COINTELPRO). *Neutralizing* meant rendering certain individuals ineffective through various means. Under the auspices of COINTELPRO the FBI and local law enforcement routinely framed or otherwise implicated revolutionaries with an array of charges ensuring that they were locked away for extensive periods and thus unable to conduct political work. Central to such activities was the illegal monitoring of thousands of innocent citizens. Established by Chief Ed Davis in 1970, the Public Disorder Intelligence Division developed files on fifty-five thousand individuals and organizations, in what obviously posed a threat to all activists (and others) in Los Angeles.[37]

In addition to being a major issue in its own right, the issue of political prisoners allowed CASA to underscore its commitment to the Black struggle. Consider, for example, a press release that CASA issued in response to George Jackson's death.

> CASA . . . a national *Mexicano* organization is proud to offer this message of solidarity in this tribute to a fallen *compañero* and class fighter George Jackson. We consider him as our own, as if he were *Mexicano* and had come from our barrios, precisely because as well as being a champion of his people he was truly a class fighter.
>
> We organize and defend workers whether or not they have the proper immigration documentation required by the state. These were the very same things which guided *compañero* George Jackson in his never-ceasing struggle against the repression of the capitalist state.[38]

CASA's expression of solidarity is interesting insofar as it attempts to claim Jackson as one "of our own," thereby erasing the differences between Blacks and Mexicanas/os. Although there is little evidence that Jackson ever mobilized on behalf of immigrant workers, such a position would likely have been in keeping with his larger political perspective. Here, CASA's approach to solidarity was not so much finding common ground as claiming and projecting its concerns and history onto others.

CASA's take on political prisoners had a slight twist from that of other groups: immigration. Because a significant portion of the Mexican-origin population was composed of immigrants, citizenship often complicated political prisoners' cases, as in the well-publicized ordeal of José Jacques "Pepe" Medina. Medina was a political activist in Mexico who was forced to flee after the 1968 student uprisings and related political activities. After coming to the United States in 1973, he became involved in organizing workers and eventually became a member of CASA. The FBI, through its surveillance activities, arrested Medina in 1976. But because of his immigrant status he was then delivered to the Immigration and Naturalization Service (INS), which sought to deport him. Medina, in turn, demanded political asylum, given that he faced political persecution if returned to Mexico, and argued that the U.S. government had "no right to deport him from lands which historically belong to the Mexican people."[39] Thus he used his case to highlight not only the problematic nature of U.S. asylum policy but also its imperialist legacy. Although the case was fraught with irregularities, the United States denied Medina's asylum request in 1977. CASA was instrumental in helping to form the José Medina Defense Committee and used the case to raise consciousness around political activism, immigration, and asylum: "We are not just fighting for Medina. We are also fighting for thousands of Haitians, Africans and other third world people fleeing fascist, US supported regimes, who have the courage to seek asylum here in the heart of imperialism. Our efforts will continue until we have turned around their policy of 'blanket asylum' to sympathizers of right wing regimes, while denying it to those who escape those regimes."[40]

CASA and the Defense Committee articulated their concerns so that they were able to link issues of immigration, political asylum, U.S. imperialism, and political prisoners. For instance, at one point the San Quentin Six attended a rally in support of Medina.[41] Besides its organizing potential, the Medina case was significant because it succeeded in forcing the INS to inform applicants in writing why their case had been denied and allowed them to challenge State Department decisions.

Aside from shared concerns over police abuse and political imprisonment, CASA supported the Black struggle to some extent in *Sin Fronteras*.[42] Like other organizations, CASA recognized the centrality of the BPP to the larger movement, although forging close ties was not a top priority. However, it is important to understand *which* Panther Party CASA supported. Recall that the Southern California chapter was nearly obliterated after the December 1969 police shoot-out and subsequent retrenchment in Oakland. It took a while for the Southern California Panthers to regroup, during which time CASA (and East Wind) were born. Thus it was the second generation of Panthers, so to speak, that CASA worked with. Eventually, Michael Zinzun, who was a Panther, left the organization and established the Coalition Against Police Abuse, which CASA joined.[43]

Despite such support, CASA's membership was not free of prejudice toward Blacks. In discussing CASA's various contradictions, one member recalled that even though the organization defined itself as multinational, it was not uncommon to hear members refer to Blacks as "*pinche mayates*" (a pejorative expression), though one CASA leader assured me that anyone using such language at a formal event would have been seriously reprimanded. Such prejudice was not inconceivable due to several factors, including the degree to which Mexican Americans had internalized the larger society's attitudes toward African Americans; Mexico's historic prejudice toward Blacks and Indians; and the racial hierarchy itself. Mexican Americans have at times taken pains to distance themselves from Blacks and participated in their denigration in order to bolster their own racial position.[44] Because of this history the Chicana/o activism of the 1960s and 1970s, particularly CASA's multinationalism, should be seen as quite radical.

CASA's interethnic activism went beyond African Americans and the BPP, however. CASA participated in such multinational formations as the Venceremos Brigade and the founding of the People's Alliance. The alliance was an effort to solidify an oppositional movement that had been forged through the July Fourth Coalition. It consisted of representatives from the Puerto Rican Socialist Party, the BPP, the International Indian Treaty Council, the American Indian Movement, the Mass Party Organizing Committee, and CASA. In its preliminary statement the alliance defined its purpose as follows: "We believe that it is necessary and possible to begin taking the first steps, nationally and locally, towards building a strategic alliance of working and oppressed peoples against our common enemy, the industrial and financial rulers and the state they control. This alliance will be born and grow out of our mutual commitment to unite our forces in joint defense against the enemy's attacks and to learn to pool our strength in counterattacks against the system of U.S. imperialism."[45]

CASA worked with American Indians through such formal channels as the People's Alliance. There is little evidence, however, that CASA attempted to forge a deeper and more sustained relationship with American Indians.

The lack of interest in American Indians contrasts with CASA's relationship to other Latinas/os. It may come as a surprise to some, but few organizations within *el movimiento* in the Los Angeles area sought to build relationships with other Latina/o groups. One reason for this was the cultural nationalist tendencies of the movement, which emphasized, not solidarity and coalition with other Latinas/os, but rather Chicanas/os' indigenous roots and history. In addition, in Southern California the ethnic Mexican population completely dominated all other Latina/o groups. There simply was not a large and consolidated Puerto Rican, Guatemalan, Cuban, or Salvadoran population in Los Angeles—that would not come until the 1980s. Though CASA was relatively nationalist, it pursued contacts with other Latina/o revolutionaries. Doing so enabled members of CASA to learn from more advanced revolutionaries and offered a degree of comfort and pleasure in working with other Latinas/os, as Chicanas/os were in the process of reconfiguring their identity. Working with Mexicans, Puerto Ricans, and Cubans fit with CASA's larger goal of building an internationalist movement, *sin fronteras*, and contributed to CASA's meeting its political soul mate, the Puerto Rican Socialist Party (PSP).

The PSP was arguably one of the leading Latina/o left organizations of the time in the United States. It emerged in 1971 when the Pro-Independence Movement transformed itself into a Marxist-Leninist organization. Although New York is considered the bastion of Puerto Rican politics in the

United States, the struggle came to California, particularly the Bay Area, in the late 1960s. Despite a much smaller presence in Southern California, CASA worked closely with the local PSP support committee and forged an even closer relationship with the PSP in New York. This alliance began at a local conference entitled "International Conference of the Americas," in which representatives of both the PSP and CASA were invited to speak. The relationship solidified as both organizations participated in events geared toward internationalist and left youth, including the World Festival of Youth and Students.[46] Eventually, CASA and the PSP developed a formal alliance based on a shared set of principles. CASA helped to sell *Claridad*, the PSP's newspaper, and the two groups supported each other's events (see figure 13), engaged in political dialogue, and had member exchanges.

Though the relationship between CASA and the PSP was not inevitable, it was hardly surprising, as they complemented each other in numerous ways. First, both organizations were internationalist and opposed to imperialism. Second, each was struggling with similar questions of identity, nation, territory, and self-determination. According to the CASA member Nativo Lopez, "[We] saw in the PSP experience very similar things to what we were dealing with, identity, the 'national question,' were we a minority within the US working class, or from the Aztlán nation, or part of México? The debates never ended. This fed the interest in maintaining a relationship with the PSP comrades."[47]

Besides the political overlap, there was a cultural affinity between CASA and the PSP. Although Puerto Rican, Mexican, and Mexican American cultures are distinct, commonalities still exist, including the Spanish language, the historical role of Catholicism and colonization, and *mestizaje*. It is conceivable to place the cultural exchange between the PSP and CASA within the context of a nascent "pan-ethnic Latina/o" identity that began to emerge in urban areas in the 1980s. Felix Padilla has explored how, for example, salsa music served to bring a diversity of Latinas/os, primarily Mexican Americans and Puerto Ricans, together in Chicago.[48] Though the Caribbean parts of Mexico are known for their *musica tropical,* salsa is not a Mexican musical form but is more associated with Cuba and Puerto Rico. But it has drawn millions of fans, Latinas/os and non-Latinas/os alike. Zoilo Cruz, a former member of the PSP, recalled that cultural identity was one of the key factors uniting various Latina/o groups at that time in Los Angeles.

> MacArthur Park was a neighborhood in Los Angeles where many Latinos, including Puerto Ricans, gathered. Music was played, picnics were organized, and political recruiting took place among the crowds.
> One important source of financial funds for the cell, in addition to the

Figure 13. Roy Brown concert flier. CASA forged close links with the Puerto Rican Socialist Party, including co-sponsoring events. Source: Box 41, folder 12, CASA Collection. Courtesy of Antonio Rodriguez and Department of Special Collections, Stanford University Libraries.

members' dues, [was] "salsa" dances. Salsa became a glue that united various Latino constituencies with Puerto Ricans as connectors between the various groups. Most of the relationships at this time were with Chicanos, including the Brown Berets, due to the fact that African American organizations were in disarray because of government repression.[49]

Perhaps because of CASA's nationalist tendencies, a true pan-ethnic Latina/o identity was never a real possibility, but there was a genuine connection that was as much political as cultural between Mexican American and Puerto Rican activists.

Between the rhetoric of Third World solidarity and the intense nationalist (albeit revolutionary) impulses that drove elements of the movement, each organization negotiated its interethnic relations with great care. Activists understood that they were on the cusp of something new requiring unprecedented levels of cooperation, but such desires had to be balanced against the community work they were engaged in as well as larger political objectives. The significant differences in how East Wind, the BPP, and CASA handled these relationships are not random but reflect each organization's political ideology, as well as the racial and class position of its membership.

While all of the Third World Left voiced a strong commitment to internationalism and multinationalism, the implementation of these politics varied by organization and place. Research by Jason Ferreira on the Third World Left in Northern California suggests there might have been more cooperation among groups in the Bay Area. Two reasons might account for these differences. First was simple demographics. Chicanas/os and Mexicanas/os were less dominant and the Latina/o population of the Bay Area was more diverse, while Asian Americans were far more numerous. A second issue was geography. Even though the Bay Area was hardly exempt from segregation, there was a great deal more diversity in working-class communities of color. Because of Los Angeles's sprawl and segregation, it was almost impossible for activists of different racial/ethnic groups to interact without cars.[50] In contrast, the geography and transportation systems of the Bay Area did not pose such an impediment. In any event, the politics of solidarity within the Third World Left were far more complex than a first glance might suggest. Moreover, many of the patterns of interaction reflect issues that we still are grappling with today.

SEVEN

Patriarchy and Revolution

Gender Relations in the Third World Left

The topic of gender relations in the New Left, particularly the Third World Left, is vast, and researchers have only begun exploring it. Much of the general literature on the movement has a de facto masculine perspective insofar as it either was authored by men or, more typically, focused on them. Nevertheless, gender permeates the Third World Left, because somewhat like race, it structures our culture, society, everyday life, and sense of self. Hence feminists have argued that "[p]art of what 'gender consciousness' embraces is recognition that one's relationship to the political world is at least partly . . . shaped by being female or male."[1]

That gender inequality was not a primary concern of the Third World Left does not negate the gendered nature of the project. Men and women brought with them a particular gender consciousness, and activists quickly learned that political work entailed the articulation of gender roles, meanings, and practices, as seen in hypermasculine representations, the predominance of male leadership, gendered divisions of labor, and the very fact that few organizations focused on gender equality itself. Indeed, Paula Giddings has observed that "a male-conscious motif ran throughout the society in the sixties."[2] Yet simply acknowledging the patriarchal nature of revolutionary nationalism hardly conveys the richness and complexity of its gender dynamics. Instead, gender relations should be viewed as a fundamental site of struggle for all participants. Many women confronted raw sexism and had to grapple with the contradictions of their organizations, while numerous men struggled with being labeled "male chauvinists." The precise nature of gender dynamics and tensions varied from group to group, depending upon a group's class position, political ideology, and racialization experience.

A discussion of gender relations first requires consideration of several contextual issues. As always, there is the business of historical context.

Though the Third World Left could certainly be categorized as patriarchal, so too could the larger society at the time. Although we still have far to go, gender equality has advanced considerably over the last thirty years. Thus, to a certain extent, the Third World Left simply reflected the gender relations of the larger society as well as those of particular racial/ethnic groups.[3]

Second, it must be appreciated that gender relations changed over the life of an organization. Sheila Rowbotham has argued that during times of revolutionary ferment women often develop a feminist consciousness, as more political space is available in which to challenge patriarchal relations.[4] As female participation in the Third World Left grew, women became increasingly aware and critical of gender inequality. The more women and men worked together, the more apparent were the contradictions between the rhetoric of freedom and equality and the lived reality, and these in turn led to organizational conflict and change.

A final issue to consider is the larger women's movement. While few members of the BPP, East Wind, or CASA actually participated in the mainstream women's movement, and while indeed many were openly hostile to it, they nevertheless benefited from the political turmoil and changing consciousness it engendered. Although most of the Third World Left eschewed what they saw as the inability of the women's movement to fully incorporate race and class into its analysis, the very presence of the movement forced activists of color to formulate their own position on race, class, and gender.[5] If Asian American women, for example, did not support feminism as articulated by white women, what did they believe?

This chapter, like the work of Tracye Matthews on the BPP, analyzes both formal and informal aspects of organizations' gender relations.[6] Formal aspects include statements and positions, organizational structures and rules, and official practices. For example, was the group represented in masculine form? Was women's liberation part of its platform? Informal aspects include everyday practices, or negotiations within the group that were not necessarily for public consumption. Such contestations, which characterized some of the most intense conflicts, included romantic relationships, sexual expectations, violence, and domestic responsibilities.

Rather than provide a complete treatment of gender relations for each organization, I aim to convey the *breadth* of gender issues.[7] In this chapter I first provide a general framework for the gender relations of the Third World Left. Drawing largely on the work of feminists of color, I argue that the Third World Left must be seen as a site of gender struggle. Specifically, it was an effort to reestablish the status and privilege of subordinated men. This was not, however, an uncontested project, for women were unwilling to submit to them and articulated diverse opinions regarding gender relations and their role as women. In the second part of the chapter I shift to the gender relations of each organization.

Though critical of its sexism, I do not wish to diminish the empowering and transformative capacity of the Third World Left. While patriarchy created tensions, reduced organizational efficacy, and warped individuals, such organizations also offered women of color an unprecedented opportunity to fight for their communities and develop themselves, and they offered men, at least those so inclined, an alternative way of claiming their masculinity. One female Panther described the empowerment she experienced: "You have to understand when I got into the party I was just sixteen, and three years later I could sit down and have meetings with doctors, lawyers, professors, the higher echelons, and get them to act any way I wanted them to." This woman's development was all the more remarkable given the options available to working-class Black women at the time. Though gender conflict could be difficult, painful, and awkward, it was revolutionary for those who managed to change their organizational culture and themselves. Many of the women of the Third World Left are highly accomplished today, and most acknowledged that their sense of themselves as capable, effective individuals began in the movement.

RADICAL POLITICAL ACTIVISM AMONG MEN AND WOMEN OF COLOR

Throughout world history the political activism of women has been devalued, if not invisible. This is not only because men are typically recognized as the leaders of movements but because analysts and writers have often treated female activists as "out of place" or deviant. Too frequently the study of social movements has followed the path of "great men," focusing on prominent individuals rather than the committed actors behind the scenes. Thankfully, a corrective is emerging in the growing literature on women and political activism, as well as in studies of nonleaders.[8]

Research on women and gender relations can be seen as the second generation of movement literature. The first generation documented and analyzed key historical movements, such as the civil rights movement, the United Farm Workers (UFW), the Asian American movement, and the BPP. Only later did scholars begin to examine the nature of gender relations, particularly the role of women, femininity, masculinity, and nonleaders. This more recent literature has begun to reveal the patriarchal nature of the movement. While summarizing this work is beyond the scope of this chapter, some key findings are crucial. For instance, Belinda Robnett has argued that women were essential to maintaining movements of this era. Despite some pronounced exceptions, including Fannie Lou Hamer of the Mississippi Freedom Democratic Party and Dolores Huerta of the UFW, most women did the behind-the-scenes, nuts-and-bolts kind of work.[9] They provided the labor that enabled organizations to achieve their goals and built the networks so crucial to successful movements. Danny Glover, in reminiscing about the BPP, voiced what growing evidence confirms: "Oh, those women. . . . Those women in the Black Panther Party, you all held it together. The men—there was a lot of chaos going on. Things were wild. But it was the women who held it all together."[10]

A second important finding is the disagreement among men and women concerning gender relations. Though many men had difficulty accepting women as their equals, a number not only altered their beliefs and practices but challenged the sexist behavior of other males. Such men understood the contradiction between the rhetoric of freedom and the practice of patriarchy, while at times incurring the disdain of other men. Equally important, however, was the dissension among women themselves. Those who openly supported patriarchy, sometimes called "loyalists," refrained from questioning traditional women's roles, whether cooking food for an event or cleaning up. They were vested in promoting the status of men as a way to enhance their community. Opposite this were those women who advocated less traditional positions.

An additional complication is the white women's movement and its relationship to woman of color and the Third World Left. Once white women realized that race was the Achilles' heel of their movement, they sought out women of color, and questions arose over the identity and location of women of color. Would they align themselves with the women's movement or with antiracist movements? Not surprisingly, most women of color desired a political path that would allow them to combine their racial, class, and gender commitments.[11] Most radical women of color did not view the white women's movement as a viable option. As one East Wind member saw it, "[S]ome sectors of the women's movement defined men as the enemy. For third world women and other white women, our enemy was defined much more broadly as the fundamental economic and political system in this country that gave rise to racism and sexism."[12] Due to political missteps and the perceived threat to the antiracist struggle, some women of color rejected the idea of feminism altogether. At a 1969 Chicana/o conference, for example, participants in a session entitled "La Chicana" declared, "It was the consensus of the group that the Chicana woman does not want to be liberated."[13] This did not necessarily mean that Chicanas were satisfied with their situation; rather, it registered their rejection of white feminism and their belief that its embrace would impose a separation from Chicano men—an unacceptable option.[14]

The tensions that women of color experienced between white feminism and antiracist struggles were exacerbated by the sanctions that those who embraced white feminism (or elements of it) risked from their ethnic communities. Such women were branded white or lesbians—both terms used as pejoratives. The message was clear: authentic Asian American, Latina, Black, and American Indian women stood by their men, struggled with them, and eschewed white feminism.

Of particular importance was the nationalism and, by extension, patriarchy that undergirded much of the activism in communities of color. Theorists have argued that most nationalisms are fundamentally masculinist projects predicated on redeeming the male subject. Indeed, Malcolm X observed that one of the most profound psychic costs of racial subordination was the emasculation of Black men. Black men (as well as Latino, Asian American, and American Indian men, albeit in modified ways) could not function as "real" men because of racial violence, terror, and subordination. White supremacy precluded men of color from earning a family wage, protecting their wife and children, and functioning as the head of the household.[15] Thus one of the main impulses of the movements of the 1960s and 1970s was to restore the manhood and privilege of men of color. Aída Hurtado has suggested that the political opening of the 1960s was largely for men and that nationalism, as the dominant ideology, reproduced patriarchy. This was the context in which women of color fought for gender equality.

> The state has incapacitated Chicano and black men so that they cannot properly provide for their families (within a liberal conception of what constitutes legitimate social arrangements for productive participation in civil society). The imprisonment and undereducation of these men of color effectively subverts their gender privilege and any trickle-down effects it may have on women from their respective groups. The crippling of these men's masculinist power further disenfranchises women in these ethnic/racial groups and puts their children at risk of genocide.
>
> What these young white men were offering Chicano and black men was an invitation to privilege. However, it was an invitation to a preestablished party in which the rules of conduct were already well set. The invitation was to a liberal vision with its masculinist underpinnings that, by its very nature, implied the subordination of women. Yet it was the best invitation these groups have received to date.
>
> . . . Masculinist underpinnings of nationalism prevented men activists in the movement from addressing gender issues, and, ultimately, the movements were unable to develop and grow into a more sophisticated

analysis. Women of color, however, did not leave their respective movements, but instead, built pockets of mobilizations around gender issues
and continued to struggle with men on behalf of their communities.[16]

Although Hurtado's analysis is rooted in the more nationalist movements,
many of these insights can be applied to the Third World Left, insofar as they
adhered to some version of revolutionary nationalism. Women of the Third
World Left generally occupied what Emma Pérez refers to as a third space, or
feminism-in-nationalism, by choosing to align themselves with and struggle
with the men of their community around race, class, *and* gender.[17]

Despite differences in how organizations approached gender issues, they
all had one commonality: none focused explicitly on women's liberation.
Over time all the organizations had to address gender as large numbers of
women joined East Wind, CASA, and the BPP. The more women and men
interacted, the more real the contradictions and tensions of sexism became,
and the more women (and some men) voiced concern and demanded change.
Nevertheless, none of the groups investigated identified gender equality as a
goal worthy of their political platforms or mission statements. While this
silence may not seem noteworthy, at least two organizations in the Third
World Left did highlight gender equality. Consider the following excerpts
from the platforms of the Young Lords and I Wor Kuen respectively.

*11) We want equality for women. Machismo must be revolutionary . . .
not oppressive.*

Under capitalism, our women have been oppressed by both the society
and our own men. The doctrine of machismo has been used by our men
to take out their frustrations against their wives, sisters, mothers, and
children. Our men must support their women in their fight for economic and social equality, and must recognize that our women are
equals in every way within the revolutionary ranks.

4) We want an end to male chauvinism and sexual exploitation.

The thousands of years of oppression under feudalism and capitalism
have created institutions and myths of male supremacy over women.
Man must fight along with sisters in the struggle for economic and
social equality and must recognize that sisters make up over half of
the revolutionary army. Sisters and brothers are equals fighting for
our people.[18]

I Wor Kuen's statement covers somewhat more ideological terrain than the
Young Lords', as it hints at the pervasive nature of patriarchy, including male
supremacy, sexual exploitation, and gender discrimination. Nonetheless, the
Young Lords took a significant step in acknowledging the problems of

machismo, male supremacy in Latin American cultures, and in condemning male terror and domination. I Wor Kuen's position is not entirely surprising given that it was a female-dominated group. Moreover, its commitment to gender equality influenced others in its orbit, including East Wind, and contributed to the organization's relatively progressive gender politics.[19] In short, some organizations consciously thought about gender issues, so the absences within East Wind, the BPP, and CASA should be read as meaningful.

THE BLACK PANTHER PARTY

The Black Panther Party (BPP) featured a highly polarized set of gender relations. On the one hand, the BPP was characterized by hypermasculine representations, embodied by Black men with guns, and its sexist, and at times misogynist, practices are legendary. On the other hand, the party offered tremendous opportunities for female empowerment, and women's participation was not only vital but recognized as such.

The Party Line

Although the BPP never included gender as part of its political demands, it left a fairly extensive written and visual record on the subject. This and the writings of former Panthers reveal a cacophony of voices. A speech by Newton, in which he argued that elements of the women's and gay liberation movements were potential allies, serves to introduce these contradictions.

> Whatever your personal opinions and your insecurities about homosexuality and the various liberation movements among homosexuals and women . . . [w]e should try to unite them in a fashion. . . . We very well know, sometimes our first instinct is to want to hit a homosexual in the mouth, and want a woman to be quiet. We want to hit a homosexual; and we want to hit the woman or shut her up because we are afraid that she might castrate us, or take the nuts that we might not have to start with.
>
> We should be careful about using those terms that might turn our friends off. The terms "faggot" and "punk" should be deleted from our vocabulary, and especially we should not attach names normally designed for homosexuals to men who are enemies of the people, such as Nixon or Mitchell. Homosexuals are not enemies of the people. [20]

To begin with, Newton is clearly speaking to Black, heterosexual men, who, it can be inferred, are assumed to be the primary political actors, while women and homosexuals are treated as secondary subjects.[21] The depth of the party's sexism and homophobia is also revealed by Newton's frank discussion of how at least some male Panthers viewed women and homosexuals—as obstacles to Black liberation and against whom violence was the norm. In light of such problematic attitudes Newton's message must be seen as radical, as he challenged a host of ingrained and regressive social practices, including physical violence, derogatory language, and misogynist and homophobic attitudes. As noted before, because the BPP accepted almost all Black people, the membership brought with them a range of attitudes and behaviors, some of which were anything but revolutionary. The BPP sought to transform such individuals through political education classes, discipline, organizational practices, and even speeches. In many ways the Newton quote is emblematic of the BPP's gender relations as a whole: they were sexist and they privileged the male subject, but they also sought to challenge patriarchy.

The mere fact that such speeches were made, however, does not reveal the full organizational reality. Though people could be disciplined for chauvinistic actions and language, individuals could not be forced to adopt new beliefs and attitudes regarding gender, men, and women.[22] This diversity of positions and attitudes was reflected on the pages of the *Black Panther*, which allows us to see how attitudes changed over time.[23]

Taken in its entirety, the *Black Panther* presents a largely male-centered organization.[24] This is evident in the number of stories and images that depict men, but also in the orientation of articles dealing with gender. Over time, however, women and their work become more visible in the publication, and depictions of their role changed. Early editions of the *Black Panther* were largely devoted to documenting the atrocities that Black men suffered at the hands of the police, as well as their efforts to organize and resist. The Black man was seen both as a victim of a brutal and unfair police system and, to a lesser extent, as a fighter (this image would develop with time). The tremendous anger of the Black community—or at least Black men—was evident in the wonderfully outrageous drawings and depictions of the white power establishment, especially those by Emory Douglas, and in the language used.[25]

Early on, women were featured primarily in supporting roles: the grieving wife, mother, or sister whose beloved husband, son, or brother had been wronged by the "pigs." Women were not regularly depicted as revolutionary agents, although some images sought to convey the strength and dignity of Black women, especially mothers. Nonetheless, there was some explicit discussion of gender roles. In one column, entitled "Sista's Section," the author wrote:

> Women cannot help but gravitate towards life—and the black man holds within the strength and the fiery passion of his struggle . . . the life of his people and his posterity. His total commitment to his life is an invitation

to the black woman to join with him in the pursuit of a life together,
removing the shackles of White Racist America and establishing a solid
foundation of blackness from which to build. . . . In terms of survival,
ie: in 1967, the black man needs a woman as a base, an anchor, a refuge,
a shelter, a haven, a place of peace, a home and institution of strength.
The black woman must incorporate all of these.[26]

Here, a woman's role is conceptualized as serving the Black man and his
needs, which are equated with revolution. Women did not exist as autonomous beings, and certainly not as independent agents and activists.[27] Such
thinking would not last, however.

With an increase in female membership, women insisted that their voices
be heard, challenged the male chauvinism of the organization, and pushed
the party to change its thinking toward Black women. Thus, over time, in
addition to the continued depiction of grieving wives and mothers, there was
a celebration of the revolutionary woman, who might or might not be
attached to a man.

> I have a message from the revolutionary sisters of babylon . . . : "Sisters
> get on your job; you have work to do." Let me tell you a little about the
> revolutionary sisters of the world.
>   We must start with sister Erica Huggins, for sister Erica has set an
> example that all oppressed women of the world can relate to. On January
> 17, 1969, sister Erica lost her very revolutionary husband when members
> of the Cultural Nationalist U.S. Organization murdered him. . . .
>   In May of the same year, sister Erica was jailed in Connecticut for
> the alleged murder of a panther brother, Alex Rackley. Since that time
> she has been subjected to torture that is extremely horrible and sense-
> less; her daughter Mai whom was only three months old, was separated
> from her. The sister is very well educated and has worked hard in the
> struggle for liberation. We should look closely at what she did and we
> should also see what is being done to her. Sister Erica held up the ban-
> ner that John died to save. She was also the acting Deputy Minister of
> Defense for the Conn. Chapter. This sister was truly on her job and we
> must try to learn from her example.[28]

Ericka Huggins is a key figure in the history of the BPP, who also captures
the gendered politics of the party. Essentially, she embodies the two tendencies of the party's official discourse on women: the dutiful wife (as seen in
the mourning widow) and the political actor in her own right. In no way
were Huggins's contributions limited to supporting her husband; she was
applauded for standing alongside her man, being a mother, and assuming a
leadership role in the BPP (deputy minister of defense, no less!) Figure 14
portrays Angela Davis and Ericka Huggins, a common juxtaposition that

BLACK WOMEN IN THE STRUGGLE FOR THE LIBERATION OF THE PEOPLE- ANGELA AND ERICKA

Figure 14. Revolutionary Black women. Source: *Black Panther,* June 12, 1971.

was used to celebrate and promote models of revolutionary Black woman-hood. In addition to such depictions of female leadership, the *Black Panther* began reporting regularly on women, particularly as they became political prisoners and suffered police abuse, and highlighted the important work women did, including leading pickets, organizing survival programs, selling the newspaper, and serving the Black community.

Participation, Leadership, and the Gendered Division of Labor

How people were integrated into the party provides a different perspective on gender relations. Though portrayed as a largely male organization, the BPP attracted many women. Kathleen Cleaver has reported that in 1969 Bobby Seale conducted a survey and determined that two-thirds of the party's membership was female.[29] While we cannot ascertain the accuracy of such figures, women clearly composed a significant percentage of the party membership. Besides constituting a large measure of the rank and file, some women attained leadership positions. Despite such steps toward equality, however, there still existed a gendered division of labor, which shaped every-day life in the BPP.

The gendered division of labor—that is, the practice of dividing tasks between men and women—is deeply entrenched globally, and the BPP was no exception. Men were concentrated in leadership and defense positions, while women were clustered in community service programs, especially those considered an extension of female duties, such as education, child care, and health services.

While party leadership was heavily male, women were allowed to occupy the highest echelons of power, the most prominent example being Elaine Brown. After Newton began acting paranoid and expelled David Hilliard from the party, Brown assumed his position as second in command, eventually becoming chair. The exact conditions of Brown's ascendancy are unclear, not least because she was "Huey's Queen" at that time. Newton subsequently fled to Cuba rather than facing another set of charges, and Brown then became chair. Brown has suggested that she gave the party a decidedly feminist flavor by placing more women on the Central Committee and emphasizing community service programs rather than armed self-defense.[30] Regardless of the merits of this decision, however, it exacerbated ongoing antagonisms within the BPP between self-defense and politics. Consequently, Brown's leadership was contested for at least two reasons: first, some disputed the decision to privilege community service over self-defense, and second, some had difficulty acknowledging female leadership.[31] Indeed, one interviewee frankly stated that he would never follow orders from a woman, as this was not the "natural" order of things. But to what extent this was a minority position is unclear, as many insisted that assignments should be based on qualifications. According to one male interviewee,

> Some of the top leadership were women. That didn't mean that sexism was eliminated immediately. But people would be called on the carpet for it. That doesn't mean that it was that way in every setting of the BPP throughout the country. I think there was a sense that men had a role and women had a role, but in Los Angeles, women had key leadership roles. In fact, the highest-ranking officer, Gwen Goodlowe, was here, the coordinator of all of Southern California. Some people didn't like her, but that was part of the struggle. You had people like Elaine who had come out of Newark, you had people like Tommy Williamson, who dealt with legal issues . . . and so there was an attempt to break down those defined roles. Again, you have a lot of dudes who didn't like them, and I would say if they didn't like them, that they should base it on not liking their politics. But if they didn't like them as a woman, fuck them. That's what I say.

Despite a range of attitudes toward female leadership, the BPP offered unprecedented opportunities for women. Women were able to challenge sexism and achieve leadership positions partly because of the value accorded *their actions*. Because participation in the BPP involved an immense workload and a willingness to risk one's life and well-being, the commitment demonstrated by female members generated a certain level of respect and thus served as a vehicle for equality. Neither CASA or East Wind offered comparable opportunities, for both organizations placed more emphasis on studying, and consequently theorizing emerged as a path to leadership, and the type of work women did in those organizations was not consistently valued.

Another factor promoting gender equality was the joint activities that men and women participated in. For example, it was somewhat difficult to deny the equality of women who participated in a shoot-out with men. As one former Panther described it, "We were in a lot of situations in which the police . . . had pulled out their guns and we had pulled out our guns, and it was a stand-off. It might have lasted two or three hours. . . . [W]hen the women were there, their lives were just as much in danger. We were in the position that we weren't tripping over who has the power. On the grassroots level, it was more about survival. Their lives were just as much in danger as the men. Therefore, they had the same rights." Other collaborative activities that supported equality included the training that men and women received. Both were required to attend political education classes, taught how to handle and care for weapons, and instructed in basic survival skills and first aid. In addition, the reality of state surveillance and harassment encouraged men and women to see themselves as comrades in struggle. A common enemy assists in erasing tensions between potentially contentious groups, however temporarily.

A final practice that contributed toward equality was the establishment of communal living facilities, called Black houses. According to one interviewee, these homes were often abandoned apartments or houses that multiple Panthers would occupy.

> Basically we lived in collectives, Black houses, community centers. It depended at what level you were functioning. If you were functioning out of the community centers or offices, then you would stay there. If you were functioning out of a section or squad, they might have a little spot, or an apartment with somebody, an abandoned one, and you just moved in. We were very mobile too, we moved around a lot so we couldn't get caught. But it was like all for one and one for all. . . . That was what kept us going. You know, if someone went hungry, we all went hungry. If somebody ate, we all ate.[32]

The military culture of the Panthers was also helpful in terms of eroding traditional gender roles, as all individuals were supposed to take turns preparing food, cleaning up, and doing household chores. Theoretically this prevented women from automatically being burdened with domestic duty, although it is unclear to what extent this was carried out. An example of how such efforts could be thwarted can be seen in East Wind, which also experimented with collective living. One interviewee recounted how a male member actually had his girlfriend (a nonmember) do his share of household duties! Such behavior obviously defeated the purpose of forging alternative cultural practices.

Still, some areas of the BPP remained distinctly gendered: the underground, for example, was disproportionately male. One former member pointed out that several women were in the underground insofar as their male partners were, but they themselves were not. Although there is evidence that women were a significant part of other undergrounds, such as New York's, which was instrumental in the development of the Black Liberation Army, the extent of female involvement in Southern California is unclear. In general, leading the troops was primarily a man's job. In Southern California, this was embodied by Geronimo Pratt, who used his army training from Vietnam to help the BPP militarily.

Another arena of uneven progress was birth control, pregnancy, and child care. Although the BPP ostensibly provided child care, it was often inadequate and less than ideal, leading some women to feel torn between their children and the party. These tensions became more pronounced as more Panther babies were born, leading to discussions and guidelines regarding contraception and culminating in a planned parenthood policy directed at both men and women.[33]

In peaceful times, there are numerous reasons why women bear children, but childbearing accrued additional meaning during this revolutionary period. The birth of Panther children was initially a cause for celebration, since raising children become a vehicle for developing alternative social arrangements and cultural practices. Indeed, there is some evidence of women having children *for* the revolution, which is somewhat different, as women are literally reproducing the movement.[34] As more women joined and gave birth, however, this placed a great strain on party resources in terms of caring for the children and pregnant women, as well as the mothers' diminished work capacity.

Panther women were also more likely to work with children than men. Establishing programs for children was disproportionately a woman's job, even for women within the leadership. For instance, at one point Ericka Huggins both directed the Oakland Community School and was elected to the Alameda County Board of Education; Assata Shakur directed a children's health clinic.[35] One woman from the Southern California chapter explained how caring for children fit with the overall tasks assigned to women. "[As] sisters, our role was soldiers also. But we taught the children, that was part of our job. It was important that our children be taught in the right manner. And we also picked up a gun just like the brothers did."

Although women's activities were concentrated in community work, such work was often valued. Community service helped people and connected the party to the larger Black population, a critical source of support. Thus, despite the central tension within the BPP between community service and self-defense, the many accomplishments of women were valued and provided an opportunity to gain status, recognition, and, in some cases, leadership positions.

The Gendered Nature of Violence in the Black Panther Party

Much has been made, and appropriately so, of the sexual and misogynist violence associated with the BPP. Some of the more egregious examples include Eldridge Cleaver's discussion of raping white women as a form of insurrection; reports that he beat his wife to the point of hospitalization; Elaine Brown's suffering from physical violence from male party members; and Assata Shakur's sexual harassment by a higher-ranking party official. While there is no denying that sexist violence existed, it would be a mistake to assume that women were the only victims of violence. In fact, most likely men were disproportionately subject to violence, which came from two sources: the party itself and the state.

Violence within the Party was extensive. Some violence was officially sanctioned, such as beating and whipping members as punishment for various infractions, whereas other violent episodes were due to anger, a loss of control, and were unauthorized. In *Last Man Standing,* Olsen describes how former Panther Julio Pratt Butler brutalized Ollie Taylor, a young male recruit. According to Olsen's account, the boy's life would have been in jeopardy if Geronimo Pratt had not intervened.[36] It is also possible that patterns of violence varied over time. For example, Brown says she ended the practice of using violence as a form of discipline, although others have disputed this claim.

Researchers have found that violence, including state violence, ultimately finds expression in our families, homes, and communities. For instance, evidence suggests that U.S. homicide rates increase during periods of wartime.[37] Though violence against women is of grave concern, as women are usually at a physical disadvantage, violence against men is also a serious problem. There are at least two reasons why violence fell disproportionately on Panther men. First, despite misogynist tendencies within the BPP, some men could not and would not beat a woman, regardless of alleged infractions. Hitting a woman who was not threatening you violated a basic tenet of acceptable behavior for some men. On the other hand, it was less transgressive for men to physically attack or beat other men, and physical violence was not unknown to those with previous gang affiliations.[38]

A second reason men were disproportionately burdened by violence was the state. This is not to deny the brutalization that Panther women endured at the hands of the police: one need only read the stories of Angela Davis, Assata Shakur, and Ericka Huggins to know that women faced harrowing circumstances. It appears, however, that such behavior may have been reserved for women who had truly incurred the wrath of the state, being charged perhaps with shooting an officer or escaping prison. In contrast, any male Panther, including "insignificant" recruits, could anticipate being physically brutalized by the police.[39] Like male Panthers, many officers were more apt to beat a man than a woman, although they certainly shot women in the course of battle. As a result, Panther men were more likely to be harassed, arrested, beaten, and incarcerated than Panther women. One former Panther offered his analysis of the gendered nature of police violence:

> You can beat a man half to death and simply say, "He struggled, he resisted," but you can't beat a woman half to death because at some point you can overcome her, even if she is tough. So that's what I mean when I say they didn't dog the women as much as they dogged us. It was politics. If it was up to them, they would've killed us every time they stopped us, but they put themselves in a position where they just couldn't kill us, because they had to answer to somebody. And if they harassed a woman and she was pregnant and lost the baby, then the media would pick up on it.

While some police may have hesitated to beat Panther women, many did not. Misogyny is not unknown among police departments, and this, coupled with racism, accounts for the harsh treatment Panther women received. It is important to bear in mind that Black women have historically been rendered as "nonwomen," and defeminized in this country. When the status of "woman" is withheld, there is no need to extend to Black women the consideration due white ones. This ideological move was partly necessary to justify chattel slavery but also served to create white, or "true," womanhood.[40] This, in turn, paved the way for police to treat Black women far worse than other women.

Male Panthers, however, as Black men, embodied the racial conflict that has gripped this country for centuries, coming to a head in the late 1960s. Black men carrying guns were a fundamental challenge to white supremacy and an attempt to defend the Black nation. The BPP was created precisely for this purpose. As men, they were assuming the role of both defenders and agents of social change and thus were seen as a more potent threat than Black women. And the police, who were charged with upholding white supremacy, responded accordingly.

CASA

The gender relations of CASA were quite different from those of the BPP. Although women made up at least half of the membership, they never achieved the leadership and visibility that Panther women did. Instead, they occupied a clearly subordinated role—though one punctuated by moments of strong female leadership. And like other women in the Third World Left they were subject to violence and sexual and emotional abuse. Although I argue that CASA had the most problematic gender relations, the women (and some men) of CASA did contest its sexism. In fact, there were intense gender struggles, but women achieved only limited success in changing the organizational culture.

The Party Line

Aside from the year 1977, which saw a whirl of activity around gender, CASA had surprisingly little to say, officially, that is, about women, gender, and (in)equality. Although hardly alone, CASA repeatedly expressed hostility toward the women's movement, which it criticized for its white and middle-class composition and inattention to issues of race and class. "In recent years, the US has seen the resurgence of the struggle for women's equality by North American women. Some Mexican women, primarily students, have been influenced peripherally. . . . This Northern American struggle has produced women who have followed the root of sexism to class oppression, but it also includes women for the ruling class who want more female court judges who can, for example, participate in the reinstatement of the death penalty, more female police to overpatrol our neighborhoods or equality just to condone their decadent sexual behavior."[41] This quote introduces several themes that permeate CASA's gender relations. Most significant is the way gender and sexuality are located within a highly economistic political ideology. Such an approach reduced gender relations and sexism to a function of capitalism, thus precluding them from being appreciated on their own terms. One consequence was that gender was treated as a highly contained topic, one abstracted from everyday life. In general, CASA viewed all women as workers but scarcely acknowledged the differing concerns that male and female workers might have. This lack of awareness was also reflected in CASA's attitudes and behaviors toward its members. Such inattention to the gendered nature of the world ultimately served to reproduce patriarchy. Moreover, CASA's antipathy toward the larger women's movement made it difficult for Chicanas to borrow elements that might have been helpful to them.

Outside 1977, CASA actively engaged in only one explicitly gendered issue: the forced sterilization of women of color. During the 1970s it was discovered that low-income women of color were being sterilized at local public hospitals. At Los Angeles County General, for example, it was found that between 1968 and 1970 the number of hysterectomies had increased 742 percent, tubal litigations 470 percent, and tubal litigations after delivery 151 percent. Not surprisingly, Mexican American and African American women were disproportionately affected. CASA participated in coalitions to end such abuses, including the National Coalition Against Sterilization, and supported lawsuits on behalf of Mexicanas. In many ways, this was a perfect issue for CASA: it was a human rights violation and a clear instance of discrimination against poor and working-class women of color. CASA's objectives in the coalition were, in addition to simply organizing Latinas, to develop "principles of unity which constitute an anti-imperialist attack against the poor to conserve profits for the imperialists."[42] While strong on class politics, such an interpretation never challenged male domination or the centrality of gender to everyday life.

Although CASA did not develop a clear political line or women's program, much can be learned by reviewing *Sin Fronteras*. For starters, there was no consistent image or set of images of women in the newspaper. Unlike the *Black Panther*, which portrayed women as either grieving mothers/wives or revolutionaries, the photographs and drawings of *Sin Fronteras* focused mostly on male subjects. Women were often visually present but were relegated largely to the background and were rarely the subject of a story or photo. Interestingly, when *Sin Fronteras* did feature photos of heroic women, they were rarely ethnic Mexicans. Instead, the newspaper was more apt to highlight Black women, including Angela Davis and Joan Bird, Puerto Rican political prisoners, and the Puertoriqueña Inez García, who was charged with murder for killing her rapist.[43] *Sin Fronteras* simply did not celebrate the revolutionary Mexicana. While images of striking and militant female workers were proudly presented, as in figure 15, their gender was irrelevant. Instead, men were typically depicted as the agents of revolution.[44] The fact that gender was not mentioned or problematized served to render male leadership as the norm and reinforced the notion that men were the principal subjects of *el movimiento* (see also figure 7).

The primary exception to this pattern of male dominance was the March 1977 issue of *Sin Fronteras*. A common strategy among the left was to devote a special issue of their publication(s) to women. This particular issue of *Sin Fronteras* coincided with International Women's Day, a regional conference entitled "Mujeres Unidas" (United Women), and a CASA forum focused on "the woman question." Thus the special issue was part of a flurry

Figure 15. Striking Mexican American women workers. CASA rarely recognized the unique concerns of female workers and members. Source: Photographer unknown. "Steelworkers in Wildcat Strike," *Sin Fronteras*, November 1975, p. 2. Courtesy of Antonio Rodriguez and Department of Special Collections, Stanford University Libraries.

of activity related to women. CASA convened the forum in response to its membership's limited understanding of gender inequality. Members of CASA "recognized that the level of consciousness within the organization on the complex aspects of the 'Woman Question' as it applies to Mexican and Latina women is very low."[45]

Of particular importance is *when* these activities occurred within CASA's history—one year before the organization's demise. Assuming that tensions existed throughout the life of the organization, it took several years for women to create the space to collectively voice their concerns effectively and for the organization to respond.

The special issue of *Sin Fronteras* published articles on the status and oppression of Mexicana workers in both Mexico and the United States, while also reporting on mass sterilizations at Los Angeles County Hospital, the political imprisonment of Latinas (mostly Puertorriqueñas), and the regional Latina conference, in which CASA women played a pivotal role. The list of demands generated by conference attendees speaks volumes about CASA's gender relations: "Support the struggle for self-determination of Latino peoples; Defeat the Bakke Decision; Demand for bilingual/bicultural programs; Demand for greater priorities on women's and children's services; Unconditional amnesty for all undocumented workers; Stop all deportation raids. . . . Stop all forced sterilization and an end to all experimental operations on Third World women."[46] The demands acknowledge the importance of the relationship between the quality of women's lives and the larger political economic picture. And while such demands would certainly improve the lives of Mexicanas, it is also true that the list barely differs from CASA's general demands.[47]

After these various initiatives, an effort was made to establish a women's group within CASA. It never materialized. This was partly because of the tremendous demands already placed on members, as well as the anxiety over how the women's group would fit within the larger organization. Specifically, there was concern that a women's caucus might be a step toward separation, something all members of CASA decried.[48] CASA, like other Third World revolutionary groups, believed ardently in the need for men and women of oppressed nationalities to work together.

The relationship between CASA's gender ideology and practice was somewhat contradictory. Although gender inequality was placed within a larger context of racial and class struggle, the reality was that gender was treated as if it were *contained*, rather than mutually constituted by the social formation. This approach enabled the male leadership to maintain gender as a separate realm.

> We must remember that the women's struggle is not a separate one. It is only one part of the struggle against all oppression. Third world women are oppressed in three ways: by capitalism, by racial prejudice, and by their own men. The last two are direct results of the first, so we can see that capitalism, as in the case of all oppressed people, is the main enemy of our women. This is very important. Women must awaken to the fact that the main fight is not with their man. Men are oppressed by the same evil, but not to such an extent. If women are not trained in the revolution, they will become obstacles and hold the revolution back.[49]

This was a fairly rigid position that did not serve women or men well. It precluded them from understanding the extent to which their lives and CASA itself were gendered and thus ensured a highly patriarchal organization that offered women few ideological tools to challenge sexism. Moreover, intended or not, such a perspective relieved men of any culpability, as ultimate responsibility for sexism was attributed to a disembodied capitalism.

> This contradiction [sexism] was expressed in direct conflict as well as in organizational narratives. In the early stages of the Chicano Movement and throughout its later years, sexism was clearly present in many forms and on many occasions. There existed a double standard of work and social life among men and women involved in the same struggle. Women did the

petty work, men did the leading. Opinions of women were belittled or ignored and rare was the woman allowed in meaningful positions of leadership. Tokenism was utilized where women who agreed with the positions
of the dominating males of the group or organization were recognized
leaders, while those who differed were ostracized as Anglo or bourgeois.

The author of this quote, Carlos Vásquez, proceeded to explain that despite
this problematic early history, things eventually improved.

[Some women] prepared to study, and to take struggle between the
sexes and within our people to the most personally expensive levels.
[They began] changing the attitudes of reactionary machismo and
chauvinism. Their commitment to love and respect women and still
be strong in their commitments to their people earned them the respect
among both men and women. As practical workers, women proved to
be the more consistent and demanding of follow through. Eventually,
the antagonisms initially caused by the women's efforts to assert their
identity, their dignity and their contributions to the people's struggles
produced creative dialogue and struggle which forced many males to
change and allowed many women to develop. Many men seeing the
energy, the talent, intelligence and efforts this unleashed, welcomed
the women. Others did not and in more subtle ways continued to carry
on their sexism and chauvinism.[50]

Vásquez's account traces the tensions inherent in the process of gender
struggle in CASA, and while the last sentence acknowledges ongoing problems, it is somewhat at odds with what interviewees reported. Essentially,
they felt that the situation did not improve and that the violence, threats,
sexual philandering, and exploitation continued. Such contrasting narratives are perhaps indicative of CASA's inability to come to terms with the
level of gender conflict and its consequences for the organization.

Participation, Leadership, and the Gendered Division of Labor

One reason why CASA women never reached the prominence that BPP
women did was that the organization placed more emphasis on study and
theoretical work. Like some graduate student seminars, discussions of political theory became sites for the performance of masculinity and male competition. Accordingly, many women, including this interviewee, felt silenced
and uncomfortable in such an arena.

Every time all of those theoretical issues would come up, the only thing
I could relate to was immigrants and unions and workers. There was this
debating and then getting off on that sort of stuff. I did it because I also
wanted to learn and be smarter. . . . [B]ut it did get many times too extreme where it was like . . . who cares?

> [CASA] was absolutely male dominated, very macho in the attitude
> of the leadership. There is no doubt about it. I didn't feel that with my
> level of experience . . . I knew how to take that on. I didn't know how
> to deal with it, and I think that most women who were serious about
> their role really felt like we were made to feel inadequate even if we
> didn't need further development. It's different to say you are in devel-
> opment from saying you are inadequate.

Although women ostensibly felt inadequate in the field of study and theory, which was only one part of the organization, it was sometimes difficult for them and for men who considered them deficient in this respect to isolate and contain such feelings. Thus, although women participated in diverse activities, it was difficult to escape the general feeling of inferiority, as it spilled into other spheres and the organization as a whole.

Because they were more comfortable and therefore more proficient in theoretical debate, which was highly valued by CASA, men were more likely to emerge as leaders. In fact, few women were acknowledged as leaders. Virtually all interviewees recognized Magdalena Mora (deceased) as brilliant and as one of the few women able to compete with men theoretically. Because she could stand her own ground in theoretical debates, she was accorded a degree of respect not given to other women, although she still suf-fered from the "emotional abuse" that other women experienced in their personal relationships. Another woman who attained leadership prominence was Isabel Rodriguez. She served for a time as the editor of *Sin Fronteras* but was eventually replaced by Carlos Vásquez. Because of this, she lost her seat on the Political Commission, leaving no woman on this governing body. While some members saw an all-male Political Commission, the highest body of the organization, as problematic, the situation was not remedied.[51]

There are several possible explanations for CASA's relative lack of suc-cess in transforming traditional gender relations. One of the problems was the division of labor. As previously noted, a division of labor is not neces-sarily bad, but there is trouble when different types of work are valued dif-ferently and are associated with essentialized forms of difference. In CASA, the *type* of work women did was often devalued. At least one interviewee suggested that in addition to their many other duties, women were largely responsible for food and cleanup at CASA events. Because this was primar-ily a female job, it was devalued. One male member described the organiza-tion's gender relations as follows:

> To me, it was just a continuation of the Chicano movement of the late
> sixties and early seventies, when the women cooked and the men did the
> work of the Chicano movement. . . . I remember some women standing

up and saying, "We're not just here to make the beans and rice for the fundraisers, we're here to do some work." And I remember for the first time thinking, "Yes, that makes sense, why should we be the workers?" Well, all the work meant what? Getting high, partying, or running home to see yourself on TV after the march. That's not work! So, that is a contradiction in itself. There were some powerful women in CASA, and the more intellectual and powerful ones would be treated with equality, but the worker bees, or *militantes*, as we called them, weren't. The women who wanted to support, get out there and organize, and work hard were delegated to a lower standard.

The result of such attitudes and behaviors was that few avenues existed for women to acquire status and respect within the organization. This stands in contrast to the BPP, where greater value was placed on community organizing, skills at which women tended to excel.

A second problem women faced was the imposition of a subjective/objective duality. Marisela Rodríguez Chávez has explored the leadership's highly disabling practice of insisting on the separation between the "subjective" and the "objective."[52] Drawing on Marxist terminology, the largely male leadership argued that women's concerns regarding sexism, including personal relationships, were subjective matters that should be handled personally, not by the organization. This was extremely frustrating and painful to many women, for it delegitimized their concerns and proved a difficult obstacle to overcome, as many "women's issues," such as child care, the division of labor, and sexual relationships, could be interpreted as "subjective." This was a great challenge for those women (and men) intent on democratizing CASA. Such an orientation also helps explain how and why CASA was able to keep its discussion of the "woman question" tightly bound to the organization's political economic analysis: gender could be discussed only insofar as it was objective.

A serious consequence of the subjective/objective duality was that it precluded the organization from addressing two key areas of life, household responsibilities and personal relationships. Because of the separation between the subjective and the objective, CASA made only limited attempts to engage in members' personal and family lives. While this may be seen as positive, given that other organizations required individuals to submit to the will of the collective, it allowed a continuation of the highly patriarchal family structure associated with Mexicana/o culture. With the absence of even a critical dialogue, the status quo is inevitably reproduced. Whereas East Wind and the BPP sought to provide alternative social arrangements for child care and other domestic responsibilities, CASA did not—with repercussions for the organization. One member was pregnant and had her first child while active in CASA.

> I remember being pregnant with Mario and never missing my Saturday morning of selling the newspaper because it was my chance to talk to the people. It was my chance to really pour my heart out. But in terms of child care, it was up to you. You figure it out. I remember when I had the baby, Evelina, she is still my best friend today, and she just bought me a bunch of stuff, presents and things for the baby. I was like, "Oh my God; I think I'm going to love you forever." As tough as she was on all of those sorts of things that were going on, as women we supported each other. But it wasn't on the organizational level at all.

Because CASA did not emphasize new cultural practices or experiment with alternative living and social arrangements, the women of CASA typically had three jobs: paid employment to support themselves and their households, volunteering with CASA, and domestic responsibilities.

At one point CASA actually discussed child raising and declared that it should be both parents' responsibility, but nothing substantive emerged from this discussion. Not surprisingly, some women found they had to leave the organization because of family demands.[53] The disparagement of women and their needs even extended to their physical well-being, as one interviewee recalled: "Magdalena Mora was really kind of symbolic. . . . Magdalena began having these severe headaches and . . . she was one of the few women who were in the leadership within CASA. And they just ridiculed her for her headaches, and it was a few of us who pushed her to go to the doctor because they didn't seem to be normal. She was dead in about a year. But that to me was symbolic of how the women were treated." This refusal to address the complexity of individual lives was a major weakness. Although not without problems, both the Panthers and East Wind experimented with collectivized child care, alternative living and social arrangements, and conflict resolution, including around romantic relationships. One member of the League of Revolutionary Struggle explained that if an organization is going to require a life-encompassing commitment, then it must be willing to engage in people's lives. While some organizations went overboard and were clearly repressive, there was a genuine need to appreciate individuals as bundles of feelings, relationships, needs, and responsibilities, instead of seeing them as atomistic beings.

Sexual Relations

Throughout the New Left, including the Third World Left, activists became romantically and sexually involved with each other. Todd Gitlin has described how women who joined activist organizations often found them-selves as part of a serial harem in which their status was derived from their lover.[54] In fact, two tendencies characterized sexual relations among activists in this period. There was the idea of free love and sexual experimentation, and there was sexual conservatism, which one reviewer, discussing the New Communist movement, described as "comparable to the Christian coalition on homosexuality." CASA embodied elements of both. In terms of the first tendency, there were among CASA's male leadership some known woman-izers who used their status to pursue sexual relationships, as the following interviewee explained.[55]

> We would talk about equality, right? And then, if you were in a car full of militant men, it was, "Hey, how about what's-her-name?" So there were contradictions of all types. The one that got me the most was sex-ism. Don't get me wrong, I'm a man struggling with sexism like all men are, but that was obvious. I mean we go to a meeting and everybody was talking about equality, "Sister so and so." And then we'd leave the meet-ing, and they were talking about how they wanted to get her in bed. It made no sense to me, and when I criticized it, it was "So what? No big thing, you are making too much out of it, man."

Such behavior suggests that at least some in the leadership viewed women as sexual objects. Not surprisingly, many women were hurt and felt used by such treatment, but when they tried to bring it up in the collective they were told that such matters were subjective and not for organizational dis-cussion. One response to this problem was to promote an alternative vision of sexual politics. Drawing on Mao's ideas of socialist morality, some opposed the casual sexual activity that was widespread within CASA, argu-ing that such behavior was not healthy for the individual or the organiza-tion. This became a major line of contention within CASA, as many felt that the leadership's sexual practices were the height of hypocrisy for an organi-zation that saw itself as the vanguard of revolutionary change.

Sexual liaisons also existed in East Wind and the BPP, but they seem to have been less damaging than in CASA—the question is why? This has been a difficult question for me to answer. When I shared this finding with col-leagues and friends, people would readily attribute the difference to ma-chismo. While I can personally attest to the deeply patriarchal nature of Chicana/o households and culture, I found this response somewhat troubling. To a certain extent, such casual assertions draw on a deep reservoir of preju-dice and condemnation of Mexicana/o culture. Moreover, preliminary evi-dence suggests that gender relations in the August Twenty-ninth Movement were not as oppressive. Although I believe that CASA's problematic gender relations stemmed primarily from its political ideology rather than simplistic cultural causes, at least two issues must be addressed, however briefly, as they are key to understanding machismo itself: Catholicism and Chicana sexuality. The extreme sexism and double standards of Catholicism, along with its glorification of virginity, permeated Mexicana/o culture, and this, coupled with colonial domination, whether from Spain or the United States, created a situation in which males had enormous control over females, whose bodies were vigorously patrolled and defended. Mexicana bodies essentially became sites of both patriarchal and anticolonial struggle.[56] Thus part of the explanation for CASA's behavior does indeed lie in the unique way that Catholicism and national oppression had shaped Mexicana/o culture. This was the history CASA inherited. To a large degree it was continued by *el movimiento*, since Chicano men were fighting to regain their manhood and, despite Chicanas' best efforts, that vision of masculinity rarely included women as equals but rather viewed them merely as helpers, caretakers, and lovers.

While this provides some historical context, it is not sufficient to explain why CASA's gender relations differed so dramatically from those of East Wind and the BPP, especially given that the late sixties and early seventies were a time of unprecedented sexual experimentation. This brings us to Chicana sexuality. While it is important not to treat Chicanas as passive victims, research suggests that they may have hesitated to embrace new sexual practices, as they tended to be more sexually conservative.[57] It was suggested by both sexes that women in CASA were not satisfied with the context in which sexual relations occurred. In particular, it is possible that Chicanas desired some commitment and exclusivity on the part of their sexual partners, which in turn led to hurt feelings and further eroded the solidarity and esprit de corps that any volunteer organization needs to function. Further widening the chasm of expectations and desires between Chicanas and Chicanos was male opportunism. More than one interviewee suggested that while some Black and Latino male activists dismissed the white counterculture as irrelevant, they did not hesitate to borrow the concept of "free love" and to belittle traditional notions of commitment and marriage as bourgeois. While sexual and romantic relationships may seem like a peripheral arena, CASA's experience demonstrates the extent to which sexuality pervades our lives, including vanguard organizations, and how it shapes larger gender relations.

EAST WIND

East Wind was arguably the most effective organization at challenging sexism and traditional gender relations. Though women in East Wind did not achieve the visibility of women in the BPP—partly because it was a collective rather than a hierarchical organization—they did not endure the domination that women in CASA or the BPP did. Although most East Wind members described the organization as sexist, insofar as it was male dominated and women had to organize to make themselves and their issues heard, there is little evidence of misogynist or physically or emotionally abusive behavior. Indeed, one woman even refuted the charge that East Wind was sexist by pointing to its strong female leadership. Several factors contributed to this exceptionalism, including the relatively weak development of a nationalist ideology within East Wind (relative to CASA and the BPP); the ability of women to unite, find a common voice, and demand change—which was partly due to the existence of a vibrant Asian American women's movement; the willingness of men to entertain change; and, perhaps most importantly, the belief that cultural change was essential to revolution.

The Party Line

Even though East Wind left a sparse written record, members of the collective were involved in *Gidra*, which, like *Sin Fronteras*, devoted a special issue to women.[58] While the special issue offers numerous insights on gender relations, gender discussions were not absent from other issues. Contributing to the special issue was recognized as important political work and figured prominently in the political development of the female participants and, perhaps to a lesser extent, the entire organization. The overall result was to place gender relations firmly on East Wind's agenda.

    Gidra reveals a great deal about how Asian American female activists defined themselves and their struggle. Like Chicana/o and Black leftists, Asian American radicals approached issues of women, men, and gender within the context of class and race. Yet they were acutely aware of the sexism of the movement itself and the need to recast feminism in light of the complex reality of women of color.

> Understanding this phenomenon [male chauvinism] and always keeping it in mind brings us to the realization that rather than condemning, putting down, separating from, fighting with, crying "chauvinist" at, or constantly competing against men—we should instead direct our energy towards giving constructive criticism to the brothers, at the same time explaining why what they have done is an act of male chauvinism. . . .
> At all times we should try to set an exemplary example of the type of women we are advocating: self-determining, strong, sensitive human beings. In this way, the struggle to end the oppression of women will be expedited as both women and men join forces to combat the existing system which perpetuates this oppression and exploitation of women.

> Since it is this system which demonstrates this same sensitivity towards poor people and people of color, we see that the woman's struggle is not and cannot be separated from the struggle of all oppressed people to gain liberation.[59]

Asian American activists not only placed the roots of patriarchy squarely at the feet of capitalism but emphasized *how* to combat it.

The special issue of *Gidra* also highlighted problems distinct to Asian American women, including the Vietnam War, the "sale" of Asian women, and the hypersexuality associated with Asian and Asian American women. This last issue illustrates the gendered nature of racism and imperialism, which activists were aware of. Scholars have demonstrated how both colonization and anti-Asian racism resulted in the production of an emasculated and desexualized male and at the same time a hypersexualized, submissive female. Such images were rooted in a distinct political economy in which Asian males were seen as economic competition and/or a moral threat. The construction of the Asian female is an overt attempt on the part of men, primarily though not entirely white men, to retain their privilege and dominance. Radical Asian Americans fought such stereotypes and sought to portray Asian American women realistically by uncovering the political economic roots of such images.[60]

Articles also emphasized the intersection of gender, race, and class, particularly in terms of Asian American women and workers. Writers examined the hardships that immigrant Asian workers faced and routinely drew upon Mao's argument that women's freedom was tied to the abolition of private property and capitalism. The sexist nature of the movement was also analyzed, as activists reviewed the causes of male chauvinism and speculated how gender relations might look under socialism or other social systems.[61] Like Blacks and Chicanas/os, Asian Americans situated male chauvinism within the context of white racism.

> There is a group of primarily Asian-American males who feel that they have been so "emasculated" by white racism that they cannot stand to see women in roles of equality or leadership in the movement. This rather subjective understanding has several serious consequences. These men fail to realize that the white stereotype of the Asian woman as a sleek and sexy Susie Wong is just as dehumanizing to Asian women as the bucktoothed-laundry man stereotype is to Asian men. . . . Second, there is a group of more "traditional" male chauvinists. . . . In general, they feel that women should be subordinate in the political movement because they are both mentally and physically weaker than men. . . . Thirdly, there is a group of primarily Asians who have had little contact

with women. Women cause political havoc among such men since they treat women according to stereotypes or fantasies, rather than as intelligent people with a political contribution to make.

The picture appears very grim, yet there are several ways out. First, women could split the movement and organize on their own. Second, women could drop out of politics altogether. Third, both men and women who are sincere about revolutionary commitment can try to struggle with the problem on a political level. . . . Clearly, the third alternative is the happiest solution and also the most feasible for people truly interested in giving the words "liberation struggles" a real meaning.[62]

Asian American women consistently and creatively voiced their frustration with the sexism of the movement. In addition to pointing out contradictions and chauvinistic behavior in essays and political analyses, they expressed themselves through stories, cartoons, poems, and forums.[63] With one notable exception—less violence—the problems that Asian American women faced did not differ significantly from those of Chicanas and Black women. Although East Wind sought to ensure female leadership at all times, some women still felt excluded from decision making and were treated as helpers rather than equals, and the collective had to contend with sexual and romantic tensions. And, when violence did threaten, it was addressed.

I received a phone call from a close sister. She asked if I would come to a meeting of some sisters who were getting together to deal with R———, a "brother" in the community. He had beat up sisters while he had been loaded. When I arrived, I saw the reason why the sisters were angry. E——— had a black eye and bruises. I was then briefed of R———'s other instances of getting loaded and beating up sisters.

The action which ensued was politically significant. When one sister lunged him, I felt my heart jump and I was ready for action but the tussle did not last long. The political significance was that the sisters showed their solidarity in a very concrete way. . . . Although many of the sisters, like myself, feel that physical violence is wrong, we chose this method to show our support because we felt that this was the only action which would make an impression on R———.[64]

This story, which I heard from an East Wind member and read in *Gidra*, was widely repeated, suggesting its exceptional nature. What is important, however, is the decision to confront the offender collectively. This kind of solidarity distinguished the women of East Wind. Similar stories circulated within CASA. In one case, the women effectively challenged the offender, but in the other, when the man was opposed, he threatened the women and his girlfriend with further violence.

Sexual relations could also be problematic in East Wind and the larger Asian American movement, but again, the political space existed to challenge it. Consider the following poem.

SISTER
Para Nuestra Hermanas (For Our Sisters) [65]

Have you seen the revolutionary sister
Rapping to the masses of the poor
    She talks about revolution—change
    She talks about redistributing wealth
    to all
She reads Mao & Marx/   Che & Lenin
She's for real
She believes in what she does
    She loves you
    She loves her people
She sleeps little/   works hard
Sometimes her eyes show it
She tries to hide it/   she smiles
She's friendly/   loves children
She talks with the junkies
And understands
She's a woman
And she loves.
She'll die
Loving you
    I understand you want to lay her.

The poem "Sister" describes the ideal revolutionary woman. She is a militant, dedicated activist but is motivated by love and manages to maintains her soft side. Because this archetype is an ideal, the suggestion that she is seen merely as an object of sexual desire is all the more damning. Although the BPP discussed such issues internally, they were not addressed so openly. The ability to publicly state a problem and have it acknowledged is highly important. Besides empowering the aggrieved individual, open discussion helps reveal the structural nature of the problem rather than having it remain an individual burden, as it was for many CASA women.

Despite such political openings, revolutionary images in *Gidra* were dominated by men. Asian American men, like African American and Chicano men, felt an urgent need, albeit slightly different, to reclaim their masculinity. A key difference was class, however. Because Japanese American men tended to come from more prosperous households, a man's inability to provide for his family was felt somewhat less acutely. Nonetheless, Nikkei

Figure 16. Revolutionary Asian woman. The Asian American movement celebrated female Asian revolutionaries. Source: Artist unknown. *Gidra* 3 (June 1971): 7.

men were all too familiar with the inability to protect their families, as seen in the internment, housing discrimination, glass ceilings, and general discrimination. In addition, society's begrudging acknowledgment of the economic and professional success of Asian American men was accompanied by a desexualization and concomitant erosion of masculinity, which may partly explain activists' fascination with guns, as Viet Nyugen has suggested.[66]

Representations of guns were widespread and deserve some mention. Guns symbolized resistance to the existing social formation, and images of people with guns signaled their revolutionary potential. Guns were not uncommon in the 1970s, although it is uncertain to what extent East Wind members actually used them. Gun images were inspired by the BPP and Asian revolutionaries, both of whom were engaged in armed struggle and served as models for many Asian American radicals. Representations of people with guns were not restricted to males: photos and drawings of Chinese and Vietnamese women carrying guns were common (see figure 16), as were detailed discussions of the role of women in Third World revolutions. For instance, the Anti-Imperialist Women's Conference (Vancouver, 1971) featured a number of Asian women. Numerous East Wind women attended

Figure 17. Asian American women activists. The women who worked on *Gidra*'s special women's issue. Source: Photograph by Mike Murase for *Gidra* 3 (January 1971): 3.

the conference, which celebrated revolutionary Asian women and sharpened the lines between white and nonwhite feminists. While Asian women were more likely to be shown with guns, Asian American women were more apt to be depicted as political activists.[67] They were shown participating in rallies, working on *Gidra*, and otherwise building the movement.

Gidra not only provided more space to express women's voices and experiences but welcomed creative work (even more than the *Black Panther*), including poetry, stories, and comics, that conveyed a range of female experiences. The final photograph (figure 17), featuring many of the women who worked on the special issue of *Gidra*, sums up the unique sense of sisterhood within the Asian American left. This photo, while seemingly insignificant, struck me as fairly remarkable. The fact that the women even *thought* to have a picture of themselves taken reflects a higher level of collective feminist consciousness than existed in either CASA or the BPP. Although women in these other organizations did things together and supported each other, those relations were largely personal and not institutionalized—even by a photograph.

Leadership, Participation, and the Division of Labor

It is difficult to compare East Wind's leadership patterns to those of the BPP and CASA because as a collective it lacked a rigid hierarchy and the power relations were thus less apparent. For example, there was no single chairperson or minister of defense in East Wind, but interviewees reported that efforts were always made to ensure a female co-chair. Nonetheless, despite the presence of some highly chauvinistic males, East Wind women enjoyed some real success in challenging patriarchy. In their ideology, unlike CASA's orthodox ideology, sexism was not reduced to a byproduct of capitalism but depicted as a relation partly constituted by capitalism that had to be fought on its own terms. Interviewees differed on the efficacy of efforts to promote female leadership. While some insisted that East Wind was characterized by powerful female leadership, others, including the following interviewee, saw it differently: "We always tried to keep some gender balance in the leadership, but we never developed women's leadership to the point where it became self-asserting. It was always dominated by [certain men], so we got into this cult of personality. There was a lot of leadership problems."

Significantly, East Wind was aware of the importance of female leadership from the beginning. Perhaps this was because East Wind was forged from several existing groups and the collective contained female members from the outset (although CASA did also). In addition, much of the female membership brought some level of feminist consciousness with them to the organization. In any event, female leadership became an issue early on.

There was a rough gendered division of labor within the leadership itself, with men concentrated in theoretical and political activities, while women focused on community outreach and organizing. Though some women participated in theoretical endeavors, others felt alienated by the emphasis on theory and political study. As one activist recalled:

> There was a period when people spent a lot of time studying. And this is a group of people who were very, very active. Everybody has to stop and reflect at some time. I think it was good to do that, but I think the group went into a weird period of study, study, study, instead of do, do, do. And in discussions like that, certain people will start talking all the time, and other people won't say anything, because they won't know what to say. It's really hard. And I know [I and other women] went through this feeling of "I can't do this. I'm not cut out for this. I'm not good enough to make it in this."

As in CASA, the culture of study had a negative impact on many women in that it made them feel inadequate—a feeling that carried over into other dimensions of their work and perhaps affected their sense of self. It should be stressed that women in East Wind and CASA were not opposed to study per se but were uncomfortable with how it was conducted and had a fear, which was not unfounded, that study was being privileged over community work. These concerns were sufficiently strong to compel a few women to separate temporarily from the organization. They rejoined when the focus returned to community service and organizing.

Female members also created their own study groups outside East Wind. Asian American women, far more than either Chicanas or Black women, gravitated toward the model of women's groups introduced by white feminists. These groups provided relatively safe spaces for Asian American women to explore a whole range of issues and to pursue political study in a more comfortable setting.[68]

The role of Asian American women's groups deserves closer consideration. Although women-only spaces were popular among all racial/ethnic groups in the 1970s, East Wind women participated in independent groups like the Asian Women's Center and Asian Sisters in far greater numbers than their sisters in the BPP and CASA.[69] Asian American women formed their own groups in response to their discomfort with the white women's movement. Besides consciousness-raising, women engaged in study and explored questions of identity and sexuality. Overall, these groups had a great impact on East Wind's gender relations. Several interviewees described their influence:

> The leadership always had women in it, and they played fairly strong roles. I remember because there was a women's movement, and the women's groups that were formed in the late sixties and early seventies were very strong. It was Chinese and Japanese women in these huge women's groups. Women were very clear about not taking a back seat or trying not to allow that to happen. CWC [Community/Workers Collective] had a discussion about women's roles, and a lot of the struggle was [about] chauvinism and things like that.

> There were a lot of women's groups for Asian women. . . . Women started talking to each other, because there was a lot of networking, and comparing notes and realizing that there were these patterns where you make coffee, you're not the one ever to speak, people don't turn to you for ideas. . . . It wasn't until people started talking to each other that they realized it was more than just the group that they were in.

> I remember there was a big citywide meeting for planning one of the demonstrations. There was maybe fifty people in a room, and everyone went around and introduced themselves. This one guy introduced him-

self and said, "And this is my wife, but she doesn't have anything to say.". . . So it wasn't like people were up in arms, but everybody just gasped. It was good in a way because it really sharpened up what women were grumbling about. And the most interesting thing about it was what she said. Everybody said, "No, let her introduce herself." And she said, "Well, I told him to say that because I don't have anything to say." And so from that women said, "Let's get together and talk." So there was a lot of groupings. After a series of meetings we developed a multimedia presentation, to sort of bring out the discussion about sexism.

To this day I cannot say that I am a feminist, and I think it's because in those days the feminist movement to us was like very middle-class white women who saw the enemy as men, and we didn't see it that way. We were really pissed off at these things that happened with men, but they weren't the enemy. And that was sort of the approach of the women's group. There was [even] a men's group that formed for a short time. It was made up of a lot of the boyfriends of the women's group. They didn't know how to deal with us.

Female members of East Wind participated in such groups and in turn they brought a feminist consciousness to the organization.

East Wind's relatively successful gender politics should not be attributed solely to women. Equally important was men's willingness, or at least tolerance, of change. While few male members might have identified as feminists at the time, most conceded that women should be treated as equals. One reason for this openness was that East Wind saw cultural change, including gender relations, as part of a larger revolutionary project. In this respect East Wind was similar to the white New Left in that it emphasized self-change as a vehicle for creating social change. Consequently, East Wind experimented with collective living and alternative cultural practices. Indeed, one male contributor to *Gidra* summarized the pervasive nature of gender relations as follows: "The women's struggle is the liberation of MEN. As women shed their roles so goes the 'masculine image,' the 'masculine ego,' and the 'masculine hang-up.' . . . The old order will be destroyed for the creation of a new, emancipated order. . . . Everyone will be free to create humanistic relationships from natural interactions. . . . Power to the Sisters."[70] Clearly, gender relations were not reduced to the "personal" or the "subjective," as in CASA, but were viewed as cultural, social, and economic relations in their own right.

A final contributor to East Wind's more egalitarian gender relations was the reduced role of nationalism. While East Wind had nationalist overtones, it did not compare to CASA and the BPP, both of which, because of their relatively more homogenous constituencies, developed more deeply entrenched nationalist ideologies and practices. In short, the lack of a strong nationalist orientation helped to erode the power of Asian American patriarchy.

The Third World Left was characterized by diverse and sometimes highly problematic gender relations, but it was a site for men and women to engage questions of gender equality and for women to develop as political leaders. Although gender relations were to a certain extent the Achilles' heel of the Third World Left, there was tremendous variation in how inequality and challenges to it were worked out and expressed. Although there is still much work to be done, this is one arena in which activists have learned from the past and in which significant progress has been made.

EIGHT

**The Third World Left Today
and Contemporary Activism**

Proposition 187; Rodney King and the 1992 uprising; Justice for Janitors; the Bus Riders' Union; the Hahn/Villaraigosa election; Three Strikes; Black-Korean tensions; globalization . . . [1] These are just some of the key events and processes that have created the contemporary political and economic landscape of Southern California. To what extent, if any, are these developments related to the 1960s and 1970s? What role might Third World Leftists have played in them? While the world, and Southern California in particular, has changed greatly over the last three decades, there are clear connections between the past and the present, although they are not always recognized. The media, for example, persist in portraying the sixties as the space of radical activism, thereby erasing any connection to contemporary efforts.[2] This is, of course, partly due to the countercultural moment of the sixties, which marked activism with a particular aesthetic,[3] but it is also due to political and economic changes. Activists in the New Left, Third World Left, and New Communist movement routinely talked about revolution, believing it was an actual possibility. In contrast, few talk about revolution today, and communism has largely been discredited. Indeed, the very term *Third World* has lost much of its currency. In short, material conditions have changed greatly. What was possible or even regarded as possible in the 1960s is not necessarily so today. While there are continuities with the past, including ongoing struggles against racism, poverty, U.S. militarism, and police abuse, there are also new challenges posed by the end of the Cold War, globalization, and heightened tensions between communities of color. In this chapter I examine contemporary activism in Los Angeles and assess where members of the Third World Left are today. I conclude with some general lessons to be learned from the experiences of the Third World Left.

While the participants of the Third World Left have changed a good deal, few have joined the corporate world or adopted right-wing politics. As Max Elbaum has observed, "[M]ost ex-party builders [builders of parties of the New Communist movement] did not retreat completely into private life or transfer allegiance to any antileft political trend. Rather, they gradually and almost invisibly meshed into the country's amorphous progressive milieu."[4] In terminology indicative of how things have changed, contemporary social justice activists identify as progressives rather than revolutionaries. This trend is certainly apparent in Los Angeles, where former members of the Third World Left are actively involved in politics, organizing, and community service. Even though the movement itself has collapsed, its legacy and impact can be seen in the greater empowerment of people of color, as well as in the coalitions and organizations forged out of the experiences and networks of that era.

Equally important have been the personal legacy and impact of the movement for individuals. Activists' participation in the Third World Left was also an intense process of personal transformation. Some people emerged from the process damaged and bitter, and in some cases tensions are still being played out by various factions. But many others were greatly empowered and have become highly productive members of society.

Upon the demise of the Third World Left, individuals focused on rebuilding their lives, making a living, and tending to their families.[5] This was an especially difficult time politically because the seventies were followed by the eighties, a period of intense conservatism in which the embers of the left were finally buried. However, as the eighties progressed, growing economic tensions and new forms of oppression, such as homelessness, immigrant bashing, and the rise of the prison-industrial complex, led to a new wave of grassroots mobilization. This work began bearing fruit in the 1990s. Not surprisingly, former members of the Third World Left, with their commitment to racial and economic justice, played important roles in these new projects. Such individuals, who carry with them a wealth of experience, have contributed actively to Los Angeles's rich political infrastructure, helping it to become one of the leading sites of progressive activism in the United States today.[6]

The current crop of progressive organizations differs from those of earlier times not only because this is a different historical moment but also because many activists have consciously tried to learn from past mistakes. Table 10 provides a partial list of contemporary Los Angeles organizations with a connection to the Third World Left, either through key individuals or, in some cases, through their emergence from previous organizations.

A review of what the former members of the Third World Left are currently doing challenges the widely held belief that radical politics is the

Table 10 *Partial list of contemporary Los Angeles organizations with links to the Third World Left*

Action for Grassroots Empowerment and Neighborhood Development
 Alternatives (AGENDA)

Asian Pacific American Labor Alliance (APALA)

California Nurses Association

Coalition Against Police Abuse (CAPA)

Community Coalition for Substance Abuse Prevention and Treatment

Community Service Organization (CSO)

Community Youth Sports & Arts Foundation

Families to Amend California's Three Strikes (FACTS)

Great Leap

Hermandad Mexicana Nacional

Hotel Employees and Restaurant Employees Union (HERE)[1]

Japanese American Community Services—Asian Involvement

Labor/Community Strategy Center

Liberty Hill Foundation

National Coalition for Redress and Reparations (NCRR)

The New Black Panther Party

One-Stop Immigration

Visual Communications (VC)

SOURCE: Compiled by author.
[1]Merged with the Union of Needletrades, Textiles, and Industrial Employees in 2004 to form UNITE HERE.

province of the young. Though few can maintain the all-encompassing commitment that revolutionary politics requires, such thinking reduces activism to a youthful pursuit and prevents us from appreciating how political commitment and work may change over the course of a life. Although the specific outcomes and trajectories of activists' lives varied greatly, patterns can still be discerned among racial/ethnic groups. These differing patterns provide a glimpse into how Southern California's racial and class structure has evolved over time and highlight the changing political landscape.

THE THIRD WORLD LEFT AT THE DAWN
OF THE TWENTY-FIRST CENTURY

Although the people I interviewed for this project were engaged in a wide variety of pursuits, most were still politically active. Many were involved in full-time political work, whether as politicians, organizers, community workers, artists, or fund-raisers, in a wide range of sectors, including labor, youth, arts, civil rights, immigrant advocacy, police abuse, and ethnic-specific work. Others had became teachers, civil servants, journalists, and administrators—careers that allowed them to pursue community activism on the side or as part of the job. Still others had redefined the nature of political activism and now contributed to the community through spiritual work and healing. No one was engaged in work that was antithetical to his or her earlier beliefs and practices.[7] Further, though most were aware of the limitations and weaknesses of the Third World Left, no one renounced it. Rather, most appreciated that it reflected a particular place and time and were thankful that they had been part of it.

Despite the diversity of careers and lifestyles that former activists assumed, there were clear patterns reflecting racial and class differences. For instance, Asian Americans were most likely to become professionals and continue their activist work in that capacity. In contrast, former Panthers struggled the most financially and sometimes emotionally. Not only were they, in the words of one activist, "the walking wounded," but their limited class mobility reflected the barriers that working-class Blacks still face. Members of CASA tended to have the primary objective of working for or with organized labor. Many eventually earned college degrees, and the labor movement itself became a vehicle for upward mobility.

CASA

Because of CASA's focus on workers, a significant percentage of the membership decided to concentrate on changing labor laws. According to one interviewee, "In CASA we were all committed to doing work for workers, which also meant most of us were going to go to law school, to work for the unions. That was the goal, to work for unions, and to do it from a legal standpoint." This was not idle talk. Although former members of CASA followed a variety of paths, including acting and work in academe and foundations, a highly visible contingent entered the labor movement. Some became involved with worker and immigration projects, such as Hermandad Mexicana Nacional and One-Stop Immigration, but many others worked for unions and went on to become labor lawyers and/or politicians aligned with the labor movement. Today there is a dense network of ties between former members of CASA who either are involved in labor itself or directly support it through legal services, foundations, progressive legislation, and community/worker services and alliances.

Although CASA never succeeded in functioning as the vanguard of the revolution, its members have been instrumental in the re-creation of a progressive labor movement in Los Angeles. When CASA began in the 1970s the national labor movement was spiraling downward, and it bottomed out when Ronald Reagan fired striking air-traffic controllers in 1980. Moreover, immigrant workers were still considered peripheral to any organizing effort. Thus there was limited institutional support for CASA's goals. Unions were indifferent, or even hostile, to the needs of such workers, and there was little public support for organized labor. Third World Left and especially Chicana/o organizations, despite their small size and marginality, were some of the few advocates for immigrant workers.

By the 1990s things had changed considerably. Organized labor, led primarily by the service unions, began to refocus on organizing workers and reaching out to a rapidly changing labor force increasingly composed of women, immigrants, and workers of color. As a result, low-wage service unions, led by groups such as Justice for Janitors and the Hotel Employees and Restaurant Employees Union (HERE), began winning some highly visible contracts and contributed to a growing sense of labor militancy that has profoundly affected not only workers' lives but the larger political culture of Southern California.[8]

One of the factors that contributed to this political shift was demographic change. Over the last several decades Southern California has been transformed by massive immigration from Latin America and Asia. Whereas in 1970 Latinas/os were 14.6 percent of Los Angeles County's population, they registered 45 percent in 2000 (see table 11). As a result, the Latina/o population is rapidly growing, while the white and Black populations are diminishing through outmigration and lower fertility rates. Such changes have profound implications for the racial and class structure of the region. Specifically, Los Angeles County has become the U.S. capital of the working poor, who are composed overwhelmingly of Latina/o immigrants. In effect, there has been a growing racial and class overlap in Los Angeles's working class: the poor are increasingly nonwhite and the wealthy are disproportionately white.[9]

Complementing these demographic and economic changes, particularly the proliferation of low-wage work, Los Angeles boasted a contingent of labor activists who had historically focused on low-wage and immigrant labor. These people did not have to be convinced that people of color, women, and immigrants should be the focal point of any union strategy: they had been talking about and trying to promote such issues for the previous twenty years, even when organized labor had dismissed such workers as unorganizable and persisted in myopically focusing on white male workers.

Table 11 *Los Angeles County population by race/ethnicity
and poverty, 2000*

Racial/Ethnic Group	% of Total Population	% beneath Poverty Line
Latino	45.0	24.2
White	31.0	8.5
Asian American	12.0	14.2
African American	9.5	24.4
American Indian	0.3	22.5

SOURCE: United Way, *A Tale of Two Cities* (Los Angeles: United Way of Greater Los Angeles, 2003), 11; United Way, *2003 State of the County Report* (Los Angeles: United Way of Greater Los Angeles, 2003), 32.

One of the more prominent such activists is María Elena Durazo, the president of HERE, Local 11. After CASA collapsed she began working for the International Ladies Garment Workers Union, an experience that showed her firsthand the transformative capacity of collective action among workers. After several years there she attended the People's College of Law and worked part time at a labor law firm that represented HERE's Local 11. This connection eventually led to a job as an organizer with the local. Unfortunately, at that time Local 11 was racist and not committed to rank-and-file leadership and democracy. "In L.A. labor's prize moment of idiocy, the leadership of the Hotel Employees and Restaurant Employees Union spent $100,000 in a 1984 lawsuit to ensure union meetings would *not* be translated into Spanish for their membership—70% of whom were Latino."[10] Sensing the untapped potential of the local, Durazo ran for office and was elected president. Besides radically reorienting the organization to meet the needs of its members, Durazo has made Local 11, like Justice for Janitors, a model of the new social movement unionism, which stresses community-labor links, direct action, democracy, and worker leadership.[11]

Although Durazo is remarkable, she did not accomplish this alone. She has effected such changes partly by her participation in a series of networks and relationships focused on a shared goal: to build a vibrant and relevant labor movement that serves the needs of low-income and immigrant workers and workers of color. These networks, a history of working together, and a sense of trust are vital to the development of effective political cultures.

Such political cultures do not evolve overnight but are built out of earlier organizing efforts and relationships.[12] Former members of CASA had created not only a network of like-minded people but seeds of resistance within the "old" labor movement that would blossom with the advent of greater institutional support.

East Wind

Most members of East Wind became professionals and continued their political involvement either through their occupations or in a volunteer capacity. Full-time activists were concentrated in community service, labor, and progressive Democratic politics, while those who had pursued less activist-oriented careers, including public sector work, still participated as volunteers in the above sectors, as well as alternative radio, youth work, healing, and teaching. Only one interviewee consciously chose to remain close to his working-class roots, despite a college degree. In keeping with the larger politics of East Wind, most were still involved in the Japanese American community, but they also engaged in pan-Asian work and often interracial work.

Just as CASA made a significant impact on the contemporary labor movement, East Wind was highly influential in the Japanese American struggle for redress and reparations. The two organizations differ, however, in that members of CASA entered the labor movement because of a set of shared commitments and a clearly defined goal. In contrast, former members of East Wind joined the League of Revolutionary Struggle (LRS), which only later became involved in the quest for redress.[13] Although not all of East Wind joined, many members did, so that the activists were able to remain fairly consolidated politically. Because the LRS's political ideology emphasized working with the most oppressed nationalities and sectors, many Japanese Americans ended up working in Chicana/o labor campaigns, such as the Watsonville strike, or in Black communities. While most Japanese Americans embraced such work, over time some resented not being able to spend more time among the Nikkei population, as the LRS did not consider Japanese Americans to be among the most oppressed. However, when Japanese Americans brought the nascent struggle for redress and reparations to the league's attention, the LRS, seeing the potential significance of the issue, decided to rally behind it. As a result, former members of East Wind working through the LRS played a prominent role in the pursuit for reparations by working with the National Coalition for Redress and Reparations.

The campaign for redress and reparations was highly significant. It was a huge step forward for a community that still struggled with the shame of internment and dealt with it primarily by repressing its past. Consequently, the initial struggle for redress was internal, as many mainstream Japanese Americans opposed the idea. Not only did the idea seem utterly implausible, but many were uncomfortable with making such demands on society. As one internee explained, "I never thought it would happen. My attitude was 'I'll believe it when I see it.' I didn't think people were sympathetic, or saw it as a hardship, or that they would even be sorry. You know, they told us that it [internment] was for our own good." This is where the leadership of revolutionary activists was so instrumental. As people used to thinking outside the box and armed with the discipline to conceive and carry out a long-term campaign, activists began shifting the discourse and attitudes of the larger Japanese American community, while at the same time making connections with potential allies. Having built this kind of base, they were then able to take the struggle to the U.S. public. At last, President Reagan, in one of his finer moments, offered a formal apology and authorized monetary reparations to internees in 1988.[14]

The Japanese American pursuit of redress and reparations was a milestone in the struggle for democracy and civil rights among U.S. people of color. This was one of the few times that the U.S. government acknowledged that it had violated the civil and human rights of a racial/ethnic minority group and offered monetary compensation. While $20,000, the amount given to internees, could never compensate for what they had lost and suffered, it was an important step in attempting to heal an open wound, as well as a move toward reconciliation and a reminder to us all of the precarious nature of freedom. The campaign for redress and reparations has become a model that other racial/ethnic groups have studied in an effort to address past grievances, including the current movement for slave reparations.[15]

While Japanese Americans continue to be active in Nikkei struggles, much of their activism has shifted toward the larger Asian/Pacific Islander (A/PI) community. This has become necessary because the A/PI population has diversified tremendously and the Nikkei continue to decline. As recently as 1970 Japanese Americans were the largest Asian American group in the region, but today they are one of the smallest. Since the 1965 Immigration Act, Chinese immigrants have been coming to Southern California in record numbers, as have Filipinas/os, Koreans, and Vietnamese, all of whom now have larger populations than Japanese Americans. Further, the Japanese American population is declining, some say vanishing, due to intermarriage, as members are marrying whites, Latinas/os, Blacks, and especially other Asians in unprecedented numbers. In addition, Southern California

Nikkei have continued to prosper economically and socially so that their income now rivals that of whites. Accordingly, while Japanese American activists still take on important community issues, such as the current struggle for a recreational center in Little Tokyo, they frequently focus on other Asian American groups when it comes to issues of class and poverty.[16]

Regardless of such shifts, Japanese Americans remain extremely important to the political landscape of Los Angeles. Because of their long history in the region, Japanese Americans have one of the most established community service traditions among A/PIs. One of the results of the Asian American movement of the 1960s and 1970s was the development of a whole series of Asian American−oriented social services. Originally built primarily, but not exclusively, by Japanese Americans, these social service organizations have long since diversified to serve a more varied and immigrant-oriented population. Many of these organizations are still led by Japanese Americans, a fact that is at times the cause of resentment but also illustrates the historical significance of this population.

The Black Panther Party

The experience of former Panthers is markedly different from that of either East Wind or CASA. In general, the lives of Panthers followed more divergent paths: Some attained national prominence, others emerged as community leaders, while still others endured material, emotional, and physical hardships. At the national level this diversity of outcomes precludes any generalizations: Assata Shakur lives in Cuba; Mumia Abu-Jamal sits on Death Row; Eldridge Cleaver became a political conservative before his death; Kathleen Cleaver is a lawyer and academic; Elaine Brown married a French industrialist; Ericka Huggins teaches yoga to educators; Angela Davis is a prominent academic; David Hilliard has sought to preserve the history of the party; Bobby Seale hawks barbecue sauce; and Huey Newton was murdered in a drug deal in 1989. While a degree of sensationalism has been attached to prominent Panthers, such has rarely been the case for the rank and file. Instead, many struggle with unresolved issues stemming from betrayals on the part of the party, the collapse of the Black Panther Party (BPP) itself, and physical and emotional problems stemming from their experiences of violence. In addition, the general poverty and limited education of much of the rank and file have prevented many Panthers from entering the middle class, in distinct contrast to Chicana/o and Asian American activists.

The differing trajectories and outcomes of activists' lives constituted one of the most pronounced differences that I found in this study. This had implications for whom I was able to contact and how they responded to me. For instance, given that many CASA members were associated with organized labor, they were relatively easy to track down, and many (except for some prominent politicians) consented to an interview. Moreover, as a Chicana, I knew some of the activists from before the project and was able to interview some highly visible CASA members early on, making contacts that in turn facilitated subsequent interviews. Asian American activists were fairly easy to locate, as they were embedded in relatively visible institutions. In addition, the small size and close-knit nature of the Japanese American community made it easy to identify potential interviewees.[17] But because Japanese Americans were so rooted in mainstream institutions, they were more reluctant to talk. While some may have been wary of an outsider, others did not wish to share this chapter of their lives. Indeed, some of those who consented to an interview requested anonymity, and one actually withdrew permission to use any material from the interview upon seeing the transcript. Even accounting for my outsider status, these experiences suggest some ambivalence among Asian American members regarding their past.

And then there were the Panthers. Finding Los Angeles Panthers was a difficult task. This was partly due to my lack of familiarity with the African American community, as well as the fact that only a handful of Southern California Panthers had become famous or highly institutionalized. Although it was relatively easy to find and contact high-profile people like Michael Zinzun of the Coalition Against Police Abuse, most Panthers were more difficult to reach, as few were attached to formal institutions. I had a major breakthrough, however, when Geronimo Pratt was released from prison in 1997. To commemorate this event, UCLA convened a forum that former Panthers attended and at which I was able to make some initial contacts. Although many Panthers were initially suspicious of me—I was asked more than once if I was with the FBI—I found that although I was a Chicana with no history in their community, there was some willingness to share their stories. Rank-and-file Panthers were painfully aware that dominant narratives of the BPP were written by party leaders or outsiders and did not necessarily reflect their experiences—which they wanted known.

Equally important, however, are the Panthers that I was *not* able to interview because they were either dead or incarcerated. No organization experienced the level of political repression that the Panthers did, and the toll can be seen in the casualties. Ward Churchill, in his analysis of state repression, found that more Panthers had been killed by the police in Los Angeles than in any other city.[18] While many Panthers were guilty of a variety of crimes, both violent and nonviolent, many were also framed and imprisoned by the state in an effort to destroy the party. One of the best examples of this is Geronimo Pratt (now known as geronimo ji Jaga), who was convicted of the 1968 murder of a white, female schoolteacher on a Santa Monica tennis court. Evidence was withheld that would have exonerated Pratt, suggesting that the state had an ulterior motive in his conviction. Specifically, the FBI had a wiretap that placed Pratt in Oakland at the time of the murder, but because of the state's desire to eliminate Pratt he ended up serving twenty-seven years for a crime he did not commit.[19] Accordingly, many former Panthers are currently, in prison, or have served time in prison, which greatly affects one's life chances.

While some of the Panthers I interviewed had completed college and become professionals, others were working in community service and/or full-time activism, while still others were just barely making it, trying to keep mind, body, and soul together. There are several reasons why former Panthers have had a harder time rebuilding their lives. For one, virtually all of the Panthers that I interviewed came from low-income working-class families. Many people from such backgrounds, regardless of their political involvement, have had a difficult time "making it" in the United States, as they must contend with inferior schools, high rates of unemployment, residential segregation, and police repression. However, these were not ordinary residents from South Central—they had been Panthers, and, as such, they had been in a state of war. Consequently, they bore many of the marks of those who have experienced intense conflict, including post-traumatic stress disorder, physical disabilities, shattered relationships, and a limited educational background and marketable set of skills.

Also contributing to the hardships that many former Panthers faced were racial and economic shifts. Many suspected, and there is considerable evidence to support the charge, that significantly more drugs began flowing into communities of color, especially Black communities, in the early 1980s. Some believed that this was the government's last attempt to stifle the political unrest that had been fermenting for decades, despite the fact that it was already in decline. Consequently, many poor communities were devastated by the waves of crack that hit the ghetto in the 1980s and the gangs that developed to manage its sale and distribution.[20]

In addition to the erosion of the social infrastructure that accompanied the crack epidemic, Black Los Angeles underwent increasing social, spatial, and economic fragmentation. Although the process of class polarization began in earnest in the late 1960s, it accelerated greatly, exacerbated by the rise of gang warfare and the drug epidemic. Middle-class and professional

Blacks found increasing opportunities in the service sector, both public and private, but low-income Blacks found fewer opportunities as the last remnants of the Fordist economy disappeared in the 1980s.[21] The subsequent "post-Fordist" economy was characterized by greater flexibility (read: less job security), a decline of the welfare state, an expansion of the service sector, heightened economic polarization, and vastly expanded incarceration. Some argue that such hardships have been intensified by greater economic competition from Latina/o immigrants, who are the preferred source of low-wage labor in the region.[22]

In response to these changes, many Blacks began leaving South Central to start a new life at the edges of Southern California. Places such as Riverside, San Bernardino, and Antelope Valley promised affordable housing and the chance to escape the problems of South Central. As a result, Los Angeles's Black population is declining relative to other groups.[23] Although African Americans are still a prominent force in Los Angeles, the community is painfully aware of what the future holds: a majority Latina/o city. Not surprisingly, many Blacks, particularly the older population, seek to cling to the past. This was evident in the 2001 mayoral race between Antonio Villaraigosa and James Hahn. Villaraigosa, a pro-labor Democrat with a long history of multiracial involvement and coalition building, lost to Hahn, a mainstream Democrat. James Hahn, the son of the legendary Kenneth Hahn, a white Los Angeles politician famous for his antiracist politics, captured the older Black vote by appealing to his father's legacy. The fact that so many African Americans would vote for the candidate who seemingly did not best represent their interests—James Hahn's record is weak at best—suggests their anxiety about the future.[24]

Los Angeles, like many other places, is in dire need of a politics and leadership that marginalized low-income residents, immigrants, and communities of color can mobilize around. This is a challenge, particularly in light of recent immigration, which has been so vast and concentrated that people have not had adequate time to adjust and learn each other's stories. Without such an incorporation process, immigrant bashing becomes more likely, as does the possibility of immigrants embracing a national racial order that denigrates African Americans. In many ways, this is one of the great challenges facing the United States: How will the racial formation be reconfigured by vast numbers of nonwhite immigrants? Developing a common framework is not easy because progressive political visions and movements don't just "happen." Rather, they are cultivated by efforts at both the grassroots and leadership levels to bring diverse communities together and to articulate sufficiently broad identities so that various groups can support each other without feeling threatened. But just as Los Angeles offers many challenges to the development of a broad-based movement for social justice, it offers many possibilities. If Los Angeles is able to forge such a movement, particularly one involving recent Asian and Latina/o immigrants, it could make a real impact on the city and serve as a model for other places.

One crucial aspect of the dynamics shaping Los Angeles is globalization. Globalization, the growing integration of capital, commodities, and people across the world, has become a major concern over the past decade, as it presents both challenges and opportunities. For the most part, we have seen a race to the bottom, as many places seek to attract capital by offering conditions that maximize profits. Yet we have also seen moments when pressure is applied to bring the wages, working conditions, and legal rights of impoverished and oppressive countries up to the standards of more prosperous ones.[25] Many observers treat globalization as an unprecedented shift ushering in a new historical era. They are both right and wrong. Although a new round of globalization may be occurring, globalization itself is hardly new. Equally profound moments of globalization occurred, for example, in 1492, or when the first shipment of African slaves arrived in the United States. In addition to such historical caveats, we must consider the geographical dimensions of globalization: globalization plays out differently across space. And given that Los Angeles is considered a "global city," with elements of both the "First World" and the "Third World," it has a distinctive character.[26] For instance, in Los Angeles, as in many other "First World" cities, labor activists must contend with industries threatening to relocate to Latin America and Asia, while at the same time activists are incorporating new populations like Mixtec immigrants into their organizing work, as large parcels of the Los Angeles landscape and economy belong to the "Third World." Thus in many ways globalization has created a new framework for activism that differs markedly from that of the 1960s and 1970s. Despite the unprecedented circumstances, however, there are continuities with the past, and most importantly, lessons to be learned. On the basis of this research as well as my own activism, I have identified the following key lessons from the Third World Left that can hopefully assist in movement building in a new era.

FOUR LESSONS OF THE THIRD WORLD LEFT

Democracy and Nonviolence

Despite its commitment to forging a more humane and socially just world, the Third World Left often fell short of its goal. Instead, it was plagued by violent, undemocratic, and abusive practices. There are many reasons for this, including the youth of the activists, the romance of violence and guns, the previous street experience of some activists, and harassment from law enforcement. The lack of a democratic culture manifested itself in several ways and seriously weakened the movement. One of the most debilitating characteristics was the cult of personality, in which leading political figures (usually men) with strong charismatic personalities unduly influenced group opinion, coerced others into supporting their agenda, and sometimes became almost revered.[27] While charismatic leaders often draw additional resources and attention to an organization, they also can stifle the leadership potential of others and create resentment on the part of the larger membership.

Democracy also suffered from various practices adopted from Marxism/ Leninism, including democratic centralism and self-criticism. Democratic centralism is a practice whereby decisions are openly debated but, once decided upon, are carried out by all members. Most members of the Third World Left (and the New Communist movement) adhered to some form of democratic centralism. Such a practice is useful insofar as it ensures that policies and decisions are executed and helps explain how a relatively small number of people could accomplish so much. But democratic centralism could also be problematic, particularly if the discussion had not been free and wide-ranging. Sometimes even *with* extensive debate, the leadership could and would decide on a course of action that was contrary to the desires of the membership. Such practices did not inspire confidence and helped account for high rates of turnover and disillusion.

Another potentially damaging practice was criticism and self-criticism. Again drawing from Marxism/Leninism, many organizations required individuals to identify their own shortcomings, as well as point out each others' weaknesses, which were to be reflected upon. Criticism and self-criticism were adopted to deal with a real problem: How to communicate short-comings of comrades so that the unit might become more effective as a whole? This was a pressing issue for the Third World Left given its goal of revolution and the discipline required to achieve it. In my interviews, many indicated that though there might have been some occasional hurt feelings, criticism, carried out in the manner intended, was an effective tool. The problems began when individuals used criticism to express personal grudges and when patterns of criticism began to reflect larger group inequalities. This was most evident in terms of gender. In certain organizations not only were women more likely to be criticized than men, but, when men were criticized, they might acknowledge the concern with a mere "Yes, I hear you, sister," and no substantive change afterwards. This defeated the purpose of the exercise, contributed to resentment, and reproduced gender inequalities.[28]

Developing appropriate forms of democracy within a social change organization is no easy task, and the lack of a democratic culture was widespread throughout most movements of the time.[29] Though the Third World Left reflected the larger culture and its inequalities, it was *trying* to be better. Activists wanted to create a new and better world and saw themselves as the vehicle for doing so. This required a fairly high level of self-awareness (or at least it should have). The challenge of building more democratic, accountable, and humane organizations is something contemporary groups are still struggling with today, and some progress has been made. Many organizations now strive to develop the leadership potential of *all* individuals so that they are able to speak their minds without being cowed by more powerful figures. In addition, many recognize the necessity of open debate and collaborative decision making, as well as the need to implement mechanisms that ensure a system of checks and balances. One factor contributing to greater democracy and openness is the leadership of women, many of whom were politicized in the sixties and seventies.

Gender/Sexuality

Though I have been somewhat critical of the gender relations of the Third World Left, gender is one arena that has undergone great transformation. The Third World Left was largely patriarchal, but it nonetheless created some powerful female activists. Participation in the Third World Left empowered men and women as they learned how to organize, challenge established power structures, become leaders, and serve the community. In short, they developed a sense of themselves as effective people. Once these women came into their own and continued their political work after the demise of the movement, they not only refused to tolerate sexism but realized they had the capacity to create more democratic and participatory organizations. Even many of the men interviewed recognized the need for gender equality and had made some efforts toward that end in their current organizing work.

The shift toward greater gender equality is evident in several ways. Most apparent is the rise of female leadership. Whereas only a few organizations among the Third World Left were female led, it is now commonplace to find women serving as executive directors of progressive organizations. In some cases they started the organizations themselves, whereas in others they rose through the ranks or were subsequently hired as directors. Women have also introduced a more collective leadership style that often promotes greater democracy. Indeed, research suggests that women in leadership tend to invest in the development of the rank and file, develop more collective approaches to decision making, and foster greater collaboration between organizations.[30] And even in male-led organizations, though to varying degrees, numerous men who emerged from the movements of the sixties and seventies recognize the need to foster greater female participation and leadership. This does not mean that patriarchy has vanished and that cases of sexual harassment and misconduct no longer surface within the activist community, but when they do, such behavior is understood to be unacceptable. Besides greater awareness among the leadership and a growing incorporation of gender analyses into organizational ideologies and training, young women today, who are a full generation removed from the Third World Left, are far less likely to tolerate the abuses that earlier activists did.[31]

Distinct but closely related to gender is sexuality, particularly homosexuality. Aside from declaring that it was the woman's revolutionary job to sleep with a brother, frank and open organizational discussions of sexuality were limited within the Third World Left, and homosexuality was largely taboo.[32] Ironically, just as the gay rights movement was blossoming and gays and lesbians were coming out of the closet, the Third World Left remained largely closed to such developments. In some cases homosexuals were actively shunned, as in struggles surrounding the participation of lesbians in International Women's Day, and at best they were expected to keep their sexual preferences quiet. Sexuality was certainly not seen as a struggle worth taking up.[33]

Fortunately, there has been some progress toward accepting queer activists within social justice organizations. In a few cases some groups have even developed a politics that includes the struggles of gays, lesbians, bisexuals, and transgendered persons. But these remain exceptions and there is still much work to be done. Far too often I have seen activists, especially young Latino and Black men, ridicule and dismiss queers and their struggle as irrelevant. This is not only cruel and insensitive but a political mistake. For only by building a broad united front of people who are working toward a shared set of goals will a dynamic movement for social change be created. Nationalist organizations in particular have remained ambivalent toward questions of gender, sexuality, and interethnic work.

Nationalism and Multiracial Politics

The Third World Left made significant progress in terms of interethnic cooperation. Although the relationships were not as deep as they might have been, this remains an important contribution that should be appreciated and built upon. Today many organizations in Los Angeles and nationally have created impressive models of multiracial activism, but many also resist it, preferring instead to focus on their own community.[34] The attraction to nationalism is understandable and has some merits insofar as it remains an important vehicle to politicize people, but it poses real political problems and challenges in demographically complex places like Los Angeles.

It is important to appreciate why oppressed people of color may favor nationalism as a political basis for mobilization. African Americans, especially low-income segments of the population, continue to face racism and segregation. Research and history indicate that race is still the most powerful basis for political consciousness among African Americans.[35] In addition, we must be sensitive to the fact that Black Angelenos are declining numerically and are confronting waning political power. These conditions help clarify why some Blacks may feel threatened and wish to focus on their own.

Latinas/os, namely Chicanas/os, also have a long history of nationalism, which, again, is understandable given how their identity and history have been erased by colonization, immigration, racism, and the "Americanization" process. Latinas/os' gravitation toward nationalist politics may intensify in the coming years, particularly as the children of immigrants grapple with difficult issues of identity, belonging, and exclusion in a society all too happy to dismiss them as criminals. Nationalist politics may also get a boost from the recent influx of Central American immigrants, who, understandably, wish to distinguish themselves from Mexicans.[36] These politics are especially complex in South Central Los Angeles, which has been transformed in recent years from a largely Black space to one that is half Latina/o. How the tension between nationalist and multinational politics will be resolved in such places is still uncertain.

A final factor to consider is the growing political power of Latinas/os. As Latinas/os begin to flex more political muscle, many of their politicians and activists have shown little interest in working with other communities of color, feeling secure in their ever-growing numbers—clearly a short-sighted view. The challenge for those interested in building a broad-based movement for social change is how to address the needs and fears that many people of color have, while at the same time working toward building a more integrated and ultimately internationalist movement.

Care must be taken not to dismiss nationalism out of hand. As Déborah Berman Santana has pointed out, not only are there multiple types of nationalism, but nationalism may be essential at particular historical moments and places.[37] So while nationalism may be entirely appropriate to the struggle of Puerto Ricans or native Hawaiians, I would argue it is not necessarily the most effective tool in contemporary Los Angeles, where multiple populations now share a potentially similar set of concerns and where the distribution of wealth and racial privilege will remain intact as long as those communities are divided. Anthony Thigpenn, a former Panther, explained, "Self-organization of a particular ethnicity or racial community can often be a legitimate form because the cultures and/or conditions of a particular community warrant that. But . . . we cannot limit ourselves to organizing just one group of people, because our vision of society is broader than that. And, if we're trying to organize on a large scale to gain real power, I don't believe there's any one ethnicity that can do it by themselves."[38]

The need for political solidarity is particularly acute among Latinas/os and African Americans. In addition to sharing the same space and similar class positions, these two groups are most likely to be pitched against each other as they fight over political and economic crumbs. Latinas/os are fast becoming the largest group in Los Angeles (and increasingly in other major cities), yet African Americans have a deeper and more established political infrastructure. Latinas/os constitute the poorest population, but Blacks continue to face the most discrimination.[39] These two groups clearly have certain commonalities and could potentially form a powerful coalition for social change, one focused on economic justice, community development, immigrant rights, and opposition to police abuse and the prison-industrial complex. All organizations need not be actively involved in all issues, but they should be aware of and sensitive to the needs and concerns of similarly positioned groups and not view them as irrelevant or, worse, as the opposition. Fortunately, some organizations have sought to bring Blacks and Latinas/os together, including the Community Coalition for Substance Abuse Prevention and Treatment (www.ccsapt.org/), Action for Grassroots Empowerment and Neighborhood Development Alternatives (AGENDA), and the Labor/Community Strategy Center (www.thestrategycenter.org/), all of which are explicitly antiracist and have a strong class analysis. Unfortunately, these organizations are still the exception.

A/PIs and committed whites must also be part of such a coalition, but Asians present special challenges because they are a highly polarized population. Although Latinas/os and Blacks are also fragmented by class and some segments have experienced significant mobility, the two still constitute a disproportionate share of the region's poor. In contrast, because of the nature of the post-1965 immigration, there is a growing number of wealthy A/PIs, a large and prosperous middle class, and a significant working class, especially among Chinese, Vietnamese, and Filipina/o immigrants. Accordingly, while much of the previous discussion applies to the thousands of A/PIs toiling away in sweatshops and the low-wage service sector, it does not necessarily apply to wealthy A/PIs, who have a different set of class interests. Indeed, as Yen Espiritu and Paul Ong have argued, class divisions limit the possibility of pan-Asian solidarity, let alone solidarity with other people of color. Such splits can be seen, for example, in tensions regarding affirmative action.[40] Many A/PIs are committed to affirmative action due to their continued experience with racism, as seen in the attack on Wen Ho Lee, employment discrimination, and hate crimes.[41] Moreover, they often have strong feelings of class solidarity, given their historic ties to the working class. Nevertheless, the potential for class conflict exists, as wealthy A/PIs may have interests antagonistic to those of workers and other communities of color. This is especially so for wealthy immigrants, who have not necessarily embraced an antiracist politics, given that they have had a far different set of experiences. But their children, who grow up in this society and have had to confront the reality of prejudice as well as interethnic contact, regardless of their class position, often see things differently. This is one indication of where political possibilities may lie.

The complicated racial and class positions of Asian Americans remind us that class cannot be equated with race and that racial formation is a dynamic process. Indeed, the existence of interethnic conflict and hostility is perhaps one of the greatest differences between the 1960s and the present. Because of immigration, economic shifts, and changing residential patterns, there are Black-Latina/o, Asian-Black, and even Latina/o-Asian tensions, whereas earlier conflict was centered on whites. The economic diversity of A/PIs makes the work of progressives all the more urgent if we wish to address economic justice issues without fostering anti-Asian racism. One example of this kind of work is the Korean Immigrant Workers Advocates (KIWA). Because whites and more established merchants are reluctant to operate retail outlets in poor communities of color, that space is left to relatively marginalized immigrant entrepreneurs, often known as ethnic middlemen. In Los Angeles that niche is largely filled by Korean immigrants. KIWA was established by progressive Korean American activists who realized that immigrant merchants, because they were located primarily in the ethnic economy and had relatively small establishments, often did not adhere to labor laws and codes. KIWA wished to support the workers, who were mostly Latina/o and Korean, but knew it had to be strategic in dealing with Korean merchants. As the campaign developed, the strategic location of the activists was key in the struggle for just wages and working conditions for the thousands of workers employed by Korean merchants.[42] Without KIWA, such conflicts could have been diluted into "cultural conflict" or, worse, could have contributed toward racism against Koreans.

KIWA's work shows the need to pay attention to racial and ethnic differences and the question of when and how to cross such lines. Yet the geography and demographics of Los Angeles suggest that while there is sufficient space for people to carve out their individual niches, there is a far greater need for people to come together. This is the challenge. This is meant, not to invalidate or call for the end of nationalism (not that that would make any difference), but to recognize its limitations, particularly in terms of gender equality, sexuality, and interethnic work. The real strength and potential of oppressed communities lie in the ties between them—a recognition of potential allies based on their economic and social location and their interests rather than simply their skin color. Until white privilege no longer exists and various groups are no longer singled out for state repression and economic exploitation, there will be a need for ethnic-specific politics. And if there is one thing the Third World Left did, it illustrated the possibility of developing relationships with others while still focusing on one's community. What is needed now is to take this one step further, for communities to work with each other, identifying their commonalities and differences, while not losing sight of their unique histories and struggles. All people of color are not the same, but they do have certain things in common, and those commonalities can often serve as the basis for shared mobilization.

Toward a More Humane Movement

The final lesson to be drawn from the Third World Left is the need to create organizations that recognize more fully the breadth and depth of people's humanity. By that I do not mean just kinder and gentler organizations but ones that are sensitive to the economic, social, intellectual, and spiritual needs of their members and how these change over time. While the Third World Left did address such issues, its efforts were highly varied. Some organizations were plagued with violence but provided collective housing; others stressed democratic practices but refused to offer child care. My interviews suggest the necessity of taking into account these needs and concerns if large, broad-based movements are to be created.

Important differences between the past and the present must be considered in any discussion of the culture and practices of social change organizations. Revolution is no longer in the air, and most activists and organizations work within more conventional frameworks. Likewise, contemporary organizations are much better funded, as they often receive foundation grants and hire full-time staff. This is dramatically different from organizations based solely on volunteer labor and the financial contributions of members and supporters. While the activists of the Third World Left may seem to have been more dedicated and selfless than today's paid staff (not necessarily so), it is difficult to sustain such activism. As people grow older their needs and concerns change. Although most movement organizations eventually collapsed, many people left politics because full-time activism became increasingly irreconcilable with the responsibilities of adulthood. Accordingly, many of the activists I talked to had specific suggestions for how organizational cultures could have been improved and could have better supported them as revolutionaries. This remains a central challenge for activists: How to transform political activism so that it is still vibrant and energetic (qualities that attract many people) but does not drain individuals to the point where they are forced to leave? When elders leave, organizations suffer from a loss of experience, expertise, and wisdom. While it is likely that radical activism will almost always be dominated by young people, organizations would benefit greatly if all age groups participated.

One of the most obvious things that organizations should and increasingly do provide is child care. Without regular, quality child care many people will be unwilling or unable to participate fully in the life of an organization. In the Third World Left, some organizations, such as the BPP, regularly provided child care (though of uneven quality), but others, such as CASA, did not. Throughout the left it was common for children to be brought to meetings lasting far into the night and simply left in a corner.[43] In fact, more than a few interviewees who were mothers regretted not doing better by their children. Such guilt should not fall on the mothers themselves but should be directed toward organizations and the movement culture as a whole. It is simply not acceptable to ask parents to choose between their children's well-being and political participation.

A distinct but related concern is the economic security that organizations can offer their members. Today organizations are composed of full- and part-time staff as well as volunteers. And while few individuals pursue a life of political activism for the money, more needs to be done to provide for the material and economic security of those who give of themselves. When asked what they might have done differently, one former Panther replied, "We should have had a plan for what we were going to do after." She was referring to the fact that the Panthers went into a state of war without a plan to deal with the human toll it would take. Consequently, there are homeless Panthers. In a society that provides only the most rudimentary safety net, organizations need to be considering these issues in innovative and creative ways.

Two key security issues are health insurance and retirement. Ironically, often standard worker concerns force individuals to leave a life of full-time activism. Granted, few organizations can afford to provide what for-profit concerns do, but there is room for improvement. One option might be medical collectives, similar to the legal ones that existed in the sixties and seventies. Another innovation pioneered by the National Organizers' Alliance is a pension plan for activist organizations.[44] Perhaps these benefits could be expanded to other needs as well. Other strategies include groups of organizations buying large buildings that can be used to house retired activists so that they are not living in dire poverty. By working collectively, small nonprofits and grassroots groups might be able to provide more opportunities and security for their members.

Burnout and intellectual development are also serious issues. Due to the intense nature of political work, burnout is a widespread problem, particularly after a long and arduous campaign. Fortunately, the idea of sabbaticals for activists is finally catching on. While still relatively few, a growing number of fellowships and sabbaticals available to longtime activists enable them to replenish themselves and pursue their interests.[45] This is especially important insofar as it can also provide an antidote to the anti-intellectualism which some organizations suffer from.

In addition, activists need to take seriously the business of conflict resolution *within* their organizations. Many activists are skilled at waging conflict and challenging the established powers, but those talents do not necessarily translate into effective communication and conflict resolution with their own colleagues. As a result, organizations may split, develop factions, and self-destruct. Sometimes these tensions are due to genuine political disagreement, in which case a separation may be necessary. But other times needless pain, rejection, and humiliation result from people's inability to communicate effectively and compassionately and handle differences. Fortunately, consultants are now available who offer affordable training to nonprofits so that their members can develop those skills.[46] Making these changes will not be easy, not only because they cost time, money, and effort, but also because they challenge one of the fundamentals of activist culture: focusing on the immediate crisis rather than the long term. As all activists know, there is never enough time and resources to do all the things that need to be done, let alone build principled and effective coalitions with like-minded individuals. But only by rethinking basic assumptions and practices will activists be able to build a new political culture.

The need for reconciliation and conflict management brings up another somewhat difficult issue. In my conversations with activists, a small but vocal number raised a distinct and diverse set of concerns ranging from a critique of the overly materialist politics of the Third World Left to the inability of organizations to recognize their members' emotional and psychological needs. I refer to these concerns as issues of spirituality. While many interviewees were so firmly grounded in a racial and class analysis that they had never even considered these issues, quite a few others had. Whether referring to the "spiritual" or to a mind/body connection, interviewees took pains to distinguish their concerns from organized religion and even the Judeo-Christian tradition.[47] Nonetheless, many saw the need for both individuals, organizations, and political cultures to address questions pertaining to the existence/nature of souls; humans' relationship to other beings (including humans, animals, and deities); healing; peace; and the importance of creating social change from within as well as without.

It is important to acknowledge the challenges of raising such concerns within a left political context.[48] While such discussions may make activists uncomfortable, to ignore such issues would only perpetuate an abiding problem of the left: its limited ability, particularly among revolutionary elements, to entertain the possibility that humans are more than political animals. Indeed, the very nature of the political animal may be more complex than imagined. As Robin Kelley has noted, "Freedom and love constitute the foundation of spirituality . . . [an] elusive and intangible force with which few scholars of social movements have come to terms."[49] It is time to break this silence and begin envisioning new ways of analyzing social movements and political activism itself if the pitfalls of the past are to be avoided.

At this point it is uncertain what the future holds for left politics in the United States, but a few things should inform any serious debate. First, although communism may be dead and much of the world appears to be accepting capitalism, it is clear that millions of people are protesting the imposition of an economic system that puts the bottom line (be it corporate or state) ahead of basic human needs. It is also evident that global hunger and misery have not abated, although the geography of human suffering does shift over time. This latest round of capitalist development is creating greater economic polarization in its wake, making the contradictions between the haves and have-nots all the more visible. As long as these conditions remain, there will be a deep desire for alternative social arrangements that will reduce human suffering and enable people to live with a modicum of dignity. In short, the *need* for a leftist politics is as great as ever. If such is the case, then a new vision will be required, and this is where the difficulty lies. Over the last few decades the right has effectively cornered the market on the "vision thing," as the left has had little to offer in response to charges of sectarianism and the collapse of communism (which proved that all left ideas were futile, right?). But without a vision of what the world might be like and how to get there, the left has little to offer people and no chance of building a broad-based movement for social change. To borrow again from Kelley's *Freedom Dreams,* the left is in dire need of dreaming.[50] Activists must dream in order to develop a vision of the kind of world they would like to live in. The visions offered must be compassionate and humane and must reach people's hearts and souls as well as their minds. Although a vision is no guarantee of successfully remaking the world, it is a necessary first step. Finally, while the content of those visions remains open and uncertain, there is a need to be wary of dogmatism, coerciveness, and sectarianism. There should be no orthodoxy. Although the U.S. left never attained the level of destruction that more institutionalized forms of Marxism/Leninism did, its character was such that it *could* have, had the power of the state been behind it. It is time for those committed to social and economic justice to come up with something new and different. I have confidence that living arrangements can be devised whereby everybody can be fed and the planet healed, but it will take a profound change and a willingness to open our hearts and minds to something entirely new and different if we wish to get there.

Notes

INTRODUCTION

1. Deciding what to call this group of activists and organizations was no easy task. Max Elbaum, in *Revolution in the Air: Sixties Radicals Turn to Lenin, Mao and Che* (New York: Verso, 2002), includes them as part of the New Communist movement, which they certainly were, but I felt that such a term deemphasized their status as people of color, which was central to their identity and this book. Conversely, to refer to them as simply part of the Black, Chicana/o, or Yellow Power movements would obscure their distinctive anticapitalist politics. While numerous like-minded organizations, especially in the seventies, called themselves "sectarian," I was concerned that such a term would not translate well across the generations. Thus I have chosen a distinctively contemporary term, the Third World Left, to refer to these organizations, in an effort to define them in a coherent fashion. I realize that not all groups or members would necessarily identify as such. Another issue of terminology concerns my use of the words *Chicana/o*, *Latina/o*, and *Mexicana/o* in this book. *Chicana/o* is used here to refer to radicalized Mexican Americans; *Latina/o* refers to any person of Latin American heritage; and *Mexicana/o* is a Spanish-language term that refers to all people of Mexican ancestry, regardless of citizenship.

2. See Eric Mann, *L.A.'s Lethal Air: New Strategies for Policy, Organizing, and Action* (Los Angeles: Labor/Community Strategy Center, 1991); Laura Pulido, "Multiracial Organizing among Environmental Justice Activists in Los Angeles," in *Rethinking Los Angeles*, ed. Michael Dear, Greg Hise, and Eric Schockman (Thousand Oaks, CA: Sage Publications, 1996), 171–89.

3. Robert Gottlieb et al., *The Next Los Angeles: The Struggle for a Livable City* (Berkeley: University of California Press, 2005); Ruth Wilson Gilmore, "You Have Dislodged a Boulder: Mothers and Prisoners in the Post-Keynsian California Landscape," *Transforming Anthropology* 8 (1 & 2): 12–38; Andy Merrifield, "The Urbanization of Labor: Living Wage Activism in the American City," *Social Text* 18 (2000): 31–53; Ruth Milkman and Kent Wong, eds., *Voices from the Front Lines: Organizing Immigrant Workers in Los Angeles* (Los

Angeles: Center for Labor Research and Education, University of California, Los Angeles, 2000); Walter Nicholls, "Forging a 'New' Organizational Infrastructure for Los Angeles's Progressive Community," *International Journal of Urban and Regional Research* 27 (2003): 881–96; Manuel Pastor Jr., "Common Ground at Ground Zero? The New Economy and the New Organizing in Los Angeles," *Antipode* 33 (2001): 260–89; Donna Houston and Laura Pulido, "The Work of Performativity: Staging Social Justice at the University of Southern California," *Environment and Planning D* 20 (2002): 401–24.

4. Karl Yoneda, *Ganbatte: Sixty-Year Struggle of a Kibei Worker* (Los Angeles: Asian American Studies Center, University of California, Los Angeles, 1983), ch. 2. On Japanese communists and on Charlotta Bass, see Scott Kurashige, "Transforming Los Angeles: Black and Japanese American Struggles for Racial Equality in the 20th Century" (PhD diss., University of California, Los Angeles, 2000), chs. 6 and 7, respectively; Gottlieb et al., *Next Los Angeles*, ch. 2; Mario García, *Memories of Chicano History: The Life and Narrative of Bert Corona* (Berkeley: University of California Press, 1994), ch. 6.

5. Laura Pulido, "The Roots of Political Consciousness among Militant Unionists and Worker Activists in Los Angeles" (working paper, Center for the Study of Southern California, University of Southern California, 1998).

6. A partial list of relevant texts includes Elaine Brown, *A Taste of Power: A Black Woman's Story* (New York: Anchor Books, 1992); Angela Davis, *Angela Davis: An Autobiography* (New York: Random House, 1974); Roxanne Dunbar-Ortiz, *Outlaw Woman: A Memoir of the War Years* (San Francisco: City Lights, 2001); James Forman, *The Making of Black Revolutionaries* (Seattle: University of Washington Press, 1997); Mario García, *Memories of Chicano History;* Todd Gitlin, *The Sixties: Years of Hope, Days of Rage* (New York: Bantam Books, 1987); Tom Hayden, *Reunion: Memoir* (New York: Collier Books, 1988); Dorothy Healey and Maurice Isserman, *California Red: A Life in the Communist Party* (Urbana: University of Illinois Press, 1993); David Horowitz, *Radical Son: A Journey through Our Times* (New York: Free Press, 1997); Elizabeth Martínez, "A View from New Mexico," *Monthly Review* 54 (2002): 79–86; Kirkpatrick Sale, *SDS* (New York: Random House, 1973); Bobby Seale, *A Lonely Rage* (New York: Bantam Books, 1978); Assata Shakur, *Assata: An Autobiography* (New York: Lawrence Hill Books, 1988). In addition, the following offer numerous first-person accounts: Fred Ho et al., eds., *Legacy to Liberation: Politics and Culture of Revolutionary Asian/Pacific America* (San Francisco: Big Red Media and AK Press, 2000); Steve Louie and Glenn Omatsu, eds., *Asian Americans: The Movement and the Moment* (Los Angeles: Asian American Studies Center, University of California, Los Angeles, 2001).

7. On African Americans, see Dan Georgakas and Marvin Surkin, *Detroit: I Do Mind Dying* (Boston: South End Press, 1998); Earl Ofari Hutchinson, *Blacks and Reds: Race and Class in Conflict, 1919–1990* (East Lansing: Michigan State University Press, 1995), chs. 12 and 13; Robin Kelley, *Freedom Dreams: The Black Radical Imagination* (Boston: Beacon Press, 2002), ch. 3; Kathleen Cleaver

and George Katsiaficas, *Liberation, Imagination, and the Black Panther Party: A New Look at the Panthers and Their Legacy* (New York: Routledge, 2001); Charles Jones, ed., *The Black Panther Party Reconsidered* (Baltimore: Black Classic Press, 1998). For a comparison between the BPP and the American Indian Movement, see Ward Churchill and Jim Vander Wall, *Agents of Repression: The FBI's Secret War against the Black Panther Party and the American Indian Movement* (Boston: South End Press, 1988). On the Chicana/o left, see "Cultures of the US Left," special issue, *Monthly Review* 54 (July–August 2002). CASA is the most well-researched organization within the Chicana/o left: see David Gutiérrez, "CASA in the Chicano Movement: Ideology and Organizational Politics in the Chicano Community, 1968–78" (Working Paper Series 5, Stanford Center for Chicano Research, Stanford University, Palo Alto, CA, 1984); Ernesto Chávez, "Imagining the Mexican Immigrant Worker: (Inter)Nationalism, Identity, and Insurgency in the Chicano Movement in Los Angeles," *Aztlán* 25 (Fall 2000): 109–35; Marisela Rodríguez Chávez, "Living and Breathing the Movement: Women in El Centro de Accion Social Autonomo, 1975–1978" (master's thesis, Arizona State University, 1997). On the Puerto Rican left, see Andrés Torres and José Velázquez, *The Puerto Rican Movement: Voices from the Diaspora* (Philadelphia: Temple University Press, 1998). On the Asian American left, see William Wei, *The Asian American Movement* (Philadelphia: Temple University Press, 1993), ch. 7; Ho et al., *Legacy to Liberation;* Louie and Omatsu, *Asian Americans.* See also Daryl Maeda, "Forging Asian American Identity: Race, Culture, and the Asian American Movement" (PhD diss., University of Michigan, 2001), and "Constructing Yellow Power: The Asian American Movement's Encounter with Black Power" (paper presented at the annual meetings of the American Studies Association, Seattle, WA, November 1998); Diane Fujino, "Japanese American Radicalism and Radical Formation" (paper presented at the National Association of Asian American Studies Conference. San Francisco, May 2003).

8. Elizabeth Martínez, "That Old White (Male) Magic," in *De Colores Means All of Us: Latina Views for a Multi-colored Century,* ed. Elizabeth Martínez (Cambridge, MA: South End Press, 1998), 21–30. Some texts that portray a largely white New Left (with the exception of the Black Panther Party) include Gitlin, *The Sixties;* Hayden, *Reunion;* Horowitz, *Radical Son;* Sale, *SDS;* Katherine Whittemore, Ellen Rosenbush, and Jim Nelson, eds., *The Sixties: Recollections of the Decade* (New York: Franklin Square Press, 1995); and Paul Jacobs and Saul Landau's *The New Radicals: A Report with Documents,* which includes a sprinkling of African American writers (New York: Vintage Books, 1966).

9. An important exception is some of the recent literature on the Asian American movement, which explicitly acknowledges its connection to Black Power (Maeda, "Constructing Yellow Power"). In Louie and Omatsu's *Asian Americans,* not only do several authors refer explicitly to the BPP, but the text is filled with imagery and slogans from Black Power, thereby establishing a connection between the two movements.

10. Jason Ferreira, "All Power to the People: A Comparative History of Third World Radicalism in San Francisco, 1968–1974" (PhD diss., University of California, Berkeley, 2003); Cynthia Young, "Soul Power: Cultural Radicalism and the Formation of a United States Third World Left" (PhD diss., Yale University, 1999).

11. Claire Kim, "The Racial Triangulation of Asian Americans," *Politics and Society* 27 (1999): 105–38; Tomás Almaguer, *Racial Fault Lines: The Historical Origins of White Supremacy in California* (Berkeley: University of California Press, 1994); Neil Foley, *The White Scourge: Mexicans, Blacks, and Poor Whites in Texas Cotton Culture* (Berkeley: University of California Press, 1997); Linda Gordon, *The Great Arizona Orphan Abduction* (Cambridge, MA: Harvard University Press, 2001); Susan Koshy, "Morphing Race into Ethnicity," *Boundary* 28 (2001): 153–94; Evelyn Nakano Glenn, *Unequal Freedom: How Race and Gender Shaped American Citizenship and Labor* (Cambridge, MA: Harvard University Press, 2002); Nicholas De Genova and Ana Ramos-Zayas, *Latino Crossings: Mexicans, Puerto Ricans, and the Politics of Race and Citizenship* (New York: Routledge, 2003).

12. Elizabeth Martínez, "Seeing More Than Black and White," in Martínez, *De Colores*, 4–20; Lisa Lowe, *Immigrant Acts: On Asian American Cultural Politics* (Durham, NC: Duke University Press, 1996), ch. 1; Edward Park and John Park, "A New American Dilemma? Asian Americans and Latinos in Race Theorizing," *Journal of Asian American Studies* 2 (1999): 289–309; Marcelo Suárez-Orozco and Mariela Páez, *Latinos: Remaking America* (Berkeley: University of California Press, 2002); Frank Wu, *Yellow: Race in America beyond Black and White* (New York: Basic Books, 2002); Silvio Torres-Saillant, "Inventing the Race," *Latino Studies* 1 (2003): 123–51. In addition, there has been an increase in scholarship exploring interethnic relations among nonwhites: Janis Faye Hutchinson, Nestor Rodriguez, and Jacqueline Hagan, "Community Life: African Americans in Multiethnic Residential Areas," *Journal of Black Studies* 27 (1996): 201–23; Jonathan Warren and France Winddance Twine, "White Americans, the New Minority," *Journal of Black Studies* 28 (1997): 200–218; Eric Yamamoto, *Interracial Justice: Conflict and Reconciliation in Post–Civil Rights America* (New York: New York University Press, 1999); Lawrence Bobo and Camille Zubrinsky, "Attitudes on Residential Integration: Perceived Status Differences, Mere In-Group Preference, or Racial Prejudice?" *Social Forces* 74 (1996): 883–909; Regina Freer, "Black Korean Conflict," in *The Los Angeles Riots: Lessons for the Urban Future*, ed. Mark Baldassare (Boulder, CO: Westview Press, 1994), 175–203; Bill Piatt, *Black and Brown in America* (New York: New York University Press, 1997).

13. On the historical uniqueness of race in Los Angeles, see Almaguer, *Racial Fault Lines*; Lawrence Guillow, "The Origins of Race Relations in Los Angeles, 1820–1880" (PhD diss., Arizona State University, 1996); Scott Kurashige, "Transforming Los Angeles." See also Richard White, "Race Relations in the American West," *American Quarterly* 38 (1986): 396–416. On the contemporary diversity of the region, see James Allen and Eugene Turner,

Changing Faces, Changing Places (Northridge: Center for Geographical Studies, California State University, Northridge, 2002); Lawrence Bobo et al., *Prismatic Metropolis: Inequality in Los Angeles* (New York: Russell Sage Foundation, 2000); Roger Waldinger and Mehdi Bozorgmehr, eds., *Ethnic Los Angeles* (New York: Russell Sage Foundation, 1996).

14. Although Chicana/o activists also asserted land claims in the southwestern United States, it was highly implausible that the United States would ever cede to such demands from a group with a tenuous claim.

15. Emphasizing the importance of land struggles, Ward Churchill has argued that "contentions over land usage and ownership have served to define the totality of the US-Indian relationships from the first moment to the present day, shaping not only the historical flow of interactions between invader and invaded, but the nature of ongoing domination of native peoples in areas such as governance and jurisdiction, identification, recognition and education." "The Earth Is Our Mother," in *The State of Native America: Genocide, Colonization, and Resistance,* ed. M. Annette Jaimes (Boston: South End Press, 1992), 139. Perhaps the two best examples of this type of activity during the sixties and seventies are Wounded Knee and Alcatraz. See Dee Brown, *Bury My Heart at Wounded Knee: An Indian History of the American West* (New York: Henry Holt, 1970); Churchill and Vander Wall, *Agents of Repression;* Peter Matthiessen, *In the Spirit of Crazy Horse* (New York: Viking Press, 1991); Troy Johnson, Joane Nagel, and Duane Champagne, *American Indian Activism: Alcatraz to the Longest Walk* (Urbana: University of Illinois Press, 1997). Overviews of land struggles include Churchill, "Earth Is Our Mother"; Rebecca Robins, "Self-Determination and Subordination," in Jaimes, *State of Native America,* 87–121. On the larger American Indian movement, see Joane Nagel, *American Indian Ethnic Renewal: Red Power and the Resurgence of Identity and Culture* (New York: Oxford University Press, 1996); Paul Chat Smith and Robert Warrior, *Like a Hurricane: The Indian Movement from Alcatraz to Wounded Knee* (New York: New Press, 1996).

Although I stress the importance of land-based conflicts, this should not diminish the importance of urban centers. Cities were key to these struggles, as they provided support, resources, and activists.

> Behind the waves of protests were numerous organizations, nearly all of them from the cities. As had happened in the Bay Area, urban communities of Indians in Minneapolis, Chicago, Los Angeles, Cleveland, Denver and other cities had transformed themselves over the course of the previous decade, shifting their main focus from Indian culture to an increased engagement in politics. Everywhere the government's relocation program had sent Indians, groups emerged to boisterously and aggressively complain about the conditions they found themselves living in. (Smith and Warrior, *Like a Hurricane,* 89)

In Los Angeles, such organizations included chapters of the American Indian Movement, the American Indian Coalition, and social service centers such as the

Los Angeles Indian Center (American Indian Movement Vertical File, American Indian Studies Center Library, University of California, Los Angeles).

16. Cleaver and Katsiaficas, *Liberation, Imagination*; Jones, *Black Panther Party Reconsidered*, 1998; Tracye Matthews, "No One Ever Asks What a Man's Place in the Revolution Is: Gender and the Politics of the Black Panther Party, 1966–1971," in Jones, *Black Panther Party Reconsidered*, 267–304; Jane Rhodes, "Fanning the Flames of Racial Discord: The National Press and the Black Panther Party," *Harvard International Journal of Press Politics* 4 (1999): 95–118; Robert Self, "To Plan Our Liberation: Black Power and the Politics of Place in Oakland California, 1965–1977," *Journal of Urban History* 26 (2000): 759–92; Hugh Pearson, *The Shadow of the Panther: Huey Newton and the Price of Black Power in America* (Reading, MA: Addison-Wesley Publishing, 1995); see also "Liberation, Imagination and the Black Panther Party," special issue of *New Political Science* 21 (June 1999).

17. *Bakke* was a 1970s lawsuit in which a University of California, Davis, medical school applicant challenged racial quotas as unconstitutional (Regents of the University of California v. Bakke, 438 U.S. 256 [1978]). This was the first major challenge to affirmative action.

18. Matt García has shown in detail how this process worked in Southern California's citrus economy. See *A World of Its Own: Race, Labor, and Citrus in the Making of Greater Los Angeles, 1900–1970* (Chapel Hill: University of North Carolina Press, 2001), ch. 2.

19. Rona Fields, "The Brown Berets: A Participant Observation Study of Social Action in the Schools of Los Angeles" (PhD diss., University of Southern California, 1970); Dionne Espinoza, "Revolutionary Sisters," *Aztlán* 26 (Spring 2001): 17–58; Ernesto Chávez, *Mi Raza Primero! Nationalism, Identity and Insurgency in the Chicano Movement in Los Angeles, 1966–1978* (Berkeley: University of California Press, 2002), ch. 2. Many thanks also to Carlos Montes for sharing his experiences with me.

20. In 1960 there were over eighty-one thousand Japanese Americans in the Los Angeles–Long Beach metropolitan area, but fewer than twenty thousand Chinese Americans and twelve thousand Filipinas/os. California Department of Industrial Relations, Fair Employment Practices Commission, "Californians of Japanese, Chinese, and Filipino Ancestry," box 69, Los Angeles Area Chamber of Commerce Collection, Department of Special Collections, University of Southern California Library, Los Angeles, 1965.

21. *Nikkei* refers to the Japanese American population in its entirety. *Issei* denotes the immigrant generation, *Nisei* the second generation, *Sansei* the third, and *Yonsei* the fourth. Many of the Japanese Americans who participated in the Third World Left were *Sansei*.

22. Maeda, "Constructing Yellow Power."

23. See Laura Pulido, "Rethinking Environmental Racism," *Annals of the Association of American Geographers* 90 (2000): 12–40, for a critique of conceptions of racism.

1. RACE AND POLITICAL ACTIVISM

1. James Allen and Eugene Turner, *The Ethnic Quilt: Population Diversity in Southern California* (Northridge: Center for Geographical Studies, California State University, Northridge, 1997), ch. 4; Philip Ethington, "Segregated Diversity: Race-Ethnicity, Space, and Political Fragmentation in Los Angeles County, 1940–1994" (unpublished manuscript, final report to the John Randolph Haynes and Dora Haynes Foundation, University of Southern California, Los Angeles, 2000).

2. Spanish for a light-skinned person.

3. Laura Pulido, *Environmentalism and Economic Justice: Two Chicano Struggles in the Southwest* (Tucson: University of Arizona Press, 1996).

4. La Raza Unida Party was actually the site of an intense struggle between Chicana/o leftists and more conservative forces. See Richard Santillan, *La Raza Unida* (Los Angeles: Tlaquilo Publications, 1973). For overviews of the movement, see Juan Gómez-Quiñones, *Chicano Politics: Reality and Promise, 1940–1990* (Albuquerque: University of New Mexico Press, 1990); Carlos Muñoz, *Youth, Identity, Power: The Chicano Movement* (New York: Verso, 1989). Ramon Gutiérrez and Jorge Mariscal have each critiqued both the movement and its scholarship. Gutiérrez has argued that although the class politics of the movement was secondary to nationalism, it in fact had the greater impact, as seen in the UFW. Mariscal, on the other hand, has pointed out that not only have the left tendencies of the movement been largely ignored, but recent postmodern scholarship, including the writings of some Chicana feminists, tends to portray the movement in monolithic (and problematic) terms, further obscuring the role of the left. Ramon Gutiérrez, "Community, Patriarchy and Individualism: The Politics of Chicano History and the Dream of Equality," *American Quarterly* 45 (1993): 44–72; Jorge Mariscal, "Left Turns in the Chicano Movement, 1965–72," *Monthly Review* 54 (2002): 59–68. For feminist critiques, see Dionne Espinoza, "Pedagogies of Nationalism and Gender: Cultural Resistance in Selected Representational Practice of Chicana/o Movement Activists, 1967–1972" (PhD diss., Cornell University, 1996); Alma García, *Chicana Feminist Thought: The Basic Historical Writings* (New York: Routledge, 1997); Elizabeth Martínez, "Chingón Politics Die Hard," in Martínez, *De Colores,* 172–81.

To date, there have only been three studies of the Chicana/o left, all focused on CASA: Ernesto Chávez, "Imagining"; David Gutiérrez, "CASA"; Marisela Rodríguez Chávez, "Living and Breathing." See also Arnoldo García, "Toward a Left without Borders," *Monthly Review* 54 (2002): 69–78.

5. Recent research has emphasized the extent to which resistance is *not* determined by domination. See Steve Pile and Michael Keith, *Geographies of Resistance* (London: Routledge, 1997), ch. 1.

6. See, for example, Stanley Sue et al., "Conceptions of Mental Illness among Asian and Caucasian American Students," *Psychological Reports* 38 (1976): 703–8; Harry Kitano and Roger Daniels, *Asian Americans: Emerging*

Minorities (Englewood Cliffs, NJ: Prentice Hall, 1988); Frank Chuman, *The Bamboo People: Japanese Americans, Their History and the Law* (Chicago: Japanese American Citizens League, 1976); Rodolfo Acuña, *Occupied America: A History of Chicanos* (San Francisco: Canfield Press, 1972); Mario Barrera, *Race and Class in the Southwest: A Theory of Racial Inequality* (Notre Dame, IN: University of Notre Dame, 1979); David Montejano, *Anglos and Mexicans in the Making of Texas, 1836–1986* (Austin: University of Texas Press, 1987).

African American studies is distinct from both Chicana/o and Asian American studies in that although it too was institutionalized in the 1960s it has a much longer history. Before Gunnar Myrdal's *An American Dilemma: The Negro Problem and Modern Democracy* (New York: Harper and Row, 1944), much of the scholarship conducted by African Americans was devoted to simply establishing the humanity of Black people. Attention subsequently shifted to documenting the gap between Blacks and whites, in what is sometimes called "gap theory." In discussing the role of the social sciences in the South, Clyde Woods writes, in *Development Arrested: The Blues and Plantation Power in the Mississippi Delta* (New York: Verso, 1998), "Slowly, the planter bloc began to view the social sciences as a useful method of officially denying their oppressive practices without resorting to the increasing unpopular biological and religious explanations of African American inferiority. Renamed 'deviance' and 'dys-functionality,' African American destitution could be blamed on the inability of certain Blacks to assimilate white standards due to 'scientifically' proven social, cultural, and psychological differences" (132).

7. On the still contentious nature of ethnic studies, see Marjorie Coeyman, "Harvard's President in the Hot-Seat," *Christian Science Monitor,* January 8, 2002, 13; "Agreement Ends UC Santa Barbara Students' Hunger Strike," *Los Angeles Times,* May 7, 1994, A27; Larry Gordon, "UCLA Strikers End Fast, Compromise Reached," *Los Angeles Times,* June 8, 1993, A1; Henry Lee, "Ten-tative Pact between UC, Hunger Strikers," *San Francisco Chronicle,* May 8, 1999, A15. For a discussion of scholarly critiques of ethnic studies and multi-cultural education, see Arthur Schlesinger, *The Disuniting of America* (New York: Norton, 1993).

8. Classic examples in Chicana/o studies include Octavio Romano's "The Anthropology and Sociology of the Mexican-Americans: The Distortion of Mexican-American History," in *Voices: Readings from El Grito: A Journal of Contemporary Mexican American Thought,* ed. Octavio Romano (Berkeley, CA: Quinto Sol, 1971), 26–39, and Arnoldo De León's *They Called Them Greasers: Anglo Attitudes toward Mexicans in Texas, 1821–1900* (Austin: University of Texas Press, 1983).

9. Asian American studies has taken the lead by focusing on Black-Asian dynamics. As Vijay Prashad has argued in *The Karma of Brown Folk* (Minneapolis: University of Minnesota, 2000), being labeled "model minorities" has forced Asian Americans to analyze their racial identity and position in ways that other groups have not had to. This is not to imply that Chicanas/os, for example, are oblivious to their (dis)connection to African Americans—as my own

story attests—but, given demographic trends and Latinas/os' impoverishment, the question of our relationship to other racially subordinated peoples has been less urgent.

Recent comparative work includes Almaguer, *Racial Fault Lines*; De Genova and Ramos-Zayas, *Latino Crossings*; Foley, *White Scourge*; Ruth Wilson Gilmore, "Fatal Couplings: Racism and Geography," *Professional Geographer* 54 (2002): 15–24; Jacalyn Harden, *Double Cross: Japanese Americans in Black and White Chicago* (Minneapolis: University of Minnesota Press, 2003); Claire Jean Kim, *Bitter Fruit: The Politics of Black-Korean Conflict in New York City* (New Haven, CT: Yale University Press, 2000); Vijay Prashad, *Everybody Was Kung Fu Fighting: Afro-Asian Connections and the Myth of Cultural Purity* (Boston: Beacon Press, 2001); Jim Lee, *Urban Triage: Racial Anxiety and Crisis in Contemporary U.S. Fiction* (Minneapolis: University of Minnesota Press, 2004); Maeda, "Constructing Yellow Power"; Wu, *Yellow*.

10. Claire Jean Kim, "Racial Triangulation."

11. Nella Larson, *Passing* (New York: Arno Press, 1969); Cherie Moraga, "La Güera," in *This Bridge Called My Back: Writings by Radical Women of Color*, ed. Cherie Moraga and Gloria Anzaldua (Latham, NY: Kitchen Table, 1983), 27–34; Adrian Piper, "Passing for White, Passing for Black," *Transition* 58 (1992): 4–32; Cheryl Harris, "Whiteness as Property," *Harvard Law Review* 106 (1993): 1709–91.

12. Dick Peet, "The Social Origins of Environmental Determinism," *Annals of the Association of American Geographers* 75 (1985): 309–33; James Blaut, *The Colonizers' Model of the World: Geographical Diffusionism and Eurocentric History* (New York: Guilford Press, 1993); David Goldberg, *Racist Culture Philosophy and the Politics of Meaning* (Oxford: Blackwell, 1993). On which came first, slavery or racist ideology, see George Fredrickson, *White Supremacy: A Comparative Study in American and South African History* (New York: Oxford University Press, 1981).

13. Antonio Gramsci, *Selections from the Prison Notebooks of Antonio Gramsci*, ed. and trans. Quintin Hoare and Geoffrey Smith (New York: International Publishers, 1987), 199 and 322. Stuart Hall has argued that Gramsci's focus on popular thought is what distinguishes his work on ideology. Hall describes common sense as "the terrain of conceptions and categories on which the practical consciousness of the masses of the people is actually formed." Stuart Hall, "Gramsci's Relevance for the Study of Race and Ethnicity," in *Stuart Hall: Critical Dialogues in Cultural Studies*, ed. David Morley and Kuan-Hsing Chen (New York: Routledge, 1996), 431.

14. George Lipsitz, *The Possessive Investment in Whiteness: How White People Profit from Identity Politics* (Philadelphia: Temple University Press, 1998). See also Ian F. Haney López, *Racism on Trial: The Chicano Fight for Justice* (Cambridge, MA: Harvard University Press, 2003).

15. Social scientists can predict the demographic ratio at which whites will move out, what is known as the "tipping point." Martin Meyerson and Edward Banfield, *Politics and the Public Interest* (Glencoe, IL: Free Press, 1955). As to

why whites do not wish to live with Blacks, see Maria Krysan, "Whites Who Say They'd Flee: Who Are They, Why Would They Leave?" *Demography* 39 (2002): 675–96. See also Douglas Massey and Nancy Denton, *American Apartheid: Segregation and the Making of the Underclass* (Cambridge, MA: Harvard University Press, 1993); Kenneth Jackson, "Race, Ethnicity and Real-Estate Appraisal," *Journal of Urban History* 4 (1980): 419–52; Gary Dymski, "Is Discrimination Disappearing? Residential Credit Market Evidence, 1992–1998," *International Journal of Social Economics* 28 (2001): 1025–45; Steve Holloway, "Exploring the Neighborhood Contingency of Race Discrimination in Mortgage Lending in Columbus, Ohio," *Annals of the Association of American Geographers* 88 (1998): 252–76. On Latino and Asian/Pacific Islanders' residential preferences, see Camille Zubrinksy Charles, "Neighborhood Racial Composition Preferences," *Social Problems* 47 (2000): 379–407.

16. Melvin Oliver and Thomas Shapiro, *Black Wealth, White Wealth: A New Perspective on Racial Inequality* (New York: Routledge, 1995).

17. Yen Le Espiritu, *Home Bound: Filipino Lives across Cultures, Communities, and Countries* (Berkeley: University of California Press, 2003). The relationship between race and class has been of long-standing interest to ethnic studies scholars. During the 1970s, when Marxism was still in vogue, scholars produced significant work that is now considered quite rigid. Two criticisms are the tendency to treat race as a given and the scant attention given to gender. See, for example, Barrera, *Race and Class;* Tomás Almaguer, "Towards the Study of Chicano Colonialism," *Aztlán* 2 (1971): 137–42, and "Ideological Distortions in Recent Chicano Historiography: The Colonial Model and Chicano Interpretation," *Aztlán* 18 (1987): 7–28; Montejano, *Anglos and Mexicans.* For an early Marxist feminist analysis, see Rosaura Sánchez, "The History of Chicanas: A Proposal for a Materialist Perspective," in *Between Borders: Essays on Mexicana/Chicana History,* ed. Adelaida del Castillo (Encino, CA: Floricanto Press, 1990), 1–29, originally presented at a 1982 conference.

18. Almaguer, *Racial Fault Lines,* 4–7. Martha Menchaca has explained Mexicans' relatively privileged position as follows: "Throughout history the Mexican Americans' Spanish ancestry protected them many times from the full impact of racial discrimination because they were part White." *Recovering History, Constructing Race: The Indian, Black, and White Roots of Mexican Americans* (Austin: University of Texas Press, 2001): 36. See also Neil Foley, "Partly Colored or Other White" (paper presented at the Labor and Working Class Historical Association Luncheon of the Organization of American Historians, St. Louis, April 1, 2000), www.lawcha.org/resources/talks/beyondbw.html (accessed April 30, 2002).

19. Benedict Anderson, *Imagined Communities: Reflections on the Origin and Spread of Nationalism* (New York: Verso, 1983). On the racial nation, see Lowe, *Immigrant Acts,* ch. 1; Bill Ong Hing, *Making and Remaking Asian America through Immigration Policy, 1850–1990* (Stanford, CA: Stanford University Press, 1993); Ian F. Haney López, *White by Law: The Legal Construction of Race* (New York: New York University Press, 1996).

20. Even this is a simplification. For example, slaves were differentiated by task, such as house and field, but also by color and paternal status. This Black/white binary also ignores American Indians.

21. Noel Ignatiev, *How the Irish Became White* (New York: Routledge, 1995); Matthew Jacobson, *Whiteness of a Different Color: European Immigrants and the Alchemy of Race* (Cambridge, MA: Harvard University Press, 1998); David Roediger, *The Wages of Whiteness: Race and the Making of the American Working Class* (London: Verso, 1991); David Roediger, *Towards the Abolition of Whiteness: Essays on Race, Politics, and Working Class History* (London: Verso, 1999). See also Karen Brodkin, *How Jews Became White Folks and What That Says about Race in America* (New Brunswick, NJ: Rutgers University Press, 1998).

22. Mia Tuan, *Forever Foreigners or Honorary Whites? The Asian Ethnic Experience Today* (New Brunswick, NJ: Rutgers University Press, 1998); Viet Nguyen, *Race and Resistance: Literature and Politics in Asian America* (Oxford: Oxford University Press, 2002). There is a large literature documenting the historical racism directed against Asian Americans; key texts include Roger Daniels, *The Politics of Prejudice: The Anti-Japanese Movement in California and the Struggle for Japanese Exclusion* (Berkeley: University of California Press, 1971); Yuji Ichioka, *The Issei: The World of the First Generation Japanese Immigrants, 1885–1924* (New York: Free Press, 1988), ch. 6; Alexander Saxton, *The Indispensable Enemy: Labor and the Anti-Chinese Movement in California* (Berkeley: University of California Press, 1975). For a personal account, see Yoneda, *Ganbatte*. For more general histories that include California, see Sucheng Chan, *Asian Americans: An Interpretive History* (Boston: Twayne, 1991), ch. 3; Ronald Takagi, *Strangers from a Different Shore: A History of Asian Americans* (New York: Penguin Books, 1989).

The contemporary status of Asian Americans and particularly the "model minority myth" are troubled by Asian Americans' diversity as well as by the unique way(s) racism operates. While several indicators suggest movement toward parity with whites and high rates of social acceptance, Asian Americans still experience racism within their various class positions, and the group as a whole still encounters multiple forms of prejudice. Three key arenas in which Asian American mobility and integration can be seen are intermarriage, economic status, and educational attainment. Intermarriage, a key indicator of social acceptance, has grown dramatically among Asians, especially Japanese Americans. See Colleen Fong and Judy Yung, "In Search of the Right Spouse," *Amerasia* 21 (1995/1996): 77–98. Although Asian American income still lags behind that of whites (even when education is controlled for), it is rapidly gaining. Paul Ong and Suzanne Hee, "Economic Diversity," in *Economic Diversity, Issues and Policies: A Public Policy report*, ed. Paul Ong (Los Angeles: Asian Pacific American Public Policy Institute and Asian American Studies Center, University of California, Los Angeles, 1994), 31–56. Finally, the sheer number of Asian Americans attending universities reflects both an upwardly mobile population and an ability to overcome historic barriers. The "yellowing" of college campuses, however, also intimates the future class composition of Asian America, although the political outcome is clearly uncertain. Dana Takagi, *The Retreat from Race: Asian-American Admissions and Racial Politics* (New Brunswick, NJ: Rutgers University Press, 1992).

Despite such mobility, Asian Americans still experience both acute and subtle racism. For instance, a close look at socioeconomic patterns reveals significant diversity among Asian Americans and obscures the poverty facing certain subgroups, such as Cambodians. Ong and Hee, "Economic Diversity"; Lucie Cheng and Philip Yang, "The 'Model Minority' Deconstructed," in *Contemporary Asian America: A Multidisciplinary Reader*, ed. Min Zhou and James Gatewood (New York: New York University Press, 2000), 459–82. In addition, although Asian Americans have made tremendous inroads in the professional sector, a "glass ceiling" limits their upward mobility. Tyler Marshall, "Asian Americans Scarce in US Corridors of Power," *Los Angeles Times*, October 21, 1997, A1, A16. Finally, Asian Americans are the victims of a significant number of hate crimes, a profound form of racism. Karen Umemoto, "From Vincent Chin to Joseph Ileto: Asian Pacific Americans and Hate Crime Policy," in *Transforming Race Relations*, ed. Paul Ong (Los Angeles: Asian Pacific American Public Policy Institute and Asian American Studies Center, University of California, Los Angeles, 2001), 243–78; Scott Kurashige, "Beyond Random Acts of Hatred: Analysing Urban Patterns of Anti-Asian Violence," *Amerasia* 26 (2000): 209–31.

Recent survey data also reflect mixed attitudes toward Asian Americans. One survey found that one-third of respondents held "very negative attitudes" toward Chinese Americans. Such a finding is consistent with the historical pattern of viewing Asian Americans as the ultimate foreigners, suggesting the extent to which the term *American* is still coded as white, regardless of one's economic status. Lisa Richardson and Hilary MacGregor, "To Be Chinese in America," *Los Angeles Times*, April 30, 2001, E1, E4. Other surveys suggest more positive assessments, but ones largely based on stereotypes. "[N]on-Asians generally speak well of Asians, citing a disposition for hard work and strong family ties as top attributes." Carla Rivera, "Asians Say They Fare Better Than Other Minorities," *Los Angeles Times*, August 20, 1993, A1, A20.

23. Neil Smith, "Homeless/Global: Scaling Places," in *Mapping the Futures: Local Cultures, Global Change*, ed. John Bird et al. (New York: Routledge, 1993), 128–43; Sallie Marston, "The Social Construction of Scale," *Progress in Human Geography* 24 (2000): 219–42. See also Andy Herod, "The Production of Scale in United States Labour Relations," *Area* 23 (1991): 114–20.

24. Michael Storper, *The Regional World: Territorial Development in a Global Economy* (New York: Guilford Press, 1997); Carolyn Cartier, *Globalizing South China* (Oxford: Blackwell, 2001). See also Doreen Massey, *Space, Place and Gender* (Minneapolis: University of Minnesota Press, 1994), 50–66 and 86–114. Despite the burgeoning literature on regions, few have attended to how race shapes them; see, however, Woods, *Development Arrested*.

25. On the distinction between class and the division of labor, see Andrew

Sayer and Richard Walker, *The New Social Economy: Reworking the Division of Labor* (Cambridge, MA: Blackwell, 1992). See also Maria Mies, *Patriarchy and Accumulation on a World Scale: Women in the International Division of Labour* (London: Zed Books, 1986); Immanuel Wallerstein, "The Construction of Peoplehood: Racism, Nationality, Ethnicity," in *Race, Nation, Class: Ambiguous Identities,* ed. Etienne Balibar and Immanuel Wallerstein (London: Verso, 1991), 71–85. To see how such divisions operate locally, see Allen Scott, "The Manufacturing Economy: Ethnic and Gender Divisions of Labor," in Waldinger and Bozorgmehr, *Ethnic Los Angeles,* 215–44.

26. Cletus Daniel, *Bitter Harvest: A History of California Farmworkers, 1870–1941* (Berkeley: University of California Press, 1981); Carey McWilliams, *Factories in the Field* (Boston: Little, Brown, 1939); Matt García, *World of Its Own.* Less appreciated is how such racial subordination enabled growers to shift the social costs of reproduction onto Mexico. Michael Burawoy, "The Functions and Reproduction of Migrant Labor," *American Journal of Sociology* 81 (1976): 1050–87.

27. This particular reading of my body is also a regional phenomenon. Outside the Southwest, my body is read differently, depending upon the local racial hierarchy. In some places I am assumed to be foreign or exotic, while in others I am offered some form of whiteness.

28. James O'Connor, *The Fiscal Crisis of the State* (New York: St. Martin's Press, 1973). On how race works in crises, see Stuart Hall, "The Politics of Mugging," in *Policing the Crisis: Mugging, the State, and Law and Order,* ed. Stuart Hall (New York: Holmes and Meier, 1978), 327–97.

29. Michael Omi and Howard Winant, *Racial Formation in the United States: From the 1960s to the 1980s* (New York: Routledge, 1986).

30. Susan Alva, quoted in Patrick McDonnell, "March Just a First Step, Latino Leaders Say," *Los Angeles Times,* June 4, 1994, B2. Latina/o youth, in particular, mobilized against what they saw as an attack on Latinas/os. Amy Pyle and Simon Romero, "Proposition 187 Fuels a New Campus Activism," *Los Angeles Times,* October 25, 1994, B1, B8. See also Mike Davis, "The Social Origins of the Referendum," *NACLA Report on the Americas* 29 (November/December 1995): 24–28; Kent Ono and John Sloop, *Shifting Borders: Rhetoric, Immigration and California's Proposition 187* (Philadelphia: Temple University Press, 2002); Otto Santa Ana, *Brown Tide Rising: Metaphors of Latinos in Contemporary American Public Discourse* (Austin: University of Texas Press, 2002).

31. Poorer Blacks were more likely to oppose the initiative than wealthy ones. Irwin Morris, "African American Voting on Proposition 187: Rethinking the Prevalence of Interminority Conflict," *Political Research Quarterly* 53 (2000): 77–89.

32. Although the majority of Black and Asian American voters supported Proposition 187, their percentages were somewhat less than the percentage of white voters who did (57 and 56 percent vs. 64 percent). Philip Martin, "Proposition 187 in California," *International Migration Review* 29 (1995): 255–63.

Nevertheless, the extent of Asian American support is significant and underscores this population's ambiguous racial position. Consider, for example, that in 1990 72 percent of the Asian American population in Los Angeles were foreign born but only about half of the Latina/o population was. Paul Ong and Tania Azores, "Asian Immigrants in Los Angeles: Diversity and Divisions," in *The New Asian Immigration in Los Angeles and Global Restructuring*, ed. Paul Ong, Edna Bonacich, and Lucie Cheng (Philadelphia: Temple University Press, 1994), 100–129. Ono and Sloop suggest that one reason for the limited attack on Asian/Pacific Islanders was that the "model minority" image helped to render them less problematic while at the same time it helped to demonize Latinas/os (Ono and Sloop, *Shifting Borders*, 162). Despite widespread prejudice toward Asian Americans in Southern California, these attitudes were overwhelmed by anti-Mexican sentiment. Indeed, there is evidence that anti-Mexican prejudice contributed toward anti-immigrant sentiment and Proposition 187. See Wayne Cornelius, "Ambivalent Reception," in *Latinos: Remaking America*, ed. Marcelo Suárez-Orozco and Mariela Páez (Berkeley: University of California Press, 2002), 165–89; Yueh-Ting Lee, Victor Ottati, and Imtiaz Hussain, "Attitudes toward 'Illegal' Immigration into the United States: California Proposition 187," *Hispanic Journal of Behavioral Sciences* 23 (2001): 430–43; Rivera, "Asians Say."

33. Charles Tilly has noted that such efforts create consolidated identities and narratives among social movements. "From Interactions to Outcomes in Social Movements," in *How Social Movements Matter*, ed. Marco Giugni, Doug McAdam, and Charles Tilly (Minneapolis: University of Minnesota Press, 1999), 263. For an insightful critique of resistance research, see Charles Montgomery, "The Trap of Race and Memory," *American Quarterly* 52 (2000): 483.

34. For a critique of Chicana/o scholarship on activism, see Gregory Rodriguez, "Taking the Oath: Why We Need a Revisionist History of Latinos in America," *Los Angeles Times*, August 20, 2000.

35. A classic study on why people do not rebel is John Gaventa's *Power and Powerlessness: Quiescence and Rebellion in an Appalachian Valley* (Urbana: University of Illinois Press, 1980).

36. Self-hate is a form of hegemonic thinking in which individuals from oppressed communities not only adopt the commonsense discourse but also assume the hostility directed toward their people and turn it on themselves and their community. In my own experience, for example, I have relatives who despise Mexicans, especially Mexican immigrants, who are an all-too-painful reminder of who they are and where they come from. The price of self-hate among oppressed groups is potentially devastating. See Kevin Johnson's discussion of his mother in *How Did You Get to Be Mexican? A White/Brown Man's Search for Identity* (Philadelphia: Temple University Press, 1999).

37. Doug McAdam, *Political Process and the Development of Black Insurgency, 1930–1970* (Chicago: University of Chicago Press, 1982).

38. Gregory Rodriguez, "Taking the Oath."

39. Resistance may range from individual foot-dragging (James Scott, *Weapons of the Weak: Everyday Forms of Peasant Resistance* [New Haven, CT:

Yale University Press, 1985], to banditry (Eric Hobsbawm, *Bandits* [New York: Pantheon Books, 1981]; Mark Rosenbaum, *Mexicano Resistance in the Southwest* [Austin: University of Texas Press, 1981]), to more collective and organized forms of resistance, such as the refusal of some Japanese Americans to sign loyalty oaths while interned (see John Okada, *No-No Boy* [Seattle: University of Washington Press, 1976]) or the innumerable slave uprisings and rebellions that characterized slavery (Herbert Aptheker, *American Negro Slave Revolts* [1943; reprint, New York: International Publishers, 1964]).

40. James Jasper, *The Art of Moral Protest: Culture, Biography, and Creativity in Social Movements* (Chicago: University of Chicago Press, 1997), 5.

41. Howard Winant, *Racial Conditions: Politics, Theory, Comparisons* (Minneapolis: University of Minnesota Press, 1994), 24.

42. Consider, for example, the GI Forum (Henry Ramos, *The American GI Forum: In Pursuit of the Dream, 1948–1983* [Houston, TX: Arte Publico, 1998]), the Japanese American Citizens League (Bill Hosokawa, *JACL in Quest of Justice* [New York: William Morrow, 1982]), and the National Association for the Advancement of Colored People (Charles Flint Kellogg, *NAACP: A History of the National Association for the Advancement of Colored People* [Baltimore: Johns Hopkins University Press, 1967]). Even more radical organizations at this time, such as the Communist Party, were preoccupied simply with survival. Healey and Isserman, *California Red*, ch. 8. But see Josh Sides, "You Understand My Condition," *Pacific Historical Review* 67 (1998): 233–57.

43. George Katsiaficas, *The Imagination of the New Left: A Global Analysis of 1968* (Boston: South End Press, 1987).

44. Eric Mann, interview with author, February 27, 2002, Los Angeles.

45. Hall, "Politics of Mugging," 347.

2. DIFFERENTIAL RACIALIZATION IN SOUTHERN CALIFORNIA

1. Mike Davis, *City of Quartz: Excavating the Future in Los Angeles* (New York: Verso, 1990), ch. 2; L. Doti and L. Schweikart, "Financing the Postwar Housing Boom in Phoenix and Los Angeles, 1945–1960," *Pacific Historical Review* 58 (1989): 173–91; Greg Hise, *Magnetic Los Angeles: Planning the Twentieth-Century Metropolis* (Baltimore: Johns Hopkins University Press, 1997); Kevin Allen Leonard, "Years of Hope, Days of Fear: The Impact of World War II on Race Relations in Los Angeles" (PhD diss., University of California, Davis, 1992); Roger Lotchin, *Fortress California, 1910–1961: From Warfare to Welfare* (New York: Oxford University Press, 1992); B. Marchand, *The Emergence of Los Angeles: Population and Housing in the City of Dreams, 1940–70* (London: Routledge and Kegan Paul, 1986); Becky Nicolaides, *My Blue Heaven: Life and Politics in the Working-Class Suburbs of Los Angeles, 1920–1965* (Chicago: University of Chicago Press, 2002); Kevin Starr, *Embattled Dreams: California in War and Peace* (New York: Oxford University Press, 2002).

2. On population expansion, see Allen and Turner, *Ethnic Quilt*; Robert Fogelson, *The Fragmented Metropolis: Los Angeles, 1850–1930* (Berkeley: University of California Press, 1993), ch. 4; John Laslett, "Historical Perspectives: Immigration and the Rise of a Distinctive Urban Region, 1900–1970," in Waldinger and Bozorgmehr, *Ethnic Los Angeles*, 39–75.

3. Lonnie Bunch, "A Past Not Necessarily Prologue: The Afro-American in Los Angeles," in *20th Century Los Angeles: Power, Promotion, and Social Conflict*, ed. Norman Klein and Martin Schiesl (Claremont: Regina Books, 1990), 103, 119. On historic Black Los Angeles, see also Susan Anderson, "A City Called Heaven," in *The City: Los Angeles and Urban Theory at the End of the Twentieth Century*, ed. Allen Scott and Edward Soja (Berkeley: University of California Press, 1996), 336–64; Keith Collins, *Black Los Angeles: The Maturing of the Ghetto, 1940–1950* (Saratoga, CA: Century Twenty One Publishers, 1980); Lawrence De Graff, "The City of Black Angels: Emergence of the Los Angeles Ghetto, 1890–1930," *Pacific Historical Review* 39 (1970): 323–52; Regina Freer, "L.A. Race Woman: Charlotta Bass and the Complexities of Black Political Development in Los Angeles," *American Quarterly* 56 (2004): 607–32; Scott Kurashige, "Transforming Los Angeles"; Josh Sides, *LA City Limits: African American Los Angeles from the Great Depression to the Present* (Berkeley: University of California Press, 2004).

4. George Harwood Phillips, "Indians in Los Angeles, 1781–1875," in *The American Indian: Past and Present*, ed. Roger Nichols (New York: McGraw-Hill College, 1999): 152; Sucheng Chan, *Asian Americans: An Interpretive History* (Boston: Twayne, 1991), 48–53; "A Forgotten Hero from a Night of Disgrace," *Los Angeles Times*, May 16, 1996, B3; Gordon DeMarco, *A Short History of Los Angeles* (San Francisco: Lexikos, 1988), 45–47; Edward Escobar, *Race, Police and the Making of a Political Identity: Mexican Americans and the Los Angeles Police Department, 1900–1945* (Berkeley: University of California Press, 1999).

5. Laslett, "Historical Perspectives," 54. On Black employment discrimination, see Sides, *LA City Limits*, ch. 3; Scott Kurashige, "Transforming Los Angeles" ch. 7; Leonard, "Years of Hope," ch. 3.

6. See Laslett, "Historical Perspectives," 54. On early industrialization, see Greg Hise, "Constructing Nature's Workshop: Industrial Districts and Urban Expansion in Southern California, 1910–1950," *Journal of Historical Geography* 27 (2001): 74–92; Edward Soja, *Postmodern Geographies: The Reassertion of Space in Critical Social Theory* (New York: Verso, 1989), ch. 8.

7. Nicolaides, *My Blue Heaven*; Greg Hise, "Home Building and Industrial Decentralization in Los Angeles: The Roots of the Postwar Urban Region," *Journal of Urban History* 19 (1993): 95–125; Robert Fishman, *Bourgeois Utopias: The Rise and Fall of Suburbia* (New York: Basic Books, 1987), ch. 6. On suburban exclusions, see D. Bartlett, "Torrance: An Industrial Garden City," *American City* 9 (1913): 312; Alida Brill, "Lakewood, California: 'Tomorrowland' at 40" in Dear, Schockman, and Hise, *Rethinking Los Angeles*, 97–112; Fogelson, *Fragmented Metropolis*, 144.

8. Kenneth Jackson, "Race, Ethnicity." As a result of such practices, African

Americans received less than 2 percent of all housing financed with federal mortgage insurance. Anderson, "City Called Heaven," 345.

9. Allen Scott and Edward Soja, "Introduction to Los Angeles," in Scott and Soja, *The City*, 8; R. F. Babcock and F. P. Bosselman, *Exclusionary Zoning: Land Use Regulation and Housing in the 1970s* (New York: Praeger, 1973); G. Miller, *Cities by Contract: The Politics of Municipal Incorporation* (Cambridge, MA: MIT Press, 1981). On how urban areas subsidize suburbs, see S. Guhathakurta and M. Wichert, "Who Pays for Growth in the City of Phoenix," *Urban Affairs Review* 33 (1998): 813–38.

10. While many have documented how sprawl erodes urban cores, less understood is *why* suburbanites seek to distance themselves from nonwhites and the poor. "That suburbanites effectively wall out those unlike themselves after arriving [in suburbia], however, suggests that a major force driving their migration is the wish to escape racial and class intermingling. In the United States, upward mobility and social status are predicated on living apart from racial and economic groups considered inferior.... Thus, it is not simply the racism of individuals but also the collectively perceived threat that race and class differences pose to homeownership and social standing that drives suburbanites to keep their territory segregated." In short, besides property values and schools, living in a largely white environment is a means of accessing whiteness and exploiting white privilege. William Sharpe and Leonard Wallock, "Bold New City or Built up 'Burb'? Redefining Contemporary Suburbia," *American Quarterly* 46 (1994): 30.

11. This does not imply that other people of color necessarily saw it as such. For instance, several authors have noted that aside from a few prominent individuals, such as Charlotta Bass, few Blacks spoke out against the internment. See Gerald Horne, *Fire This Time: The Watts Uprising and the 1960s* (Charlottesville: University Press of Virginia, 1995), 321; Scott Kurashige, "Transforming Los Angeles," ch. 7. Nevertheless, internment had huge implications for how Japanese Americans were perceived and treated by white Angelenos, which, in turn, affected the racial status of other racial/ethnic groups.

12. On Los Angeles's Nikkei population, see Donald Teruo Hata Jr. and Nadine Ishitani Hata, "Asian-Pacific Angelinos: Model Minorities and Indispensable Scapegoats," in Klein and Schiesl, *20th Century Los Angeles*, 71; Lon Kurashige, *Japanese American Celebration and Conflict: A History of Ethnic Identity and Festival, 1934–1990* (Berkeley: University of California Press, 2002), ch. 1; Valerie Matsumoto, "Japanese American Women and the Creation of Urban Nisei Culture in the 1930s," in *Over the Edge: Remapping the American West*, ed. V. Matsumoto and B. Allmendinger (Berkeley: University of California Press, 1999), 291–306; John Moddell, *The Economics of Racial Accommodation: Japanese Americans of Los Angeles, 1900–1942* (Urbana: University of Illinois Press, 1977). On the internment itself, see Allan Bosworth, *America's Concentration Camps* (New York: Norton, 1967); Roger Daniels, Sandra Taylor, and Harry Kitano, *Japanese Americans: From Relocation to Redress* (Seattle: University of Washington Press, 1991); Roger Daniels, *The Decision to Relocate*

the Japanese Americans (Philadelphia: J. B. Lippincott, 1975); Audrie Girdner and Anne Loftis, *The Great Betrayal: The Evacuation of the Japanese-Americans during World War II* (New York: Macmillan, 1970).

13. John Moddell, cited in Horne, *Fire This Time,* 32.

14. Lon Kurashige, *Japanese American Celebration,* ch. 4; Kariann Yokota, "From Little Tokyo to Bronzeville and Back: Ethnic Communities in Transition" (master's thesis, University of California, Los Angeles, 1996); William Warren, "Maps: A Spatial Approach to Japanese American Communities in Los Angeles," *Amerasia* 13 (1986–87): 137–51.

15. Jose Cardenas, "History of WWII Gets the Latino Perspective," *Los Angeles Times,* May 27, 2002, B1, B8; Mario García, "Americans All: The Mexican American Generation and the Politics of Wartime Los Angeles, 1941–45," in *The Mexican American Experience: An Interdisciplinary Anthology,* ed. Rodolfo de la Garza et al. (Austin: University of Texas Press, 1985), 201–12; Nelson Peery, *Black Fire: The Making of an American Revolutionary* (New York: New Press, 1994).

16. Mary Dudziak, *Cold War Civil Rights: Race and the Image of American Democracy* (Princeton, NJ: Princeton University Press, 2000).

17. Grace Lee Boggs, *Living for Change: An Autobiography* (Minneapolis: University of Minnesota Press, 1998), 53–54.

18. On the Communist Party's silence on the Japanese internment, see Healey and Isserman, *California Red,* 86. They also note that although Blacks and Mexicanos/as were welcomed at Communist Party club meetings, there was not a deep connection. See, however, Sides, "You Understand." Early ethnic radicalism in Los Angeles can be seen in Horne, *Fire This Time,* 5; Fujino, "Japanese American Radicalism"; Scott Kurashige, "Transforming Los Angeles," ch. 6; Yuji Ichioka, "A Buried Past: Early Issei Socialists and the Japanese Community," *Amerasia* 1 (1971): 1–25; Yoneda, *Ganbatte*; Ichioka, *The Issei,* ch. 4; Mario García, *Memories of Chicano History,* ch. 6; Douglas Monroy, "Anarquismo y Comunismo: Mexican Radicalism and the Communist Party in Los Angeles during the 1930s," *Labor History* 24 (1983): 34–59; Douglas Monroy, *Rebirth: Mexican Los Angeles from the Great Migration to the Great Depression* (Berkeley: University of California Press, 1999); Gottlieb et al., *Next Los Angeles,* ch. 2.

19. Horne, *Fire This Time,* 5.

20. In 1970, the Hispanic category included Salvadorans, Guatemalans, Other Central Americans, Mexicans, and Other Hispanic. Of the 1,400,000 Hispanics counted in Los Angeles County, 1,114,000 (80 percent) were of Mexican origin, and approximately 75 percent of these were native born. In 1970 the following groups made up the Asian American category: Japanese, Chinese, Vietnamese, Filipino, Korean, Asian Indian, and Other Asians. The total Asian American population was 256,200 in Los Angeles County, or 2.6 percent of the entire population. Japanese Americans constituted 47 percent of this group, Chinese Americans 21 percent, and Filipinos 17 percent. For historic and geographic

overviews of both groups in Southern California, see Allen and Turner, *Ethnic Quilt*, chs. 4 and 5.

The 1970 census was taken on the eve of what would become one of the largest immigration waves in U.S. history. Because of the 1965 Immigration Act, which dismantled racial quotas, as well as political and economic crises in Latin America, millions of Asians and Latinas/os, including large numbers of Central Americans, came to the United States. Ruben Rumbaut, "Origins and Destinies: Immigration to the United States since World War II," *Sociological Forum* 9 (1994): 583–621. Los Angeles was their destination of choice, and this immigration has dramatically reconfigured the politics and demographics of the region (see table 11).

21. Mauricio Mazón, *The Zoot-Suit Riots: The Psychology of Symbolic Annihilation* (Austin: University of Texas Press, 1984); Escobar, *Race, Police,* 84–90; Eduardo Obregón Pagán, *Murder at the Sleepy Lagoon: Zoot Suits, Race and Riot in Wartime L.A.* (Chapel Hill: University of North Carolina Press, 2003); Francisco Balderrama and Raymond Rodriguez, *Decade of Betrayal: Mexican Repatriation in the 1930s* (Albuquerque: University of New Mexico Press, 1995); George Sánchez, *Becoming Mexican American: Ethnicity, Culture, and Identity in Chicano Los Angeles, 1900–1945* (New York: Oxford University Press, 1993), ch. 10; Leonard, "Years of Hope," chs. 6 and 7. See also Kevin Leonard, "In the Interest of All Races: African Americans and Interracial Cooperation in Los Angeles during and after World War II," in *Seeking El Dorado: African Americans in California,* ed. Lawrence De Graaf, Kevin Mulroy, and Quintard Taylor (Los Angeles: Autry Museum of Western Heritage, 2001), 309–40.

22. T. Bowden and D. Mayborn, "Confidentiality Report of a Survey in Metropolitan Los Angeles, California," box 101, record group 95, Division of Research and Statistics, Home Owners Loan Corporation, Records Relating to the City Survey Files, 1935–40, National Archives and Records Administration, College Park, MD.

23. Leonard, "Years of Hope," 43–45. This observation was substantiated by a handful of interviews I conducted with Mexican American veterans who voiced surprise at white southern soldiers' hostility toward Blacks but not Latinos. Some were warned by white soldiers against associating with Blacks, as their status and reputation would be diminished.

24. Paul Weeks, "700 March for Integration of Torrance Tract," *Los Angeles Times,* June 30, 1963, 1, 12.

25. William Peterson, "Success Story, Japanese American Style," *New York Times Magazine,* January 9, 1966, 21–22, 33, 36, 38, 40–43; Barbara Varon, "The Japanese Americans: Comparative Occupational Status, 1960 and 1950," *Demography* 4 (1967): 817; "Success Story of One Minority Group in US," *US News and World Report,* December 26, 1966, reprinted in *Roots: An Asian American Reader,* ed. Amy Tachiki et al. (Los Angeles: University of California, Los Angeles, Asian American Studies Center, 1971), 6–9; David Bell, "The Tri-

umph of Asian Americans," *New Republic,* July 15 and 22, 1985, 24–26. For critiques, see Keith Osajima, "Asian Americans as the Model Minority," in Zhou and Gatewood, *Contemporary Asian America,* 449–58; Prashad, *Karma of Brown Folk.*

26. Don Nakanishi, "Surviving Democracy's 'Mistake': Japanese Americans and the Enduring Legacy of Executive Order 9066," *Amerasia* 19 (1993): 20.

27. Research suggests that light-skinned Latinas/os fare better than darker-skinned ones. Edward Telles and Edward Murguia, "Phenotype Discrimination and Income Differences among Mexican Americans," *Social Science Quarterly* 71 (1990): 682–96; Christina Gómez, "The Continual Significance of Skin Color," *Hispanic Journal of Behavioral Sciences* 22 (2000): 94–103; John Logan, "How Race Counts for Hispanic Americans" (working paper, Lewis Mumford Center, State University of New York, Albany, 2003).

28. Lawrence De Graaf, "African American Suburbanization in California, 1960 through 1990," in De Graaf, Mulroy, and Taylor, *Seeking El Dorado,* 405–49.

29. The National Advisory Commission on Civil Disorders commissioned a major survey of white attitudes toward Blacks that was published in 1971. While some findings may have represented "progress" from previous decades, I still find them alarming. For instance, 56 percent believed that Negro disadvantages in jobs and housing were due to Black deficiencies, while 51 percent opposed any laws that would prevent residential discrimination. Angus Campbell, *White Attitudes towards Black People* (Ann Arbor: Institute for Social Research, University of Michigan, 1971), 4.

30. Richard Preston, "The Changing Form and Structure of the Southern California Metropolis," *California Geographer* 12 (1971): 11; Allen Scott, "Manufacturing Economy," 216.

31. Laslett, "Historical Perspectives," 65. On earlier Mexican employment patterns, see Monroy, *Rebirth,* ch. 3; Ricardo Romo, *East Los Angeles: History of a Barrio* (Austin: University of Texas Press, 1983), ch. 6; George Sánchez, *Becoming Mexican American,* ch. 9.

32. California Department of Industrial Relations, Fair Employment Practices Commission, "Negroes and Mexican Americans in South and East Los Angeles: Changes between 1960 and 1965," 1965, p. 28, box 69, Los Angeles Area Chamber of Commerce Collection, Department of Special Collections, University of Southern California Library, Los Angeles. See also Leo Grebler, Joan Moore, and Ralph Guzman, *The Mexican American People, the Nation's Second Largest Minority* (New York: Free Press, 1970); Institute of Industrial Relations, University of California, Los Angeles, *Hard Core Unemployment and Poverty in Los Angeles* (Washington, DC: U.S. Department of Commerce, Area Redevelopment Administration, 1965).

33. Allen Scott, "Manufacturing Economy," 223. See also William Crigler, "The Employment Status of Blacks in Los Angeles: Ten Years after the Kerner Commission Report" (PhD diss., Claremont Graduate School, 1979).

34. The situation has since changed with Latina immigrants now dominating domestic work. Pierrette Hondagneu-Sotelo, *Doméstica: Immigrant Work-*

ers *Cleaning and Caring in the Shadows of Affluence* (Berkeley: University of California Press, 2001).

35. Hondagneu-Sotelo, *Doméstica*.

36. Ivan Light and Elizabeth Roach, "Self-Employment: Mobility Ladder or Economic Lifeboat?" in Waldinger and Bozorgmehr, *Ethnic Los Angeles*, 199. These figures should be interpreted with caution, however, as they are based on a small sample (N = less than 50). Other researchers, however, have found high rates of self-employment among Japanese Americans. Sheila Henry, *Cultural Persistence and Socio Economic Mobility: A Comparative Study of Assimilation among Armenians and Japanese in Los Angeles* (San Francisco: R & E Research Associates, 1978), 62–63; California Department of Industrial Relations, Fair Employment Practices Commission, "Californians of Japanese, Chinese and Filipino Ancestry," box 69, Los Angeles Area Chamber of Commerce Collection, Department of Special Collections, University of Southern California Library, Los Angeles, 1965; Varon, "Japanese Americans."

37. Scott Kurashige, "Transforming Los Angeles," ch. 2; Moddell, *Economics of Racial Accommodation*; Daniels, Taylor, and Kitano, *Japanese Americans*.

38. Guy Kurose, interviewed in Martin Wong, "Art Ishi and Guy Kurose," *Giant Robot*, Spring 1998, 77.

39. Leonard, "Years of Hope," 61–62; Laslett, "Historical Perspectives," 55.

40. Allen Scott, "Manufacturing Economy," 222.

41. Joe Feagin and Melvin Sikes, *Living with Racism: The Black Middle-Class Experience* (New York: Beacon Press, 1994); Leland Saito, *Race and Politics: Asian Americans, Latinos, and Whites in a Los Angeles Suburb* (Urbana: University of Illinois Press, 1998).

42. Ethington, "Segregated Diversity."

43. Allen Scott, *Metropolis: From Division of Labor to Urban Form* (Berkeley: University of California Press, 1988), ch. 9; Allen Scott, "High Technology Industrial Development in the San Fernando Valley and Ventura County," in Scott and Soja, *The City*, 276–310; Robin Law, Jennifer Wolch, and Lois Takahashi, "Defenseless Territory: Workers, Communities, and the Decline of Military Production in Los Angeles," *Environment and Planning C: Government and Policy* 11 (1993): 291–315.

44. Los Angeles Times, "*Los Angeles Times* 1965: Market and Media," box 118, Los Angeles Area Chamber of Commerce Collection, Department of Special Collections, University of Southern California Library, Los Angeles. See also Rob Kling, Spencer Olin, and Mark Poster, "The Emergence of Postsuburbia: An Introduction," in *Postsuburban California: The Transformation of Orange County since World War II*, ed. Rob Kling, Spencer Olin, and Mark Poster (Berkeley: University of California Press, 1995), 1–30; Allen Scott, *Metropolis*, ch. 9.

45. Quoted in Martin Schiesl, "Designing the Model Community: The Irvine Company and Suburban Development, 1950–88," in Kling, Olin, and Poster, *Postsuburban California*, 68. See also De Graaf, "African American Suburbanization."

46. Researchers found that 30 percent of the housing occupied by Spanish speakers throughout the Southwest was substandard. Grebler, Moore, and Guzman, *Mexican American People*, 251–52.

47. California Department of Industrial Relations, "Negroes and Mexican Americans," 23.

48. Ibid.

49. The San Gabriel Valley was one of the top destinations for Mexican and Asian Americans. Saito, *Race and Politics*; see also Wei Li, "Anatomy of a New Ethnic Settlement: The Chinese Ethnoburb in Los Angeles," *Urban Studies* 35 (1998): 479–501.

50. Carlos Montes, interview with author, May 26, 2000, Los Angeles. The cultural exchange between Black and Mexican Angelenos is evident in gang activity, low-riding, graffiti, clothing, hairstyles, musical borrowing, as seen in groups like War and Ozomatli, and the club scene of the 1940s and 1950s. Gaye Johnson, "A Sifting of Centuries: Afro-Chicano Interaction and Popular Musical Culture in California, 1960–2000," in *Decolonial Voices: Chicana and Chicano Cultural Studies in the 21st Century*, ed. A. Aldama and Naomi Quiñones (Bloomington: University of Indiana Press, 2002), 316–29; Matt Garcia, *World of Its Own*, ch. 6.

51. Biliana Ambrecht and Harry Pachon, "Ethnic Mobilization in a Mexican American Community: An Exploratory Study of East Los Angeles, 1965–1972," *Western Political Quarterly* 29 (1974): 513–14. On Mexican Americans' efforts to claim whiteness and nonwhiteness, respectively, see Foley, "Partly Colored"; López, *Racism on Trial*.

3. THE POLITICIZATION OF THE THIRD WORLD LEFT

1. McAdam, *Political Process*.

2. For important exceptions, see Darryl Maeda, "Constructing Yellow Power"; Yuri Kochiyama, "The Impact of Malcolm X on Asian American Politics and Activism," in *Blacks, Latinos, and Asians in Urban America: Status and Prospects for Politics and Activism*, ed. James Jennings (Westport, CT: Praeger, 1994), 129–41; Wong, "Yellow Power." Such recognition has been less evident in Chicana/o studies, although see López, *Racism on Trial*.

3. Quoted in June Rustan, "Inside Out and Upside Down: An Interview with Anne Braden," *Colorlines* 4 (Spring 2001): 30.

4. Key texts include McAdam, *Political Process*; Paulo Freire, *The Pedagogy of the Oppressed* (New York: Continuum, 1981); George Lipsitz, *A Life in the Struggle: Ivory Perry and the Culture of Opposition* (Philadelphia: Temple University Press, 1988); James Scott, *Weapons of the Weak*.

5. Jasper, *Art of Moral Protest*, ch. 2.

6. Some examples are Elaine Brown, *Taste of Power*; Angela Davis, *Angela Davis*; Forman, *Making of Black Revolutionaries*; Boggs, *Living for Change*; Jose Angel Gutiérrez, *The Making of a Chicano Militant* (Madison: University of Wisconsin Press, 1999); Huey Newton, *Revolutionary Suicide* (New York:

Writers and Readers Publishing, 1995); Assata Shakur, *Assata* (New York: Lawrence Hill Books, 1988).

7. Freire, *Pedagogy of the Oppressed*, 31–32.

8. Alex Haley, *The Autobiography of Malcolm X* (1964; reprint, New York: Ballantine Books, 1992); Komozi Woodward, *A Nation within a Nation: Amiri Baraka (LeRoi Jones) and Black Power Politics* (Chapel Hill: University of North Carolina Press, 1999); Diane Fujino, "To Serve the Movement," in Ho et al., *Legacy to Liberation*, 257–66; Jacques Levy, *Cesar Chavez: Autobiography of La Causa* (New York: Norton, 1975); Rigoberta Menchú, *I, Rigoberta Menchú: An Indian Woman in Guatemala*, ed. Elisabeth Burgos-Debray, trans. Ann Wright (New York: Verso, 1984).

9. On white activists, see Kenneth Keniston, *Young Radicals: Notes on Committed Youth* (New York: Harcourt, Brace and World, 1968); James Elden and David Schweitzer, "New Third Party Radicalism: The Case of the California Peace and Freedom Party," *Western Political Quarterly* 24 (December 1971): 761–74; Rebecca Klatch, "The Counterculture, the New Left, and the New Right," in *Cultural Politics and Social Movements*, ed. Marcy Darnovsky, Barbara Epstein, and Richard Flacks (Philadelphia: Temple University Press, 1995), 74–89; Richard Flacks, *Youth and Social Change* (Chicago: Markham, 1971); Richard Flacks, "Who Protests: The Social Bases of the Student Movement," in *Protest! Student Activism in America*, ed. J. Foster and D. Long (New York: William Morrow, 1970), 134–57. On nonwhite activists, see Anthony Orum and Amy Orum, "The Class and Status Bases of Negro Student Protest," *Social Science Quarterly* 49 (1968): 521–33; Maurice Pinard, Jerome Kirk, and Donald Von Eschen, "Process of Recruitment in the Sit-In Movement," in *The Black Revolt: The Civil Rights Movement, Ghetto Uprisings, and Separatism*, ed. James Geschwender (Englewood Cliffs, NJ: Prentice Hall, 1971), 184–97; Biliana Ambrecht, *Politicizing the Poor: The Legacy of the War on Poverty in a Mexican American Community* (New York: Praeger, 1976).

10. Andrew Barlow, "The Student Movement of the 1960s and the Politics of Race," *Journal of Ethnic Studies* 19 (1991): 1–22.

11. Horowitz, *Radical Son*, 423.

12. Laura Pulido, "The Interior Life of Politics," *Ethics, Place and Environment* 6 (2003): 46–52.

13. Linda Chávez, *An Unlikely Conservative: The Transformation of an Ex-liberal, or, How I Became the Most Hated Hispanic in America* (New York: Basic Books, 2002); Ward Connerly, *Creating Equal: My Fight against Race Preferences* (San Francisco: Encounter Books, 2000); Dinesh D'Souza, *What's So Great about America* (New York: Penguin Books, 2000); Shelby Steele, *The Content of Our Character: A New Vision of Race in America* (New York: Perennial Press, 1990); Andrew Peyton Thomas, *Clarence Thomas: A Biography* (San Francisco: Encounter Books, 2002).

14. Gitlin, *The Sixties*, 67.

15. Mario García, *Memories of Chicano History*, ch. 6; Lorena Oropeza, "La Batalla Está Aqui!" (PhD diss., Cornell University, 1996), 72; Sides, "You Under-

stand My Condition"; Fujino, "Japanese American Radicalism"; Scott Kurashige, "Transforming Los Angeles," ch. 8; Gerald Horne, *Black Liberation/Red Scare: Ben Davis and the Communist Party* (University of Delaware Press, 1994).

16. Black communists were dismayed when the CPUSA, following the Soviet Union, disavowed Stalin. Stalin was embraced by many nonwhite leftists because of his work on national minorities. Nelson Peery, interview with author, February 26, 1999, Los Angeles; Harry Haywood, *Black Bolshevik: Autobiography of an Afro-American Communist* (Chicago: Liberator Press, 1978), ch. 22. See also Harry Haywood, *Negro Liberation* (New York: International Publishers, 1948); Hutchinson, *Blacks and Reds*, ch. 9.

17. Healey and Isserman, *California Red*, 208; Hutchinson, *Blacks and Reds;* Robin Kelley, *Hammer and Hoe: Alabama Communists during the Great Depression* (Chapel Hill: University of North Carolina Press, 1990); Mark Solomon, *The Cry Was Unity: Communists and African Americans, 1917–36* (Jackson: University Press of Mississippi Press, 1998).

18. On conflict between the New and Old Left, see Gitlin, *The Sixties*, 176. Generational tensions did exist within CASA when Bert Corona was pushed out by younger activists. David Gutiérrez, "CASA in the Chicano Movement," 13; Mario García, *Memories of Chicano History*, 308–14.

19. Brodkin, *How Jews Became White Folks;* Paul Buhle, "Themes in American Jewish Radicalism," in *The Immigrant Left in the United States*, ed. Paul Buhle and Dan Georgakas (Albany: State University of New York Press, 1996), 77–118; Horowitz, *Radical Son*, parts 1 and 2; Gitlin, *The Sixties*, 24–26; Flacks, "Who Protests"; George Sánchez, " 'What's Good for Boyle Heights Is Good for the Jews': Creating Multiracialism on the Eastside during the 1950s," *American Quarterly* 56 (2004): 633–61.

20. Tuan, *Forever Foreigners*, ch. 4.

21. McAdam, *Political Process*.

22. Bob Sipchen, "Labor of Love," *Los Angeles Times*, March 9, 1997, E1, E8.

23. Others have suggested that the federal government's reluctance to protect civil rights activists in the South contributed to the rise of more militant Black politics. Gitlin, *The Sixties*, 136–46; Hayden, *Reunion*, 63–66.

24. Escobar, *Race, Police*. See also López, *Racism on Trial*.

25. Scott Kurashige, "Transforming Los Angeles," ch. 6.

26. California Governor's Commission on the Los Angeles Riots, *Violence in the City—An End or a Beginning?* (Los Angeles, 1965), 1; Horne, *Fire This Time*. See also Robert Fogelson, *The Los Angeles Riots* (Salem, NH: Ayer, 1988); U.S. National Advisory Commission on Civil Disorders, *Report of the National Advisory Commission on Civil Disorders* (Washington, DC: Government Printing Office, 1968).

27. Horne, *Fire This Time*, 141.

28. Walter Raine, "Los Angeles Riot Study: The Ghetto Merchant Survey" (Working Paper MR-98, Institute of Government and Public Affairs, University of California, Los Angeles, 1967); Raymond Murphy and James Watson, "The

Structure of Discontent" (Working Paper MR-92, Institute of Government and Public Affairs, University of California, Los Angeles, 1967).

For examples of attacks against the police, see Horne, *Fire This Time*, 81. Research suggests that the incidence of police abuse was actually lower than most Blacks believed. One study found that over 60 percent of Blacks living in the curfew zone felt that the police used unnecessary force in arrests, beat people in custody, and searched homes unnecessarily. However, only 13 percent had actually experienced unnecessary force in an arrest, while 1 percent had been beaten while in custody, and 6 percent had had their homes searched. Nonetheless, 45 percent of respondents had experienced lesser forms of police abuse, including offensive language and being unnecessarily stopped and searched. Nathan Cohen, "Los Angeles Riot Study: Summary and Implications for Policy" (Working Paper MR-103, Institute of Government and Public Affairs, University of California, Los Angeles, 1967). Certainly, it is conceivable that past abuses would contribute to heightened anxiety, belief in police misconduct, and anger toward law enforcement. Consider the following quote: "If they stop a white man, they don't bother him, but a Negro they hope to find dope or pills or stolen merchandise. . . . You are tense and nervous, looking for them at all times. Even the children are afraid. They start running when they see the police because they have heard how the policemen beat their fathers and brothers, they have seen how they stop them for nothing" (quoted in Murphy and Watson, "Structure of Discontent," 24–27).

29. Bruce Tyler, "Black Radicalism in Southern California, 1950–1982" (PhD diss., University of California, Los Angeles, 1983); Murphy and Watson, "Structure of Discontent"; Horne, *Fire This Time*, ch. 7. One survey found that 76 percent of Blacks held unfavorable attitudes toward Chief Parker. David Sears, "Los Angeles Riot Study: Political Attitudes of Los Angeles Negroes" (working paper, Institute of Government and Public Affairs, University of California, Los Angeles, 1967), 8. For histories of the LAPD, see Terry McDermott, "Behind the Bunker Mentality," *Los Angeles Times*, June 11, 2000; Joe Domanick, *To Protect and Serve* (New York: Pocket Books, 1994).

30. Roy Nakano, "Them Bad Cats: Past Images and Asian American Street Gangs," *Gidra* 5 (January 1973): 4–7; Jeff Furumura, Tom Okabe, and Roy Nakano, "Them Bad Cats: Part II," *Gidra* 5 (June 1973): 1, 5–7; James Diego Vigil, *Barrio Gangs: Street Life and Identity in Southern California* (Austin: University of Texas Press, 1988).

31. The McCone Commission reported that a very small percentage of African Americans participated in and/or supported the Watts riot, but subsequent studies suggest otherwise. One study estimated that 20 percent of curfew zone residents participated and that an additional 35–40 percent were "active spectators." David Sears and John McConahay, "Los Angeles Riot Study: Riot Participation" (working paper, Institute of Government and Public Affairs, University of California, Los Angeles, 1967), 3, 10. Moreover, approximately one-third of Blacks viewed the rebellion favorably. Cohen, "Los Angeles Riot Study,"

4. On gender differences, see Sears and McConahay, "Los Angeles Riot Study," 13; Murphy and Watson, "Structure of Discontent," 34.

32. California Governor's Commission, *Violence in the City*, 5.

33. Joan Moore and Ralph Guzman, "New Wind from the Southwest," *Nation* 30 (May 1966): 645–48.

34. The shift toward a bipolar racial order was most apparent in the electoral arena, culminating in the 1973 election of Tom Bradley. Raphael Sonenshein, *Politics in Black and White: Race and Power in Los Angeles* (Princeton, NJ: Princeton University Press, 1993). However, see also Fernando Guerra, "Ethnic Politics in Los Angeles: The Emergence of Black, Jewish, Latino and Asian Office Holders" (PhD diss., University of Michigan, 1990). Heather Rose Parker, in "The Elusive Coalition: African American and Chicano Political Organizing in Los Angeles" (PhD diss., University of California, Los Angeles, 1996), has argued that Blacks' greater visibility was due to the Chicano community's limited institutional development, but equally important, I suggest, is the general recognition of Blacks as *the* oppressed minority group. On Black politics more generally, see David Scoble, "Negro Politics in Los Angeles: The Quest for Power" (Working Paper MR-89, Institute of Government and Public Affairs, University of California, Los Angeles, 1967).

35. Project 100,000, devised by Secretary of Defense Robert McNamara, sought to increase the number of men eligible for military service by targeting those who did not qualify. Packaged as a Great Society Program that would teach valuable skills, Project 100,000 focused on language skills and supplemental education to prepare for the military exam. Because military personnel were classified as only "Caucasian" and "non-Caucasian," it is uncertain how many Latinos served, but it appears that there was significant minority participation. Half of all the men recruited under Project 100,000 fought in Vietnam, of which over 50 percent were Black. Jorge Mariscal, *Aztlán and Viet Nam: Chicano and Chicana Experiences of the War* (Berkeley: University of California Press, 1999), 20; Lisa Hsiao, "Project 100,000," *Viet Nam Generation* 2 (Spring 1989): 14–37.

36. Mariscal, *Aztlán and Viet Nam*, 27; Ron Vera, "Observations on the Chicano Relationship to Military Service in Los Angeles County," *Aztlán* 1 (Fall 1970): 33.

37. Consider the pride and celebration of the 442nd battalion, in which Japanese Americans emerged as one of the most decorated units of World War II.

38. Oropeza, "La Batalla Está Aqui!" 110.

39. One survey found that Mexican Americans, monolingual Spanish speakers in particular, were more opposed to the war than either whites or Blacks. Charles Ornelas and Michael Gonzalez, "The Chicano and the War," *Aztlán* 2 (Spring 1971): 23–35. This opposition was also expressed in public protest. Ron Ridenour, "April 22: Out Now!" *Los Angeles Advocate*, April 15–30, 1972, 11–14.

40. This tension affected the larger antiwar movement. For example, in 1972, Chicana/o activists struggled with the National Peace Action Coalition

(NPAC) because they wanted the issue of deportation to have equal status with the war. Ridenour, "April 22," 13.

41. Oropeza, "La Batalla Está Aquí!" 126–27; Asian Coalition, "Asian Coalition: On the White Anti-War Movement," *Gidra* 5 (March 1973): 20.

42. See the special issue of *Regeneración* (vol. 6, 1970) dedicated to Rubén Salazar; "National Chicano Moratorium Committee," *La Causa* 1 (December 1970): 6. For a different perspective, see California State Advisory Committee to the U.S. Commission on Civil Rights, *Police-Community Relations in East Los Angeles, California* (Washington, DC: Government Printing Office, 1970). On LAPD and Chicana/o activists more generally, see "L.A. Police vs. Mexican Americans," *Los Angeles News Advocate*, February 2, 1972, 1, 3.

43. William Wei has argued that the rise of the Asian American movement was largely due to the convergence of college-age Asian Americans and opposition to the Vietnam War (*Asian American Movement*, 1).

44. Consequently, much of the Asian American antiwar activism was campus based. Alan Ota, "Moratorium Day," *Gidra* 1 (1969): 2.

45. Wei, *Asian American Movement*, 38.

46. Ridenour, "April 22," 13–14.

47. See also Warren Furutani, "The March," *Gidra* 2 (February 1970): 5, 8.

48. Quote in Miriam Ching Louie, "Yellow, Brown and Red: Towards an Appraisal of Marxist Influences on the Asian American Movement" (unpublished manuscript, Oakland, CA, 1991), 8. Blacks and Chicanas/os were also influenced by international events, but not to the same degree. See, for example, Cynthia Young, "Havana in Harlem," *Science and Society* 65 (2001): 12–38.

49. See also Evelyn Yoshimura, "G.I.'s and Asian Women," *Gidra* 3 (January 1971): 4, 15. For a more general discussion, see Cynthia Enloe, *Bananas, Beaches and Bases: Making Feminist Sense of International Politics* (Berkeley: University of California Press, 1989).

50. For example, the High Potential Program at the University of California, Los Angeles, was designed especially for students of color and became an important meeting ground for radical activists. I.M., "High Potential at UCLA," *Gidra* 1 (September 1969): 1.

51. Two important instances of Black student activism are the creation of the Third World College at the University of California, San Diego, and the Third World Liberation Front at San Francisco State University (box 42, "Third World Strike," 1969, Twentieth Century Organizational Files, Southern California Library). On Black student activism in Los Angeles, see Brown, *Taste of Power*, 110–12. The relationship between students and the Black Panther Party needs further investigation. While the BPP worked closely with student groups, there were tensions between the students (petty bourgeoisie) and the people from the street (lumpen proletariat).

52. Yen Le Espiritu, *Asian American Panethnicity: Bridging Institutions and Identities* (Philadelphia: Temple University Press, 1992).

53. Black Student Union, "Education for Our People," box 38, collection 50,

Special Collections, UCLA Library. Murray was the BPP's minister of education and an English instructor, and the TWLF believed he was fired for political reasons. San Francisco Strike Committee, "On Strike, Shut It Down," box 42, "Third World Strike," Twentieth Century Organizational Files, Southern California Library; Mike Murase, "Ethnic Studies and Higher Education for Asian Americans," in *Counterpoint: Perspectives on Asian America*, ed. Emma Gee (Los Angeles: Asian American Studies, University of California, Los Angeles, 1976), 206.

54. Editorial Staff of Asian American Political Alliance, "Asian Studies: The Concept of Asian Studies," *Asian American Political Alliance* 1 (October 1969).

55. Murase, "Ethnic Studies," 206.

56. The significance of California State University, Long Beach, in the development of the Third World Left is critical. As part of the California State University system, it accepted a greater percentage of high school graduates than the University of California, thus making it more accessible to first-generation college students. In addition, Long Beach's location attracted a cross section of students, whereas UCLA, ensconced in Westwood, was a world away from the ghetto and barrio. If not for UCLA's High Potential Program, the campus would have been relevant for a relatively small number of minority activists.

57. St. Mary's, a private college in Northern California, recruited Black and Chicana/o students from Los Angeles.

4. SERVING THE PEOPLE AND VANGUARD POLITICS

1. On Mexican and Japanese American politics in Los Angeles, see Ernesto Chávez, *Mi Raza Primero!* ch. 1; Scott Kurashige, "Transforming Los Angeles," ch. 8.

2. Wei, *Asian American Movement*, 1.

3. On the intransigence of the white establishment, see Diane McWhorter, *Carry Me Home: Birmingham, Alabama* (New York: Simon and Schuster, 2001); Gitlin, *The Sixties*, 136–46.

4. Chana Kai Lee, *For Freedom's Sake: The Life of Fannie Lou Hamer* (Urbana: University of Illinois Press, 1999).

5. Stokely Carmichael and Charles Hamilton, *Black Power: The Politics of Liberation in America* (New York: Vintage Books, 1967). Activists were also influenced by Franz Fanon, *The Wretched of the Earth* (New York: Grove Press, 1963).

6. Elaine Brown, *Taste of Power*, 126–27.

7. Carmichael and Hamilton, *Black Power*; John McCartney, *Black Power Ideologies: An Essay in African-American Political Thought* (Philadelphia: Temple University Press, 1992); Woodward, *Nation within a Nation*.

8. Hayden, *Reunion*, 162. SNCC actually voted on whether to expel white members (164). Below are two contrasting views of this shift. David Horowitz saw it in largely anti-Semitic terms:

The Panthers were not alone among black radicals in their attacks on Jews. In 1966, Stokely Carmichael and the leaders of SNCC had expelled whites from the civil-rights movement. Since Jews were a near majority of the whites in these organizations, and had played a strategic role in organizing and funding the struggle, it was clear to everyone that they were the primary target of the assault. . . . Jews had funded the movement, devised its legal strategies, and provided support for its efforts in the media and in the universities—and wherever else they had power. More than *half* the freedom riders who had gone to the southern states were Jews, although Jews constituted only 3% of the population. It was an unprecedented show of solidarity from one people to another. . . . But . . . the black leaders of the movement had unceremoniously expelled the Jews from their ranks. (*Radical Son*, 225, 277)

In contrast, Eric Mann, also Jewish, interpreted these events as follows:

We had come to Newark in the tradition of the students who went South . . . but in 1967–68, there was a period of tremendous Black consciousness, [giving rise to] the Black Power movement, and white organizers were not appropriate at that moment in history. . . . Several NCUP [Newark Community Union Project] leaders agreed with the general concepts of Black Power but did not see why they could not retain a few white organizers. [They told us,] "We are leaders in our own movement, you are very valuable organizers, we trust you, and think you can help the cause." So they didn't ask us to leave, but we all knew a historical period was coming to an end, the transition from civil rights to a Black Liberation movement. And, one at a time, [we left]. (Interview with author, February 27, 2002, Los Angeles)

9. Gerry Silva, interview with author, June 14, 2002, Santa Monica, CA; Helen Toribio, "Dare to Struggle," in Ho et al., *Legacy to Liberation*, 31–49; Tram Quang Nguyen, "Caring for the Soul of Our Community," in Louie and Omatsu, *Asian Americans*, 285–97.

10. Carlos Montes, interview with author, May 26, 2000, Los Angeles.

11. James Forman, "1967: High Tide of Black Resistance," International Affairs Commission, Student Nonviolent Coordinating Committee, James Forman File, Southern California Library, Los Angeles, 24.

12. Mann, interview.

13. A. Belden Fields, *Trotskyism and Maoism: Theory and Practice in France and the United States* (Brooklyn, NY: Autonomedia, 1989), ch. 5; Gitlin, *The Sixties*, 382–91; Andrew Moss, "SDS: Heavy Weather Ahead," *Dock of the Bay*, p. 5, box 2, collection 50, Special Collections, UCLA Library; Sale, *SDS*.

14. Bernadine Dohrn, "Notes from the Underground," *Contempt!* p. 4, box 1, collection 50, Special Collections, UCLA Library; Shinya Ono, "A Weatherman: You Do Need a Weatherman to Know Which Way the Wind Blows," in Jacobs, *Weatherman*, 227–74; Weather Underground, *Prairiefire: The Politics of*

Revolutionary Anti-Imperialism, folder 29, carton 12, Social Protest Collection, Bancroft Library, University of California, Berkeley.

15. Peace and Freedom Party and Black and Chicano Caucus, "The Third World," box 138, collection 50, Special Collections, UCLA Library. See also "Editorial: BPP and PFP," *Black Panther*, March 16, 1968, 3; *Peace and Freedom News*, special issue, May 6, 1968.

16. See, for example, George Breitman, *On Black Nationalism and Self-Determination* (New York: Pathfinder Press, 1970); Communist Party USA, *Toward Chicano Liberation*, 1971, Communist Party USA Conventions File, Southern California Library; *Revolutionary Union, The Chicano Struggle and the Struggle for Socialism*, adopted by the Revolutionary Communist Party, 1975, Revolutionary Union File, Southern California Library; Olga Rodríguez, *The Politics of Chicano Liberation* (New York: Pathfinder Press, 1977); Henry Winston, "Black and White—One Class, One Fight," 1972, Community Party USA Conventions File, Southern California Library; Communist Collective of the Chicano Nation (M-L), "Report to the Communist Collective of the Chicano Nation on the Chicano National-Colonial Question," *Proletariat* 4 (Spring 1974); Communist League, *Regional Autonomy for the Indian Peoples!* (San Francisco: Proletarian Publishers, n.d.); Communist Labor Party, "Analysis of the National Question in the Negro Nation," *Proletariat* 1 (Fall 1975): 36–37. Thanks to Cynthia Cuza for sharing her materials with me. Although I found position papers on Puerto Ricans and American Indians, I did not find any from major organizations analyzing the position of Asian Americans.

17. Healey and Isserman, *California Red*, 185, see also 208–9.

18. Ibid., 208–9; Angela Davis, *Angela Davis*, 188–89.

19. Edward Soja, *Thirdspace: Journeys to Los Angeles and Other Real-and-Imagined Places* (Cambridge, MA: Blackwell, 1996).

20. The Communist Party (Marxist-Leninist) was an offshoot of the Black Workers' Congress that lasted from approximately 1978 to 1983. It had no official tie to the CPUSA. Elbaum, *Revolution in the Air*, 236–37, 159.

21. Fields, *Trotskyism and Maoism*, 200–202; Jim O'Brien, "American Leninism in the 1970s," *Radical America* 11 and 12 (Winter 1977–78): 39–43; Elbaum, *Revolution in the Air*, ch. 4.

22. Harold Nelson, "The Defenders: A Case Study of an Informal Police Organization," in Geschwender, *Black Revolt*, 79–95; geronimo ji Jaga, "Every Nation Struggling to Be Free Has a Right to Struggle," *New Political Science* 21 (June 1999): 241–42; Black Panther Party, *The Black Panther Party: Speech by John Hullet, Interview with Stokely Carmichael, Report from Lowndes County* (New York: Merit, 1966).

23. *Black Panther*, November 6, 1971, 15; "L.A. Panthers Begin Free Breakfast Program," *Black Panther*, June 14, 1969, 3. See also JoNina Abron, "Serving the People: The Survival Programs of the Black Panther Party," in Charles Jones, *Black Panther Party Reconsidered*, 177–12. Survival programs were not considered revolutionary themselves, but rather as necessary to serve the community until it was ready to assume a revolutionary position.

24. Elaine Brown, *Taste of Power*, ch. 14; Michael Clemons and Charles Jones, "Global Solidarity: The Black Panther Party in the International Arena," *New Political Science* 21 (June 1999): 177–203; John McCartney, "The Influences of the Black Panther Party on the Vanguard Party of the Bahamas, 1972–1987," *New Political Science* 21 (June 1999): 205–15; "Solidarity Activities Calendar, Year 1971," *Black Panther*, January 9, 1971; Huey Newton, "To the National Liberation Front of South Vietnam," in *To Die for the People: The Writings of Huey P. Newton*, ed. Toni Morrison (New York: Writers and Readers Publishing, 1995), 178–81.

25. Huey Newton, "On the Defection of Eldridge Cleaver from the Black Panther Party and the Defection of the Black Panther Party from the Black Community," in *The Black Panthers Speak*, ed. Eric Foner (New York: Da Capo Press, 1995), 272–78; Kathleen Cleaver, "Back to Africa," in Charles Jones, *Black Panther Party Reconsidered*, 236–40; Donald Cox, "The Split in the Party," *New Political Science* 21 (June 1999): 171–76.

26. On the demise of the BPP, see Ollie Johnson III, "Explaining the Demise of the Black Panther Party: The Role of Internal Factors," in Charles Jones, *Black Panther Party Reconsidered*, 391–414. On state repression, see Jim Fletcher, Tanaquil Jones, and Sylvere Lotringer, *Still Black, Still Strong: Survivors of the War against Black Revolutionaries* (New York: Semiotext[e], 1993), 9–56 and 205–20; Huey Newton, *The War against the Panthers: A Study of Repression in America* (New York: Harlem River Press, 1996); Churchill and Vander Wall, *Agents of Repression*; Elaine Brown, *Taste of Power*, chs. 10 and 11; Kevin O'Reilly, *Racial Matters: The FBI's Secret File on Black America, 1960–1972* (New York: Free Press, 1989), ch. 9. On the Los Angeles Police Department, see Frank Donner, *Protectors of Privilege: Red Squads and Police Repression in Urban America* (Berkeley: University of California Press, 1990), ch. 7; Citizens Research and Investigation Committee and Louis Tackwood, *The Glass House Tapes* (New York: Avon, 1973).

27. Elaine Brown, *Taste of Power*, 122–24.

28. Ron Wilkins, interview with author, June 14, 2000, Los Angeles. See also Dolly Veale, "Richard Aoki," in Ho et al., *Legacy to Liberation*, 326; Pearson, *Shadow of the Panther*, 108; Robert Allen, *Black Awakening in Capitalist America: An Analytic History* (Trenton, NJ: Africa World Press, 1992), 82.

29. Elaine Brown, *Taste of Power*, ch. 8; Church League of America, "Special Report: Discussion and Death—US Style," 1969, box 50, folder 38, collection 50, Special Collections, UCLA Library. On the murders in the party, see Elaine Brown, "What Ever Happened to the Black Panther Party? Part II," *Black Panther*, November 20, 1976, 10, 22; Tyler, "Black Radicalism," 364–66. In defense of US, see Scot Ngozi-Brown, "The US Organization, Maulana Karenga, and Conflict with the Black Panther Party: A Critique of Sectarian Influences on Historical Discourse," *Journal of Black Studies* 28 (November 1997): 157–70. Thanks to Alex Alonso for this citation.

30. Dial Togerson, "Police Seize Panther Fortress in 4-Hour Gunfight, Arrest," *Los Angeles Times*, December 9, 1969, 1, 3, 32.

31. Wei, *Asian American Movement*, 1.

32. Espiritu, *Asian American Panethnicity*, ch. 2. On the challenges of developing such an identity, see Edward Long, "Reflections in a Slanted Eye," *Gidra* 1 (June 1969): 2.

33. Diane Fujino has argued, in "Japanese American Radicalism," that the demise of the Japanese American left was triggered by both state repression and the Communist Party's turning its back on noncitizens. On pre–World War II radicalism, see Carlos Bulosan, *America Is in the Heart* (Seattle: University of Washington Press, 1973); Yoneda, *Ganbatte*; Ichioka, "A Buried Past"; Mark Lai, "A Historical Survey of the Chinese Left in America," in Gee, *Counterpoint*, 63–80; Robert Lee, "The Hidden World of Asian Immigrant Radicalism," in Buhle and Georgakas, *Immigrant Left*, 256–88.

The politically conservative nature of the Nikkei community can be seen in a 1967 survey finding that 84 percent of Sansei were opposed to Black Power and that many felt that Blacks could solve their problems by emphasizing hard work, getting an education, and ceasing their "unruly" behavior. Lon Kurashige, *Japanese American Celebration*, 155. A reluctance to identify with other minorities was also evident, as one commentator noted: "The formation of organizations of Orientals is also similar in nature to the strategy of the Negroes and Mexican Americans. Yet, why should we follow the strategy of the Negro or Mexican American when our problems are not the same as the Negro or Mexican American?" Long, "Reflections," 2.

34. Wei, *Asian American Movement*, 25–26.

35. Fujino, "To Serve the Movement," 257–66; Eric Nakamura, "Yuri Kochiyama," *Giant Robot*, Spring 1998, 62–65; Veale, "Richard Aoki," 319–34; Martin Wong, "Gang of Four," *Giant Robot*, Spring 1998, 70–71; Boggs, *Living for Change*; Jennifer Jung Hee Choi, "At the Margins of Asian American Political Experience," *Amerasia Journal* 25 (1999): 18–40; Shinya Ono, "Finding a Home Community," in Louie and Omatsu, *Asian Americans*, 263–50. Yoshimura's actual participation in the SLA is open to debate and may have been more a media product. Some interviewees felt that it was inappropriate to include Yoshimura in this list, as the SLA's status as a political organization was dubious. See, however, Ann O'Neill, "A Radical Change in Lifestyle," *Los Angeles Times*, January 11, 2000, A1, A16.

36. It should be noted, however, that a progressive faction of the Japanese American Citizens League did exist and played a pivotal role in the development of Yellow Power. *Amerasia* Staff, "An Interview with Warren Furutani," *Amerasia* 1 (1971): 70–76.

37. Louie, "Yellow, Brown and Red," 3. This is not to deny tensions between radical youth and more conservative forces within the Japanese American community. Lon Kurashige, *Japanese American Celebration*, ch. 5. See also Ho et al., *Legacy to Liberation*; Louie and Omatsu, *Asian Americans*; Wei, *Asian American Movement*.

38. There is no definitive work on the development of the Asian American movement in Los Angeles, but partial accounts include Mo Nishida, "Where Do

We Go From Here?" *Gidra* 6 (April 1974): 20–21; Susie Ling, "The Mountain Movers," *Amerasia* 15 (1989): 51–67; Roy Nakano, "Marxist-Leninist Organizing," 1984, unpublished manuscript, Asian American Studies Center Reading Room, University of California at Los Angeles; Lon Kurashige, *Japanese American Celebration,* ch. 5. See also Ho et al., *Legacy to Liberation;* Louie and Omatsu, *Asian Americans;* Wei, *Asian American Movement.*

39. Many thanks to Warren Furutani for this insight. Interview with author, July 17, 2002, Los Angeles.

40. Amy Uyematsu, "The Emergence of Yellow Power," *Gidra* 1 (October 1969): 8–11.

41. Wei, *Asian American Movement,* 45; Ling, "Mountain Movers," 53.

42. Nishida, "Where Do We Go?" 20; Mo Nishida, "Shitamachi," *Amerasia Journal* 15 (1989): 126–34.

43. Mike Murase, "Toward Barefoot Journalism," in Gee, *Counterpoint,* 307–19.

44. A similar crisis existed among Chinese Americans. Wei, *Asian American Movement,* 14.

45. "Alan Nishio," *East Wind Magazine* 1 (1982), www.aamovement.net/history/eastwind/nishio (accessed April 6, 2005). On the internment and family tension, see Donna Nagata, "The Japanese American Internment," *Journal of Traumatic Stress* 3 (1990): 47–69; Lon Kurashige, *Japanese American Celebration,* 95.

46. On the drug crisis, see Ray Tasaki, comments as participant in the discussion "Gang Culture, Youth Culture and Activism," Japanese American National Museum, Los Angeles, May 22, 1999; Linda Iwataki, "Ain't I a Woman?" *Gidra* 6 (April 1974): 22–24; Steve Tatsukawa, "Gardena: Part One: A Saga of Youth, Drugs, and Middle Class Misery," *Gidra* 5 (July 1973): 6–8; Art Ishi, quoted in Wong, "Yellow Power," 76–77; Peggy Holter, "Asian Community Beset with Woes," *Los Angeles News Advocate,* April 15–30, 1972, 1, 3, 5.

47. Janice Tanaka, *When You're Smiling: The Deadly Legacy of Internment,* DVD (Los Angeles: Visual Communications, 1999). Art Ishi, comments as participant in the discussion "Gang Culture, Youth Culture and Activism," Japanese American National Museum, Los Angeles, May 22, 1999. A cursory review of the *Rafu* did not reveal references to youth dying of heart attacks, but there were numerous obituaries of young people. See, for instance, March 3, 1971, and January 13, 1971, 3.

48. On Asian American Hardcore, see Fred Ho, "Moritsugu 'Mo' Nishida," in Ho et al., *Legacy to Liberation,* 301–3; Ray Tasaki, "Where There Is Oppression," in Louie and Omatsu, *Asian Americans,* 81–86. On the Yellow Brotherhood, see Mike Murase, "Yellow Brotherhood," *Gidra* 1 (July 1969): 1, 8; Seigo Hayashi, "Yellow Brotherhood," *Gidra* 2 (April 1970): 8; Gary Asamura, "The Unsung Heroes of the Yellow Brotherhood," *Amerasia Journal* 15 (1989): 156–58. See also Gary Asamura, Art Ishi, and Nick Nagatoni, comments as participants in the discussion "Gang Culture, Youth Culture and Activism," Japanese American National Museum, Los Angeles, May 22, 1999; June Miyaji, "Asian

Street Sisters," *Gidra* 3 (March 1971): 4. On JACS-AI, see Linda Iwataki, "Ai Means Love," *Gidra* 2 (December 1970): 4; Nishida, "Shitamachi," 126–28.

49. Ling, "Mountain Movers," 57; Kathy Masaoka, comments as participant in the discussion "Gang Culture, Youth Culture and Activism," Japanese American National Museum, Los Angeles, May 22, 1999. See also Miyaji, "Asian Street Sisters," 4.

50. For a partial list of such organizations, see Nishida, "Where Do We Go?" 21.

51. Nakano, "Marxist-Leninist Organizing," 6.

52. Mo Nishida, quoted in Ho, "Moritsugu 'Mo' Nishida," 305.

53. Some members did not wish to pursue a more political path and formed the New People's Hardcore. See "Collective Remapping," *Gidra* 3 (October 1971): 20–21.

54. Mo Nishida, in Ho, "Moritsugu 'Mo' Nishida" (interview), 301. See also League of Revolutionary Struggle, *Statements on the Founding of the League of Revolutionary Struggle* (Oakland, CA: Getting Together Publications, 1978), courtesy of Mark Masaoka; "Statement by East Wind on Its Unity with the League, April 1979," *Unity*, April 6–19, 1979, 4.

55. Ignacio García, *Chicanismo: The Forging of a Militant Ethos among Mexican Americans* (Tucson: University of Arizona Press, 1997), 3. For overviews and critiques of the movement, see Gómez-Quiñones, *Chicano Politics*; Muñoz, *Youth, Identity, Power*; John García, "The Chicano Movement: Its Legacy for Politics and Policy," in *Chicanas/Chicanos at the Crossroads: Social, Economic, and Political Change*, ed. David Maciel and Isidro Ortiz (Tucson: University of Arizona Press, 1996), 83–107; Ramon Gutiérrez, "Community, Patriarchy," 44–72.

56. Henry Ramos, *The American GI Forum: In Pursuit of the Dream, 1948–1983* (Houston, TX: Arte Publico Press, 1998); Benjamin Márquez, *LULAC: The Evolution of a Mexican American Political Organization* (Austin: University of Texas Press, 1993), ch. 3. On Mexican Americans and whiteness, see Neil Foley, "Becoming Hispanic: Mexican Americans and Whiteness," in *White Privilege: Essential Readings on the Other Side of Racism*, ed. Paula Rothenberg (New York: Worth, 2002), 49–59; *La Prensa*, "A Poignant Defense of the Whiteness of Mexicans," in *Testimonio: A Documentary History of the Mexican American Struggle for Civil Rights*, ed. F. Arturo Rosales (Houston, TX: Arte Público Press, 2000), 173.

57. *Mestizaje* refers to the racial mixing that characterizes Mexico.

58. On youth organizing, see Juan Gómez-Quiñones, *Mexican Students por La Raza: The Chicano Student Movement in Southern California, 1967–1977* (Santa Barbara, CA: Editorial La Causa, 1978); Armando Navarro, *Mexican American Youth Organization: Avant-garde of the Chicano Movement in Texas* (Austin: University of Texas Press, 1995); Dolores Delgado Bernal, "Chicana School Resistance and Grassroots Leadership" (PhD diss., University of California, Los Angeles, 1997).

On La Raza Unida Party, see Jose Angel Gutiérrez, *Making of a Chicano*

Militant; Armando Navarro, *The Cristal Experiment: A Chicano Struggle for Community Control* (Madison: University of Wisconsin Press, 1998); Santillan, *La Raza Unida*. Some have argued that the La Raza Unida was less popular in California than Texas because of reduced discrimination. "In California it was very difficult to organize people around La Raza Unida party because they felt that they hadn't really sensed real discrimination. I remember so many people telling me, 'You don't know what discrimination is until you've come from Texas.' Or, 'I'm from parts of Colorado', or, 'I'm from New Mexico, and I'll tell you what discrimination is." Richard Martinez, oral history interview, 1990, conducted by Carlos Vásquez, UCLA Oral History Program, for the California State Government Oral History Program, 102 and 103, Special Collections, UCLA Library.

On the Crusade for Justice, see Ernesto Vigil, *The Crusade for Justice: Chicano Militancy and the Government's War on Dissent* (Madison: University of Wisconsin Press, 1999). On Chávez and the United Farm Workers, see Levy, *Cesar Chavez*; Craig Jenkins, *The Politics of Insurgency: The Farm Worker Movement in the 1960s* (New York: Columbia University Press, 1985); Sam Kushner, *Long Road to Delano* (New York: International Publishers, 1975). On La Alianza, see Peter Nabakov, *Tijerina and the Courthouse Raid* (Albuquerque: University of New Mexico Press, 1970); Reies Lopez Tijerna, *Mi lucha por la tierra* (Mexico: Fondo de Cultura Economica, 1978).

59. National Chicano Liberation Conference, "El Plan Espiritual de Aztlán," in Rosales, *Testimonio*, 361.

60. Bill Gallegos, interview with author, April 15, 1999, Los Angeles.

61. Critics of the Chicana/o movement point out that few Mexican citizens lived in the Southwest at the time of conquest (1848). This is true but overlooks the fact that the Treaty of Guadalupe Hidalgo surrendered one-third of Mexico's national territory to the United States—a deep, collective psychic wound.

62. Ernesto Chávez, *Mi Raza Primero!* ch. 2; Edward Escobar, "The Dialectics of Repression," *Journal of American History* 79 (March 1993): 1483–1514; Espinoza, "Pedagogies of Nationalism"; Marguerite Marín, *Social Protest in an Urban Barrio: A Study of the Chicano Movement, 1966–1974* (New York: University Press of America, 1991), 144–66; Rona Fields, "The Brown Berets: A Participant Observation Study of Social Action in the Schools of Los Angeles" (PhD diss., University of Southern California, 1970); David Sánchez, *Expedition through Aztlan* (La Puente: Perspectiva Publicaciones, 1978), ch. 1. See also www.brownberets.org/bbhistory.html.

The Berets had a political program that was similar to the Panthers' but also called for the return of Aztlán and the opening of U.S. borders. "Brown Beret 13-Point Political Program," *La Causa*, December 1970, 16–17.

63. "On the Black and White Revolutionary's Relation to the Chicano Struggle," *La Causa*, March 1971, 7.

64. Ernesto Chávez, *Mi Raza Primero!* 50.

65. *Mutualistas* are mutual aid societies for working-class Mexicans.

66. Ernesto Chávez, *Mi Raza Primero!* ch. 5; Mario García, *Memories of*

Chicano History 290–91; "History of CASA," box 1, folder 5, CASA Collection, Special Collections, Stanford University Libraries, Palo Alto, CA (hereafter "CASA Collection"); David Gutiérrez, "CASA," 9–13.

67. Quoted in Mario García, *Memories of Chicano History*, 296.

68. Marisela Rodríguez Chávez, "Living and Breathing," 8. On CFLT's case, see "Chicano Trio Jailed in Dopepusher Killing," *Los Angeles News Advocate*, January 15–31, 1972, 7.

69. Mario García, *Memories of Chicano History*, 310; David Gutiérrez, "CASA," 13. For a different interpretation, see "History of CASA."

70. "C.A.S.A. Salutes National Chicano Forum," p. 3, box 2, folder 11, CASA Collection.

71. David Gutiérrez, "CASA," 11 and 22. On CASA's view of the base, see "Growth of the Organization/Recruitment Efforts," box 1, folder 2, CASA Collection.

72. "Plan de Ataque a la Ley Rodino," Boletín Interno, box 1, folder 2, CASA Collection; "Campaign of National Resistance," Internal Bulletin, box 1, folder 2, CASA Collection; "United Farmworkers," Boletín Interno, box 21, folder 5, CASA Collection.

73. Marisela Rodríguez Chávez, "Living and Breathing," 44; "Membership," in "By-Laws of CASA," box 1, folder 1, CASA Collection.

74. "Principles and Statutes of the Centro Legal of CASA—Hermandad General de Trabajadores," box 1, folder 3, CASA Collection.

75. FBI Memorandum, "Regarding CASA and the Committee to Free Los Tres (CFLT)," January 29, 1975, box 25, folder 1, CASA Collection; FBI Memorandum, "Regarding CASA," November 16, 1975, box 25, folder 2, CASA Collection; FBI Memorandum, "Regarding CASA-MAPA," January 31, 1973, box 24, folder 10, CASA Collection.

76. Resignation Memorandum, "From Carlos Vásquez to National Coordinating Committee," December 26, 1977, box 2, folder 4, CASA Collection; Memorandum, "Mass Resignation," n.d., box 1, folder 5, CASA Collection.

5. IDEOLOGIES OF NATION, CLASS, AND RACE

1. Alan Nadel, *Flatlining on the Field of Dreams: Cultural Narratives in the Films of President Reagan's America* (New Brunswick, NJ: Rutgers University Press, 1997), ch. 2; Michael Ryan and Douglas Kellner, *Camera Politica: The Politics and Ideology of Contemporary Hollywood Film* (Bloomington: Indiana University Press, 1988), 277–79.

2. Fanon Che Wilkins, "In the Belly of the Beast: Black Power, Anti-Imperialism, and the African Liberation Solidarity Movement, 1968–1975" (PhD diss., New York University, 2001); Cedric Robinson, *Black Marxism: The Making of the Black Radical Tradition* (London: Zed Books, 1983), 1.

3. Bill Gallegos, interview with author, April 14, 1999, Los Angeles. Race relations historically have been a challenge to the left precisely because it sought to address racism. Healey and Isserman, *California Red*, 126–28; Kelley, *Ham-*

mer and Hoe, ch. 5; Oscar Berland, "The Emergence of the Communist Perspective on the 'Negro Question' in America: 1919–1931, Part One," *Science and Society* 63 (Winter 1999–2000): 411–42; Shakur, *Assata,* 191–92.

4. Chicanas/os did not join the CPUSA in large numbers because of the party's reluctance to engage with nationalist struggles, its embrace of the Democratic Party, and the fact that alternatives existed. The ATM, for instance, described the CPUSA's treatment of Mexican Americans as one of "chauvinism and betrayal." Quoted in "The Betrayal of the Communist Party USA on the Chicano National Question," *Red Banner* 1 (Winter 1976–77): 43 (courtesy of Lian Hurst Mann). Nonetheless, some, such as Evelina Alarcon, joined the party and have remained committed members. Alarcon was active in the Chicana/o movement and recalls being called a communist. She decided that if communists supported bilingual education, the United Farm Workers, and affirmative action, then indeed she was. Evelina Alarcon, untitled speech presented at "Our History of Revolutionary Struggle: A New Raza Left Perspective," California State University, Los Angeles, March 13, 1999.

5. In truth, some joined particular organizations simply due to circumstance. Thus one might join a group, for example, largely because of a friend. Accordingly, while some made highly conscious decisions to join organizations, there was also a randomness to such affiliations across all racial/ethnic groups.

6. Antonio Rodriguez, "Editorial, National Chicano Forum," *Sin Fronteras,* June 1976, 6.

7. David Gutiérrez, "CASA," 14–15. On Aztlán, see Rodolfo Anaya and Francisco Lomeli, *Aztlán: Essays on the Chicano Homeland* (Albuquerque: University of New Mexico Press, 1989); John R. Chávez, *The Lost Land: The Chicano Image of the Southwest* (Albuquerque: University of New Mexico Press, 1989); Gloria Anzaldúa, *Borderlands: La Frontera* (San Francisco: Aunt Lute Books, 1987); Rafael Pérez-Torres, "Refiguring Aztlán," *Aztlán* 22 (Fall 1997): 15–37.

8. Quoted in "The Basic Aspects of the National Question," n.d., p. 1, box 39, folder 11, CASA Collection, Special Collections, Stanford University Libraries, Palo Alto, CA (hereafter "CASA Collection").

9. David Gutiérrez, *Walls and Mirrors: Mexican Americans, Mexican Immigrants and the Politics of Ethnicity* (Berkeley: University of California Press, 1995).

10. After the 1968 massacre in Mexico City, the Mexican government waged a "dirty war" against leftists. Hector Tobar, "Shroud Comes off Fate of 'Disappeared' Radical," *Los Angeles Times,* December 19, 2001, A1, A24; James Smith and Mark Fineman, "Mexicans Shine Light on State's Dark Secrets," *Los Angeles Times,* December 9, 2001, A1, A40; Geoffrey Mohan, "Family Torn Asunder in Battle with Government," *Los Angeles Times,* December 28, 2001, A1, A26; James Smith, "One Family Paid Dearly in 'Dirty War,'" *Los Angeles Times,* December 11, 2001, A1, A16.

11. The INS was abolished and replaced by the Department of Homeland Security in 2002.

12. CASA Hermandad General de Trabajadores, "We Make a Call," box 7, folder 1, CASA Collection.

13. "CASA General Brotherhood of Workers Salutes National Chicano Forum," p. 2, box 2, folder 11, CASA Collection.

14. "América es un Continente—No un País," *Sin Fronteras*, October 1976.

15. Ernesto Chávez, "Imagining the Mexican Immigrant Worker," 109–35.

16. CASA Secretaría de Información y Propaganda, "Seminars for Study Group Leaders," box 6, folder 9, CASA Collection, emphasis added.

17. "CASA General Brotherhood," 2.

18. Ideological conflict also existed with the Socialist Workers' Party and the October League. For instance, some argued that Mexican Americans were not a nation but an oppressed people and that the correct demand should be for regional autonomy.

19. On the emergence of the ATM, see "History of the August 29th Movement," in Rosales, *Testimonio*, 394–99; Gallegos, interview; CASA, "Internal Document, Memo to Militantes and Afiliados," box 7, folder 9, CASA Collection. On the LRUP, see Santillan, *La Raza Unida*.

20. August Twenty-ninth Movement, "Fan the Flames: A Revolutionary Position on the Chicano National Question," p. 1, box 25, folder 1, CASA Collection.

21. August Twenty-ninth Movement, "CASA Attacks the Chicano Movement," pamphlet, p. 2, box 25, folder 8, CASA Collection.

22. August Twenty-ninth Movement, "CASA Attacks," 3.

23. CASA, "Internal Document," 1; August Twenty-ninth Movement, "CASA Attacks."

24. Elbaum, *Revolution in the Air*, ch. 7.

25. East Wind's ideology may appear less consolidated partly because of the difficulty I had ascertaining it. Diane Fujino has suggested that one reason for this is that East Wind's history has not been adequately summarized. This is a crucial point: an essential part of creating a historical narrative is *responding* to others' interpretations. Wei's *Asian American Movement* is one of the few texts to discuss the Asian American left, but most activists dismiss his perspective as hostile. Both Fred Ho et al., *Legacy to Liberation*, and Louie and Omatsu, *Asian Americans*, are partly responses to Wei's work but are quite recent. Hopefully this book will also serve to inspire more conversations and revisions. Thanks, Diane.

26. Mo Nishida, interview with author, May 7, 2000, Los Angeles. On the role of study, see Miriam Ching Louie, "Yellow, Brown, and Red," 14; Ling, "Mountain Movers"; Wei, *Asian American Movement*, 207.

27. See also "Luis" in Miriam Ching Louie's "Yellow, Brown and Red," 8; "A History of the Red Guard Party," *I.W.K. Journal*, May 1975, 81–88.

28. Miriam Ching Louie, "Yellow, Brown and Red." One Asian American activist recalled, "I was a Panther, I got a Red Book, I said, 'This Motherfucker's Asian.' I got an identity thing out of that." In Wong, "Art Ishi," 77.

29. Marx believed that communist revolutions would first occur in indus-

trialized countries led by urbanized, working classes, which neither Russia or China had. Mao reevaluated the role of the peasantry on the basis of his own experiences and concluded that it had revolutionary potential. In addition, Mao promoted the democratic participation of the masses and introduced the concept of the "Third World." Mao Tse-tung, *Mao Zedong: An Anthology of His Writings*, ed. A. Fremantle (New York: Mentor Books, 1962). See also Philip Short, *Mao: A Life* (New York: Henry Holt, 2000); Mao Tse-tung, *On Guerilla Warfare*, 2nd ed., trans. Samuel B. Griffith (Urbana: University of Illinois Press, 2000), and *Quotations from Chairman Mao Tse-tung; or, Little Red Book* (San Francisco: China Books and Periodicals, 1990).

30. For example, see Amilcar Cabral, *Unity and Struggle: Speeches and Writings* (New York: Monthly Review, 1982). For a critique, see Henry Winston, *Strategy for a Black Agenda: A Critique of New Theories of Liberation in the United States and Africa* (New York: International Publishers, 1973).

31. Ronaldo Munck, *The Difficult Dialogue: Marxism and Nationalism* (London: Zed Books, 1986), 120.

32. The Collective, "Asian Nation," *Gidra* 3 (October 1971): 16.

33. Merilynne Quon, "Individually We Contributed, Together We Made a Difference," in Louie and Omatsu, *Asian Americans*, 218.

34. The Collective, "Asian Nation," 18. The *Gidra* article was actually a popularized version of the original text.

35. Shinya Ono, "Finding a Home Community," 267.

36. See also Wei, *Asian American Movement*, 228–29; Nakano, "Marxist-Leninist Organizing," 11. On other Asian American groups and nationalism, see "Opportunism in the Asian Movement, Wei Min She/Revolutionary Union," *I.W.K. Journal*, May 1975, 19–21.

37. Quon, "Individually We Contributed," 217.

38. Shinya Ono, "Finding a Home Community," 266.

39. Jim Lee, "The Soul of Little Tokyo: Political Archaeologies of Asian American Activism" (paper presented at the annual meetings of the American Studies Association, Washington, DC, November 2001); Little Tokyo Anti-Eviction Task Force, "Redevelopment in Los Angeles' Little Tokyo," in Gee, *Counterpoint*, 327–33; Lon Kurashige, *Japanese American Celebration*, ch. 5. On contemporary land use struggles in Little Tokyo, see "Little Tokyo Recreation Center," http://reccenter.ltsc.org (accessed April 6, 2005).

40. Warren Furutani, interview with author, July 17, 2002, Los Angeles; *Amerasia* Staff, "Interview with Warren Furutani," 70–76.

41. Storefront People, "Storefront: Cooperation over Competition," *Gidra* 4 (January 1972): 3.

42. Quoted in Nakano, "Marxist-Leninist Organizing," 8.

43. "A Rap with Ms. Henderson," *Come Unity*, August 1972, 4.

44. Quoted in Nakano, "Marxist-Leninist Organizing," 7.

45. Rod Bush, *We Are Not What We Seem: Black Nationalism and Class Struggle in the American Century* (New York: New York University Press, 1999), 3; Alphonso Pinkney, *Red, Black, and Green: Black Nationalism in the*

United States (Cambridge: Cambridge University Press, 1976). On specific movements, see McCartney, *Black Power Ideologies*, ch. 2; Woodward, *Nation within a Nation*; Emory Tolbert, *The UNIA and Black Los Angeles: Ideology and Community in the American Garvey Movement* (Los Angeles: Center for Afro-American Studies, University of California, Los Angeles, 1980); Ula Taylor, "Negro Women Are Great Thinkers as Well as Doers," *Journal of Women's History* 12 (Summer 2000): 104–26; John Henrick Clarke, *Marcus Garvey and the Vision of Africa* (New York: Vintage Books, 1974); Haley, *Autobiography of Malcolm X*; Robert Allen, *Black Awakening*. For critiques, see Harold Cruse, *The Crisis of the Negro Intellectual* (New York: Quill, 1984); Winston, *Strategy*.

46. Berland, "Emergence"; Susan Campbell, "Black Bolsheviks and Recognition of African Americans' Right to Self-Determination by the Communist Party, USA," *Science and Society* 58 (Winter 1994): 440–70; Haywood, *Black Bolshevik*, ch. 9; Earl Ofari Hutchinson, *Blacks and Reds*, ch. 3; Kelley, *Hammer and Hoe*, 13; Robinson, *Black Marxism*, 301–11.

47. William Julius Wilson, *The Declining Significance of Race: Blacks and Changing American Institutions* (Chicago: University of Chicago Press, 1980).

48. Karl Marx, *The Eighteenth Brumaire of Louis Bonaparte* (Moscow: Progress Publishers, 1972), 63.

49. Thanks to Ruth Wilson Gilmore for this insight.

50. Prime evidence includes Black unemployment and incarceration rates. Jacqueline Jones, *American Work: Four Centuries of Black and White Labor* (New York: Norton, 1998); Michael Goldfield, *The Color of Politics: Race and the Mainsprings of American Politics* (New York: New Press, 1997); Manning Marable, *How Capitalism Underdeveloped Black America: Problems in Race, Political Economy, and Society* (Boston: South End Press, 1983); William Julius Wilson, *When Work Disappears: The World of the New Urban Poor* (New York: Alfred A. Knopf, 1996); Jerome Miller, *Search and Destroy* (Cambridge: Cambridge University Press, 1996); Michael Tonry, *Malign Neglect: Race, Crime, and Punishment in America* (New York: Oxford University Press, 1996); Ruth Wilson Gilmore, *Golden Gulag: Labor, Land, State, and Opposition in Globalizing California* (Berkeley: University of California Press, forthcoming).

51. Georgakas and Surkin, *Detroit, I Do Mind Dying*; Earl Ofari Hutchinson, *Blacks and Reds*, ch. 2. See also Self, "To Plan Our Liberation."

52. Pearson, *Shadow of the Panther*, 95.

53. David Hilliard, "Black Student Unions," in Foner, *Black Panthers Speak*, 124–27.

54. Consider this quote from Newton: "The Nation of Islam sought to reform black prisoners and criminals, the BPP sought to rechannel them: 'Instead of trying to eliminate these activities—numbers, hot goods, drugs—I attempted to channel them into significant community actions. . . . Many brothers who were burglarizing and participating in similar pursuits began to contribute weapons and material to community defense.'" Huey Newton in Chris Booker, "Lumpenization: A Critical Error of the Black Panther Party," in Charles

Jones, *Black Panther Party Reconsidered*, 341; Errol Henderson, "Black Nationalism and Rap Music," *Journal of Black Studies* 26 (January 1996): 308–39. See also Winston, *Strategies*, 218.

55. Pearson, *Shadow of the Panther*, 97.

56. Healey and Isserman, *California Red*, 211; Winston, *Strategies*, 218.

57. David Hilliard, "The Ideology of the Black Panther Party," in Foner, *Black Panthers Speak*, 122. For different interpretations, see Winston, *Strategies*, ch. 12; Huey Newton, "Reply to William Patterson: September 19, 1970," in Newton, *To Die for the People*, 163–77.

58. Huey Newton, "Huey Newton Talks to the Movement about the Black Panther Party, Cultural Nationalism, SNCC, Liberals, and White Revolutionaries," in Foner, *Black Panthers Speak*, 52.

59. Pinkney, *Red, Black and Green*, 127.

60. Linda Harrison, "On Cultural Nationalism," in Foner, *Black Panthers Speak*, 151.

61. Ngozi-Brown, "US Organization." On US more generally, see Scot Brown, "Resistance and Memory: The US Organization and Reflections on Utopian Aspirations during Turbulent Times" (paper presented at the annual meetings of the Oral History Association, San Diego, CA, October 2002); Clyde Halisi and James Mtume, *The Quotable Karenga* (Los Angeles: US Organization, 1967); Elaine Brown, "What Ever Happened to the Black Panther Party?" *Black Panther*, November 1976, 10; Tyler, "Black Radicalism."

62. Newton, "Huey Newton Talks," 50.

63. Maeda, "Constructing Yellow Power." See also Regina Jennings, "Poetry of the Black Panther Party," *Journal of Black Studies* 29 (September 1998): 106–29; Erika Doss, "Revolutionary Art Is a Tool for Liberation," *New Political Science* 21 (1999): 245–59.

64. Linda Harrison, "On Cultural Nationalism," 151. See also Brown, "What Ever Happened?" 10.

65. Errol Henderson, "Black Nationalism." On cultural praxis and the BPP, see Jane Rhodes, "Cultures of Black Nationalism: The Self-Fashioning of the Black Panther Party" (paper presented at the annual meeting of the American Studies Association, Seattle, WA, November 1998). For a critique of fetishizing cultural artifacts, see Angela Davis, "Afro Images: Politics, Fashion and Nostalgia," in *Soul: Black Power, Politics, and Pleasure*, ed. Monique Guillory and Richard Green (New York: New York University Press, 1998), 23–31. For exemplary analyses of cultural and economic processes, see George Lipsitz, "World Cities and World Beat: Low-Wage Labor and Transnational Culture," *Pacific Historical Review* 68 (1999): 213–31; Stuart Hall's "The Politics of Mugging," in Hall, *Policing the Crisis*, 327–97.

66. According to Bobby Seale, "When we use the term 'pig,' for example, we are referring to people who systematically violate peoples' Constitutional rights—whether they be monopoly capitalists or police. The term is now being adopted by radicals, hippies and minority peoples." "Bobby Seale Explains Panther Politics: An Interview," in Foner, *Black Panthers Speak*, 82.

67. Huey Newton, "Black Capitalism Re-Analyzed I: June 5, 1971," in Newton, *To Die for the People*, 105–6. For a critique, see Winston, *Strategies*, 219.

68. Davis, *Angela Davis*, 161.

69. Elaine Brown, *Taste of Power*, 109.

70. For a comparison of the 1966 and 1972 programs, see Newton, *War against the Panthers*, 119–26.

71. Huey Newton, "Speech Delivered at Boston College, November 18, 1970," in Newton, *To Die for the People*, 31–32.

72. Huey Newton, "Resolutions and Declarations: December 5, 1970," in Newton, *To Die for the People*, 39–43. See also George Katsiaficas, "Organization and Movement: The Case of the Black Panther Party and the Revolutionary People's Constitutional Convention of 1970," in Cleaver and Katsiaficas, *Liberation, Imagination*, 141–55.

6. THE POLITICS OF SOLIDARITY

1. Newton, "To the National Liberation Front," 178–81; Nguyen Thi Dinh, "Letter from Nguyen Thi Dinh: October 31, 1970," in Newton, *To Die for the People*, 182–85.

2. "Chinese Want No Identity Errors," *Los Angeles Examiner*, January 6, 1942. See also Carolyn See, *On Gold Mountain* (New York: Vintage Books, 1996), 256. Even Koreans and Filipinos distinguished themselves from Japanese Americans during this period, although earlier, Japanese Americans differentiated themselves from the Chinese. Espiritu, *Asian American Panethnicity*, 21–23.

3. On the KDP, see Toribio, "Dare to Struggle," 31–45; "Getting Together Interview with Katipunan ng mga Demokratikong Pilipino," *Getting Together*, September–October 1973; and "Part II, Katipunan ng mga Demokratikong Pilipino," *Getting Together*, October 1973. On I Wor Kuen, see *I.W.K. Journal: The Political Organ of the I Wor Kuen*; Fred Ho, "Fists for Revolution," in Ho et al., *Legacy to Liberation*, 3–13; Fred Ho and Steve Yip, "Alex Hing," in Ho et al., *Legacy to Liberation*, 279–96.

4. This thinking continues in the present. For instance, Louie and Omatsu's *Asian Americans* reinscribes the centrality of African Americans to the Asian American movement, while figuring Latinas/os and American Indians as much more marginal.

5. Karen Umemoto, "Asian American Students in the San Francisco State College Strike, 1964–1968" (master's thesis, University of California, Los Angeles, 1989), 5. On the significance of the strike, see Wei, *Asian American Movement*, 15–20; Lloyd Wake, "Reflections on the San Francisco State Strike," *Amerasia* 15 (1989): 43–47; Mo Nishida, "A Revolutionary Nationalist Perspective on the San Francisco State Strike," *Amerasia* 15 (1989): 69–79.

6. San Francisco State Strike Committee, "On Strike, Shut It Down," box 42, "Third World Strike," Twentieth Century Organizational Files, Southern California Library, Los Angeles, 1969.

7. Dylan Rodriguez, "Thinking Solidarity across Generations: Richard Aoki and the Relevance of Living Legacies," *Shades of Power* 1 (Summer 1998): 10–11, 14; Veale, "Richard Aoki," 319–34. The evidence indicates that the Panthers attended at least one Red Guard rally: "About 150 to 200 people attended to hear the Red Guard talk about its Ten Point program, saving the Chinese playground, and pig brutality in the community. The rally was bi-lingual (Chinese and English). David Hilliard, Chief of Staff of the Black Panther Party was the guest speaker. The Panthers were there to show unity with the people in the Asian community." *Red Guard*, April 1969, 7. I learned about the Pittsburgh chapter of the Brown Berets at a panel discussion entitled "Chicana Brown Berets," organized by Dionne Espinoza at the University of California, San Diego, May 26, 1998.

Also worth mentioning are the number of Asian American women who have devoted themselves to the Black struggle, including Grace Lee Boggs, Nobuko Miyamoto, and Yuri Kochiyama. However, it should be pointed out that much of their engagement was personal rather than organizational. Moreover, each of these women had quite different relationships to the Asian American movement. See Choi, "At the Margins"; Fujino, "To Serve the Movement"; *Revolutionary Worker*, "Yuri Kochiyama: With Justice in Her Heart," in Ho et al., *Legacy to Liberation*, 269–78; Eric Nakamura, "Nobuko Miyamoto: Grain of Sand," *Giant Robot*, Spring 1998, 72–73; Nobuko Miyamoto, interview with author, June 4, 2002, Los Angeles.

8. Shakur, *Assata*, 200.

9. Although the Red Guard subsequently merged with I Wor Kuen, its origins were closely tied to the Panthers. See Ho and Yip, "Alex Hing," 279–96; Wei, *Asian American Movement*, 207–10; "A History of the Red Guard Party," *I.W.K. Journal* 2 (May 1975): 81–88; and various issues of the *Red Guard Community News*.

10. Evelyn Yoshimura, interview with author, February 9, 2000, Los Angeles.

11. Miyamoto is a performing artist and activist. She participated in Storefront and is committed to multiracial solidarity. Her experience has been portrayed in the play *A Grain of Sand*. See also Nakamura, "Nobuko Miyamato," and Miyamoto, interview.

12. Freer, "Black-Korean Conflict"; Nadine Koch and Eric Schockman, "Riot, Rebellion or Civil Unrest?" in *Community in Crisis: The Korean American Community after the Los Angeles Civil Unrest of April 1992*, ed. George O. Totten II and Eric Schockman (Los Angeles: Center for Multiethnic and Transnational Studies, University of Southern California, 1994), 47–93; Edward Park, "Our L.A.?" in *Rethinking Los Angeles*, ed. Michael Dear, Eric Schockman, and Greg Hise (Thousand Oaks, CA: Sage Publications, 1996), 153–68.

13. Mo Nishida, interview with author, May 7, 2000, Los Angeles. I should point out that other members of East Wind refuted Nishida's account and objected to its inclusion.

14. Ling, "Mountain Movers," 61–63; Yoshimura, interview.

15. Peggy Holter, "Asian Community Beset with Woes," *Los Angeles News Advocate*, April 15–30, 1972, 1, 3, 5.

16. Some interviewees insisted that the SLA was actually a criminal group rather than a political organization.

17. For a caricature of this tendency, see Tom Wolfe, *Radical Chic and Mau Mauing the Flak Catchers* (New York: Farrar, Straus and Giroux, 1970). Note that Wolfe offers Black and Chicano case studies but not an Asian American one.

18. Bobby Seale, *Seize the Time* (Baltimore: Black Classic Press, 1991), 210–11.

19. Gitlin, *The Sixties,* 349, 351.

20. For examples of dedicated lawyers, see Jack Olsen, *Last Man Standing: The Tragedy and Triumph of Geronimo Pratt* (New York: Doubleday, 2000); Shakur, *Assata.* On lawyering and radicals, see Seale, *Seize the Time,* 203–7; Nathan Hakman, "Old and New Left Activity in the Legal Order: An Interpretation," *Journal of Social Issues* 27 (1971): 105–21. Thanks to Barry Litt for telling me about Bar Sinister.

21. Eldridge Cleaver, "A Letter from Eldridge Cleaver," n.d., Eldridge Cleaver Vertical File, Southern California Library, Los Angeles; *Peace and Freedom News,* May 6, 1968, and July 25, 1968, both in carton 12, folder 13, Social Protest Collection, Bancroft Library, University of California, Berkeley. For an overview, see Elden and Schweitzer, "New Third Party Radicalism."

22. Seale, *Seize the Time,* 208–9.

23. Students for a Democratic Society, "SDS Resolution on the Black Panther Party," in Foner, *Black Panthers Speak,* 227.

24. For detailed discussions of these events, see A. Belden Fields, *Trotskyism and Maoism,* 191–98; Gitlin, *The Sixties,* 388; Sale, *SDS,* ch. 23.

25. Elaine Brown, *Taste of Power,* 209.

26. Shirl Buss, personal communication, April 21, 2000.

27. See, for example, Charles Jones, "Talkin' the Talk and Walkin' the Walk: An Interview with Panther Jimmy Slater," in Charles Jones, *Black Panther Party Reconsidered,* 149.

28. Leonard Peltier, quoted in Lee Lew-Lee's video *All Power to the People: The Black Panther Party and Beyond* (Los Angeles: Electronic News Group, 1996). Below are the platforms of the Red Guard, Young Lords, and Brown Berets, respectively. The similarities are obvious. Note also that each program changed over time.

THE RED GUARD'S POLITICAL PROGRAM

(1) We want freedom. We want the power to determine the destiny of our people, the Asian community.

(2) We want decent housing, fit for the shelter of human beings.

(3) We want education for our people that exposes the true nature of this decadent American society. We want education that teaches us our true history and our true role in the present-day society.

(4) We want all Asian men to be exempt from military service.

(5) We want an immediate end to POLICE BRUTALITY AND MURDER OF ASIAN PEOPLE.

(6) We want freedom for all Asian men held in federal, state, county, and city prisons and jails.

(7) We want all Asian people when brought to trial to be tried in a court by a jury of their peer group or people from the Asian communities, as defined by the Constitution of the United States.

(8) We want adequate and free medical facilities available for the people in the Asian community.

(9) We want full employment for our people and an end to their exploitation.

(10) We demand that the United States government recognize the People's Republic of China, Democratic Republic of Vietnam, National Liberation Front, Democratic People of Korea.

(11) We demand that the United States government halt the rape of land.

(SOURCE: *Red Guard Community News,* April 1969, 10–11)

YOUNG LORDS' PARTY 13-POINT PROGRAM AND PLATFORM

(1) We Want Self-determination for Puerto Ricans—liberation on the island and inside the United States.

(2) We want self-determination for all Latinos.

(3) We want liberation of all third world people.

(4) We are revolutionary nationalists and oppose racism.

(5) We want community control of our institutions and land.

(6) We want a true education of our creole culture and Spanish language.

(7) We oppose capitalists and alliances with traitors.

(8) We oppose the Amerikkkan military.

(9) We want freedom for all political prisoners.

(10) We want equality for women. Machismo must be very revolutionary . . . not oppressive!

(11) We fight anti-communism with international unity.

(12) We believe armed self-defense and armed struggle are the only means to liberation.

(13) We want a socialist society.

(SOURCE: *Palante* (n.d., reprint) in *The Black Panthers Speak,* 235–38)

THE BROWN BERETS' 13 POINT POLITICAL PROGRAM

(1) We want all land that was stolen from our people returned.

(2) We demand the immediate end to the occupation of our community by the fascist police.

(3) We want an end to the robbery of our communities by capitalistic businessmen.

(4) We want all Chicanos exempt from military service.

(5)   We want all Chicanos in all jails released.

(6)   We demand a judicial system relevant to Chicanos and therefore administered by Chicanos.

(7)   We demand Chicano control of Chicano education.

(8)   We want full employment for all Chicanos.

(9)   We demand housing fit for human beings.

(10) We demand an end to the destruction of our land and air by the corrupt capitalist ruling class.

(11) We demand that all border lands be open to La Raza whether born north or south of the "fence."

(12) We as Chicanos stand in solidarity with all revolutionary people who are engaged in the struggle for self-determination and freedom.

(13) We denounce the U.S. System—Capitalism and imperialism.

(SOURCE: *La Causa*, December 1970, 16–17)

On the Black Berets, see the interview with Joaquin Lujan and Richard Moore, "Antonio y Rito—Presente!" *Voces Unidas* 11 (Spring 2001): 5–21.

29. Carlos Montes, interview with author, May 26, 2000, Los Angeles.

30. See also Katsiaficas, "Organization and Movement," esp. 151–53.

31. For a sampling of *Black Panther*'s reportage on Chicana/o issues, see "Cannery Workers Fight Discrimination and Union Bias," *Black Panther*, June 16, 1973, 7; Brown Caucus of the Peace and Freedom Party, "Mexican Americans Fight Racism," *Black Panther*, May 4, 1968, 2; "Bobby Seale Meets Cesar Chavez," *Black Panther*, May 12, 1973, 5; "Cesar Chavez, Bobby and Elaine Exchange Messages of Solidarity," *Black Panther*, April 21, 1973, 7, 14.

32. "Cesar Chavez, Bobby," 14. For more general reportage on the UFW, see "Chavez Calls for Grape Boycott," *Black Panther*, April 28, 1973, 6, 14; "Growers, Teamsters Losing Battle with Farm Workers," *Black Panther*, May 26, 1973, 6.

33. "A New Wounded Knee?" *Black Panther*, 26 May 26, 1973, 6; "Another Broken Treaty at Wounded Knee," *Black Panther*, April 21, 1973, 7. See also "'Longest Walk' Ends in D.C. with 5-Day Protest," *Black Panther*, July 29, 1978, 3.

34. Michael Zinzun, interview with author, September 15, 2000, Los Angeles.

35. Marisela Rodríguez Chávez, "Living and Breathing," 73.

36. "Support Rally for Chavis & Wilmington 10," *Sin Fronteras* 3 (August 1976). The Wilmington 10 were convicted for defending a Black church against a Ku Klux Klan attack in 1971.

37. In the 1980s several organizations sued the City of Los Angeles. *Coalition Against Police Abuse v. Superior Court*, 170 Cal. App. 3d 888 (1985). The suit was settled out of court, with the LAPD not admitting to any wrongdoing but paying almost $2 million in legal fees and compensation. Domanick, *To Protect and Serve*, 294–95.

38. CASA, "Solidarity Message on the Occasion of a Tribute to George

Jackson," box 40, folder 2, CASA Collection, Special Collections, Stanford University Libraries, Palo Alto, CA (hereafter "CASA Collection"). George Jackson was a field marshal in the BPP who was convicted of robbery and given an indeterminate sentence. Jackson was a leader both in and outside prison and was shot to death by a prison guard on August 21, 1971. See Angela Davis, *Angela Davis*, 250–79; George Jackson, Jonathon Jackson, and Jean Genet, *Soledad Brother: The Prison Letters of George Jackson* (New York: Lawrence Hill, 1994); George Jackson, *Blood in My Eye* (Baltimore: Black Classic Press, 1990); and the special issue of the *Black Panther*, "George Jackson Lives," *Black Panther*, August 1971.

39. "Medina Deportation Hearing Postponed," *Sin Fronteras* 3 (October 1976): 1.

40. Peter Schey, quoted in "We Are Not Just Fighting for Jose Medina, but for Countless Others," *Sin Fronteras* 3 (November 1977): 5. See also Lourdes Castañeda, "Pro-Medina National Demonstrations—January 8th," *Sin Fronteras* 3 (December 1976): 3; Jose Rodriguez, "US Lingers with Class Action Suit of Medina," *Sin Fronteras* 4 (January/February 1978): 5; Jose Rodriguez, "Medina Case Sets Precedent," *Sin Fronteras* 4 (March 1978): 3; "Political Asylum for Pepe Medina Denied by State Dept. and INS," *Sin Fronteras* 3 (April 1977): 1, 3; "The Demand of the People Is Clear: Political Asylum for Jose Medina Now!" *Sin Fronteras* 3 (July 1977): 1.

41. Adelaida del Castillo, "National Call for Political Asylum, Medina Hearing Postponed Again," *Sin Fronteras* 3 (January 1977): 1.

42. See, for example, "Joann Little Acquitted," *Sin Fronteras* 2 (September 1975); "Support Rally for Chavis."

43. Zinzun, interview. See also "Activists Hit Police Abuse," *Sin Fronteras* 2 (June 1976); Lourdes Castañeda, "CAPA Exposes Police Abuse Presenting Concrete Evidence," *Sin Fronteras* 4 (October 1977).

44. On race and ethnicity in Latin America, see Peter Wade, *Race and Ethnicity in Latin America* (London: Pluto Press, 1997); on anti-Black sentiment in Mexico, see Menchaca, *Recovering History*, ch. 2; on Mexican Americans and whiteness, see Foley, "Becoming Hispanic." For evidence of Black hostility toward Mexicans Americans in Los Angeles, see Chicano Ad Hoc Committee, undated letter, box 26, folder 5, CASA Collection.

45. "Organizational Proposal Adopted at National Conference to Build a People's Alliance," box 39, folder 13, CASA Collection; People's Alliance, "Press Release: National 'People's Alliance' Formed at DC Conference," box 39, folder 13, CASA Collection.

46. On the relationship between CASA and Puerto Rican activists, see letter, November 15, 1976, box 23, folder 3, CASA Collection; letter regarding Puerto Rican solidarity, box 41, folder 13, CASA Collection.

47. Quoted in Victor Rodriguez, "Boricuas, African Americans, and Chicanos in the 'Far West': Notes on the Puerto Rican Pro-Independence Movement in California, 1960s-1980s," in *Latino Social Movements: Historical and Theoret-*

ical Perspectives; A New Political Science Reader, ed. Rodolfo Torres and George Katsiaficas (New York: Routledge, 1999), 99. On the Los Angeles chapter of the Puerto Rican Socialist Committee, see correspondence dated November 15, 1976, box 41, folder 13, CASA Collection. On the Puerto Rican Socialist Party itself, see Partido Socialista Puertorriqueño, Manuel de Organizacion, box 41, folder 5, CASA Collection.

48. Felix Padilla, *Latino Ethnic Consciousness: The Case of Mexican Americans and Puerto Ricans in Chicago* (Notre Dame, IN: University of Notre Dame Press, 1985).

49. Zoilo Cruz, quoted in Victor Rodriguez, "Boricuas, African Americans," 97.

50. Jason Ferreria, "Venceremos! Los Siete de la Raza and Third World Radicalism in San Francisco, 1969–1975" (paper presented at the annual meeting of the American Studies Association, Houston, TX, November 2002). See also Horacio Ramírez, "Music and Mobilization: The Sounds and Rhythms of San Francisco's Gay Latino Alliance, 1975–1983" (paper presented at the annual meeting of the American Studies Association, Houston, TX, November 2002).

Los Angeles and San Francisco are two very different urban regions that have historically been in competition. Although DeLeon focuses on municipal politics and McGirr emphasizes grassroots activism, their respective texts convey the very different political cultures of the two regions. Richard DeLeon, *Left Coast City: Progressive Politics in San Francisco, 1975–1991* (Lawrence: University of Kansas Press, 1992); Lisa McGirr, *Suburban Warriors: The Origins of the New American Right* (Princeton, NJ: Princeton University Press, 2001).

7. PATRIARCHY AND REVOLUTION

1. Sue Tolleson Rinehart, *Gender Consciousness and Politics* (New York: Routledge, 1992), 32.

2. Paula Giddings, *When and Where I Enter: The Impact of Black Women on Race and Sex in America* (New York: Quill William Morrow, 1984), 314.

3. Safiya Bukhari-Alston, "On the Question of Sexism within the Black Panther Party," *Black Panther,* Fall/Winter 1993, 4.

4. Sheila Rowbotham, *Women, Resistance and Revolution* (New York: Vintage Books, 1974).

5. Giddings, *When and Where,* ch. 27. Such divisions were also due to blunders by white feminists. For instance, white women did not invite Black women to one of the first major feminist conferences because of worries they would shift the agenda too heavily toward racism. Elbaum, *Revolution in the Air,* 137. On the women's movement, see Ruth Rosen, *The World Split Open: How the Modern Women's Movement Changed America* (New York: Penguin Books, 2000); Bernice Carroll, "Women Take Action," *Women's Studies International Forum* 12 (1989): 3–24.

6. Matthews, "No One Ever Asks," 267–304.

7. For more detailed and comprehensive coverage, see Elaine Brown, *Taste of*

Power; Kathleen Cleaver, "Women, Power and Revolution," *New Political Science,* June 1999, 231–36; Angela Davis, *Angela Davis;* Giddings, *When and Where,* ch. 27; Regina Jennings, "Why I Joined the Party," in Charles Jones, *Black Panther Party Reconsidered,* 257–65; Angela LeBlanc-Ernest, "The Most Qualified Person to Handle the Job: Black Panther Party Women, 1966–1982," in Charles Jones, *Black Panther Party Reconsidered,* 305–34; Matthews, "No One Ever Asks"; Madalynn Rucker and JoNina Abron, "Comrade Sisters," in *Unrelated Kin: Race and Gender in Women's Personal Narratives,* ed. Gwendolyn Etter-Lewis and Michèle Foster, 139–67 (New York: Routledge, 1996); Shakur, *Assata.*

On gender relations within CASA, see Marisela Rodríguez Chávez, "Living and Breathing." Since there has been no scholarly study of East Wind, an analysis of its gender relations does not exist. However, on gender relations and the role of women within the larger Asian American movement, see Miya Iwataki, "The Asian Women's Movement: A Retrospective," *East Wind* 2 (Spring/Summer 1983): 35–41; Ling, "Mountain Movers"; Malcolm's Mother [Anonymous], "My Son Malcolm," *Amerasia* 15 (1989): 110–13; Quon, "Individually We Contributed." The Institute for Multiracial Justice in the San Francisco Bay Area also recently convened the forum "Listen to Your Mama!" featuring Black, Asian American, and American Indian women active in the Third World Left. Thanks to Betita Martinez for sharing the video of this event.

8. On women's political activism, see Choi, "At the Margins"; Bettye Collier-Thomas and V. P. Franklin, *Sisters in the Struggle: African American Women in the Civil Rights–Black Power Movement* (New York: New York University Press, 2001); Vicki Crawford, Jacqueline A. Rouse, and Barbara Woods, eds., *Women in the Civil Rights Movement: Trailblazers and Torchbearers, 1941–1965* (New York: Carlson Publishing, 1990); Espinoza, "Revolutionary Sisters"; Fujino, "To Serve the Movement"; Giddings, *When and Where;* Cynthia Hamilton, "Women in Politics," *Women's Studies International Forum* 12 (1989): 129–35; Ling, "Mountain Movers"; Glenn Omatsu, "Always a Rebel: An Interview with Kazu Iijima," *Amerasia* 13 (1986–87): 83–98; Mary Pardo, *Mexican American Women Activists: Identity and Resistance in Two Los Angeles Communities* (Philadelphia: Temple University Press, 1998); Belinda Robnett, *How Long? How Long? African-American Women in the Struggle for Civil Rights* (New York: Oxford University Press, 1997); Margaret Rose, "Women in the United Farm Workers" (PhD diss., University of California, Los Angeles, 1988); Cynthia S'thembile West, "Revisiting Female Activism in the 1960s: The Newark Branch Nation of Islam," *Black Scholar* 26 (1996): 41–59; Ula Taylor, "The Historical Foundation of Black Feminist Theory and Praxis," *Journal of Black Studies* 29 (November 1998): 234–53. On the activism of nonleaders, see Soo-Young Chin, *Doing What Had to Be Done: The Life Narrative of Dora Yum Kim* (Philadelphia: Temple University Press, 1999); Lipsitz, *Life in the Struggle.*

9. Robnett, *How Long, How Long?;* Charles Payne, "Men Led, but Women Organized" in Crawford, Rouse, and Woods, *Women,* 1–12. On Fannie Lou

Hamer and Dolores Huerta, respectively, see Chana Kai Lee, *For Freedom's Sake*, and Rose, "Women."

10. Quoted in Kathleen Cleaver, "Women, Power and Revolution," 236.

11. In the 1980s women of color began actively theorizing their politics, which illustrated these multiple commitments. Key texts include Gloria Anzaldúa, *Making Face, Making Soul/Hacienda Caras: Creative and Critical Perspectives by Feminists of Color* (San Francisco: Aunt Lute Books, 1990); Patricia Hill Collins, *Black Feminist Thought: Knowledge, Consciousness, and the Politics of Empowerment* (New York: Routledge, 2000); Kimberlé Crenshaw, "Whose Story Is It Anyway?" in *Race-ing Justice, En-gendering Power: Essays on Anita Hill, Clarence Thomas, and the Construction of Social Reality* (New York: Pantheon Books, 1992), 402–40; Angela Davis, *Women, Race and Class* (New York: Random House, 1983); bell hooks, *Ain't I a Woman? Black Women and Feminism* (Boston: South End Press, 1981); Chandra T. Mohanty, Ann Russo, and Lourdes Torres, eds., *Third World Women and the Politics of Feminism* (Bloomington: Indiana University Press, 1991); Cherie Moraga and Gloria Anzaldúa, eds., *This Bridge Called My Back: Writings by Radical Women of Color* (New York: Kitchen Table, 1983); Chela Sandoval, "US Third World Feminism," *Genders* 19 (1991): 1–24; Sonia Shah, ed., *Dragon Ladies: Asian American Feminists Breathe Fire* (Boston: South End Press, 1997).

12. Quon, "Individually We Contributed," 210.

13. Quoted in Enriqueta Longeaux y Vasquez, "The Women of La Raza," in *Chicana Feminist Thought: The Basic Historical Writings*, ed. Alma García (New York: Routledge, 1997), 29.

14. Chicanas had not yet fully articulated what would eventually become Chicana feminism. For an overview and chronology, see Alma García, *Chicana Feminist Thought*.

15. On the masculinity of men of color, see David Abalos, *The Latino Male: A Radical Redefinition* (Boulder, CO: Lynne Rienner, 2002); Hazel Carby, *Race Men* (Cambridge, MA: Harvard University Press, 1998); Ray Gonzalez, ed., *Muy Macho: Latino Men Confront Their Manhood* (New York: Anchor Books, 1996); Thelma Golden, *Black Male: Representations of Masculinity in Contemporary American Art* (New York: Whitney Museum of American Art, 1994); Andrea Hunter and James Dixon, "Hidden Voices of Black Men," *Journal of Black Studies* 25 (September 1994): 20–40; Karen Leong, "A Distinct and Antagonistic Race: Constructions of Chinese Manhood in the Exclusionist Debates, 1869–1878," in *Across the Great Divide: Cultures of Manhood in the American West*, ed. Matthew Basso, Laura McCall, and Dee Garceau (New York: Routledge, 2001), 131–48; Viet Nguyen, "The Remasculinization of Chinese America: Race, Violence, and the Novel," *American Literary History* 12 (Spring/Summer 2000): 130–57; Robert Staples, *Black Masculinity: The Black Male's Role in American Society* (San Francisco: Black Scholar Press, 1982); Robert Tanaka, "Sansei Male Personhood, Corporate Sexuality and Ms. Madeline Girbaud," *Journal of Ethnic Studies*, 17 (1989): 1–22; Eric Wat, *The Making of a Gay Asian Community: An Oral History of Pre-AIDS Los Angeles*

(Lanham, MD: Rowman and Littlefield, 2002); Maxine Baca Zinn, "Chicano Men and Masculinity," *Journal of Ethnic Studies* 10 (Summer 1982): 29–44. On masculinity more generally, see R. W. Connell, *Masculinities* (Berkeley: University of California Press, 1995).

16. Aída Hurtado, *The Color of Privilege: Three Blasphemies on Race and Feminism* (Ann Arbor: University of Michigan Press, 1996), 98, 100, 116. Note that she refers only to Chicano and Black men, continuing the exclusion of Asian Americans.

17. Emma Pérez, *The Decolonial Imaginary: Writing Chicanas into History* (Bloomington: Indiana University Press, 1999), 33.

18. "Young Lords Party 13-Point Program and Platform," in Foner, *Black Panthers Speak*, 237; "12-Point Platform and Program, I Wor Kuen," in Ho et al., *Legacy to Liberation*, 406.

19. On I Wor Kuen, see Ho, "Fists for Revolution," 3–13. It is not entirely fair to critique East Wind's lack of a gender statement because it did not articulate any platform and left no official written record.

20. Huey Newton, "The Women's Liberation and Gay Liberation Movement," in Newton, *To Die for the People*, 152, 154.

21. Consider also the Eight Points of Attention, of which the seventh reads, "Do not take liberties with women." That the writers deemed it necessary and appropriate to include such behavioral guidelines assumes a male membership and its sometimes problematic behavior toward women. Black Panther Party, "8 Points of Attention," reprinted in Charles Jones, *Black Panther Party Reconsidered*, 476.

22. Individuals, depending upon their age, personality, and chapter, also had radically different experiences. See Rucker and Abron, "Comrade Sisters."

23. On the *Black Panther* newspaper itself, see Christian Davenport, "Reading the 'Voice of the Vanguard,'" in Charles Jones, *Black Panther Party Reconsidered*, 193–209; Jane Rhodes, "The Black Panther Newspaper," *Media History* 7 (2001): 151–58.

24. See Doss's discussion on the BPP's representation of Black masculinity in "Revolutionary Art."

25. For examples of such reportage, see the front-page story of the July 18, 1970, issue of the *Black Panther*; "Randy Williams Has Shown Love, Respect, and Dedication to His People," *People's New Service*, April 30, 1970, 2–3; "Entire Family Brutalized by Memphis Pigs," *Black Panther*, June 12, 1971, 5; "Entire Family Beaten and Jailed," *Black Panther*, February 6, 1971, 5; Carol Rucker, "Panther Kidnapped and Beaten by Special Gestapo Pigs," *Black Panther*, February 6, 1971, 7; "Fascist Storm Troopers Wage Cowardly Attack on N.C.C.F. Office . . . Ohio," *Black Panther*, July 11, 1970, 3.

26. Judy Hart, "Sista's Section: Black Womanhood, No. 1," *Black Panther*, July 20, 1967, 11, 14.

27. Regina Jennings, in her analysis of Panther poetry, has pointed out that early female poets even adopted masculine voices when advocating revolution. Jennings, "Poetry," 123.

28. Kansas City Chapter, Black Panther Party, "Revolution and Women," *Black Panther*, March 15, 1970, 5. Note that the spelling of Huggins's first name shifts between "Erica" and "Ericka." I follow the spelling of whatever source I am drawing from.

29. Kathleen Cleaver, "Women, Power and Revolution," 234.

30. Brown, *Taste of Power*, ch. 17.

31. Others also suspected Brown was an informant. See Lee Lew-Lee's video, *All Power to the People.*

32. For a more critical position, see Rucker and Abron, "Comrade Sisters," 148.

33. LeBlanc-Ernest, "Most Qualified Person," 319–20; Rucker and Abron, "Comrade Sisters," 156.

34. LeBlanc-Ernest, "Most Qualified Person," 319.

35. "Ericka Huggins Elected to County Education Board," *Oakland Community Learning Center News*, April–May 1976, 1–2; Shakur, *Assata.*

36. Olsen, *Last Man Standing*, 56. Butler was later revealed to be an informant.

37. Dane Archer and Rosemary Gartner, *Violence and Crime in Cross-National Perspective* (New Haven, CT: Yale University Press, 1984).

38. On the context of Black male violence, see Anthony King, "Understanding Violence among Young African American Males," *Journal of Black Studies* 28 (September 1997): 79–96.

39. See, however, Rucker, "Panther Kidnapped," 7.

40. Angela Davis, "Reflections on the Black Woman's Role in the Community of Slaves," in *The Angela Y. Davis Reader*, ed. Joy James, 111–28 (Oxford: Basil Blackwell, 1998); Ruth Frankenberg, *White Women, Race Matters: The Social Construction of Whiteness* (Minneapolis: University of Minnesota Press, 1993); Evelyn Nakano Glenn, "From Servitude to Service Work: Historical Continuities in the Racial Division of Paid Reproductive Labor," *Signs* 18 (Autumn 1982): 1–43.

41. Evelina Márquez and Margarita Ramirez, "Women's Task Is to Gain Liberty," *Sin Fronteras*, March 1977, *Sin Fronteras* Collection, Chicano Studies Library, University of California, Los Angeles; hereafter referred to as "*Sin Fronteras* Collection."

42. "Committee to Stop Forced Sterilization," p. 5, box 1, folder 7, CASA Collection, Special Collections, Stanford University Libraries, Palo Alto, CA; hereafter referred to as "CASA Collection." According to a *Sin Fronteras* article, "Some of the women who were sterilized were told that they must sign the consent forms because they were poor, Mexican, and had already had enough children." March 1978, *Sin Fronteras* Collection. See also "Stop Forced Sterilization Now!" pamphlet, p. 1, box 28, folder 8, CASA Collection; letter from National Coalition Against Sterilization Abuse to Enrique Vela, October 26, 1976, box 23, folder 3, CASA Collection. See also Adelaida del Castillo, "Sterilization: An Overview," and Carlos Velez-Ibañez, "Se Me Acabó la Canción: An Ethnography of Non-consenting Sterilization among Mexican Women in Los Angeles," in *Mexican American Women in the United States: Struggles Past*

and Present, ed. Magdalena Mora and Adelaida del Castillo, 65–70 and 71–93 (Los Angeles: Chicano Studies Research Center, University of California, Los Angeles), 1980.

43. "Inez García Gains Victory," *Sin Fronteras,* January 1976, 3; "Joan Little Acquitted," *Sin Fronteras,* September 1975, *Sin Fronteras* Collection.

44. An exception was Magdalena Mora, who wrote a regular column, *El Engrane,* which featured her photo.

45. Boletin Interno Local, 3, February 21, 1977, p. 3, box 21, folder 5, CASA Collection.

46. Margarita Ramirez, "300 Women Attend Latina Conference," *Sin Fronteras,* April 1977, *Sin Fronteras* Collection.

47. Although CASA women in Seattle identified at least three problematic behaviors on the part of men in the organization—patronizing attitudes, double standards, and men "ignoring the fact that their comrades are women"—there is no evidence of such issues being raised at the conference. Letter and notes from Jana Adkins to Evelina Marquez, June 17, 1977, p. 2, box 8, folder 2, CASA Collection.

48. Marisela Rodríguez Chávez, "Living and Breathing," 57. See also letter to Evelina Márquez from Jana Adkins, June 17, 1977. Interestingly, this letter was written by a white female member on behalf of the Seattle CASA women to the Los Angeles office in an effort to make women's issues more prominent in the organization.

49. "The Woman Question," box 28, folder 8, CASA Collection.

50. Carlos Vásquez, "The Chicano Movement—A Step, Part 10," *Sin Fronteras,* November 1977, 10.

51. Marisela Rodríguez Chávez, "Living and Breathing," 66.

52. Marisela Rodríguez Chávez, "Living and Breathing," ch. 3.

53. On parental responsibilities, see "Boletin Interno Local," Local Committee, Los Angeles, February 21, 1977, p. 9, box 21, folder 5, CASA Collection. On family demands, see "Transfer Report of Cecilia Gurrola." July 18, 1977, box 21, folder 2, CASA Collection.

54. Gitlin, *The Sixties,* 371.

55. Marisela Rodríguez Chávez notes that numerous men had extramarital affairs and some actually became romantically involved with women in order to draw them into CASA. "Living and Breathing," 67.

56. Antonia Castañeda has explored the complex relations surrounding colonization, sexuality, and female bodies in "Sexual Violence in the Politics and Policies of Conquest," in *Building with Our Hands: New Directions in Chicana Studies,* ed. Adela de la Torre and Beatríz Pesquera (Berkeley: University of California Press, 1993), 15–33. On Chicanas' response to La Virgin/Malinche dualism, see Aída Hurtado, "The Politics of Sexuality in the Gender Subordination of Chicanas," in *Living Chicana Theory,* ed. Carla Trujillo (Berkeley: Third Woman Press, 1998), 383–428.

57. Luciana Lira, Mary Koss, and Nancy Russo, "Mexican American Women's Definitions of Rape and Sexual Abuse," *Hispanic Journal of Behav-*

ioral Sciences 21 (1999): 236–65; J. Baldwin, S. Whiteley, and J. Baldwin, "The Effect of Ethnic Group on Sexual Activities Related to Contraception and STDs," *Journal of Sex Research* 29 (1992): 189–205; T. Baird, "Mexican Adolescent Sexuality," *Hispanic Journal of Behavioral Sciences* 15 (1993): 402–17; A. Padilla and T. Baird, "Mexican American Adolescent Sexual Knowledge," *Hispanic Journal of Behavioral Sciences* 13 (1990): 95–104; Patricia Zavella, "Playing with Fire: Gendered Construction of Chicana/Mexicana Sexuality," in *The Gender/Sexuality Reader: Culture, History, Political Economy,* ed. Roger Lancaster and Micaela di Leonardo (New York: Routledge, 1997), 392–408. Thanks to Gloria Gonzalez-Lopez for introducing me to this literature.

58. This is a major methodological shortcoming on my part. By relying on *Gidra,* I risk attributing to East Wind the actions and attitudes of a larger group of Asian American activists. When possible, I try to differentiate between East Wind and the larger Los Angeles Asian American movement. Fortunately, the fact that *Gidra* was so heavily Japanese American helps bridge the gap somewhat. Wei, *Asian American Movement,* 106. See also Murase, "Toward Barefoot Journalism," 1, 43–46.

59. Linda Iwataki, "Women's HerStory," *Gidra* 3 (January 1971): 12.

60. On the sexualization of Asian and Asian American women, see Sumi Cho, "Asian Pacific American Women and Racialized Sexual Harassment," in *Making More Waves: New Writing by Asian American Women,* ed. Elaine Kim and Lilia Villanueva (New York: Beacon Press, 1997), 164–73; Elaine Kim, *Dangerous Women: Gender and Korean Nationalism* (New York: Routledge, 1997); Lynn Lu, "Critical Visions: The Representation and Resistance of Asian Women," in Shah, *Dragon Ladies,* 17–28. On gender and the nation, see Leong, "Distinct and Antagonistic Race."

Activists highlighted problematic attitudes by reproducing advertisements for Asian women. See, for example, p. 3 of *Gidra* (January 1971) for the following advertisement, "Oriental women are different. They are among the most respected in the world. They are famous for being unselfish, faithful, kind, trusting, and obedient. They are dedicated to pleasing their man who is their whole life. Ask anyone who is fortunate enough to be married to one, and thousands upon thousands are! . . . You, too, can have a lovely, unspoiled and feminine Japanese wife!" Quoted in *Gidra* 4 (April 1972): 3.

61. Yvonne Wong Nishio, "Power to the Workers," *Gidra* 3 (January 1971): 6; Vivian Matsushige, "A Woman's Life Story," *Gidra* 3 (January 1971): 7; Wilma Chen, "Movement Contradiction," *Gidra* 3 (January 1971): 8; Killer Fawn, "In the Movement Office," *Gidra* 3 (January 1971): 13; Mike Yamamoto, "Male Perspective," *Gidra* 3 (January 1971): 13; Iwataki, "Women's HerStory," 9, 12.

62. Chen, "Movement Contradiction."

63. For example, consider the graphic portrayal of the female body in Laura Takamaga and Evelyn Yoshimura, "An American Fiasco," *Gidra* 5 (November 1973): 13, and "An Addict's Wife," *Gidra* 3 (March 1971): 5. Such representations would have been inconceivable in either *Sin Fronteras* or the *Black Pan-*

ther. See also "Women and Men," *Gidra* 3 (August 1971): 14. For examples of poetry, see "Sister," *Gidra* 6 (1974): 24, and "I Am an Asian Woman," *Gidra* 5 (January 1973): 14.

64. "Narrative: A Personal Account," *Gidra* 2 (October 1970): 8.

65. "Sister," *Gidra* 6 (1974): 24.

66. Viet Nguyen, "Remasculinization of Chinese America," 130.

67. For an exception, see the photograph of Evelyn Yoshimura in China. *Gidra* 6 (April 1974): 42.

68. Carol Mochizuki, "I Hate My Wife for Her Flat Yellow Face . . . ," *Gidra* 3 (June 1971): 6; Ling, "Mountain Movers"; "Asian Women's Center," *Gidra* 5 (January 1973): 14; "Asian Women's Center," *Gidra* 5 (December 1973): 15; Takamaga and Yoshimura, "An American Fiasco," 13. For a more general overview, see Iwataki, "Asian Women's Movement."

69. Both Chicana and Black women were also organizing among themselves, but I found no evidence that women from CASA and the BPP participated significantly in such formations.

70. Yamamoto, "Male Perspective," 13.

8. THE THIRD WORLD LEFT TODAY AND CONTEMPORARY ACTIVISM

1. See Santa Ana, *Brown Tide Rising*; Mike Davis, "Social Origins"; Robert Gooding-Williams, *Reading Rodney King, Reading Urban Uprising* (New York: Routledge, 1993); Harold Meyerson, "The Red Sea," *LA Weekly,* April 28–May 4, 2000, 17–20; Mike Davis, "Runaway Train Crashes Buses," *Nation,* September 18, 1995, 270–74; Erin Texeira, "Generation Gap Seen in Black Support for Hahn," *Los Angeles Times,* May 5, 2001, B1, B11; David Shichor and Dale Sechrest, *Three Strikes and You're Out: Vengeance as Public Policy* (Thousand Oaks, CA: Sage Publications, 1996); Freer, "Black Korean Conflict"; Edna Bonacich et al., *Global Production: The Apparel Industry in the Pacific Rim* (Philadelphia: Temple University Press, 1994).

2. Consider, once again, *Field of Dreams,* especially the scene where Amy Madigan, delighted to be taking on a conservative school board, says with relish, "It's just like the sixties!" See also Nadel, *Flatlining,* ch. 2.

3. See, for example, Angela Davis, "Afro Images."

4. Elbaum, *Revolution in the Air,* 310. See also Jack Whalen and Richard Flacks, *Beyond the Barricades: The Sixties Generation Grows Up* (Philadelphia: Temple University Press, 1989). Important exceptions to this pattern are those who became conservative radicals. See Horowitz, *Radical Son.*

5. Whalen and Flacks found that many activists were lost after the demise of the New Left, as they had delayed key decisions regarding marriage, work, and family. *Beyond the Barricades,* ch. 4.

6. Nicholls, "Forging a 'New' Organizational Infrastructure"; Pastor, "Common Ground"; Gottlieb et al., *Next Los Angeles.*

7. This conclusion is drawn from a biased sample: I only interviewed those that either I knew to be politically active or other interviewees referred me to. Thus I did not interview those who had either closed the door on this chapter of their lives or for whatever reason declined to talk to me.

8. Meyerson, "Red Sea"; Roger Waldinger et al., "Justice for Janitors," *Dissent* 47 (Winter 1997): 37–44; Nancy Cleeland, "LA Area Now a Model for Labor Revival," *Los Angeles Times*, September 6, 1996, A1, A20; Merrifield, "Urbanization of Labor"; Milkman and Wong, *Voices from the Front Lines*; Stuart Silverstein, "Going to Work in LA," *Los Angeles Times*, February 22, 1996, D1, D3; Ruth Milkman, *Organizing Immigrants: The Challenge for Unions in Contemporary California* (Ithaca, NY: Cornell University Press, 2000).

9. Allen and Turner, *Changing Faces, Changing Places*, ch. 5. Paul Moore et al., *The Other Los Angeles: Working Poor in the City of the 21st Century* (Los Angeles: Los Angeles Alliance for a New Economy, 2000); Paul Ong and Evelyn Blumenberg, "Income and Racial Inequality in Los Angeles," in Scott and Soja, *The City*, 311–35.

10. Dave Gardetta, "True Grit: Clocking Time with the Janitors' Organizer Rocio Saenz," *L.A. Weekly* 15 (1993): 23.

11. María Elena Durazo, "María Elena Durazo," in Milkman and Wong, *Voices from the Front Lines*, 11–22; Lou Siegel, "LRR Voices: Local 11 Takes on LA," *Labor Research Review* 20 (1993): 21–23; Bob Spichen, "Labor of Love," *Los Angeles Times*, March 9, 1997, E1, E8.

12. Nicholls, "Forging a 'New' Organizational Infrastructure," 24–25.

13. Elbaum, *Revolution in the Air*, 235; League of Revolutionary Struggle, *Statements*; League of Revolutionary Struggle, *Peace, Justice, Equality and Socialism* (Oakland, CA: Getting Together Publications, 1986).

14. Mitchell Maki et al., *Achieving the Impossible Dream: How Japanese Americans Obtained Redress* (Urbana: University of Illinois Press, 1999); Daniels, Taylor, and Kitano, *Japanese Americans*, part 7.

15. Eric Yamamoto, "What's Next? Japanese American Redress and African American Reparations," *Amerasia* 25 (1999): 1–17.

16. On A/PI demographics, see Allen and Turner, *Changing Faces, Changing Places*, ch. 6. On economic diversity, see Ong and Hee, "Economic Diversity"; Ong and Blumenberg, "Income and Racial Inequality." On interracial marriage, see Fong and Yung, "In Search"; Tuan, *Forever Foreigners*, 31–36; Wu, *Yellow*, ch. 7.

Activism around Little Tokyo dates back to the redevelopment efforts of the 1970s. On the current struggle, see http://reccenter.ltsc.org.

17. Thanks to Tony Osumi and Jenni Kuida for help with contacts.

18. Ward Churchill, "To Disrupt, Discredit and Destroy: The FBI's Secret War against the Black Panther Party," in Cleaver and Katsiaficas, *Liberation, Imagination*, 109.

19. Olsen, *Last Man Standing*.

20. Gary Webb, *Dark Alliance: The CIA, the Contras, and the Crack Cocaine*

Explosion (New York: Seven Stories, 1999); Mike Davis, *City of Quartz*, ch. 5; Cynthia Hamilton, *Apartheid in America* (Los Angeles: Labor/Community Strategy Center, 1987).

21. Melvin Oliver, James Johnson, and William Farrell, "Anatomy of a Rebellion," in *Reading Rodney King, Reading Urban Uprising*, ed. Robert Gooding-Williams (New York: Routledge, 1993), 117–41.

22. Latina/o immigrants are routinely blamed for Black unemployment and poverty. With some notable exceptions, however, such as the janitorial industry, evidence suggests that Latina/o immigration has had a mixed impact. For instance, Ong and Valenzuela found that while Latina/o immigration affected Black joblessness (but not earnings), equally important was the role of institutional racism and employer discrimination. Paul Ong and Abel Valenzuela, "The Labor Market: Immigrant Effects and Racial Disparities," in Waldinger and Bozorgmehr, *Ethnic Los Angeles*, 165–91. Likewise, Waldinger and Lichter argue that immigration has contributed to "African Americans being 'pulled' rather than 'pushed' out of their employment concentrations." Roger Waldinger and Michael Lichter, *How the Other Half Works: Immigration and the Social Organization of Labor* (Berkeley: University of California Press, 2003), 209. See also J. Kirschenman and K. Neckerman, "We'd Love to Hire Them, but . . . : The Meaning of Race for Employers," in *The Urban Underclass*, ed. C. Jencks and P. Peterson (Washington, DC: Brookings Institution, 1991), 203–32.

23. Allen and Turner, *Changing Faces, Changing Places*, ch. 4

24. James Rainey and Jeffrey Rabin, "Hahn and Villaraigosa Now Must Shift Focus," *Los Angeles Times*, April 12, 2001, A1, A17; Texeira, "Generation Gap Seen." Hahn and Villaraigosa faced off again in 2005, and once again the Black vote was pivotal. The outcome of this election was different, however, as Villaraigosa won easily. Michael Finnegan, "In Testy Debate, Hahn and Villaraigosa Appeal for the Support of Black Voters," *Los Angeles Times*, April 10, 2005, B1, B6.

25. Laura Pulido, "Restructuring and the Contraction and Expansion of Environmental Rights in the US," *Environment and Planning A* 26 (1994): 915–36; Liza Featherstone, *Students against Sweatshops* (New York: Verso, 2002); Miriam Ching Yoon Louie, *Sweatshop Warriors: Immigrant Women Workers Take on the Global Factory* (Boston: South End Press, 2001).

26. Janet Abu-Lughod, *New York, Chicago, Los Angeles: America's Global Cities* (Minneapolis: University of Minnesota Press, 2000).

27. Although far fewer, such female leaders also existed. Some have suggested that Carmen Chow of I Wor Kuen was such a figure.

28. On the culture of the New Communist movement, see Elbaum, *Revolution in the Air*, ch. 8.

29. For example, the Southern Christian Leadership Conference under Martin Luther King Jr. was less democratic than either the Student Non-violent Coordinating Committee or the Congress of Racial Equality. Akinleye Umoja, "The Ballot and the Bullet," *Journal of Black Studies* 29 (March 1999): 570.

30. Carol Mueller, "Ella Baker and the Origins of Participatory Democracy,"

in Crawford, Rouse, and Woods, *Women in the Civil Rights Movement*, 51–70; Pardo, *Mexican American Women Activists*; Alice Eagley and Mary Johannesen-Schmidt, "The Leadership Styles of Men and Women," *Journal of Social Issues* 57 (2001): 781–97.

31. See, for example, Emily Woo Yamasaki, "Perspective of a Revolutionary Feminist" in Ho et al., *Legacy to Liberation*, 47–51.

32. For a different perspective, see Jennifer Ting, "The Power of Sexuality," *Journal of Asian American Studies* 1 (1998): 65–82.

33. Huey Newton, "The Women's Liberation and Gay Liberation Movements," in Newton, *To Die for the People*, 152–55; Wat, *Making of a Gay Asian Community*, 93–101.

34. On the challenges of multiracial organizing, see Pulido, "Multiracial Organizing."

35. Thomas Durant, "Race and Class Consciousness among Lower and Middle-Class Blacks," *Journal of Black Studies* 27 (1997): 334–51.

36. On Central Americans, see Nora Hamilton and Norma Stoltz Chinchilla, *Seeking Community in a Global City: Guatemalans and Salvadorans in Los Angeles* (Philadelphia: Temple University Press, 2001).

37. See Deborah Berman Santana, "No Somos Unicos: The Status Question from Manila to San Juan," *Centro* 11 (Fall 1999): 127–40.

38. Anthony Thigpenn, in "The View from the Ground: Organizers Speak out on Race," *Colorlines* 3 (Summer 2000): 16–17.

39. On Latina/o poverty, see Moore et al., *The Other Los Angeles;* on Black and Chicana/o political infrastructure, see Parker, "Elusive Coalition"; on racial discrimination, see Logan, "How Race Counts."

40. David Savage, "Affirmative Action Case Splits Asian Americans," *Los Angeles Times*, March 30, 2003, A30; Yen Espiritu and Paul Ong, "Class Constraints on Racial Solidarity among Asian Americans," in Ong, Bonacich, and Cheng, *New Asian Immigration*, 295–321.

41. "Scientist Says Race Was a Factor in US Spy Case," *Los Angeles Times*, January 16, 2002, A17; Elizabeth Kelly, "Claims against Abercrombie Detailed," *Los Angeles Times*, June 18, 2003, C2; Umemoto, "From Vincent Chin"; Scott Kurashige, "Beyond Random Acts."

42. On Korean merchants, see Pyong Gap Min, *Caught in the Middle: Korean Merchants in America's Multiethnic Cities* (Berkeley: University of California Press, 1996). On KIWA, see Tram Nguyen, "Showdown in K-Town," *Colorlines* 4 (Spring 2001): 26–29. See also KIWA's Web site: www.kiwa.org.

43. Marisela Rodríguez Chávez, "Living and Breathing," 69.

44. See the National Organizers' Alliance Web site: www.noacentral.org/pension.html.

45. Innovative programs include UCLA's Community/Scholars' Program (www.sppsr.ucla.edu), the Bannerman Fellowship (www.bannermanfellowship.org), and the Vallecitos Mountain Refuge Fellowship Program (www.vallecitos.org/refuge_fellowship.html).

46. On the need for reconciliation among communities of color, see Yamamoto, *Interracial Justice.*

47. The only religion openly acknowledged by interviewees was Buddhism.

48. Indeed, one manuscript reviewer insisted that any reference to spirituality should be eliminated from this book.

49. Kelley, *Freedom Dreams,* 12.

50. Kelley, *Freedom Dreams,* 12.

Selected Bibliography

Abalos, David. *The Latino Male: A Radical Redefinition.* Boulder, CO: Lynne Rienner, 2002.

Abron, JoNina. "Serving the People: The Survival Programs of the Black Panther Party." In *The Black Panther Party Reconsidered,* edited by Charles Jones, 177–92. Baltimore: Black Classic Press, 1998.

Abu-Lughod, Janet. *New York, Chicago, Los Angeles: America's Global Cities.* Minneapolis: University of Minnesota Press, 2000.

Acuña, Rodolfo. *Occupied America: A History of Chicanos.* San Francisco: Canfield Press, 1972.

Allen, James, and Eugene Turner. *Changing Faces, Changing Places: Mapping Southern California.* Northridge: Center for Geographical Studies, California State University, Northridge, 2002.

———. *The Ethnic Quilt: Population Diversity in Southern California.* Northridge: Center for Geographical Studies, California State University, Northridge, 1997.

Allen, Robert. *Black Awakening in Capitalist America: An Analytic History.* Trenton, NJ: Africa World Press, 1992.

Almaguer, Tomás. "Ideological Distortions in Recent Chicano Historiography: The Colonial Model and Chicano Interpretation." *Aztlán* 18 (1987): 7–28.

———. *Racial Fault Lines: The Historical Origins of White Supremacy in California.* Berkeley: University of California Press, 1994.

———. "Towards the Study of Chicano Colonialism." *Aztlán* 2 (1971): 137–42.

Ambrecht, Biliana. *Politicizing the Poor: The Legacy of the War on Poverty in a Mexican American Community.* New York: Praeger, 1976.

Ambrecht, Biliana, and Harry Pachon. "Ethnic Mobilization in a Mexican American Community: An Exploratory Study of East Los Angeles, 1965–1972." *Western Political Quarterly* 29 (1974): 500–519.

Amerasia Staff. "An Interview with Warren Furutani." *Amerasia* 1 (1971): 70–76.

Anaya, Rodolfo, and Francisco Lomeli. *Aztlán: Essays on the Chicano Homeland.* Albuquerque: University of New Mexico Press, 1989.

Anderson, Benedict. *Imagined Communities: Reflections on the Origin and Spread of Nationalism.* New York: Verso, 1983.

Anderson, Susan. "A City Called Heaven." In *The City: Los Angeles and Urban Theory at the End of the Twentieth Century,* edited by Allen Scott and Edward Soja, 336–64. Berkeley: University of California Press, 1996.

Anzaldúa, Gloria. *Borderlands: La Frontera.* San Francisco: Aunt Lute Books, 1987.

———. *Making Face, Making Soul/Haciendo Caras: Creative and Critical Perspectives by Feminists of Color.* San Francisco: Aunt Lute Books, 1990.

Aptheker, Herbert. *American Negro Slave Revolts.* 1943. Reprint, New York: International Publishers, 1964.

Archer, Dane, and Rosemary Gartner. *Violence and Crime in Cross-National Perspective.* New Haven, CT: Yale University Press, 1984.

Asamura, Gary. "The Unsung Heroes of the Yellow Brotherhood." *Amerasia* 15 (1989): 156–58.

Babcock, R. F., and F. P. Bosselman. *Exclusionary Zoning: Land Use Regulation and Housing in the 1970s.* New York: Praeger, 1973.

Baird, T. "Mexican Adolescent Sexuality: Attitudes, Knowledge, and Sources of Information." *Hispanic Journal of Behavioral Sciences* 15 (1993): 402–17.

Balderrama, Francisco, and Raymond Rodriguez. *Decade of Betrayal: Mexican Repatriation in the 1930s.* Albuquerque: University of New Mexico Press, 1995.

Baldwin, J., S. Whiteley, and J. Baldwin. "The Effect of Ethnic Group on Sexual Activities Related to Contraception and STDs." *Journal of Sex Research* 29 (1992): 189–205.

Barlow, Andrew. "The Student Movement of the 1960s and the Politics of Race." *Journal of Ethnic Studies* 19 (1991): 1–22.

Barrera, Mario. *Race and Class in the Southwest: A Theory of Racial Inequality.* Notre Dame, IN: University of Notre Dame Press, 1979.

Bartlett, D. "Torrance: An Industrial Garden City." *American City* 9 (1913): 310–14.

Bell, David. "The Triumph of Asian-Americans." *New Republic,* July 15 and 22, 1985, 24–26, 28–31.

Berland, Oscar. "The Emergence of the Communist Perspective on the 'Negro Question' in America: 1919–1931, Part One." *Science and Society* 63 (Winter 1999/2000): 411–32.

Bernal, Dolores Delgado. "Chicana School Resistance and Grass Roots Leadership." PhD diss., University of California, Los Angeles, 1997.

Black Panther Party. *The Black Panther Party: Speech by John Hullet, Interview with Stokely Carmichael, Report from Lowndes County.* New York: Merit, 1966.

Blaut, James. *The Colonizers' Model of the World: Geographical Diffusionism and Eurocentric History.* New York: Guilford Press, 1993.

"Bobby Seale Explains Panther Politics: An Interview." In *The Black Panthers Speak,* edited by Eric Foner, 82. New York: Da Capo Press, 1995.

Bobo, Lawrence, Mel Oliver, James Johnson, and Abel Valenzuela. *Prismatic Metropolis: Inequality in Los Angeles.* New York: Russell Sage Foundation, 2000.

Bobo, Lawrence, and Camille Zubrinsky. "Attitudes on Residential Integration: Perceived Status Differences, Mere In-Group Preference, or Racial Prejudice?" *Social Forces* 74 (1996): 883–909.

Boggs, Grace Lee. *Living for Change: An Autobiography.* Minneapolis: University of Minnesota Press, 1998.

Bonacich, Edna, Lucie Cheng, Norma Chinchilla, Nora Hamilton, and Paul Ong. *Global Production: The Apparel Industry in the Pacific Rim.* Philadelphia: Temple University Press, 1994.

Booker, Chris. "Lumpenization: A Critical Error of the Black Panther Party." In *The Black Panther Party Reconsidered,* edited by Charles Jones, 337–62. Baltimore: Black Classic Press, 1998.

Bosworth, Allan. *America's Concentration Camps.* New York: W. W. Norton, 1967.

Breitman, George. *On Black Nationalism and Self-Determination.* New York: Pathfinder Press, 1970.

Brill, Alida. "Lakewood, California, 'Tomorrowland' at 40." In *Rethinking Los Angeles,* edited by Michael Dear, Eric Schockman, and Greg Hise, 97–112. Thousand Oaks, CA: Sage Publications, 1996.

Brodkin, Karen. *How Jews Became White Folks and What That Says about Race in America.* New Brunswick, NJ: Rutgers University Press, 1998.

Brown, Dee. *Bury My Heart at Wounded Knee: An Indian History of the American West.* New York: Henry Holt, 1970.

Brown, Elaine. *A Taste of Power: A Black Woman's Story.* New York: Anchor Books, 1992.

Buhle, Paul. "Themes in American Jewish Radicalism." In *The Immigrant Left in the United States,* edited by Paul Buhle and Dan Georgakas, 77–118. Albany: State University of New York Press, 1996.

Buhle, Paul, and Dan Georgakas, eds. *The Immigrant Left in the United States.* Albany: State University of New York Press, 1996.

Bulosan, Carlos. *America Is in the Heart.* Seattle: University of Washington Press, 1973.

Bunch, Lonnie. "A Past Not Necessarily Prologue: The Afro-American in Los Angeles." In *20th Century Los Angeles: Power, Promotion, and Social Conflict,* edited by Norman Klein and Martin Schiesl, 101–30. Claremont, CA: Regina Books, 1990.

Burawoy, Michael. "The Functions and Reproduction of Migrant Labor." *American Journal of Sociology* 81 (1976): 1050–87.

Bush, Rod. *We Are Not What We Seem: Black Nationalism and Class Struggle in the American Century.* New York: New York University Press, 1999.

Cabral, Amilcar. *Unity and Struggle: Speeches and Writings.* New York: Monthly Review, 1982.

California Department of Industrial Relations. Fair Employment Practices Commission. "Californians of Japanese, Chinese, and Filipino Ancestry." 1965. Box 69, Los Angeles Area Chamber of Commerce Collection, Department of Special Collections, University of Southern California Library, Los Angeles.

California Department of Industrial Relations. Fair Employment Practices Commission. "Negroes and Mexican Americans in South and East Los Angeles: Changes between 1960 and 1965." 1965. Box 69, Los Angeles Area Chamber of Commerce Collection, Department of Special Collections, University of Southern California Library, Los Angeles.

California Governor's Commission on the Los Angeles Riots. *Violence in the City—An End or a Beginning?* Los Angeles, 1965.

California State Advisory Committee to the U.S. Commission on Civil Rights. *Police-Community Relations in East Los Angeles, California.* Washington, DC: Government Printing Office, 1970.

Campbell, Angus. *White Attitudes towards Black People.* Ann Arbor: Institute for Social Research, University of Michigan, 1971.

Campbell, Susan. "Black Bolsheviks and Recognition of African Americans' Right to Self-Determination by the Communist Party, USA." *Science and Society* 58 (Winter 1994): 440–70.

Carby, Hazel. *Race Men.* Cambridge, MA: Harvard University Press, 1998.

Carmichael, Stokely, and Charles Hamilton. *Black Power: The Politics of Liberation in America.* New York: Vintage Books, 1967.

Carroll, Bernice. "Women Take Action." *Women's Studies International Forum* 12 (1989): 3–24.

Cartier, Carolyn. *Globalizing South China.* Oxford: Blackwell, 2001.

Castañeda, Antonia. "Sexual Violence in the Politics and Policies of Conquest." In *Building with Our Hands: New Directions in Chicana Studies,* edited by Adela de la Torre and Beatríz Pesquera, 15–33. Berkeley: University of California Press, 1993.

Chan, Sucheng. *Asian Americans: An Interpretive History.* Boston: Twayne, 1991.

Charles, Camille Zubrinsky. "Neighborhood Racial Composition Preferences." *Social Problems* 47 (2000): 379–407.

Chávez, Ernesto. "Imagining the Mexican Immigrant Worker: (Inter)Nationalism, Identity, and Insurgency in the Chicano Movement in Los Angeles." *Aztlán* 25 (Fall 2000): 109–35.

———. *Mi Raza Primero! Nationalism, Identity and Insurgency in the Chicano Movement in Los Angeles, 1966–1978.* Berkeley: University of California Press, 2002.

Chávez, John. *The Lost Land: The Chicano Image of the Southwest.* Albuquerque: University of New Mexico Press, 1989.

Chávez, Linda. *An Unlikely Conservative: The Transformation of an Ex-liberal, or, How I Became the Most Hated Hispanic in America.* New York: Basic Books, 2002.

Chávez, Marisela Rodríguez. "Living and Breathing the Movement: Women in

El Centro de Accion Social Autonomo, 1975–1978." Master's thesis, Arizona State University, 1997.

Cheng, Lucie, and Philip Yang. "The 'Model Minority' Deconstructed." In *Contemporary Asian America: A Multidisciplinary Reader*, edited by Min Zhou and James Gatewood, 459–82. New York: New York University Press, 2000.

Chin, Soo-Young. *Doing What Had to Be Done: The Life Narrative of Dora Yum Kim*. Philadelphia: Temple University Press, 1999.

Cho, Sumi. "Asian Pacific American Women and Racialized Sexual Harassment." In *Making More Waves: New Writing by Asian American Women*, edited by Elaine Kim and Lilia Villanueva, 164–73. New York: Beacon Press, 1997.

Choi, Jennifer Jung Hee. "At the Margins of Asian American Political Experience: The Life of Grace Lee Boggs." *Amerasia* 25 (1999): 18–40.

Chuman, Frank. *The Bamboo People: Japanese Americans, Their History and the Law*. Chicago: Japanese American Citizens League, 1976.

Churchill, Ward. "The Earth Is Our Mother." In *The State of Native America: Genocide, Colonization, and Resistance*, edited by M. Annette Jaimes, 139–88. Boston: South End Press, 1992.

———. "To Disrupt, Discredit and Destroy: The FBI's Secret War against the Black Panther Party." In *Liberation, Imagination, and the Black Panther Party: A New Look at the Panthers and Their Legacy*, edited by Kathleen Cleaver and George Katsiaficas, 78–122. New York: Routledge, 2001.

Churchill, Ward, and Jim Vander Wall. *Agents of Repression: The FBI's Secret War against the Black Panther Party and the American Indian Movement*. Boston: South End Press, 1988.

Citizens Research and Investigation Committee and Louis Tackwood. *The Glass House Tapes*. New York: Avon, 1973.

Clarke, John. *Marcus Garvey and the Vision of Africa*. New York: Vintage Books, 1974.

Cleaver, Kathleen. "Back to Africa: The Evolution of the International Section of the Black Panther Party, 1969–72." In *The Black Panther Party Reconsidered*, edited by Charles Jones, 211–54. Baltimore: Black Classic Press, 1998.

———. "Women, Power and Revolution." *New Political Science* 21 (June 1999): 231–36.

Cleaver, Kathleen, and George Katsiaficas. *Liberation, Imagination, and the Black Panther Party: A New Look at the Panthers and Their Legacy*. New York: Routledge, 2001.

Clemons, Michael, and Charles Jones. "Global Solidarity: The Black Panther Party in the International Arena." *New Political Science* 21 (1999): 177–203.

Cohen, Nathan. "Los Angeles Riot Study: Summary and Implications for Policy." Working Paper MR-103, Institute of Government and Public Affairs, Los Angeles.

Collier-Thomas, Bettye, and V. P. Franklin. *Sisters in the Struggle: African American Women in the Civil Rights–Black Power Movement*. New York: New York University Press, 2001.

Collins, Keith. *Black Los Angeles: The Maturing of the Ghetto, 1940–1950.* Saratoga, CA: Century Twenty One Publishing, 1980.

Collins, Patricia Hill. *Black Feminist Thought: Knowledge, Consciousness, and the Politics of Empowerment.* New York: Routledge, 2000.

Communist Collective of the Chicano Nation (M-L). "Report to the Communist Collective of the Chicano Nation on the Chicano National—Colonial Question." *Proletariat* 4 (Spring 1974).

Communist Labor Party. "Analysis of the National Question in the Negro Nation." *Proletariat* 1 (Fall 1975): 36–37.

Communist League. *Regional Autonomy for the Indian Peoples!* San Francisco: Proletarian Publishers, n.d.

Connell, R. W. *Masculinities.* Berkeley: University of California Press, 1995.

Connerly, Ward. *Creating Equal: My Fight against Race Preferences.* San Francisco: Encounter Books, 2000.

Cornelius, Wayne. "Ambivalent Reception." In *Latinos: Remaking America,* edited by Marcelo Suárez-Orozco and Mariela Páez, 165–89. Berkeley: University of California Press, 2002.

Cox, Donald. "The Split in the Party." *New Political Science* 21 (1999): 171–76.

Crawford, Vicki, Jacqueline A. Rouse, and Barbara Woods, eds. *Women in the Civil Rights Movement: Trailblazers and Torchbearers, 1941–1965.* New York: Carlson Publishing, 1990.

Crenshaw, Kimberlé. "Whose Story Is It Anyway?" In *Race-ing Justice, Engendering Power: Essays on Anita Hill, Clarence Thomas, and the Construction of Social Reality,* edited by Toni Morrison, 402–40. New York: Pantheon Books, 1992.

Crigler, William. "The Employment Status of Blacks in Los Angeles: Ten Years after the Kerner Commission Report." PhD diss., Claremont Graduate School, 1979.

Cruse, Harold. *The Crisis of the Negro Intellectual.* New York: Quill, 1984.

"Cultures of the US Left." Special issue, *Monthly Review* 54 (July–August 2002).

Daniel, Cletus. *Bitter Harvest: A History of California Farmworkers, 1870–1941.* Berkeley: University of California Press, 1981.

Daniels, Roger. *The Decision to Relocate the Japanese Americans.* Philadelphia: J. B. Lippincott, 1975.

———. *The Politics of Prejudice: The Anti-Japanese Movement in California and the Struggle for Japanese Exclusion.* Berkeley: University of California Press, 1977.

Daniels, Roger, Sandra Taylor, and Harry Kitano. *Japanese Americans: From Relocation to Redress.* Seattle: University of Washington Press, 1991.

Davenport, Christian. "Reading the 'Voice of the Vanguard.'" In *The Black Panther Party Reconsidered,* edited by Charles Jones, 193–209. Baltimore: Black Classic Press, 1998.

Davis, Angela. "Afro Images: Politics, Fashion and Nostalgia." In *Soul: Black*

Power, Politics, and Pleasure, edited by Monique Guillory and Richard Green, 23–31. New York: New York University Press, 1998.

———. *Angela Davis: An Autobiography.* New York: Random House, 1974.

———. "Reflections on the Black Woman's Role in the Community of Slaves." In *The Angela Y. Davis Reader,* edited by Joy James, 111–28. Oxford: Blackwell, 1998.

———. *Women, Race and Class.* New York: Random House, 1983.

Davis, Mike. *City of Quartz: Excavating the Future in Los Angeles.* New York: Verso, 1990.

———. "Runaway Train Crashes Buses." *Nation,* September 18, 2001, B1, B11.

———. "The Social Origins of the Referendum." *NACLA Report on the Americas* 29 (November/December 1995): 24–28.

De Genova, Nicholas, and Ana Ramos-Zayas. *Latino Crossings: Mexicans, Puerto Ricans, and the Politics of Race and Citizenship.* New York: Routledge, 2003.

De Graaf, Lawrence. "African American Suburbanization in California, 1960 through 1990." In *Seeking El Dorado: African Americans in California,* edited by Lawrence De Graaf, Kevin Mulroy, and Quintard Taylor, 405–49. Los Angeles: Autry Museum of Western Heritage, 2001.

———. "The City of Black Angels: Emergence of the Los Angeles Ghetto, 1890–1930." *Pacific Historical Review* 39 (1970): 323–52.

De Graaf, Lawrence, Kevin Mulroy, and Quintard Taylor, eds. *Seeking El Dorado: African Americans in California.* Los Angeles: Autry Museum of Western Heritage, 2001.

De León, Arnoldo. *They Called Them Greasers: Anglo Attitudes toward Mexicans in Texas, 1821–1900.* Austin: University of Texas Press, 1983.

Dear, Michael, Eric Schockman, and Greg Hise, eds. *Rethinking Los Angeles.* Thousand Oaks, CA: Sage Publications, 1996.

Del Castillo, Adelaida. "Mexican Women in Organization." In *Mexican Women in the United States: Struggles Past and Present,* edited by Magdalena Mora and Adelaida del Castillo, 7–16. Los Angeles: Chicano Studies Research Center Publications, University of California, Los Angeles, 1980.

———. "Sterilization: An Overview." In *Mexican Women in the United States: Struggles Past and Present,* edited by Magdalena Mora and Adelaida del Castillo, 65–70. Los Angeles: Chicano Studies Research Center Publications, University of California, Los Angeles, 1980.

DeLeon, Richard. *Left Coast City: Progressive Politics in San Francisco, 1975– 1991.* Lawrence: University of Kansas Press, 1992.

DeMarco, Gordon. *A Short History of Los Angeles.* San Francisco: Lexikos, 1988.

Dinh, Nguyen Thi. "Letter from Nguyen Thi Dinh: October 31, 1970." In *To Die for the People: The Writings of Huey P. Newton,* edited by Toni Morrison, 182–85. New York: Writers and Readers Publishing, 1995.

Domanick, Joe. *To Protect and Serve.* New York: Pocket Books, 1994.

Donner, Frank. *Protectors of Privilege: Red Squads and Police Repression in Urban America*. Berkeley: University of California Press, 1990.

Doss, Erika. "Revolutionary Art Is a Tool for Liberation." *New Political Science* 21 (1999): 245–59.

Doti, L., and L. Schweikart. "Financing the Postwar Housing Boom in Phoenix and Los Angeles, 1945–1960." *Pacific Historical Review* 58 (1989): 173–91.

D'Souza, Dinesh. *What's So Great about America*. New York: Penguin Books, 2000.

Dudziak, Mary. *Cold War Civil Rights: Race and the Image of American Democracy*. Princeton, NJ: Princeton University Press, 2000.

Dunbar-Ortiz, Roxanne. *Outlaw Woman: A Memoir of the War Years*. San Francisco: City Lights, 2001.

Durant, Thomas. "Race and Class Consciousness among Lower and Middle-Class Blacks." *Journal of Black Studies* 27 (1997): 334–51.

Durazo, María Elena. "María Elena Durazo." In *Voices from the Front Lines: Organizing Immigrant Workers in Los Angeles*, edited by Ruth Milkman and Kent Wong, 11–22. Los Angeles: Center for Labor Research and Education, 2000.

Dymski, Gary. "Is Discrimination Disappearing? Residential Credit Market Evidence, 1992–1998." *International Journal of Social Economics* 28 (2001): 1025–45.

Eagley, Alice, and Mary Johannesen-Schmidt. "The Leadership Styles of Men and Women." *Journal of Social Issues* 57 (2001): 781–97.

Editorial Staff of *Asian American Political Alliance*. "Asian Studies: The Concept of Asian Studies." *Asian American Political Alliance* 1 (October 1969).

Elbaum, Max. *Revolution in the Air: Sixties Radicals Turn to Lenin, Mao and Che*. New York: Verso, 2002.

Elden, James, and David Schweitzer. "New Third Party Radicalism: The Case of the California Peace and Freedom Party." *Western Political Quarterly* 24 (December 1971): 761–74.

Enloe, Cynthia. *Bananas, Beaches and Bases: Making Feminist Sense of International Politics*. Berkeley: University of California Press, 1989.

Escobar, Edward. "The Dialectics of Repression." *Journal of American History* 79 (1993): 1483–1514.

———. *Race, Police and the Making of a Political Identity: Mexican Americans and the Los Angeles Police Department, 1900–1945*. Berkeley: University of California Press, 1999.

Espinoza, Dionne. "Pedagogies of Nationalism and Gender: Cultural Resistance in Selected Representational Practice of Chicana/o Movement Activists, 1967–1972." PhD diss., Cornell University, 1996.

———. "Revolutionary Sisters." *Aztlán* 26 (Spring 2001): 17–58.

Espiritu, Yen Le. *Asian American Panethnicity: Bridging Institutions and Identities*. Philadelphia: Temple University Press, 1992.

———. *Home Bound: Filipino Lives across Cultures, Communities, and Countries*. Berkeley: University of California Press, 2003.

Espiritu, Yen Le, and Paul Ong. "Class Constraints on Racial Solidarity among Asian Americans." In *The New Asian Immigration in Los Angeles and Global Restructuring*, edited by Paul Ong, Edna Bonacich, and Lucie Cheng, 295–321. Philadelphia: Temple University Press, 1994.

Ethington, Philip. "Segregated Diversity: Race-Ethnicity, Space, and Political Fragmentation in Los Angeles County, 1940–1994." Unpublished manuscript, final report to the John Randolph Haynes and Dora Haynes Foundation, University of Southern California, Los Angeles.

Fanon, Franz. *The Wretched of the Earth.* New York: Grove Press, 1963.

Feagin, Joe, and Melvin Sikes. *Living with Racism: The Black Middle-Class Experience.* New York: Beacon Press, 1994.

Featherstone, Liza. *Students against Sweatshops.* New York: Verso, 2002.

Ferreira, Jason. "All Power to the People: A Comparative History of Third World Radicalism in San Francisco, 1968–1974." PhD diss., University of California, Berkeley, 2003.

Fields, A. Belden. *Trotskyism and Maoism: Theory and Practice in France and the United States.* Brooklyn, NY: Autonomedia, 1989.

Fields, Rona. "The Brown Berets: A Participant Observation Study of Social Action in the Schools of Los Angeles." PhD diss., University of Southern California, 1970.

Fishman, Robert. *Bourgeois Utopias: The Rise and Fall of Suburbia.* New York: Basic Books, 1987.

Flacks, Richard. "Who Protests: The Social Bases of the Student Movement." In *Protest! Student Activism in America*, edited by J. Foster and D. Long, 134–57. New York: William Morrow, 1970.

———. *Youth and Social Change.* Chicago: Markham, 1971.

Fletcher, Jim, Tanaquil Jones, and Sylvere Lotringer. *Still Black, Still Strong: Survivors of the War against Black Revolutionaries.* New York: Semiotext(e), 1993.

Fogelson, Robert. *The Fragmented Metropolis: Los Angeles, 1850–1930.* Berkeley: University of California Press, 1993.

———. *The Los Angeles Riots.* Salem, NH: Ayer, 1988.

Foley, Neil. "Becoming Hispanic: Mexican Americans and Whiteness." In *White Privilege: Essential Readings on the Other Side of Racism*, edited by Paula Rothenberg, 49–59. New York: Worth, 2002.

———. "Partly Colored or Other White." Paper presented at the Labor and Working Class Historical Association Luncheon of the Organization of American Historians, St. Louis, April 1, 2000. www.lawcha.org/resources/talks/beyondbw.html (accessed April 30, 2002).

———. *The White Scourge: Mexicans, Blacks, and Poor Whites in Texas Cotton Culture.* Berkeley: University of California Press, 1997.

Foner, Eric, ed. *The Black Panthers Speak.* New York: Da Capo Press, 1995.

Fong, Colleen, and Judy Yung. "In Search of the Right Spouse." *Amerasia* 21 (1995/1996): 77–98.

Forman, James. *The Making of Black Revolutionaries*. Seattle: University of Washington Press, 1997.

Frankenberg, Ruth. *White Women, Race Matters: The Social Construction of Whiteness*. Minneapolis: University of Minnesota Press, 1993.

Fredrickson, George. *White Supremacy: A Comparative Study in American and South African History*. New York: Oxford University Press, 1981.

Freer, Regina. "Black Korean Conflict." In *The Los Angeles Riots: Lessons for the Urban Future*, edited by Mark Baldassare, 175–203. Boulder, CO: Westview Press, 1994.

———. "L.A. Race Woman: Charlotta Bass and the Complexities of Black Political Development in Los Angeles." *American Quarterly* 56 (2004): 607–32.

Freire, Paulo. *The Pedagogy of the Oppressed*. New York: Continuum, 1981.

Fujino, Diane. "Japanese American Radicalism and Radical Formation." Paper presented at the National Association of Asian American Studies Conference. San Francisco, May 2003.

———. "To Serve the Movement." In *Legacy to Liberation: Politics and Culture of Revolutionary Asian/Pacific America*, edited by Fred Ho with Carolyn Antonio, Diane Fujino, and Steve Yip, 257–66. San Francisco: Big Red Media and AK Press, 2000.

García, Alma. *Chicana Feminist Thought: The Basic Historical Writings*. New York: Routledge, 1997.

García, Arnoldo. "Toward a Left without Borders." *Monthly Review* 54 (2002): 69–78.

García, Ignacio. *Chicanismo: The Forging of a Militant Ethos among Mexican Americans*. Tucson: University of Arizona Press, 1997.

García, John. "The Chicano Movement: Its Legacy for Politics and Policy." In *Chicanas/Chicanos at the Crossroads: Social, Economic, and Political Change*, edited by David Maciel and Isidro Ortiz, 83–107. Tucson: University of Arizona Press, 1996.

García, Mario. "Americans All: The Mexican American Generation and the Politics of Wartime Los Angeles, 1941–45." In *The Mexican American Experience: An Interdisciplinary Anthology*, edited by Rodolfo de la Garza, Frank Bean, Charles Bonjean, Ricardo Romo, and Rodolfo Alvarez, 201–12. Austin: University of Texas Press, 1985.

———. *Memories of Chicano History: The Life and Narrative of Bert Corona*. Berkeley: University of California Press, 1994.

———. *United We Win: The Rise and Fall of the La Raza Unida*. Tucson: Mexican American Studies Research Center, University of Arizona, 1989.

García, Matt. *A World of Its Own: Race, Labor, and Citrus in the Making of Greater Los Angeles, 1900–1970*. Chapel Hill: University of North Carolina Press, 2001.

Gardener, R. *Grito! Reies Tijerina and the New Mexico Land Grant War of 1967*. Indianapolis: Bobbs-Merrill, 1970.

Gardetta, Dave. "True Grit: Clocking Time with the Janitors' Organizer Rocio Saenz." *L.A. Weekly* 15 (1993): 16–24, 26.

Gaventa, John. *Power and Powerlessness: Quiescence and Rebellion in an Appalachian Valley.* Urbana: University of Illinois Press, 1980.

Gee, Emma, ed. *Counterpoint: Perspectives on Asian America.* Los Angeles: Asian American Studies Center, University of California, Los Angeles, 1976.

Georgakas, Dan, and Marvin Surkin. *Detroit: I Do Mind Dying.* Boston: South End Press, 1998.

Geschwender, James, ed. *The Black Revolt: The Civil Rights Movement, Ghetto Uprisings, and Separatism.* Englewood Cliffs, NJ: Prentice Hall, 1971.

Giddings, Paula. *When and Where I Enter: The Impact of Black Women on Race and Sex in America.* New York: Quill William Morrow, 1984.

Gilmore, Ruth Wilson. "Fatal Couplings: Racism and Geography." *Professional Geographer* 54 (2002): 15–24.

———. *Golden Gulag: Labor, Land, State, and Opposition in Globalizing California.* Berkeley: University of California Press, forthcoming.

———. "You Have Dislodged a Boulder: Mothers and Prisoners in the Post-Keynsian California Landscape." *Transforming Anthropology* 8 (1 & 2): 12–38.

Girdner, Audrie, and Anne Loftis. *The Great Betrayal: The Evacuation of the Japanese-Americans during World War II.* New York: Macmillan, 1970.

Gitlin, Todd. *The Sixties: Years of Hope, Days of Rage.* New York: Bantam Books, 1987.

Glenn, Evelyn Nakano. "From Servitude to Service Work: Historical Continuities in the Racial Division of Paid Reproductive Labor." *Signs* 18 (Autumn 1992): 1–43.

———. *Unequal Freedom: How Race and Gender Shaped American Citizenship and Labor.* Cambridge, MA: Harvard University Press, 2002.

Goldberg, David. *Racist Culture: Philosophy and the Politics of Meaning.* Oxford: Blackwell, 1993.

Golden, Thelma. *Black Male: Representations of Masculinity in Contemporary American Art.* New York: Whitney Museum of American Art, 1994.

Goldfield, Michael. *The Color of Politics: Race and the Mainsprings of American Politics.* New York: New Press, 1997.

Gómez, Christina. "The Continual Significance of Skin Color." *Hispanic Journal of Behavioral Sciences* 22 (2000): 94–103.

Gómez-Quiñones, Juan. *Chicano Politics: Reality and Promise, 1940–1990.* Albuquerque: University of New Mexico Press, 1990.

———. *Mexican Students por la Raza: The Chicano Student Movement in Southern California, 1967–1977.* Santa Barbara, CA: Editorial La Causa, 1978.

Gonzalez, Ray, ed. *Muy Macho: Latino Men Confront Their Manhood.* New York: Anchor Books, 1996.

Gooding-Williams, Robert. *Reading Rodney King, Reading Urban Uprising.* New York: Routledge, 1993.

Gordon, Linda. *The Great Arizona Orphan Abduction.* Cambridge, MA: Harvard University Press, 2001.

Gottlieb, Robert, Mark Vallianatos, Regina M. Freer, and Peter Dreier. *The Next Los Angeles: The Struggle for a Livable City.* Berkeley: University of California Press, 2005.

Gramsci, Antonio. *Selections from the Prison Notebooks of Antonio Gramsci.* Edited and translated by Quintin Hoare and Geoffrey Smith. New York: International Publishers, 1987.

Grebler, Leo, Joan Moore, and Ralph Guzman. *The Mexican-American People, the Nation's Second Largest Minority.* New York: Free Press, 1970.

Guerra, Fernando. "Ethnic Politics in Los Angeles: The Emergence of Black, Jewish, Latino and Asian Office Holders." PhD diss., University of Michigan, 1990.

Guhathakurta, S., and M. Wichert. "Who Pays for Growth in the City of Phoenix." *Urban Affairs Review* 33 (1998): 813–38.

Guillow, Lawrence. "The Origins of Race Relations in Los Angeles, 1820–1880." PhD diss., Arizona State University, 1996.

Gutiérrez, David. "CASA in the Chicano Movement: Ideology and Organizational Politics in the Chicano Community, 1968–78." Working Paper 5, Stanford Center for Chicano Research, Stanford University, Palo Alto, CA, 1984.

———. *Walls and Mirrors: Mexican Americans, Mexican Immigrants and the Politics of Ethnicity.* Berkeley: University of California Press, 1995.

Gutiérrez, Jose Angel. *The Making of a Chicano Militant: Lessons from Cristal.* Madison: University of Wisconsin Press, 1999.

Gutiérrez, Ramon. "Community, Patriarchy and Individualism: The Politics of Chicano History and the Dream of Equality." *American Quarterly* 45 (1993): 44–72.

Hakman, Nathan. "Old and New Left Activity in the Legal Order: An Interpretation." *Journal of Social Issues* 27 (1971): 105–21.

Haley, Alex. *The Autobiography of Malcolm X.* 1964. Reprint, New York: Ballantine Books, 1992.

Halisi, Clyde, and James Mtume. *The Quotable Karenga.* Los Angeles: US Organization, 1967.

Hall, Stuart. "Gramsci's Relevance for the Study of Race and Ethnicity." In *Stuart Hall: Critical Dialogues in Cultural Studies,* edited by David Morley and Kuan-Hsing Chen, 411–40. New York: Routledge, 1996.

———, ed. *Policing the Crisis: Mugging, the State, and Law and Order.* New York: Holmes and Meier, 1978.

———. "The Politics of Mugging." In *Policing the Crisis: Mugging, the State, and Law and Order,* edited by Stuart Hall, 327–97. New York: Holmes and Meier, 1978.

Hamilton, Cynthia. *Apartheid in America.* Los Angeles: Labor/Community Strategy Center, 1987.

———. "Women in Politics." *Women's Studies International Forum* 12 (1989): 129–35.

Hamilton, Nora, and Norma Stoltz Chinchilla. *Seeking Community in a Global*

City: Guatemalans and Salvadorans in Los Angeles. Philadelphia: Temple University Press, 2001.

Harden, Jacalyn. *Double Cross: Japanese Americans in Black and White Chicago.* Minneapolis: University of Minnesota Press, 2003.

Harris, Cheryl. "Whiteness as Property." *Harvard Law Review* 106 (1993): 1709–91.

Harrison, Linda. "On Cultural Nationalism." In *The Black Panthers Speak,* edited by Eric Foner, 151. New York: Da Capo Press, 1995.

Hata, D. T., Jr., and N. I. Hata. "Asian-Pacific Angelinos: Model Minorities and Indispensable Scapegoats." In *20th Century Los Angeles: Power, Promotion, and Social Conflict,* edited by Norman Klein and Martin Schiesl, 61–99. Claremont, CA: Regina Books, 1990.

Hayden, Tom. *Reunion: Memoir.* New York: Collier Books, 1988.

Haywood, Harry. *Black Bolshevik: Autobiography of an Afro-American Communist.* Chicago: Liberator Press, 1978.

———. *Negro Liberation.* New York: International Publishers, 1948.

Healey, Dorothy Ray, and Maurice Isserman. *California Red: A Life in the Communist Party.* Urbana: University of Illinois Press, 1993.

Henderson, Errol. "Black Nationalism and Rap Music." *Journal of Black Studies* 26 (January 1996): 308–39.

Henry, Sheila. *Cultural Persistence and Socio Economic Mobility: A Comparative Study of Assimilation among Armenians and Japanese in Los Angeles.* San Francisco: R & E Research Associates, 1978.

Herod, Andy. "The Production of Scale in United States Labour Relations." *Area* 23 (1991): 114–20.

Hing, Bill Ong. *Making and Remaking Asian America through Immigration Policy, 1850–1990.* Stanford, CA: Stanford University Press, 1993.

Hise, Greg. "Constructing Nature's Workshop: Industrial Districts and Urban Expansion in Southern California, 1910–1950." *Journal of Historical Geography* 27 (2001): 74–92.

———. "Home Building and Industrial Decentralization in Los Angeles: The Roots of the Postwar Urban Region." *Journal of Urban History* 19 (1993): 95–125.

———. *Magnetic Los Angeles: Planning the Twentieth-Century Metropolis.* Baltimore: Johns Hopkins University Press, 1997.

Ho, Fred. "Fists for Revolution." In *Legacy to Liberation: Politics and Culture of Revolutionary Asian/Pacific America,* edited by Fred Ho, Carolyn Antonio, Diane Fujino, and Steve Yip, 3–13. San Francisco: Big Red Media and AK Press, 2000.

———. "Moritsugu 'Mo' Nishida." In *Legacy to Liberation: Politics and Culture of Revolutionary Asian/Pacific America,* edited by Fred Ho, Carolyn Antonio, Diane Fujino, and Steve Yip, 297–317. San Francisco: Big Red Media and AK Press, 2000.

Ho, Fred, Carolyn Antonio, Diane Fujino, and Steve Yip, eds. *Legacy to Libera-*

tion: Politics and Culture of Revolutionary Asian/Pacific America. San Francisco: Big Red Media and AK Press, 2000.

Ho, Fred, and Steve Yip. "Alex Hing." In *Legacy to Liberation: Politics and Culture of Revolutionary Asian/Pacific America*, edited by Fred Ho, Carolyn Antonio, Diane Fujino, and Steve Yip, 279–96. San Francisco: Big Red Media and AK Press, 2000.

Hobsbawm, Eric. *Bandits*. New York: Pantheon Books, 1981.

Holloway, Steve. "Exploring the Neighborhood Contingency of Race Discrimination in Mortgage Lending in Columbus, Ohio." *Annals of the Association of American Geographers* 88 (1998): 252–76.

Hondagneu-Sotelo, Pierrette. *Doméstica: Immigrant Workers Cleaning and Caring in the Shadows of Affluence*. Berkeley: University of California Press, 2001.

hooks, bell. *Ain't I A Woman? Black Women and Feminism*. Boston: South End Press, 1981.

Horne, Gerald. *Black Liberation/Red Scare: Ben Davis and the Communist Party*. University of Delaware Press, 1994.

———. *Fire This Time: The Watts Uprising and the 1960s*. Charlottesville: University Press of Virginia, 1995.

Horowitz, David. *Radical Son: A Journey through Our Times*. New York: Free Press, 1997.

Hosokawa, Bill. *JACL in Quest of Justice*. New York: William Morrow, 1982.

Houston, Donna, and Laura Pulido. "The Work of Performativity: Staging Social Justice at the University of Southern California." *Environment and Planning D* 20 (2002): 401–24.

Hsiao, Lisa. "Project 100,000." *Vietnam Generation* 2 (Spring 1989): 14–37.

Hunter, Andrea, and James Dixon. "Hidden Voices of Black Men." *Journal of Black Studies* 25 (September 1994): 20–40.

Hurtado, Aída. *The Color of Privilege: Three Blasphemies on Race and Feminism*. Ann Arbor: University of Michigan Press, 1996.

———. "The Politics of Sexuality in the Gender Subordination of Chicanas." In *Living Chicana Theory*, edited by Carla Trujillo, 383–428. Berkeley, CA: Third Woman Press, 1998.

Hutchinson, Earl Ofari. *Blacks and Reds: Race and Class in Conflict, 1919–1990*. East Lansing: Michigan State University Press, 1995.

Hutchinson, Janis Faye, Nestor Rodriguez, and Jacqueline Hagan. "Community Life: African Americans in Multiethnic Residential Areas." *Journal of Black Studies* 27 (1996): 201–23.

Ichioka, Yuji. "A Buried Past: Early Issei Socialists and the Japanese Community." *Amerasia* 1 (1971): 1–25.

———. *The Issei: The World of the First Generation Japanese Immigrants, 1885–1924*. New York: Free Press, 1988.

Ignatiev, Noel. *How the Irish Became White*. New York: Routledge, 1995.

Institute of Industrial Relations, University of California, Los Angeles. *Hard*

Core Unemployment and Poverty in Los Angeles. Washington, DC: U.S. Department of Commerce, Area Redevelopment Administration, 1965.

Iwataki, Miya. "The Asian Women's Movement: A Retrospective." *East Wind* 2 (Spring/Summer 1983): 35–41.

Jackson, George. *Blood in My Eye.* Baltimore: Black Classic Press, 1990.

Jackson, George, Jonathon Jackson, and Jean Genet. *Soledad Brother: The Prison Letters of George Jackson.* New York: Lawrence Hill, 1994.

Jackson, Kenneth. "Race, Ethnicity, and Real Estate Appraisal." *Journal of Urban History* 4 (1980): 419–52.

Jacobs, Harold, ed. *Weatherman.* Palo Alto, CA: Ramparts Press, 1970.

Jacobs, Paul, and Saul Landau. *The New Radicals: A Report with Documents.* New York: Vintage Books, 1966.

Jacobson, Matthew. *Whiteness of a Different Color: European Immigrants and the Alchemy of Race.* Cambridge, MA: Harvard University Press, 1998.

Jaga, geronimo ji. "Every Nation Struggling to Be Free Has a Right to Struggle." *New Political Science* 21 (June 1999): 237–44.

Jasper, James. *The Art of Moral Protest: Culture, Biography, and Creativity in Social Movements.* Chicago: University of Chicago Press, 1997.

Jenkins, Craig. *The Politics of Insurgency: The Farm Worker Movement in the 1960s.* New York: Columbia University Press, 1985.

Jennings, Regina. "Poetry of the Black Panther Party." *Journal of Black Studies* 29 (September 1998): 106–29.

———. "Why I Joined the Party." In *The Black Panther Party Reconsidered,* edited by Charles Jones, 257–65. Baltimore: Black Classic Press, 1998.

Johnson, Gaye. "A Sifting of Centuries: Afro-Chicano Interaction and Popular Musical Culture in California, 1960–2000." In *Decolonial Voices: Chicana and Chicano Cultural Studies in the 21st Century,* edited by A. Aldama and Naomi Quiñones, 316–29. Bloomington: University of Indiana Press, 2002.

Johnson, Kevin. *How Did You Get to Be Mexican? A White/Brown Man's Search for Identity.* Philadelphia: Temple University Press, 1999.

Johnson, Ollie III. "Explaining the Demise of the Black Panther Party: The Role of Internal Factors." In *The Black Panther Party Reconsidered,* edited by Charles Jones, 391–414. Baltimore: Black Classic Press, 1998.

Johnson, Troy, Joane Nagel, and Duane Champagne. *American Indian Activism: Alcatraz to the Longest Walk.* Urbana: University of Illinois Press, 1997.

Jones, Charles, ed. *The Black Panther Party Reconsidered.* Baltimore: Black Classic Press, 1998.

———. "Talkin' the Talk and Walkin' the Walk: An Interview with Panther Jimmy Slater." In *The Black Panther Party Reconsidered,* edited by Charles Jones, 147–53. Baltimore: Black Classic Press, 1998.

Jones, Jacqueline. *American Work: Four Centuries of Black and White Labor.* New York: Norton, 1998.

Katsiaficas, George. *The Imagination of the New Left: A Global Analysis of 1968.* Boston: South End Press, 1987.

———. "Organization and Movement: The Case of the Black Panther Party and the Revolutionary People's Constitutional Convention of 1970." In *Liberation, Imagination and the Black Panther Party: A New Look at the Panthers and Their Legacy*, edited by Kathleen Cleaver and George Katsiaficas, 141–55. New York: Routledge, 2001.

Kelley, Robin. *Freedom Dreams: The Black Radical Imagination*. Boston: Beacon Press, 2002.

———. *Hammer and Hoe: Alabama Communists during the Great Depression*. Chapel Hill: University of North Carolina Press, 1990.

Kellogg, Charles Flint. *NAACP: A History of the National Association for the Advancement of Colored People*. Baltimore: Johns Hopkins University Press, 1967.

Keniston, Kenneth. *Young Radicals: Notes on Committed Youth*. New York: Harcourt, Brace and World, 1968.

Kim, Claire Jean. *Bitter Fruit: The Politics of Black-Korean Conflict in New York City*. New Haven, CT: Yale University Press, 2000.

———. "The Racial Triangulation of Asian Americans." *Politics and Society* 27 (1999): 105–38.

Kim, Elaine. *Dangerous Women: Gender and Korean Nationalism*. New York: Routledge, 1997.

King, Anthony. "Understanding Violence among Young African American Males." *Journal of Black Studies* 28 (September 1997): 79–96.

Kirschenman, J., and K. Neckerman. "We'd Love to Hire Them, but . . . : The Meaning of Race for Employers." In *The Urban Underclass*, edited by Christopher Jencks and P. Peterson, 203–32. Washington, DC: Brookings Institution, 1991.

Kitano, Harry, and Roger Daniels. *Asian Americans: Emerging Minorities*. Englewood Cliffs, NJ: Prentice Hall, 1988.

Klatch, Rebecca. "The Counterculture, the New Left, and the New Right." In *Cultural Politics and Social Movements*, edited by Marcy Darnovsky, Barbara Epstein, and Richard Flacks, 74–89. Philadelphia: Temple University Press, 1995.

Klein, Norman, and Martin Schiesl, eds. *20th Century Los Angeles: Power, Promotion, and Social Conflict*. Claremont, CA: Regina Books, 1990.

Kling, Rob, Spencer Olin, and Mark Poster. "The Emergence of Postsuburbia: An Introduction." In *Postsuburban California: The Transformation of Orange County since World War II*, edited by Rob Kling, Spencer Olin, and Mark Poster, 1–30. Berkeley: University of California Press, 1995.

———, eds. *Postsuburban California: The Transformation of Orange County since World War II*. Berkeley: University of California Press, 1995.

Koch, Nadine, and Eric Schockman. "Riot, Rebellion or Civil Unrest?" In *Community in Crisis: The Korean American Community after the Los Angeles Civil Unrest of April 1992*, edited by George O. Totten II and Eric Schockman, 47–93. Los Angeles: Center for Multiethnic and Transnational Studies, University of Southern California, 1994.

Kochiyama, Yuri. "The Impact of Malcolm X on Asian American Politics and

Activism." In *Blacks, Latinos, and Asians in Urban America: Status and Prospects for Politics and Activism,* edited by James Jennings, 129–41. Westport, CT: Praeger, 1994.

Koshy, Susan. "Morphing Race into Ethnicity." *Boundary* 28 (2001): 153–94.

Krysan, Maria. "Whites Who Say They'd Flee: Who Are They, Why Would They Leave?" *Demography* 39 (2002): 675–96.

Kurashige, Lon. *Japanese American Celebration and Conflict: A History of Ethnic Identity and Festival, 1934–1990.* Berkeley: University of California Press, 2002.

Kurashige, Scott. "Beyond Random Acts of Hatred: Analysing Urban Patterns of Anti-Asian Violence." *Amerasia* 26 (2000): 209–31.

———. "Transforming Los Angeles: Black and Japanese American Struggles for Racial Equality in the 20th Century." PhD diss., University of California, Los Angeles, 2000.

Kushner, Sam. *Long Road to Delano.* New York: International Publisher, 1975.

La Prensa. "A Poignant Defense of the Whiteness of Mexicans." In *Testimonio: A Documentary History of the Mexican American Struggle for Civil Rights,* edited by Arturo F. Rosales, 173. Houston, TX: Arte Publico Press, 2000.

Lai, Mark. "A Historical Survey of the Chinese Left in America." In *Counterpoint: Perspectives on Asian America,* edited by Emma Gee, 63–80. Los Angeles: Asian American Studies Center, University of California, Los Angeles, 1976.

Larson, Nella. *Passing.* New York: Arno Press, 1969.

Laslett, John. "Historical Perspectives: Immigration and the Rise of a Distinctive Urban Region, 1900–1970." In *Ethnic Los Angeles,* edited by Roger Waldinger and Mehdi Bozorgmehr, 39–75. New York: Russell Sage Foundation, 1996.

Law, Robin, Jennifer Wolch, and Lois Takahashi. "Defenseless Territory: Workers, Communities, and the Decline of Military Production in Los Angeles." *Environment and Planning C: Government and Policy* 11 (1993): 291–315.

League of Revolutionary Struggle. *Peace, Justice, Equality and Socialism.* Oakland, CA: Getting Together Publications, 1986.

———. *Statements on the Founding of the League of Revolutionary Struggle.* Oakland, CA: Getting Together Publications, 1978.

LeBlanc-Ernest, Angela. "The Most Qualified Person to Handle the Job: Black Panther Party Women, 1966–1982." In *The Black Panther Party Reconsidered,* edited by Charles Jones, 305–34. Baltimore: Black Classic Press, 1998.

Lee, Chana Kai. *For Freedom's Sake: The Life of Fannie Lou Hamer.* Urbana: University of Illinois Press, 1999.

Lee, Jim. *Urban Triage: Racial Anxiety and Crisis in Contemporary U.S. Fiction.* Minneapolis: University of Minnesota Press, 2004.

Lee, Robert. "The Hidden World of Asian Immigrant Radicalism." In *The Immigrant Left in the United States,* edited by Paul Buhle and Dan Georgakas, 256–88. Albany: State University of New York Press, 1996.

Lee, Yueh-Ting, Victor Ottati, and Imtiaz Hussain. "Attitudes toward 'Illegal'

Immigration into the United States: California Proposition 187." *Hispanic Journal of Behavioral Sciences* 23 (2001): 430–43.

Leonard, Kevin Allen. "In the Interest of All Races: African Americans and Interracial Cooperation in Los Angeles during and after World War II." In *Seeking El Dorado: African Americans in California,* edited by Lawrence De Graaf, Kevin Mulroy, and Quintard Taylor, 309–40. Los Angeles: Autry Museum of Western Heritage, 2001.

———. "Years of Hope, Days of Fear: The Impact of World War II on Race Relations in Los Angeles." PhD diss., University of California, Davis, 1992.

Leong, Karen. "A Distinct and Antagonistic Race: Constructions of Chinese Manhood in the Exclusionist Debates, 1869–1878." In *Across the Great Divide: Cultures of Manhood in the American West,* edited by Matthew Basso, Laura McCall, and Dee Garceau, 131–48. New York: Routledge, 2001.

Levy, Jacques. *Cesar Chavez: Autobiography of La Causa.* New York: Norton, 1975.

Lew-Lee, Lee. *All Power to the People: The Black Panther Party and Beyond.* Video. Los Angeles: Electronic News Group, 1996.

Li, Wei. "Anatomy of a New Ethnic Settlement: The Chinese Ethnoburb in Los Angeles." *Urban Studies* 35 (1998): 479–501.

Light, Ivan, and Elizabeth Roach. "Self-Employment: Mobility Ladder or Economic Lifeboat?" In *Ethnic Los Angeles,* edited by Roger Waldinger and Mehdi Bozorgmehr, 193–213. New York: Russell Sage Foundation, 1996.

Ling, Susie. "The Mountain Movers." *Amerasia* 15 (1989): 51–67.

Lipsitz, George. *A Life in the Struggle: Ivory Perry and the Culture of Opposition.* Philadelphia: Temple University Press, 1988.

———. *The Possessive Investment in Whiteness: How White People Profit from Identity Politics.* Philadelphia: Temple University Press, 1998.

———. "World Cities and World Beat: Low-Wage Labor and Transnational Culture." *Pacific Historical Review* 68 (1999): 213–31.

Lira, Luciana, Mary Koss, and Nancy Russo. "Mexican American Women's Definitions of Rape and Sexual Abuse." *Hispanic Journal of Behavioral Sciences* 21 (1999): 236–65.

Logan, John. "How Race Counts for Hispanic Americans." Working paper, Lewis Mumford Center, State University of New York, Albany, 2003.

Longeaux y Vasquez, Enriqueta. "The Women of La Raza." In *Chicana Feminist Thought: The Basic Historical Writings,* edited by Alma García, 29–31. New York: Routledge, 1997.

López, Ian F. Haney. *Racism on Trial: The Chicano Fight for Justice.* Cambridge, MA: Harvard University Press, 2003.

———. *White by Law: The Legal Construction of Race.* New York: New York University Press, 1996.

Lotchin, Roger. *Fortress California, 1910–1961: From Warfare to Welfare.* New York: Oxford University Press, 1992.

Louie, Miriam Ching Yoon. *Sweatshop Warriors: Immigrant Women Workers Take on the Global Factory.* Boston: South End Press, 2001.

———. "Yellow, Brown and Red: Towards an Appraisal of Marxist Influences on the Asian American Movement." Unpublished manuscript, Oakland, CA, 1991.

Louie, Steve, and Glenn Omatsu, eds. *Asian Americans: The Movement and the Moment*. Los Angeles: Asian American Studies Center, University of California, Los Angeles, 2001.

Lowe, Lisa. *Immigrant Acts: On Asian American Cultural Politics*. Durham, NC: Duke University Press, 1996.

Lu, Lynn. "Critical Visions: The Representation and Resistance of Asian Women." In *Dragon Ladies: Asian American Feminists Breathe Fire*, edited by Sonia Shah, 17–28. Boston: South End Press, 1997.

Lujan, Joaquin, and Richard Moore. "Antonio y Rito—Presente!" *Voces Unidas* 11 (Spring 2001): 5–21.

Maeda, Daryl. "Constructing Yellow Power: The Asian American Movement's Encounter with Black Power." Paper presented at the annual meetings of the American Studies Association, Seattle, WA, November 1980.

———. "Forging Asian American Identity: Race, Culture, and the Asian American Movement." PhD diss., University of Michigan, 2001.

Maki, Mitchell, Harry Kitano, Megan Berthold, and Roger Daniels. *Achieving the Impossible Dream: How Japanese Americans Obtained Redress*. Urbana: University of Illinois Press, 1999.

Malcolm's Mother [Anonymous]. "My Son Malcolm." *Amerasia* 15 (1989): 110–13.

Mann, Eric. *L.A.'s Lethal Air: New Strategies for Policy, Organizing, and Action*. Los Angeles: Labor/Community Strategy Center, 1991.

Mao Tse-tung. *Mao Zedong: An Anthology of His Writings*. Edited by A. Fremantle. New York: Mentor, 1962.

———. *On Guerilla Warfare*. 2nd ed. Translated by Samuel B. Griffith. Urbana: University of Illinois Press, 2000.

———. *Quotations from Chairman Mao Tse-tung; or, Little Red Book*. 1972. San Francisco: China Books and Periodicals, 1990.

Marable, Manning. *How Capitalism Underdeveloped Black America: Problems in Race, Political Economy, and Society*. Boston: South End Press, 1983.

Marchand, B. *The Emergence of Los Angeles: Population and Housing in the City of Dreams, 1940–70*. London: Routledge and Kegan Paul, 1986.

Marin, Marguerite. *Social Protest in an Urban Barrio: A Study of the Chicano Movement, 1966–1974*. New York: University Press of America, 1991.

Mariscal, Jorge, ed. *Aztlán and Viet Nam: Chicano and Chicana Experiences of the War*. Berkeley: University of California Press, 1999.

———. "Left Turns in the Chicano Movement, 1965–72." *Monthly Review* 54 (2002): 59–68.

Márquez, Benjamin. *LULAC: The Evolution of a Mexican American Political Organization*. Austin: University of Texas Press, 1993.

Marston, Sallie. "The Social Construction of Scale." *Progress in Human Geography* 24 (2000): 219–42.

Martin, Philip. "Proposition 187 in California." *International Migration Review* 29 (1995): 255–63.

Martínez, Elizabeth. "Chingón Politics Die Hard." In *De Colores Means All of Us: Latina Views for a Multi-colored Century,* edited by Elizabeth Martínez, 172–81. Cambridge, MA: South End Press, 1998.

———, ed. *De Colores Means All of Us: Latina Views for a Multi-colored Century.* Cambridge, MA: South End Press, 1998.

———. "Seeing More Than Black and White." In *De Colores Means All of Us: Latina Views for a Multi-colored Century,* edited by Elizabeth Martínez, 4–20. Cambridge, MA: South End Press, 1998.

———. "That Old White (Male) Magic." In *De Colores Means All of Us: Latina Views for a Multi-colored Century,* edited by Elizabeth Martínez, 21–30. Cambridge, MA: South End Press, 1998.

———. "A View from New Mexico." *Monthly Review* 54 (2002): 79–86.

Marx, Karl. *The Eighteenth Brumaire of Louis Bonaparte.* Moscow: Progress Publishers, 1972.

Massey, Doreen. *Space, Place and Gender.* Minneapolis: University of Minnesota Press, 1994.

Massey, Douglas, and Nancy Denton. *American Apartheid: Segregation and the Making of the Underclass.* Cambridge, MA: Harvard University Press, 1993.

Matsumoto, Valerie. "Japanese American Women and the Creation of Urban Nisei Culture in the 1930s." In *Over the Edge: Remapping the American West,* edited by V. Matsumoto and B. Allmendinger, 291–306. Berkeley: University of California Press, 1999.

Matthews, Tracye. "No One Ever Asks What a Man's Place in the Revolution Is: Gender and the Politics of the Black Panther Party 1966–1971." In *The Black Panther Party Reconsidered,* edited by Charles Jones, 267–304. Baltimore: Black Classic Press, 1998.

Matthiessen, Peter. *In the Spirit of Crazy Horse.* New York: Viking Press, 1991.

———. *Sal si Puedes: Cesar Chavez and the New American Revolution.* New York: Random House, 1969.

Mazón, Mauricio. *The Zoot-Suit Riots: The Psychology of Symbolic Annihilation.* Austin: University of Texas Press, 1984.

McAdam, Doug. *Political Process and the Development of Black Insurgency, 1930–1970.* Chicago: University of Chicago Press, 1982.

McCartney, John. *Black Power Ideologies: An Essay in African-American Political Thought.* Philadelphia: Temple University Press, 1992.

———. "The Influences of the Black Panther Party on the Vanguard Party of the Bahamas, 1972–1987." *New Political Science* 21 (1999): 205–15.

McGirr, Lisa. *Suburban Warriors: The Origins of the New American Right.* Princeton, NJ: Princeton University Press, 2001.

McWhorter, Diane. *Carry Me Home: Birmingham, Alabama.* New York: Simon and Schuster, 2001.

McWilliams, Carey. *Factories in the Field.* Boston: Little, Brown, 1939.

Menchaca, Martha. *Recovering History, Constructing Race: The Indian, Black, and White Roots of Mexican Americans*. Austin: University of Texas Press, 2001.

Menchú, Rigoberta. *I, Rigoberta Menchú: An Indian Woman in Guatemala*. Edited by Elisabeth Burgos-Debray. Translated by Ann Wright. New York: Verso, 1984.

Merrifield, Andy. "The Urbanization of Labor: Living Wage Activism in the American City." *Social Text* 18 (2000): 31–53.

Meyerson, Harold. "The Red Sea: How the Janitors Won Their Strike." *L.A. Weekly*, April 28- May 4, 2000, 17–20.

Meyerson, Martin, and Edward Banfield. *Politics and the Public Interest*. Glencoe, IL: Free Press, 1955.

Mies, Maria. *Patriarchy and Accumulation on a World Scale: Women in the International Division of Labour*. London: Zed Books, 1986.

Milkman, Ruth. *Organizing Immigrants: The Challenge for Unions in Contemporary California*. Ithaca, NY: Cornell University Press, 2000.

Milkman, Ruth, and Kent Wong, eds. *Voices from the Front Lines: Organizing Immigrant Workers in Los Angeles*. Los Angeles: Center for Labor Research and Education, University of California, Los Angeles, 2000.

Miller, G. *Cities by Contract: The Politics of Municipal Incorporation*. Cambridge, MA: MIT Press, 1981.

Miller, Jerome. *Search and Destroy: African-American Males in the Criminal Justice System*. New York: Cambridge University Press, 1996.

Min, Pyong Gap. *Caught in the Middle: Korean Merchants in America's Multiethnic Cities*. Berkeley: University of California Press, 1996.

Moddell, John. *The Economics of Racial Accommodation: Japanese Americans of Los Angeles, 1900–1942*. Urbana: University of Illinois Press, 1977.

Mohanty, Chandra T., Ann Russo, and Lourdes Torres, eds. *Third World Women and the Politics of Feminism*. Bloomington: Indiana University Press, 1991.

Monroy, Douglas. "Anarquismo y Comunismo: Mexican Radicalism and the Communist Party in Los Angeles during the 1930s." *Labor History* 24 (1983): 34–59.

———. *Rebirth: Mexican Los Angeles from the Great Migration to the Great Depression*. Berkeley: University of California Press, 1999.

Montejano, David. *Anglos and Mexicans in the Making of Texas, 1836–1986*. Austin: University of Texas Press, 1987.

Montgomery, Charles. "The Trap of Race and Memory." *American Quarterly* 52 (2000): 478– 513.

Moore, Joan, and Ralph Guzman. "New Wind from the Southwest." *Nation* 30 (1966): 645–48.

Moore, Paul, Patrice Wagonhurst, Jessica Goodheart, David Runsten, Ernrico Marcelli, Pascale Joassart-Marcelli, and John Medearis. *The Other Los Angeles: Working Poor in the City of the 21st Century*. Los Angeles: Los Angeles Alliance for a New Economy, 2000.

Moraga, Cherie. "La Güera." In *This Bridge Called My Back: Writings by Rad-

ical Women of Color, edited by Cherie Moraga and Gloria Anzaldúa, 27–34. Latham, NY: Kitchen Table, 1983.

Moraga, Cherie, and Gloria Anzaldúa, eds. *This Bridge Called My Back: Writings by Radical Women of Color.* Latham, NY: Kitchen Table, 1983.

Morris, Irwin. "African American Voting on Proposition 187: Rethinking the Prevalence of Interminority Conflict." *Political Research Quarterly* 53 (2000): 77–89.

Mueller, Carol. "Ella Baker and the Origins of Participatory Democracy." In *Black Women in United States History,* edited by Vicki Crawford, Jacqueline A. Rouse, and Barbara Woods, 51–70. Brooklyn, NY: Carlson Publishing, 1990.

Munck, Ronaldo. *The Difficult Dialogue: Marxism and Nationalism.* London: Zed Books, 1986.

Muñoz, Carlos. *Youth, Identity, Power: The Chicano Movement.* New York: Verso, 1989.

Murase, Mike. "Ethnic Studies and Higher Education for Asian Americans." In *Counterpoint: Perspectives on Asian America,* edited by Emma Gee, 205–23. Los Angeles: Asian American Studies, University of California, Los Angeles, 1976.

———. "Toward Barefoot Journalism." In *Counterpoint: Perspectives on Asian America,* edited by Emma Gee, 307–19. Los Angeles: Asian American Studies, University of California, Los Angeles, 1976.

Murphy, Raymond, and James Watson. "The Structure of Discontent: The Relationship between Social Structure, Grievance and Support for the Los Angeles Riot." Working Paper MR-92, Institute of Government and Public Affairs, University of California, Los Angeles, 1967.

Myrdal, Gunnar. *An American Dilemma: The Negro Problem and Modern Democracy.* New York: Harper and Row, 1944.

Nabakov, Peter. *Tijerina and the Courthouse Raid.* Albuquerque: University of New Mexico Press, 1970.

Nadel, Alan. *Flatlining on the Field of Dreams: Cultural Narratives in the Films of President Reagan's America.* New Brunswick, NJ: Rutgers University Press, 1997.

Nagata, Donna. "The Japanese American Internment." *Journal of Traumatic Stress* 3 (1990): 47–69.

Nagel, Joane. *American Indian Ethnic Renewal: Red Power and the Resurgence of Identity and Culture.* New York: Oxford University Press, 1996.

Nakamura, Eric. "Nobuko Miyamoto: Grain of Sand." *Giant Robot,* Spring 1998, 72–73.

———. "Yuri Kochiyama." *Giant Robot,* Spring 1998, 62–65.

Nakanishi, Don. "Surviving Democracy's 'Mistake': Japanese Americans and the Enduring Legacy of Executive Order 9066." *Amerasia* 19 (1993): 7–35.

Nakano, Roy. "Marxist-Leninist Organizing in the Asian American Community: Los Angeles, 1969–79." Unpublished manuscript, Asian American Studies Center Reading Room, Los Angeles, 1984.

National Chicano Liberation Conference. "El Plan Espiritual de Aztlan." In *Testimonio: A Documentary History of the Mexican American Struggle for Civil Rights*, edited by Arturo F. Rosales, 361. Houston, TX: Arte Publico Press, 2000.

Navarro, Armando. *The Cristal Experiment: A Chicano Struggle for Community Control*. Madison: University of Wisconsin Press, 1998.

———. *Mexican American Youth Organization: Avant-garde of the Chicano Movement in Texas*. Austin: University of Texas Press, 1995.

Nelson, Harold. "The Defenders: A Case Study of an Informal Police Organization." In *The Black Revolt: The Civil Rights Movement, Ghetto Uprisings, and Separatism*, edited by James Geschwender, 79–95. Englewood Cliffs, NJ: Prentice Hall, 1971.

Newton, Huey. "Black Capitalism Re-Analyzed I: June 5, 1971." In *To Die for the People: The Writings of Huey P. Newton*, edited by Toni Morrison, 105–6. New York: Writers and Readers Publishing, 1995.

———. "On the Defection of Eldridge Cleaver from the Black Panther Party and the Defection of the Black Panther Party from the Black Community." In *The Black Panthers Speak*, edited by Eric Foner, 272–78. New York: Da Capo Press, 1995.

———. "Resolutions and Declarations: December 5, 1970," in *To Die for the People: The Writings of Huey P. Newton*, edited by Toni Morrison, 39–43. New York: Writers and Readers Publishing, 1995.

———. *Revolutionary Suicide*. New York: Writers and Readers Publishing, 1995.

———. "Speech Delivered at Boston College, November 18, 1970," in *To Die for the People: The Writings of Huey P. Newton*, edited by Toni Morrison, 31–32. New York: Writers and Readers Publishing, 1995.

———. *To Die for the People: The Writings of Huey P. Newton*. Edited by Toni Morrison. New York: Writers and Readers Publishing, 1995.

———. "To the National Liberation Front of South Vietnam: August 29, 1970." In *To Die for the People: The Writings of Huey P. Newton*, edited by Toni Morrison, 178–81. New York: Writers and Readers Publishing, 1995.

———. *The War against the Panthers: A Study of Repression in America*. New York: Harlem River Press, 1996.

Ngozi-Brown, Scot. "The US Organization, Maulana Karenga, and Conflict with the Black Panther Party: A Critique of Sectarian Influences on Historical Discourse." *Journal of Black Studies* 28 (November 1997): 157–70.

Nguyen, Tram. "Caring for the Soul of Our Community." In *Asian Americans: The Movement and the Moment*, edited by Steve Louie and Glenn Omatsu, 285–97. Los Angeles: Asian American Studies Center, University of California, Los Angeles, 2001.

———. "Showdown in K-Town." *Colorlines* 4 (Spring 2001): 26–29.

Nguyen, Viet. *Race and Resistance: Literature and Politics in Asian America*. Oxford: Oxford University Press, 2002.

———. "The Remasculinization of Chinese America: Race, Violence, and the Novel." *American Literary History* 12 (Spring/Summer 2000): 130–57.

Nicholls, Walter. "Forging a 'New' Organizational Infrastructure for Los Angeles's Progressive Community." *International Journal of Urban and Regional Research* 27 (2003): 881–96.

Nicolaides, Becky. *My Blue Heaven: Life and Politics in the Working-Class Suburbs of Los Angeles, 1920–1965.* Chicago: University of Chicago Press, 2002.

Nishida, Mo. "A Revolutionary Nationalist Perspective on the San Francisco State Strike." *Amerasia* 15 (1989): 69–79.

———. "Shitamachi." *Amerasia* 15 (1989): 126–34.

O'Brien, Jim. "American Leninism in the 1970s." *Radical America* 11/12 (Winter 1977–78): 27–62.

O'Connor, James. *The Fiscal Crisis of the State.* New York: St. Martin's Press, 1973.

Okada, John. *No-No Boy.* Seattle: University of Washington Press, 1976.

Oliver, Melvin, James Johnson, and William Farrell. "Anatomy of a Rebellion." In *Reading Rodney King, Reading Urban Uprising*, edited by Robert Gooding-Williams, 117–41. New York: Routledge, 1993.

Oliver, Melvin, and Thomas Shapiro. *Black Wealth, White Wealth: A New Perspective on Racial Inequality.* New York: Routledge, 1995.

Olsen, Jack. *Last Man Standing: The Tragedy and Triumph of Geronimo Pratt.* New York: Doubleday, 2000.

Omatsu, Glenn. "Always a Rebel: An Interview with Kazu Iijima." *Amerasia* 13 (1986–87): 83–98.

Omi, Michael, and Howard Winant. *Racial Formation in the United States: From the 1960s to the 1980s.* New York: Routledge, 1986.

Ong, Bill Hing. *Making and Remaking Asian America through Immigration Policy, 1850–1990.* Stanford, CA: Stanford University Press, 1993.

Ong, Paul, and Tania Azores. "Asian Immigrants in Los Angeles: Diversity and Divisions." In *The New Asian Immigration in Los Angeles and Global Restructuring*, edited by Paul Ong, Edna Bonacich and Lucie Cheng, 100–129. Philadelphia: Temple University Press, 1994.

Ong, Paul, and Evelyn Blumenberg. "Income and Racial Inequality in Los Angeles." In *The City: Los Angeles and Urban Theory at the End of the Twentieth Century*, edited by Allen Scott and Edward Soja, 311–35. Berkeley: University of California Press, 1996.

Ong, Paul, Edna Bonacich and Lucie Cheng, eds. *The New Asian Immigration in Los Angeles and Global Restructuring.* Philadelphia: Temple University Press, 1994.

Ong, Paul, and Suzanne Hee. "Economic Diversity." In *Economic Diversity, Issues and Policies: A Public Policy Report*, edited by Paul Ong, 31–56. Los Angeles: Asian Pacific American Public Policy Institute and Asian American Studies Center, University of California, Los Angeles, 1994.

Ong, Paul, and Abel Valenzuela. "The Labor Market: Immigrant Effects and

Racial Disparities." In *Ethnic Los Angeles*, edited by Roger Waldinger and Mehdi Bozorgmehr, 165–91. New York: Russell Sage Foundation, 1996.

Ono, Kent, and John Sloop. *Shifting Borders: Rhetoric, Immigration and California's Proposition 187*. Philadelphia: Temple University Press, 2002.

Ono, Shinya. "Finding a Home Community." In *Asian Americans: The Movement and the Moment*, edited by Steve Louie and Glenn Omatsu, 262–73. Los Angeles: Asian American Studies Center, University of California, Los Angeles, 2001.

———. "A Weatherman: You Do Need a Weatherman to Know Which Way the Wind Blows." In *Weatherman*, edited by Harold Jacobs, 227–74. Palo Alto, CA: Ramparts Press, 1970.

O'Reilly, Kevin. *Racial Matters: The FBI's Secret File on Black America, 1960–1972*. New York: Free Press, 1989.

Ornelas, Charles, and Michael Gonzalez. "The Chicano and the War." *Aztlán* 2 (1971): 23–35.

Oropeza, Lorena. "La Batalla Está Aqui!" PhD diss., Cornell University, 1996.

Orum, Anthony, and Amy Orum. "The Class and Status Bases of Negro Student Protest." *Social Science Quarterly* 49 (1968): 521–33.

Osajima, Keith. "Asian Americans as the Model Minority." In *Contemporary Asian America: A Multidisciplinary Reader*, edited by Min Zhou and James Gatewood, 449–58. New York: New York University Press, 2000.

Padilla, A., and T. Baird. "Mexican American Adolescent Sexual Knowledge." *Hispanic Journal of Behavioral Sciences* 13 (1990): 95–104.

Padilla, Felix. *Latino Ethnic Consciousness: The Case of Mexican Americans and Puerto Ricans in Chicago*. Notre Dame, IN: University of Notre Dame Press, 1985.

Pagán, Eduardo Obregón. *Murder at the Sleepy Lagoon: Zoot Suits, Race and Riot in Wartime L.A.* Chapel Hill: University of North Carolina Press, 2003.

Pardo, Mary. *Mexican American Women Activists: Identity and Resistance in Two Los Angeles Communities*. Philadelphia: Temple University Press, 1998.

Park, Edward. "Our LA?" In *Rethinking Los Angeles*, edited by Michael Dear, Eric Schockman, and Greg Hise, 153–68. Thousand Oaks, CA: Sage Publications, 1996.

Park, Edward, and John Park. "A New American Dilemma? Asian Americans and Latinos in Race Theorizing." *Journal of Asian American Studies* 2 (1999): 289–309.

Parker, Heather Rose. "The Elusive Coalition: African American and Chicano Political Organizing in Los Angeles." PhD diss., University of California, Los Angeles, 1996.

Pastor, Manuel, Jr. "Common Ground at Ground Zero? The New Economy and the New Organizing in Los Angeles." *Antipode* 33 (2001): 260–89.

Payne, Charles. "Men Led, but Women Organized." In *Women in the Civil Rights Movement*, edited by Vicki Crawford, Jacqueline A. Rouse, and Barbara Woods, 1–12. New York: Carlson Publishing, 1990.

Pearson, Hugh. *The Shadow of the Panther: Huey Newton and the Price of Black Power in America*. Reading, MA: Addison-Wesley Publishing, 1994.

Peery, Nelson. *Black Fire: The Making of an American Revolutionary*. New York: New Press, 1994.

Peet, Dick. "The Social Origins of Environmental Determinism." *Annals of the Association of American Geographers* 75 (1985): 309–33.

Pérez, Emma. *The Decolonial Imaginary: Writing Chicanas into History*. Bloomington: Indiana University Press, 1999.

Perez-Torres, Rafael. "Refiguring Aztlán." *Aztlán* 22 (Fall 1977): 15–37.

Peterson, William. "Success Story, Japanese American Style." *New York Times Magazine*, January 9, 1966, 21–22, 33, 36, 38, 40–43.

Phillips, George Harwood. "Indians in Los Angeles, 1781–1875." In *The American Indian: Past and Present*, edited by Roger Nichols, 143–63. New York: McGraw-Hill College, 1999.

Piatt, Bill. *Black and Brown in America*. New York: New York University Press, 1997.

Pile, Steve, and Michael Keith. *Geographies of Resistance*. London: Routledge, 1997.

Pinard, Maurice, Jerome Kirk, and Donald Von Eschen. "Process of Recruitment in the Sit-In Movement." In *The Black Revolt: The Civil Rights Movement, Ghetto Uprisings, and Separatism*, edited by James Geschwender, 184–97. Englewood Cliffs, NJ: Prentice Hall, 1971.

Pinkney, Alphonso. *Red, Black and Green: Black Nationalism in the United States*. Cambridge: Cambridge University Press, 1976.

Piper, Adrian. "Passing for White, Passing for Black." *Transition* 58 (1992): 4–32.

Prashad, Vijay. *Everybody Was Kung Fu Fighting: Afro-Asian Connections and the Myth of Cultural Purity*. Boston: Beacon Press, 2001.

———. *The Karma of Brown Folk*. Minneapolis: University of Minnesota Press, 2000.

Preston, Richard. "The Changing Form and Structure of the Southern California Metropolis." *California Geographer* 12 (1971): 4–20.

Pulido, Laura. *Environmentalism and Economic Justice: Two Chicano Struggles in the Southwest*. Tucson: University of Arizona Press, 1996.

———. "The Interior Life of Politics." *Ethics, Place and Environment* 6 (2003): 46–52.

———. "Multiracial Organizing among Environmental Justice Activists in Los Angeles." In *Rethinking Los Angeles*, edited by Michael Dear, Eric Schockman, and Greg Hise, 171–89. Thousand Oaks, CA: Sage Publications, 1996.

———. "Restructuring and the Contraction and Expansion of Environmental Rights in the US." *Environment and Planning A* 26 (1994): 915–36.

———. "Rethinking Environmental Racism: White Privilege and Urban Development in Southern California." *Annals of the Association of American Geographers* 90 (2000): 12–40.

———. "The Roots of Political Consciousness among Militant Unionists and

Worker Activists in Los Angeles." Working paper, Center for the Study of Southern California, University of Southern California, Los Angeles, 1998.

Quon, Merilynne Hamano. "Individually We Contributed, Together We Made a Difference." In *Asian Americans: The Movement and the Moment*, edited by Steve Louie and Glenn Omatsu, 207–19. Los Angeles: Asian American Studies Center, University of California, Los Angeles, 2001.

Raine, Walter. "Los Angeles Riot Study: The Ghetto Merchant Survey." Working Paper MR-98, Institute of Government and Public Affairs, University of California, Los Angeles, 1967.

Ramos, Henry. *The American GI Forum: In Pursuit of the Dream, 1948–1983.* Houston, TX: Arte Público Press, 1998.

Revolutionary Worker. "Yuri Kochiyama: With Justice in Her Heart." In *Legacy to Liberation: Politics and Culture of Revolutionary Asian/Pacific America,* edited by Fred Ho with Carolyn Antonio, Diane Fujino and Steve Yip, 269–78. San Francisco: Big Red Media and AK Press, 2000.

Rhodes, Jane. "The Black Panther Newspaper." *Media History* 7 (2001): 151–58.

———. "Fanning the Flames of Racial Discord: The National Press and the Black Panther Party." *Harvard International Journal of Press Politics* 4 (1999): 95–118.

Rinehart, Sue Tolleson. *Gender Consciousness and Politics.* New York: Routledge, 1992.

Robins, Rebecca. "Self-Determination and Subordination." In *The State of Native America: Genocide, Colonization, and Resistance,* edited by M. Annette Jaimes, 87–121. Boston: South End Press, 1992.

Robinson, Cedric. *Black Marxism: The Making of the Black Radical Tradition.* London: Zed Books, 1983.

Robnett, Belinda. *How Long? How Long? African-American Women in the Struggle for Civil Rights.* New York: Oxford University Press, 1997.

Rodriguez, Dylan. "Thinking Solidarity across Generations: Richard Aoki and the Relevance of Living Legacies." *Shades of Power* 1 (Summer 1998): 10–14.

Rodríguez, Olga. *The Politics of Chicano Liberation.* New York: Pathfinder Press, 1977.

Rodriguez, Victor. "Boricuas, African Americans, and Chicanos in the 'Far West': Notes on the Puerto Rican Pro-Independence Movement in California, 1960s–1980s." In *Latino Social Movements: Historical and Theoretical Perspectives; A New Political Science Reader,* edited by Rodolfo Torres and George Katsiaficas, 79–109. New York: Routledge, 1999.

Roediger, David. *Towards the Abolition of Whiteness: Essays on Race, Politics, and Working Class History.* London: Verso, 1999.

———. *The Wages of Whiteness: Race and the Making of the American Working Class.* London: Verso, 1991.

Romano, Octavio. "The Anthropology and Sociology of the Mexican-Americans: The Distortion of Mexican-American History." In *Voices: Readings from El Grito: A Journal of Contemporary Mexican American Thought,* edited by Octavio Romano, 26–39. Berkeley, CA: Quinto Sol, 1971.

Romo, Ricardo. *East Los Angeles: History of a Barrio.* Austin: University of Texas Press, 1983.

Rosales, F. Arturo, ed. *Testimonio: A Documentary History of the Mexican American Struggle for Civil Rights.* Houston, TX: Arte Público Press, 2000.

Rose, Margaret. "Women in the United Farm Workers." PhD diss., University of California, Los Angeles, 1988.

Rosen, Ruth. *The World Split Open: How the Modern Women's Movement Changed America.* New York: Penguin Books, 2000.

Rosenbaum, Mark. *Mexicano Resistance in the Southwest.* Austin: University of Texas Press, 1981.

Rowbotham, Sheila. *Women, Resistance and Revolution.* New York: Vintage Books, 1974.

Rucker, Madalynn, and JoNina Abron. "Comrade Sisters." In *Unrelated Kin: Race and Gender in Women's Personal Narratives,* edited by Gwendolyn Etter-Lewis and Michèle Foster, 139–67. New York: Routledge, 1996.

Rumbaut, Ruben. "Origins and Destinies: Immigration to the United States since World War II." *Sociological Forum* 9 (1994): 583–621.

Rustan, June. "Inside Out and Upside Down: An Interview with Anne Braden." *Colorlines* 4 (2001): 30–33.

Ryan, Michael, and Douglas Kellner. *Camera Politica: The Politics and Ideology of Contemporary Hollywood Film.* Bloomington: Indiana University Press, 1988.

Sabagh, Georges, and Mehdi Bozorgmehr. "Population Change: Immigration and Ethnic Transformation." In *Ethnic Los Angeles,* edited by Roger Waldinger and Mehdi Bozorgmehr, 79–107. New York: Russell Sage Foundation, 1996.

Saito, Leland. *Race and Politics: Asian Americans, Latinos, and Whites in a Los Angeles Suburb.* Urbana: University of Illinois Press, 1998.

Sale, Kirkpatrick. *SDS.* New York: Random House, 1973.

Sánchez, David. *Expedition through Aztlan.* La Puente: Perspectiva Publicaciones, 1978.

Sánchez, George. *Becoming Mexican American: Ethnicity, Culture, and Identity in Chicano Los Angeles, 1900–1945.* New York: Oxford University Press, 1993.

———. " 'What's Good for Boyle Heights Is Good for the Jews': Creating Multiracialism on the Eastside during the 1950s." *American Quarterly* 56 (2004): 633–61.

Sánchez, Rosaura. "The History of Chicanas: A Proposal for a Materialist Perspective." In *Between Borders: Essays on Mexicana/Chicana History,* edited by Adelaida del Castillo, 1–29. Encino, CA: Floricanto Press, 1990.

Sandoval, Chela. "U.S. Third World Feminism." *Genders* 19 (1991): 1–24.

Santa Ana, Otto. *Brown Tide Rising: Metaphors of Latinos in Contemporary American Public Discourse.* Austin: University of Texas Press, 2002.

Santana, Deborah Berman. "No Somos Unicos: The Status Question from Manila to San Juan." *Centro* 11 (Fall 1999).

Santillan, Richard. *La Raza Unida.* Los Angeles: Tlaquilo Publications, 1973.

Saxton, Alexander. *The Indispensable Enemy: Labor and the Anti-Chinese Movement in California.* Berkeley: University of California Press, 1971.

Sayer, Andrew, and Richard Walker. *The New Social Economy: Reworking the Division of Labor.* Cambridge, MA: Blackwell, 1992.

Schiesl, Martin. "Designing the Model Community: The Irvine Company and Suburban Development, 1950–88." In *Postsuburban California: The Transformation of Orange County since World War II,* edited by Rob Kling, Spencer Olin, and Mark Poster, 55–91. Berkeley: University of California Press, 1991.

Schlesinger, Arthur. *The Disuniting of America.* New York: Norton, 1993.

Scoble, David. "Negro Politics in Los Angeles: The Quest for Power." Working Paper MR-89, Institute of Government and Public Affairs, University of California, Los Angeles 1967.

Scott, Allen. "High Technology Industrial Development in the San Fernando Valley and Ventura County." In *The City: Los Angeles and Urban Theory at the End of the Twentieth Century,* edited by Allen Scott and Edward Soja, 276–310. Berkeley: University of California Press, 1996.

———. "The Manufacturing Economy: Ethnic and Gender Divisions of Labor." In *Ethnic Los Angeles,* edited by Roger Waldinger and Mehdi Bozorgmehr, 215–44. New York: Russell Sage Foundation, 1996.

———. *Metropolis: From Division of Labor to Urban Form.* Berkeley: University of California Press, 1988.

Scott, Allen, and Edward Soja, eds. *The City: Los Angeles and Urban Theory at the End of the Twentieth Century.* Berkeley: University of California Press, 1996

———. "Introduction to Los Angeles." In *The City: Los Angeles and Urban Theory at the End of the Twentieth Century,* edited by Allen Scott and Edward Soja, 1–21. Berkeley: University of California Press, 1996.

Scott, James. *Weapons of the Weak: Everyday Forms of Peasant Resistance.* New Haven, CT: Yale University Press, 1985.

Seale, Bobby. *A Lonely Rage.* New York: Bantam Books, 1978.

———. *Seize the Time.* Baltimore: Black Classic Press, 1991.

Sears, David. "Los Angeles Riot Study: Political Attitudes of Los Angeles Negroes." Working paper, Institute of Government and Public Affairs, University of California, Los Angeles, 1967.

Sears, David, and John McConahay. "Los Angeles Riot Study: Riot Participation." Working paper, Institute of Government and Public Affairs, University of California, Los Angeles, 1967.

Sears, David, and T. M. Tomlinson. "Riot Ideology in Los Angeles: A Study of Negro Attitudes." In *The Black Revolt: The Civil Rights Movement, Ghetto Uprisings, and Separatism,* edited by James Geschwender, 375–401. Englewood Cliffs, NJ: Prentice Hall, 1971.

See, Carolyn. *On Gold Mountain*. New York: Vintage Books, 1996.

Self, Robert. "To Plan Our Liberation: Black Power and the Politics of Place in Oakland California, 1965–1977." *Journal of Urban History* 26 (2000): 759–92.

Shah, Sonia, ed. *Dragon Ladies: Asian American Feminists Breathe Fire*. Boston: South End Press, 1997.

Shakur, Assata. *Assata: An Autobiography*. New York: Lawrence Hill Books, 1988.

Sharpe, William, and Leonard Wallock. "Bold New City or Built up 'Burb'? Redefining Contemporary Suburbia." *American Quarterly* 46 (1994): 1–30.

Shichor, David, and Dale Sechrest. *Three Strikes and You're Out: Vengeance as Public Policy*. Thousand Oaks, CA: Sage Publications, 1996.

Short, Philip. *Mao: A Life*. New York: Henry Holt, 2000.

Sides, Josh. *LA City Limits: African American Los Angeles from the Great Depression to the Present*. Berkeley: University of California Press, 2004.

———. "You Understand My Condition." *Pacific Historical Review* 67 (1998): 233–57.

Siegel, Lou. "LRR Voices: Local 11 Takes on LA." *Labor Research Review* 20 (1993): 21–23.

Smith, Neil. "Homeless/Global: Scaling Places." In *Mapping the Futures: Local Cultures, Global Change*, edited by John Bird, B. Curtis, T. Putnam, and G. Robertson, 128–43. New York: Routledge, 1993.

Smith, Paul Chat, and Robert Warrior. *Like a Hurricane: The Indian Movement from Alcatraz to Wounded Knee*. New York: New Press, 1996.

Soja, Edward. *Postmodern Geographies: The Reassertion of Space in Critical Social Theory*. New York: Verso, 1989.

———. *Thirdspace: Journeys to Los Angeles and Other Real-and-Imagined Places*. Cambridge, MA: Blackwell, 1996.

Solomon, Mark. *The Cry Was Unity: Communists and African Americans, 1917–36*. Jackson: University Press of Mississippi, 1998.

Sonenshein, Raphael. *Politics in Black and White: Race and Power in Los Angeles*. Princeton, NJ: Princeton University Press, 1993.

Staples, Robert. *Black Masculinity: The Black Male's Role in American Society*. San Francisco: Black Scholar Press, 1982.

Starr, Kevin. *Embattled Dreams: California in War and Peace*. New York: Oxford University Press, 2002.

———. *Material Dreams: Southern California through the 1920's*. New York: Oxford University Press, 1990.

Steele, Shelby. *The Content of Our Character: A New Vision of Race in America*. New York: Perennial Press, 1990.

Storper, Michael. *The Regional World: Territorial Development in a Global Economy*. New York: Guilford Press, 1997.

Students for a Democratic Society. "SDS Resolution on the Black Panther Party." In *The Black Panthers Speak*, edited by Eric Foner, 227. New York: Da Capo Press, 1995.

Suárez-Orozco, Marcelo, and Mariela Páez. *Latinos: Remaking America.* Berkeley: University of California Press, 2002.

"Success Story of One Minority Group in the US." *US News and World Report,* December 26, 1966. Reprinted in *Roots: An Asian American Reader,* edited by Amy Tachiki, Eddie Wong, and Franklin Odo, 6–9. Los Angeles: Asian American Studies Center, University of California, Los Angeles, 1971.

Sue, Stanley, Nathaniel Wagner, Davis Ja, Charlene Margullis, and Louise Lew. "Conceptions of Mental Illness among Asian and Caucasian American Students." *Psychological Reports* 38 (1976): 703–8.

Takagi, Dana. *The Retreat from Race: Asian-American Admissions and Racial Politics.* New Brunswick, NJ: Rutgers University Press, 1992.

Takagi, Ronald. *Strangers from a Different Shore: A History of Asian Americans.* New York: Penguin Books, 1989.

Tanaka, Janice. *When You're Smiling: The Deadly Legacy of Internment.* DVD. Los Angeles: Visual Communications, 1999.

Tanaka, Robert. "Sansei Male Personhood, Corporate Sexuality and Ms. Madeline Girbaud." *Journal of Ethnic Studies* 17 (1989): 1–22.

Tasaki, Ray. "Where There Is Oppression." In *Asian Americans: The Movement and the Moment,* edited by Steve Louie and Glenn Omatsu. Los Angeles: Asian American Studies Center, University of California, Los Angeles, 2001.

Taylor, Ula. "The Historical Foundation of Black Feminist Theory and Praxis." *Journal of Black Studies* 29 (November 1998): 234–53.

———. "Negro Women Are Great Thinkers as Well as Doers." *Journal of Women's History* 12 (Summer 2000): 104–26.

Telles, Edward, and Edward Murguia. "Phenotype Discrimination and Income Differences Among Mexican Americans." *Social Science Quarterly* 71 (1990): 682–96.

Thomas, Andrew Peyton. *Clarence Thomas: A Biography.* San Francisco: Encounter Books, 2002.

Tijerna, Reies Lopez. *Mi lucha por la tierra.* Mexico: Fondo de Cultura Economica, 1978.

Tilly, Charles. "From Interactions to Outcomes in Social Movements." In *How Social Movements Matter,* edited by Marco Giugni, Doug McAdam, and Charles Tilly, 253–70. Minneapolis: University of Minnesota Press, 1999.

Ting, Jennifer. "The Power of Sexuality." *Journal of Asian American Studies* 1 (1998): 65–82.

Tolbert, Emory. *The UNIA and Black Los Angeles: Ideology and Community in the American Garvey Movement.* Los Angeles: Center for Afro-American Studies, University of California, Los Angeles, 1980.

Tonry, Michael. *Malign Neglect: Race, Crime, and Punishment in America.* New York: Oxford University Press, 1996.

Toribio, Helen. "Dare to Struggle: The KDP and Filipino American Politics." In *Legacy to Liberation: Politics and Culture of Revolutionary Asian/Pacific America,* edited by Fred Ho, Carolyn Antonio, Diane Fujino and Steve Yip, 31–49. San Francisco: Big Red Media and AK Press, 2000.

Torres, Andrés, and José Velázquez. *The Puerto Rican Movement: Voices from the Diaspora*. Philadelphia: Temple University Press, 1998.

Torres-Saillant, Silvio. "Inventing the Race." *Latino Studies* 1 (2003): 123–51.

Tuan, Mia. *Forever Foreigners or Honorary Whites? The Asian Ethnic Experience Today*. New Brunswick, NJ: Rutgers University Press, 1998.

Tyler, Bruce. "Black Radicalism in Southern California, 1950–1982." PhD diss., University of California, Los Angeles, 1983.

Umemoto, Karen. "Asian American Students in the San Francisco State College Strike, 1964–1968." Master's thesis, University of California, Los Angeles, 1989.

———. "From Vincent Chin to Joseph Ileto: Asian Pacific Americans and Hate Crime Policy." In *Transforming Race Relations*, edited by Paul Ong, 243–78. Los Angeles: Asian Pacific American Public Policy Institute and Asian American Studies Center, University of California, Los Angeles, 2001.

Umoja, Akinleye. "The Ballot and the Bullet." *Journal of Black Studies* 29 (March 1999): 558–78.

United Way. *A Tale of Two Cities: Promise and Peril in Los Angeles*. Los Angeles: United Way of Greater Los Angeles, 2003.

———. *2003 State of the County Report*. Los Angeles: United Way of Greater Los Angeles, 2003.

U.S. National Advisory Commission on Civil Disorders. *Report of the National Advisory Commission on Civil Disorders*. Washington, DC: Government Printing Office, 1968.

Varon, Barbara. "The Japanese Americans: Comparative Occupational Status, 1960 and 1950." *Demography* 4 (1967): 809–19.

Veale, Dolly. "Richard Aoki." In *Legacy to Liberation: Politics and Culture of Revolutionary Asian/Pacific America*, edited by Fred Ho, Carolyn Antonio, Diane Fujino, and Steve Yip, 183–96. San Francisco: Big Red Media and AK Press, 2000.

Velez-Ibañez, Carlos. "Se Me Acabó la Canción: An Ethnography of Non-consenting Sterilization among Mexican Women in Los Angeles." In *Mexican Women in the United States: Struggles Past and Present*, edited by Magdalena Mora and Adelaida del Castillo, 71–93. Los Angeles: Chicano Studies Center Publications, 1980.

Vera, Ron. "Observations on the Chicano Relationship to Military Service in Los Angeles County." *Aztlán* 1 (Fall 1970): 27–37.

"The View from the Ground: Organizers Speak out on Race." *Colorlines* 3 (Summer 2000): 16–17.

Vigil, Ernesto. *The Crusade for Justice: Chicano Militancy and the Government's War on Dissent*. Madison: University of Wisconsin Press, 1999.

Vigil, James Diego. *Barrio Gangs: Street Life and Identity in Southern California*. Austin: University of Texas Press, 1988.

Wade, Peter. *Race and Ethnicity in Latin America*. London: Pluto Press, 1997.

Wake, Lloyd. "Reflections on the San Francisco State Strike." *Amerasia* 15 (1989): 43–47.

Waldinger, Roger, and Mehdi Bozorgmehr, eds. *Ethnic Los Angeles.* New York: Russell Sage Foundation, 1996.

Waldinger, Roger, C. Erickson, Ruth Milkman, D. Mitchell, Abel Valenzuela, Kent Wong, and Maurice Zeitlin. "Justice for Janitors." *Dissent* 47 (Winter 1997): 37–44.

Waldinger, Roger, and Michael Lichter. *How the Other Half Works: Immigration and the Social Organization of Labor.* Berkeley: University of California Press, 2003.

Wallerstein, Immanuel. "The Construction of Peoplehood: Racism, Nationality, Ethnicity." In *Race, Nation, Class: Ambiguous Identities,* edited by Etienne Balibar and Immanuel Wallerstein, 71–85. London: Verso, 1991.

Warren, Jonathan, and France Winddance Twine. "White Americans, the New Minority." *Journal of Black Studies* 28 (1997): 200–218.

Warren, William. "Maps: A Spatial Approach to Japanese American Communities in Los Angeles." *Amerasia* 13 (1986–87): 137–51.

Wat, Eric. *The Making of a Gay Asian Community: An Oral History of Pre-AIDS Los Angeles.* Lanham, MD: Rowman and Littlefield, 2002.

Webb, Gary. *Dark Alliance: The CIA, the Contras, and the Crack Cocaine Explosion.* New York: Seven Stories, 1999.

Wei, William. *The Asian American Movement.* Philadelphia: Temple University Press, 1993.

West, Cynthia S'thembile. "Revisiting Female Activism in the 1960s: The Newark Branch Nation of Islam." *Black Scholar* 26 (1996): 41–59.

Whalen, Jack, and Richard Flacks. *Beyond the Barricades: The Sixties Generation Grows Up.* Philadelphia: Temple University Press, 1989.

White, Richard. "Race Relations in the American West." *American Quarterly* 38 (1986): 396–416.

Whittemore, Katherine, Ellen Rosenbush, and Jim Nelson, eds. *The Sixties: Recollections of the Decade.* New York: Franklin Square Press, 1995.

Wilkins, Fanon Che. "In the Belly of the Beast: Black Power, Anti-Imperialism, and the African Liberation Solidarity Movement, 1968–1975." PhD diss., New York University, 2001.

Wilson, William Julius. *The Declining Significance of Race: Blacks and Changing American Institutions.* Chicago: University of Chicago Press, 1980.

———. *When Work Disappears: The World of the New Urban Poor.* New York: Alfred A. Knopf, 1996.

Winant, Howard. *Racial Conditions: Politics, Theory, Comparisons.* Minneapolis: University of Minnesota Press, 1994.

Winston, Henry. *Strategy for a Black Agenda: A Critique of New Theories of Liberation in the United States and Africa.* New York: International Publishers, 1973.

Wolfe, Tom. *Radical Chic and Mau-Mauing the Flak Catchers.* New York: Farrar, Straus and Giroux, 1970.

Wong, Martin. "Art Ishi and Guy Kurose." *Giant Robot,* Spring 1998, 77.

———. "Gang of Four." *Giant Robot,* Spring 1998, 70–71.

Woods, Clyde. *Development Arrested: The Blues and Plantation Power in the Mississippi Delta*. New York: Verso, 1998.

Woodward, Komozi. *A Nation within a Nation: Amiri Baraka (LeRoi Jones) and Black Power Politics*. Chapel Hill: University of North Carolina Press, 1999.

Wu, Frank. *Yellow: Race in America beyond Black and White*. New York: Basic Books, 2002.

Yamamoto, Eric. *Interracial Justice: Conflict and Reconciliation in Post–Civil Rights America*. New York: New York University Press, 1999.

———. "What's Next? Japanese American Redress and African American Reparations." *Amerasia* 25 (1999): 1- 17.

Yamasaki, Emily Woo. "Perspective of a Revolutionary Feminist." In *Legacy to Liberation: Politics and Culture of Revolutionary Asian/Pacific America*, edited by Fred Ho with Carolyn Antonio, Diane Fujino, and Steve Yip, 47–51. San Francisco: Big Red Media and AK Press, 2000.

Yokota, Kariann. "From Little Tokyo to Bronzeville and Back: Ethnic Communities in Transition." Master's thesis, University of California, Los Angeles, 1996.

Yoneda, Karl. *Ganbatte: Sixty-Year Struggle of a Kibei Worker*. Los Angeles: Asian American Studies Center, University of California, Los Angeles, 1983.

Young, Cynthia. "Havana in Harlem." *Science and Society* 65 (2001): 12–38.

———. "Soul Power: Cultural Radicalism and the Formation of a United States Third World Left." PhD diss., Yale University, 1999.

Zavella, Patricia. "Playing with Fire: Gendered Constructions of Chicana/Mexicana Sexuality." In *The Gender/Sexuality Reader: Culture, History, Political Economy*, edited by Roger Lancaster and Micaela di Leonardo, 392–408. New York: Routledge, 1997.

Zhou, Min, and James Gatewood, eds. *Contemporary Asian America: A Multidisciplinary Reader*. New York: New York University Press, 2000.

Zinn, Maxine Baca. "Chicano Men and Masculinity." *Journal of Ethnic Studies* 10 (1982): 29–44.

Index

on, 149, 186–93, 289n21; growth, 99; interethnic politics, 166, 167–70; international solidarity work, 98–99; leadership struggles, 100, 190; life span, 9–10; lumpen proletariat and, 142, 143–46; Marxism and, 123; origins, 9, 70–71, 80, 96, 121; Peace and Freedom Party relations with, 164; People's Alliance membership, 176; police attack on Southern California Chapter headquarters, 105; police repression and, 71, 96–98, 224–25; political activity, 99–100, 164; political prisoners, 173–74, 225; prominence, 3, 19, 162, 170; public images of, 6; as revolutionary nationalists, 124; SDS relationship to, 161, 162, 165–66; self-defense emphasis, 6, 50, 68, 96, 97–98, 99, 145; sexism in, 145, 149, 165, 166, 186–89, 193–94; Southern California Chapter, 100–105; survival programs, 6, 50, 96, 98, 190, 193, 268n23; Ten-Point Programs, 96, 97, 146, 151, 167, *168*; UFW relations with, 168–69; underground, women in the, 192; US compared, 104, 147–48, 152; US relations with, 104, 149–50, 166; violence in, 193–94; white support of, 98, 166, 170; women leaders, 188–89, 190; women's liberation movement and, 186–89; women's roles in, 183, 187–89, 193, 289n27
Black Panthers of Lowndes County (Alabama), 96
Black Power: civil rights movement and, 89, 90–91, 92; effect on white radicals, 93–95; as inspiration for other racial/ethnic power movements, 91–92; New Left and, 93
Black Power (Carmichael & Hamilton), 90
Blacks: Asian Americans and, 160; class distinctions, 44–45; class polarization, 225–26; crack cocaine epidemic, 225; cultural nationalism, 146–49; de-

feminization of Black women, 194; discrimination by other racial/ethnic groups, 56–58; emasculation of men, 184; employment in Los Angeles, 47–50, *48*; immigration effects on, 29; Japanese Americans and, 57–58; as lumpen proletariat, 143–44; as most oppressed group, 163–64; political mobilization, 60; social-structural oppression, 97–98; unemployment blamed on Latinas/os, 226, 295n2; urban housing segregation and, 23
Black Workers Congress, 95
Boggs, Grace Lee, 106, 281n7
Booker, Chris, 144, 145
BPP. *See* Black Panther Party
Braden, Anne, 60
Brotherhood House (Casa Carnalismo), 118
Brown, Elaine, 90, 100, 101, 104, 151, 168, 193, 223; BPP leadership, 190, 193
Brown, H. Rap, 92
Brown, Joe, 166
Brown, Roy, *178*
Brown Berets, 7, 19, 92, 115, 162; 13-point political program, 283–84n28; activities, 116; antiwhite rhetoric, 172; BPP relations with, 167, 168; condemnation of PL, 165; ideology, 116–17; origins, 115–16; political diversity, 117; Young Citizens for Chicano Action and, 92
Brown Power, Black Power and, 92
Burnout, 236
Buss, Shirl, 166
Butler, Julio Pratt, 193

California: agriculture, Mexicana/o labor for, 27; Proposition 187, 28–29, 251n32. *See also* Los Angeles; San Francisco; Southern California
California Coalition Treaty, 94
California Communist League, 2, 5
California Nurses Association, 217
California State University, Long Beach, 82, 83, 266n56

Hewitt, Masai, 104
Hilliard, David, 104, 146, 158, 190, 223, 281n7
Hispanics: populations in Los Angeles in 1970, 256n20. *See also* Chicanas/os; Latinas/os
Ho Chi Min, 78
Hollywood, support of left-wing causes, 166
Home Owners Loan Corporation, 37, 42–43
Homosexuals, 186–87, 230. *See also* Gay rights movement
Hondagneu-Sotelo, Pierrette, 50
Horne, Gerald, 41, 70
Horowitz, David, 62, 266n8
Hotel Employees and Restaurant Employees Union (HERE), 2, 217, 219, 220
Housing, 37; prices for racial/ethnic groups in Los Angeles, 55–56, 55; residential segregation, 15–16, 16, 23, 53–55, 260n46
Huerta, Dolores, 183
Huggins, Ericka (Erica), 188, 189, 192, 194, 223
Huggins, John, 98, 104, 147
Hurtado, Aída, 184–85

Illegal aliens. *See under* Workers, undocumented
Immigrants: as a labor problem, 7; Asian populations in Southern California, 219, 220, 222; attitudes toward, 117–18; CASA advocacy of, 118, 119, 121, 171, 172; eschewed by U.S. labor unions, 130; racism and, 226; white advocacy for, 171, 172
Imperialism, 128–29; racism and, 127–28; Vietnam War as, 77, 78
Intercommunalism, 151–52
Interethnic politics: of BPP, 162–63, 167–70; of CASA, 170–71, 176–79; of East Wind, 123, 154–56, 160–62
International Conference of the Americas, 177

International Indian Treaty Council, 176
International Longshoremen's and Warehousemen's Union, 40
International organizations, 95
International Women's Day, 155, 172, 196, 230
Ishi, Art, 105
I Wor Kuen, 2, 95, 113, 154, 281n7, 295n27; gender equality, 185, 186

Jackson, George, 174
JACS-AI (Japanese American Community Services-Asian Involvement), 109, 110, 111, 217
Japanese American Citizens League, 40, 106, 270n36
Japanese American Community Services–Asian Involvement (JACS-AI), 109, 110, 111, 217
Japanese American internment (World War II), 38–40, 44, 108–9, 255n11, 256n18; redress and reparation campaign, 221–22
Japanese Americans, 8, 222–23, 224; African American relations with, 57–58; behavioral expectations, 109; drug abuse, 108, 109; economic mobility, 52, 223; employment in Los Angeles, 50–52, 51; gang membership, 108, 110; immigrant generations, terminology, 244n21; in manufacturing jobs, 61–62; as model minority, 106, 155; Nikkei, 8, 109, 139, 222, 223, 244n21, 270n33; Nisei, 44; not perceived as people of color, 136; political agitation, discomfort with, 106, 270n3; population in Los Angeles, 222, 244n20; in racial hierarchies, 43–44; residential segregation, 53–54; Sansei, 108–9, 270n33; socioeconomic diversity, 110, 223; soldiers in World War II, 44, 264n37; Third World identity of leftists, 136–37; upward mobility, 44, 136, 249–50n22. *See also* Asian Americans

Compositor: BookMatters, Berkeley
Indexer: Jeanne C. Moody
Text: 10/13 Aldus
Display: ITC Franklin Gothic

CPSIA information can be obtained
at www.ICGtesting.com
Printed in the USA
FSOW02n1204180917
38900FS

9 780520 245204